Arabic Political Memoirs
and Other Studies

By the same author:

Arabic Political Memoirs
and Other Studies

Elie Kedourie

Professor of Politics
London School of Economics and Political Science

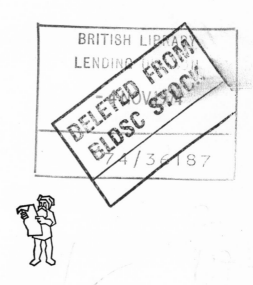

FRANK CASS: LONDON

First published 1974 in Great Britain by
FRANK CASS AND COMPANY LIMITED
67 Great Russell Street, London WC1B 3BT, England

and in United States of America by
FRANK CASS AND COMPANY LIMITED
c/o International Scholarly Book Services, Inc.
P.O. Box 4347, Portland, Oregon 97208

Copyright © 1974 Elie Kedourie

ISBN 0 7146 3041 1

Library of Congress Catalog Card No. 73–93193

Printed in Great Britain by William Clowes & Sons, Limited,
London, Beccles and Colchester

Contents

Preface

This book constitutes the continuation and complement of a work, *The Chatham House Version and Other Middle-Eastern Studies*, published in 1970. Both works are concerned with certain themes prominent in recent middle-eastern history, namely the influence of great-power, and particularly British policies in the region; the character of middle-eastern, and particularly Arab, politics and political thought during the last hundred years or so; and the fate of so-called minorities, and particularly the Jews of the Arab world, caught as they were in the cross-fire of antagonistic ideologies and of international conflicts. While in the earlier work the theme of British attitudes and policies loomed largest, the major theme of this book is the failure of constitutionalism in the middle east during the last hundred years or so, the transformation of a native tradition of autocratic rule into a European-style absolutism, and the increasing radicalization of political thought which accompanied this transformation. There is no doubt that the conflict in Palestine between Zionism and Arab nationalism has greatly contributed to this radicalization, and Palestine is the focus on which converge the two other minor themes of the work, British policy, and the fate of the Jews in the Arab world.

The nineteen chapters which make up this book were written over the last ten years or so. Chapters 8 and 19, and a large part of Chapter 1 are published here for the first time. Details of earlier publication in respect of the other chapters follow:

Chapter 1 incorporates parts of a chapter on 'The Middle East 1900–1945' contributed to *The New Cambridge Modern History, volume xii: The Shifting Balance of World Forces 1898–1945*, 2nd edition, 1968.

Chapter 2 is based on an article, '*Hizb*: the Arab Lands', contributed to *The Encyclopaedia of Islam*, new edition.

Chapter 3 appeared in *Middle Eastern Studies*, vol. 3 no. 1 (October 1966).

Chapter 4 appeared in *The Jewish Journal of Sociology*, vol. ix no. 1 (June 1967).

Chapter 5 appeared in *Middle Eastern Studies*, vol. 9 no. 1 (January 1973).

Chapter 6 appeared in *The Jewish Journal of Sociology*, vol. vi no. 2 (December 1964).

Chapter 7 appeared in *Middle Eastern Studies*, vol. 8 no. 2 (May 1972).

Chapter 9 appeared in *The New York Review of Books* (23 November 1967).

Chapter 10 appeared in *Art International and The Lugano Review*, vol. xvii no. 4 (April 1973).

Chapter 11 appeared in *Encounter*, vol. xxxix no. 5 (November 1972).

Chapter 12 appeared in *The U.S.S.R. and The Middle East*, edited by M. Confino and S. Shamir and published by Wiley, 1973.

Chapter 13 appeared in *The Arab-Israeli Dispute*, published by the Institute for the Study of Conflict, 1971.

Chapter 14 appeared in *Middle Eastern Studies*, vol. 2 no. 2 (January 1966).

Chapter 15 appeared in *Middle Eastern Studies*, vol. 6 no. 3 (October 1970).

Chapter 16 appeared in *Middle Eastern Studies*, vol. 7 no. 1 (January 1971).

Chapter 17 appeared in *Middle Eastern Studies*, vol. 7 no. 3 (October 1971).

Chapter 18 appeared in *Middle Eastern Studies*, vol. 2 no. 4 (July 1966).

I am most grateful to the editors and publishers of the publications listed above for kindly allowing republication in this book. Crown copyright records appear by permission of the Controller, Her Majesty's Stationery Office.

I am greatly obliged to the Central Research Fund of the University of London and to the Government Research Division of the London School of Economics and Political Science for enabling me to obtain books and documents not available in this country, and to the Warden and Fellows of St. Antony's College, Oxford for having made it possible for me to consult documents in the National Archives, Washington.

I would also very much like to thank the staffs of the Public Record Office, London, of the National Archives, Washington, and of the Archives du Ministère des Affaires Etrangères, Paris for their constant and ready helpfulness.

London School of Economics and Political Science   E.K.
February 1974

1. The Fate of Constitutionalism in the Middle East

Constitutional government is usually—and rightly—said to originate in western Europe, where it is the distant—and quite unforeseen—outcome of the militarization and barbarization which overtook, after the ninth century, the settled and prosperous lands of the western Roman empire. Constitutional government may be described as limited government, or as a government of checks and balances, or as representative and responsible government; again it may be associated with the existence of various powerful and substantial interests in society which other interests are powerless permanently to suppress, and which the government is not in a position to destroy. But however constitutional government is described, and whatever the particular social structure with which it may be associated, we may safely say that it is far removed from, if not antithetical to, what usually obtains in 'oriental despotism' where the ruling institution is subject to no control by the subjects and where, to use Wittfogel's formulation, the state is stronger than society.

'Oriental despotism' is the régime which most of the middle east has traditionally known; more precisely the term may serve to describe the Ottoman empire and its military and administrative institutions, which were at their most efficient during the sixteenth and part of the seventeenth century. Whatever may be said about Ottoman society at large, there can be no doubt that these institutions at the end of the eighteenth century were manifestly in decline. This decline meant, in particular, that the hold of the sultan and his servants over large areas of the empire became weak, and there arose in the provinces powerful interests which were not amenable to central control. Whether a'yans and derebeys in Rumelia and Anatolia, or mamlukes in Baghdad and Cairo, or local potentates like Jazzar of Acre, Zahir al-'Umar of Nablus, or Ali Pasha of Janina, one may compare them, without being seriously misleading, to those feudal barons of western Europe who, in retrospect, are seen to have shared in the making of a society in which constitutional and limited government could function and have reality.

In fact, the decay of the Ottoman ruling institution and the growth of provincial and local interests able to assert themselves resulted, on one occasion, in a state of affairs which again bears some resemblance to the politics of feudal Europe. Shortly after the accession of

1

Mahmud II, in 1808, leading a'yans and derebeys from Rumelia and Anatolia came to Istanbul at the invitation of the grand vizier. They were accompanied by large retinues which camped on the outskirts of the capital. These local potentates proceeded to negotiate with the grand vizier and the principal officials and officers of the central government. The result of their negotiation was the instrument known as the *sened-i ittifaq* or deed of agreement, which the sultan, in spite of disliking it, found himself compelled to ratify. It is not so much the detailed provisions of the *sened* which are relevant, as the fact that by ratifying it, the sultan recognized the standing of these local potentates and conceded them a say in the affairs of the empire.[1] Turkish historians have likened the *sened* to Magna Carta, and provided that this is taken to be no more than an analogy, it is not seriously misleading.

The *sened*, however, proved to have no future. Under Mahmud II and his successors the centralizing absolutism of the Ottoman government with the help of European military and administrative techniques, gained new life and vigour. Those interests which had found their opportunity in the decay of the central ruling institution, and which might perhaps have led to some kind of constitutionalism and representative government were one by one more or less violently shorn of their power and made to submit to the will of the sultan and his servants. When a constitution finally came in the Ottoman empire, it was not the expression and symbol of compromise between state and society; it was a benevolent 'grant' by the absolute sovereign to his subjects, the parody rather than the analogue of what obtained in western Europe.

As it happened the parody was first enacted not in Istanbul, but in an outlying province which, however, was only nominally an Ottoman dependency. The Bey of Tunis Ahmad (1837–55) attracted by the example of Muhammad Ali in Egypt, wanted to make himself an independent and powerful potentate by the same methods which seemed to have brought the Pasha of Egypt such success. He decided to create a modern army and navy and to introduce manufactures into Tunis. His projects came to nought, but he plunged Tunisian finances into disorder, and entangled himself and his successors in a net of indebtedness to European bankers. His disastrous activities gave European Powers—France and Great Britain in particular—a much greater influence in Tunisian affairs: France because she was a powerful neighbour in Algeria, and Great Britain because it was then British policy to prevent French control over Tunisia. Under Ahmad's successor, Muhammad Bey (1855–9), the consuls of these two Powers suggested, in 1857, that Tunisia should emulate the Ottoman example and enact 'reforms' similar to those promised the previous year by the *Khatt-i Humayun*. The Bey proclaimed his intention to institute these 'reforms' in the *'ahd al-aman* and ensure to all security of the person, and equality in taxation and before the law. In the event, these 'reforms' meant the creation of a new centralized bureaucracy staffed by the officials of the Bey and their clients—a bureaucracy more grasping and less responsive to the grievances of the subject than the traditional, seemingly corrupt, ramshackle and arbitrary institutions. When the 'reforms' were proclaimed in 1857, the Bey indicated his intention to grant a constitution. It was in fact his successor Muhammad as-Sadiq (1859–82) who did so in January 1861. This constitution set up a grand council of sixty members partly appointed by the Bey, and partly co-opted. The councillors were chosen among ministers, high officials, senior officers and notables. The constitution laid down that the Bey and his ministers were responsible to the grand council whose approval was necessary for new laws to be enacted, old laws to be changed, expenditure to be increased, the army and the navy to be equipped or enlarged. What in effect happened was that the grand council was packed with the followers and clients of the Bey's powerful minister, the mamluke Mustafa the Khaznadar who, sheltering behind the façade of an ostensibly all-powerful assembly could exercise the most absolute and irresponsible power. In a remarkable letter written a year after the constitution came into effect, lieutenant-colonel Campenon, the head of the French military mission, discussed the character of the new régime:

This supreme Council [he wrote from Tunis to the French minister of war on 31 May 1862] combines the powers of the Legislative Assembly, of the Senate, of the *conseil d'état*, of the court of appeal and of the *cour des comptes*. The guarantees which the governed in constitutional states find in the division of powers exist no more here, and one is at a loss to explain how the European consuls who, as I have said above, took part in the drafting of the Tunisian Constitution, could have been accomplices in the monstrous creation of this supreme Council where all powers are mixed up and which is no more than a reminiscence of the old Turkish divans. It is true that the life of the Beys is no longer threatened daily, but only on condition that their power and their intervention in public affairs become non-existent. At the side of the Head of State, reduced to the role of a do-nothing king (*roi fainéant*), a permanent committee composed of ten members of the Supreme Council watches daily. This Committee, called the committee of ordinary affairs (*de service ordinaire*), receives complaints concerning illegal actions done either by the Bey or by any other individual. It is made up of the most influential mamlukes.

This is the crown of the whole edifice. The Tunisian Constitution, the liberalism of which is lauded by some journalists, leads to the formation of a council of ten, a kind of vigilance commission similar to that invented by the French assembly of 1849. Power, influence, wealth, all is concentrated in it, and the situation of the Regency is perfectly summed up in these lucid words which General Bonaparte addressed to the Egyptian population: Is there a beautiful woman? She is for the mamlukes. A fine horse? It is for the mamlukes. Money, fruitful trees, fertile land? They are all for the mamlukes.

Campenon went on to make the point that what the Bey's subjects wanted was not to be crushed by high taxation, to be administered by as few officials as possible and to have their cases tried locally and expeditiously. The 'reforms' of 1857–61 changed all this. Previously the subject depended in administrative matters on the *qa'id*, and in judicial on the *qadi*, the Bey having in both cases ultimate say: as Campenon picturesquely put it, the subject was

eaten by two men, but only by two. Today when almost all the powers of the *qa'id* and the *qadi* have passed to the [new] tribunals, he is eaten by all the members of these tribunals. He used to accept the decision of the local judge because it was a prompt decision, and only in grave issues would he appeal to the Sovereign. Today, the inhabitant of Gabes, which is 80 leagues from Tunis, who wants to appeal from a judgement rendered by the local tribunal, has to go to Tunis. And even after a journey so costly for him, he does not enjoy the privilege of personally rehearsing his grievances before the Bey. It is yet another committee issuing from the supreme Council, a number of these detested mamlukes transformed into a court of appeal, who will annul or confirm the first verdict.

Everything, then, has suddenly changed in the customs of this Arab population hitherto so immobile; the seeds of discontent have therefore not been tardy in appearing. A few months ago, twelve hundred inhabitants of Tunis went to the Bardo carrying the banners of those marabouts most venerated by the people. They went to ask the Bey to deliver them from innovations and to prevent the export of wheat. The Bey did not give in and ordered the ring-leaders to be imprisoned. There is no doubt that, had he weakened, grave disorders would have broken out in the European quarter of Tunis.

This was because the Mamlukes, with their sly policy, have not failed to tell the natives: The reforms against which you protest are not our work, but that of the Christians. Their consuls have imposed them by force. You must therefore submit and await better times.[2]

This constitutional régime did not last very long. To obtain more revenue, at the end of 1863 the *mejba*, a poll-tax which was anyway unpopular, was raised from 36 to 72 piastres. A large element of the Tunisian population then consisted of nomad or semi-sedentary tribes who had not yet been brought under full control by the central government. They rose in rebellion, their battle-cry being: 'No more mamlukes, no more *mejba*, no more constitution.'[3] The rebellion was eventually put down, but the constitution was suspended, never to be activated again.

Constitutionalism was next introduced into another autonomous province of the Ottoman empire—Egypt. Here too it was a 'grant' from the ruler, Isma'il. While there was no European pressure for its introduction, there is no doubt that Isma'il, so eager to make Egypt a part of Europe, considered a constitution and a chamber of deputies an indispensable sign of modernity like railways or an opera house: 'Whereas,' began his rescript of 22 October 1866, 'the great uses and benefits of assemblies (*majalis shura*) have been observed in civilized states, I have been in hopes of constituting an assembly in Egypt, the members of which would be elected from amongst the people. I thank God that I have seen the inhabitants of our country to possess the ability and aptitudes to realize such a hope; we have therefore agreed to establish this assembly.'[34] The *majlis shura al-nuwwab* which he thus established consisted of 75 members elected for three years. The electors, as the electoral decree prescribed (article VII) were the '*omdas* whom the decree describes as 'notables appointed according to the wishes of the population'! Isma'il did not have a mamluke caste such as existed in Tunis who would use the assembly for arrogating power to themselves. He himself was the undisputed and absolute ruler of Egypt. The assembly, elected by the '*omdas* who were of course his creatures, was given no powers and existed in effect for purposes of parade. The story is well-known of Isma'il insisting that his assembly should, following the best European models, divide into a government side and an opposition side, and the regulations for the conduct of *majlis* business which Isma'il issued testify to his anxiety that the assembly should behave in the most decorous and correct manner. Thus article XXXV (the regulations extended to 61 articles) enjoined the assembly 'to respect the right of the minority during debates. The minority should be listened to and their observations heard.'[5]

Nothing much was heard of Isma'il's assembly until 1879. Pressed that year by his creditors, and by the Powers, and threatened with a drastic curtailment both in his income and in his prerogatives, he imagined to convoke the assembly once more (it seems to have last met in 1876), in order on the one hand that it should be the mouthpiece of his own schemes; and on the other to make it seem that the quarrel was not between himself and his creditors, but between them and the Egyptian people over whom he, Isma'il, presided as a mere constitutional monarch. Cromer describes very well Isma'il's probable train of thought:

> He [Isma'il] knew that Europeans laid much stress on the will of the people. They had large talking assemblies, termed Parliaments, to whose will Kings and Emperors were obliged to conform. Such institutions were,

of course, wholly unsuitable for Egypt. Nevertheless, would it not be possible to hoist those Franks with their own petard? It was, indeed, difficult to deal with the French. They scarcely made a pretence of caring for anything but the interests of the French creditors . . . .

The case of the English was different. . . . They were easily carried away by phrases such as the popular will, constitutional government, and so on . . . With a people such as this, a great deal might be done. Might not an acute ruler so adapt his language as to suit a foreign public, whilst his acts would be in strict conformity with his own wishes and personal interests? The British Government must not be openly defied. . . . But surely if a scheme were devised which would present matters to the British Government and public in a form to which they were accustomed, if their most cherished institutions were apparently copied in Egypt, if the Egyptian people were to express their own views through their own representatives, then the bait would take. An Egyptian Parliament should, therefore, be assembled. The representatives of the Egyptian people should express their devotion to the Khedive, and their satisfaction with his system of government. They would reject as insulting the imputation that the country was bankrupt. They would demur to the changes in the system of taxation proposed by the European advisers of their Sovereign. Those changes were unjust, and, moreover, . . . the fresh taxation would fall on the representatives themselves rather than on the people whom, by a bold flight of the imagination, they were presumed to represent. But they would devise another system which would be more equitable. The representatives of the people, who were rich, would preserve their former privileges, but they would make large sacrifices in order to enable Egypt to meet its financial engagements. It was true that these sacrifices would fall, not on themselves, but on their fellow-countrymen in more humble classes of society. But the result would be the same. The interest of the debt would be paid. The members of the Egyptian Parliament must be left to devise their own scheme. That was essential. Otherwise, constitutional government would be a mere farce. Their patriotism would revolt at the idea of any foreign interference. For the future it must cease. The European Ministers must be dismissed.

When all this was done, it would not be necessary to talk any more of Parliaments or of popular representation. The necessity for their existence would have passed away.[6]

All this was indeed done, but availed Isma'il nothing. He was deposed and his son Tawfiq reigned in his stead. Some three years of complicated manœuvres and intrigues ensued, between the Khedive, still unsure of his position, ministers such as Sharif and Barudi intent perhaps on transferring to themselves the absolute power of the ruler —as the Tunisian mamlukes had done—and the army officers led by 'Urabi, who soon found themselves the effective masters of the state. Sharif, Barudi and other public men found it useful—as Isma'il had latterly done—to speak the language of constitutionalism; while the army officers proclaimed that the aim of their movement was to put an end to the absolutism which had ruined Egypt. When Tawfiq succeeded his father, he appointed Sharif chief minister. Sharif lost no time in preparing draft laws enlarging both the franchise and the powers of the assembly. Tawfiq, suspicious of Sharif's designs, dismissed him and adjourned the assembly which had been convoked by his father a few months earlier. It was not to meet again until October 1881 when Sharif was again in power and—what is more important—'Urabi's *coup d'état* had taken place. The pressures on Tawfiq were now more powerful than they had been in 1879, and he finally agreed—on 7 February 1882—to a law which made ministers collectively and individually responsible to the assembly, which required its assent to legislation and gave it control over the budget. It is quite clear that Tawfiq assented to this law only under the pressure of 'Urabi and the officers who were now in effect the ultimate arbiters in the state, and for whom this was a convenient way of transferring power from the Khedive to themselves. The assembly of 1879 was continued in being and allowed to exercise these considerably enlarged powers. It sat for a few months until the collapse of 'Urabi's movement. It proved to be, during this period, as pliant and obedient an instrument in the hands of the military dictatorship as it had been earlier, in Isma'il's hands.[7] There is no reason to believe that 'Urabi, had he continued in power, would have been less cavalier with the assembly than successive Egyptian governments proved to be under the constitutional monarchy in 1924–52.[8]

Constitutionalism and representative government became an issue and a battle-cry in the latter half of the eighteen-seventies, not only in Egypt but in the centre of the Ottoman empire itself. The immediate reason was the parlous financial and military situation in the last years of Abd al-'Aziz, but the demand for a parliament was, more remotely and more significantly, an outcome of the *tanzimat* by which, for half a century and more, the Ottoman rulers had been refashioning—and revolutionizing—their society. These *tanzimat* conjured up a class of European-educated officials some of whom, sensitive to the new tensions and injustices created by their reforms, from the 1860s began to subject the *tanzimat* to radical criticism and to argue that the remedy for the Empire lay not in administrative reforms initiated and directed by an absolutist state, but rather in constitutional and representative government which was both the secret of European superiority, and in profound consonance with the genuine traditions of Islam itself. These Young Ottoman notions found a follower in Midhat Pasha, a high official and minister, who, with a few colleagues, saw in the disturbed conditions of 1876 an opportunity to realize these ideals. A military *coup d'état* deposed Abd al-'Aziz on 30 March 1876, and another *coup d'état* deposed his successor Murad on 1 September of the same year. Abd al-Hamid II was chosen to succeed Murad after Midhat had made sure that he would be agreeable to the 'granting' of a constitution and a parliament. Between September and the promulgation of the constitution of 23 December 1876, there was a sharp struggle between Midhat and the sultan over its terms. But it would be more illuminating to describe the struggle as one concerning the ultimate power in the state. And this struggle was not between sultan and people. In the circumstances of the Ottoman empire then and long afterwards it was quite out of the question for the people to control or curb the ruling institution. The struggle was rather between two competing absolutisms, that of the Sultan and that of doctrinaire officials and officers who (in this respect similar to the mamlukes of Tunis, and to 'Urabi and his fellows) utilized constitutional and representative devices to divest the traditional ruler of his power to their own benefit. In saying this one is not necessarily impugning Midhat's sincerity—though there is enough in his actions and those of his followers in 1876 to raise powerful suspicions—but it remains true—does it not?—that if Brutus topples Caesar, Brutus will sit in Caesar's seat. We may give Abd al-Hamid this credit at least, that in exiling Midhat on 5 February 1877, he knew what issues were at stake.

The constitution 'granted' in December 1876 gave the parliament for which it provided very few, hardly any, powers. This parliament, chosen by means of indirect elections, met for a short session from March to June 1877; another parliament, freshly elected, met on 13 December 1877 and was prorogued *sine die* on 14 February 1878. The sultan, unlike Isma'il, in Egypt, happened to have no use for a parliament; whilst those who might have had some use for it, Midhat and his sympathizers (the analogues of Sharif in Egypt and of the mamlukes of Tunis) were threatening the sultan's power.

But the sultan having prevented putting it to the test, the Young Ottoman contention that salvation lay in making ministers responsible to a popular assembly and in encouraging local and provincial self-government remained a mere argument, an unfulfilled promise the ghost of which haunted the intellectual and official classes in the three decades of Hamidian rule which followed. The Hamidian period saw a continuation of the trends to modernization and centralization which were dominant all through the nineteenth century in the Ottoman empire. 'It would not be an exaggeration,' writes Professor Bernard Lewis, 'that it was in these early years of the reign of Abdulhamid that the whole movement of the *tanzimat*, of legal, administrative and educational reform reached its fruition and its climax. And so, too, did the tendencies, already discernible under the *tanzimat* régime towards a new centralized and unrestrained despotism.'[9] One may in fact go on to argue that it was the very success of Hamidian policies in promoting education—both civilian and military—and in developing railways and telegraphs which brought about the downfall of the régime. More and more young men—eventually to become officers and officials—were exposed to European-style education and ideas, and thus became disaffected towards the régime which had set up the schools and colleges in which they were educated, while improved communications spread these ideas to remote corners of the empire where they had hardly penetrated before. As a result, scepticism about the legitimacy of the traditional Ottoman institutions, a toleration, an expectation of change—whether peaceful or violent—became widespread among the educated classes. Again, the increase in centralization and absolutism in the three decades of Hamidian rule itself made easier the success of a *coup d'état*, the authors of which had now only to neutralize or topple the supreme authority in the state, i.e. the sultan, for them in turn to gain control of the empire and its military and administrative organization.

This is what in effect happened in the Young Turk Revolution of 1908. In July of that year a group of young conspiratorial officers in the third army corps stationed in Macedonia (with its headquarters in Salonika) started a mutiny which rapidly spread in the corps and in the second army corps stationed in Edirne. When it looked as though the troops which the sultan despatched from Izmir against the mutineers were in sympathy with them, the sultan capitulated and on 24 July restored the constitution of 1876 as the Salonika officers had demanded. But it became rapidly clear that the empire was not to be governed on constitutional, parliamentary lines. Until April 1909, there was an uneasy and indecisive sparring for power between the officers organized into a Committee of Union and Progress and Abd al-Hamid whose position was of course profoundly shaken but who still had some power and much influence. The Young Turk officers were by no means popular with the traditional mass of Ottoman soldiers, or with those officers who had been promoted from the ranks and had not been exposed to European political doctrines which the Young Turks had imbibed in Abd al-Hamid's military schools and colleges. These 'ranker' officers incited soldiers of the first army corps stationed in Istanbul to mutiny on the night of 12–13 April, to the cry that the religion was in danger. This provoked a so-called 'Army of Deliverance' to march from Salonika on Istanbul, which they reached on 23 April. They crushed the counter-mutiny and the Committee of Union and Progress deposed

the sultan and reigned in his place.[10] It then became speedily apparent
that autocracy was not transformed into constitutional government;
rather the sultan's power passed to the officers who had dared to
depose him. True, there were elections and there was a parliament,
but it was not the deputies who controlled the government; on the
contrary it was the government who manipulated elections and controlled the parliament. Power lay elsewhere; it was held by the officers
who had carried out the *coup d'état* of July 1908, and who had foiled
the counter *coup* of April 1909. As was shortly to be seen, such power
was not amenable to constitutional limitation; gained through a *coup
d'état*, it could be destroyed—not limited—only through a similar
coup d'état. In 1911 there was a split within the committee and opposition to its rule began to grow. The Unionists therefore dissolved the
chamber of deputies in January 1912, and held a general election
in which all but six of the returned members supported the government. This election became known as 'the big-stick election'. In
July a group of officers known as the 'Saviour Officers' organized a
movement in the army which succeeded in bringing down the Unionist government. The sultan, Mehmed Reshad—Abd al-Hamid's
successor and now a mere figurehead—appointed a new government,
ratifying the choice of the 'Saviour Officers'. The Unionist parliament was dissolved. In January 1913, a group of Unionist officers,
led by Colonel Enver Bey, one of the authors of the original *coup* in
1908, burst into the Sublime Porte, where the cabinet was meeting,
and in the *fracas* which ensued one of them shot the minister of war
dead. The cabinet was forced to resign at the point of the gun, and
until the end of the first world war, Unionist domination in the empire
went unchallenged and unquestioned. The yearning of the official
and educated classes for a modern constitutional parliamentary
government thus finally found fulfillment in the replacement of the
sultan's stable traditional autocracy by unstable military rule in
which rulers gained and maintained their position by a constant
and ready appeal to the sword. We may say in retrospect that for the
Ottoman empire and its successors the events of 1908–14 have an
archetypal significance. They establish a modern and now familiar
pattern of army intervention in politics—intervention planned and
carried out by young officers in the belief that the European ideologies which inspire them can provide remedies for their political and
social ills. These events also exemplify the crisis in representation
which has increasingly overtaken middle-eastern politics. The
traditional rulers shared the same universe of discourse with their
subjects, and in the course of the centuries autocracy had come to be
mediated, tempered or checked by intermediate bodies which had
either—like the *millets*—been instituted by the authorities for ease

and convenience of government, or, like the Janissaries, had arrogated to themselves, owing to the decay of the ruling institution, a quasi-independent position in the state. The officers and officials who now began to carry out *coups d'état* were isolated by their European ideas from the still traditional society the fate of which they were resolved to shape and direct. Again, the new centralized absolutism, of which these officers were the product and outcome, largely destroyed or emasculated the traditional intermediate bodies which had effectively if informally 'represented' the main interests of society and had served as their link with the central authority. In the European-style elections individual voters elected the candidates agreeable to the authorities, and the resultant parliaments could neither control nor check the government which had brought them into being. Representative institutions in fact signified an actual decrease of representativeness in the Ottoman body politic.

This decline is still apparent and just as marked under Mustafa Kemal's régime after the first world war. In his westernizing policies, Ataturk was the direct heir of the men of the *tanzimat* and the Young Turks. *Tanzimat* and constitutionalism were in reality opposites since the mass of the people, if they were given a voice in government, would have rejected with incomprehension and loathing much of their enlightened rulers' policies. Kemalist Turkey was an absolutism in which a small minority had the power to indoctrinate the majority and tell them how best to order their lives. Kemalist administrative absolutism survived Ataturk's death by a decade or so. Its dominance was in the end broken, but by members of the ruling minority falling out among themselves. The Republicans in power were visibly losing their nerve. Their slackened grip over the country encouraged the people to manifest their hatred and dislike of the government and resulted in a landslide victory for the Democrats. When these latter came to power in 1950, they were the first Turkish ruling group since the beginning of western reforms to pay some heed to the actual inclinations and desires of the population. But their decade in office showed that it was still possible for the rulers to manipulate elections and representative assemblies. They were removed from office in 1960 by a military *coup d'état* the authors of which, however, objected not so much to the Democrats' electoral and parliamentary practices as to their 'reactionary' proclivities in allowing the Turkish people to indulge in unwestern and un-Enlightened activities. It is too early yet to come to a judgement on Turkish politics since 1960. If we are optimists, we may say that at last constitutionalism will have a chance to survive.

The other middle-eastern state which proclaimed a constitution before the first world war was Iran. The conditions here were quite different from those obtaining in the Ottoman empire. Iran had not been touched by European influences during the nineteenth century to anything like the same extent as the Ottoman empire, and had certainly not been subjected to that sustained and radical westernization which the Ottoman sultans from Mahmud II to Abd al-Hamid had initiated and carried through. The Iranian army, in particular, remained weak and backward, useless in war against a European enemy and hardly more useful in maintaining internal security. The most successful attempt at modernizing the army had been that of Nasir al-Din Shah (1848–96). In 1879 he engaged Russian officers to train and command a Persian cossack brigade which until the reforms of Riza Shah (1925–41) remained practically the only modern—and effective—military formation in Iran. As a large modernized army did not exist, so its fateful concomitant, a numerous and important class of European-trained army officers, was likewise absent. By the same token, Iran remained an old-fashioned Oriental despotism, largely innocent of the centralized and levelling absolutism which was the consequence of the Ottoman reforms.

But of course Iran could not remain immune from European influence, whether political, economic or intellectual. Russia and Great Britain confronted each other in Iran as elsewhere in Central Asia and were always seeking to establish and increase their influence and destroy that of their rivals. The European economy, world-wide in its extension, sooner or later brought Iran within its network through the activities of financiers and concession-hunters. The telegraph, first introduced in 1858 and extended after 1862 into a large network by a British concern, the Indo-European Telegraph Company, may stand as a symbol and index of the steady and cumulative increase of European influence in Iran. Beyond all these was the intellectual ferment which contact with Europe created and which until the last decade of the nineteenth century affected a few, albeit an influential few, of the learned and official classes.

The disturbance which European activity and European influences created in Iran is indicated by the so-called tobacco protest of 1891–2. Iran had known internal disturbances during the reign of Nasir al-Din Shah, the most serious of which were those messianic uprisings which the Babis fomented in the first years of his reign; but the tobacco protest had certain new features lacking in traditional agitations—which were to recur in the events leading to the grant of a constitution in 1906. The increasing intercourse between Europe and Iran had subjected the economy and public finances of Iran to great stress. It seemed to the government that an easy way of repairing its finances was to grant, against immediate payment, monopolistic concessions, to exploit one or other of Iran's resources.

In 1890 the shah granted to a British concessionaire a monopoly of the production, sale and export of Iranian tobacco. The concession aroused widespread opposition in the country and it is interesting to examine which groups in Iranian society initiated and organized this opposition. The monopoly was seen as a threat to their interests by the native merchants and money-lenders, and they were prompt in voicing their objections. They were supported by the *ulama*, whose Shi'ism did not enjoin the same utterly passive obedience to the earthly ruler which was current in areas of Sunni dominance. Twelver Shi'ism, established as the official religion of Iran since Safawid times, considered the twelfth descendant of the Caliph Ali, who had vanished in infancy, as the legitimate ruler of the Muslim community, the Hidden Imam who would one day return to establish a reign of righteousness. In the meantime the authority to interpret the Holy Law was vested in the *mujtahids*, the theologians who, by their knowledge of holy writ and of precedents, are qualified to express the intentions of the Hidden Imam. The temporal ruler, whose authority would disappear at the coming of the Hidden Imam, was therefore bound to respect the authority of these *mujtahids* and to defer to their pronouncements. Two other features of Shi'ism served to enhance the position of the *ulama* and to make their concerted opposition to the ruler formidable. In the first place, some of the most revered shrines of Shi'ism, Karbala, Najaf and Kazimayn, lay in Ottoman Mesopotamia outside the control of the shah, and in them were to be found some of the most eminent *mujtahids* of the Shi'a world whose pronouncements would receive the ready and respectful acquiescence of the devout masses. And it is this popular devotion which, in the second place, gave the Iranian *ulama* influence and power in Iranian society. In the tobacco protest, these *ulama*, fortified by *fatwas* emanating from *mujtahids* in Iran and Mesopotamia, exerted their influence—which proved decisive—against the concession. Their power was shown to be such that when they declared a boycott of tobacco and prohibited all forms of smoking, their prohibition was universally obeyed. The *ulama* no doubt acted out of dislike for infidels and foreigners whose ways and whose ideas they shrewdly suspected of subverting sooner or later the traditional religion. As the struggle against the shah showed signs of being successful, they no doubt also came to enjoy this demonstration of their power and influence. The third group which worked with the merchants and *ulama* in organizing and sustaining the agitation was rather different, less numerous and seemingly less powerful, but in retrospect it proves to have been the most significant. This group believed that the ills of Iran originated in its traditional institutions and the only efficacious remedy was a radical one. In other words, these were the westernizers who were themselves westernized whether at first or at second-hand. The Iranian western-izers, necessarily drawn from the official and intellectual classes, were a small group who began to propagate their views in the last two decades or so of Nasir al-Din's reign. But they had to proceed very circumspectly, for in a country where religion had such a strong hold, a damaging charge of heresy could easily be levelled against them. To parry such a threat it would seem that some of them deliberately adopted the tactic of presenting their European notions in a Muslim garb. One of the most prominent of these reformers, Malkam Khan, openly discussed these tactics in an article on 'Persian Civilisation', published by *The Contemporary Review* in 1891. 'As then Islam . . .', he wrote 'is an ocean in which are accumulated all the sciences of the past times of Asia . . . then for any new law or new principle you wish to promulgate, you can find in that ocean many precepts and maxims which support and confirm what you want to introduce. As to the principles which are found in Europe, which constitute the root of your civilization, we must get hold of them somehow, no doubt; but instead of taking them from London or Paris, instead of saying this comes from such an ambassador, or that is advised by such a government (which will never be accepted), it will be very easy to take the same principle and to say that it comes from *Islam,* and that this can be soon proved. We have had some experience in this direction. We found that ideas which were by no means accepted when coming from your agents in Europe, were accepted at once with the greatest delight when it was proved that they were latent in Islam. I can assure you that the little progress which we see in Persia and Turkey, especially in Persia, is due to this fact, that some people have taken your European principles, and instead of saying that they came from Europe, from England, France or Germany, have said: "We have nothing to do with Europeans; these are the true principles of our own religion (and, indeed, that is quite true) which have been *taken* by Europeans!" That has had a marvellous effect at once.' This again was exactly the tactic which his associate, the famous Jamal al-Din al-Afghani (1838–97), pursued in Iran and elsewhere. For these modernizers the protest against the tobacco concession could be widened into a protest against the régime as a whole and could be made the occasion for demanding a limitation of the shah's power.

These three groups, then, merchants, men of religion and mod-ernizers, though their motives were certainly not identical, found it possible to act in concert. Their agitation, thanks to the telegraph, spread across the whole of Iran. Supported by the Russians who were afraid that the tobacco monopoly would increase the power and influence of their British rivals, it succeeded in eliciting a popular response such that the shah had no alternative but to cancel the concession.

The cancellation was a great blow to the authority of the régime. By giving in so unconditionally to pressure and popular agitation it cast doubt on its legitimacy and implicitly admitted the charges of despotism, greed and corruption which the more extreme of its critics had made. The tobacco protest publicized grievances which were to be heard again in 1905–6, when a constitution was granted and it made familiar the notion that the shah and the government could be checkmated and perhaps overthrown by a popular uprising. The murder of Nasir al-Din Shah in 1896 showed the influence of the ideas spread during the tobacco protest, and the murder itself gave them further currency. The shah was murdered at the instigation of Jamal al-Din al-Afghani by a follower of his, Mirza Muhammad Riza. The murderer was essentially a simple man and politically quite unsophisticated. What he had to say in justification of his deed is therefore striking. He had murdered in the first place to avenge Afghani 'that holy man and true descendant of the Prophet', whom the shah had seized and forcibly deported from Iran in 1891; but what moved him even more was the spectacle of 'thousands of poor Persian subjects who have fled from their own dear country from the hand of oppression and tyranny, and have perforce adopted the most miserable means of earning a livelihood . . . After all,' he went on, 'these flocks of your sheep need a pasture in which they may graze, so that their milk may increase, and that they may be able both to suckle their young and to support your milking; not that you should constantly milk them as long as they have milk to give, and when they have none, should devour their flesh from their body. Your sheep are all gone and scattered: this is the result of tyranny which you see.' For these reasons he had murdered the shah, and in no uncertain words threatened that if Nasir al-Din's successor did not mend his father's ways, he would suffer the same fate: 'If . . . he likewise adopts this practice and conduct, then this crooked load will never reach the halting-place.' When asked how he could reconcile his anxiety for his country with a deed which could possibly precipitate disorder and confusion, he replied: 'Yes, that is true, but look at the histories of the Franks: so long as blood was not shed to accomplish lofty aims, the object in view was not attained.'

Under Muzaffar al-Din Shah (1896–1907) the same conditions which led to the discontent of merchants, *ulama* and modernizers continued and perhaps worsened. Iran was becoming more and more enmeshed in the world economy and embroiled in foreign debt to service and repay which required more revenues. This strained the Iranian fiscal system and evoked loud protests against foreign exploitation, official corruption and maladministration. Secret societies, or *anjumans*, became active. They were dedicated to the spread, particularly among the intellectual and official classes, of reforming and modernizing notions. In 1904, in particular, various groups decided to come together and concert measures for the overthrow of despotism. A secret meeting of some sixty persons held on 28 May 1904, agreed on a programme of action consisting of eighteen articles, the sixteenth of which speaks of 'the bringing about of revolution'. The modernizers, as has been said, were always very careful to avoid any imputation of heresy, and it is interesting in this connexion to note that article fourteen of this programme required that whatever was circulated by the committee should conform to the laws of Islam so that no member could be accused of heresy, and article seventeen required members not to take part in other than Islamic religious assemblies. Shortly afterwards, in February 1905, another group, known as the Secret Society, was formed the object of which, as stated in its programme, was to awaken the people to their rights, to remove tyranny and to seek ways of reforming abuses. In 1905 discontent came to a head, and there was widespread and open agitation against the shah, his ministers, and against Russian influence which was great and increasing. The Russo-Japanese war of 1904, in which a Christian European Power was signally defeated at the hands of an Oriental Power, and the Russian Revolution which followed the war, no doubt contributed to the effervescence, but the specific grievance which set in train the events leading to the grant of a constitution was the introduction of a new customs tariff in 1903 which the merchants considered onerous and oppressive. In 1905, the tariffs were enforced with greater severity and there were protests in various cities. In particular, a group of Tehran merchants took sanctuary in the shrine of Shah Abd al-Azim near the capital, whence they demanded redress for their grievances. The shah was then abroad, and his heir who was acting as regent pacified them by promising redress upon the shah's return. In the ensuing months tension between government and people both in the capital and in the provinces did not abate. Incidents indicative of this tension were the ill-treatment of a *mulla* by the governor of Qazvin, the administration of the bastinado on the orders of the governor to a prominent religious leader in Kirman, and the firing by a troop of soldiers on a crowd demonstrating against the governor of Mashhad. These incidents in turn further exacerbated the situation. In December, the prime minister accused some merchants of having raised the price of sugar; he seized them and had them bastinadoed. This led a group of merchants to protest by taking sanctuary in a Tehran mosque, where they were joined by a number of prominent *ulama* and their popular following. From this mosque they were expelled by a crowd at the instigation of another *mulla*, who was on the side of the authorities. The protesters and their following thereupon left the city for the sanctuary of Shah Abd al-Azim, where at the end there were some 2,000 of them. A month afterwards there was still no prospect of their being dislodged. There they were, financed, provisioned and encouraged by their friends and perhaps also by prominent men who wanted to intrigue against the prime minister. To put an end to a state of affairs injurious to his authority and prestige, the shah issued an autograph letter to his prime minister which promised equality before the law, a code and the setting up of a ministry of justice to supervise its execution. This was presumably in response to a demand which one of the secret societies had made public the previous May. The shah's promise satisfied the protesters and they returned to Tehran. But it soon appeared that the promises were not being implemented and the agitation revived. The secret societies and the *ulama* who sympathized with them denounced despotism and put continuously before the public the shah's un-fulfilled promise. In June, the prime minister tried to expel from Tehran two influential preachers; riots ensued and once again a large number of *ulama*, merchants and others took sanctuary, this time in Qum; the merchants and artisans of Tehran went on strike and the bazaars were closed; on 19 July another group took sanctuary in the gardens of the British legation and so many joined them that by the beginning of August it was estimated that some 12,000 were camping in the gardens. Just as he felt compelled to give in on the previous January, so now again the shah retreated, dismissed his prime minister, and on 5 August issued a rescript setting up a national consultative assembly. Elections were held in September, and on 7 September, the shah opened the assembly. It speedily proceeded to draft and vote on a Fundamental Law which the shah signed on 30 December. A supplementary Fundamental Law was promulgated on 7 October 1907.

When the agitation first began it was directed against financial and fiscal oppressions, and what its leaders openly demanded was the promulgation of a code of laws and reform in the administration of justice. The setting-up of constitutional and representative govern-ment may therefore be seen as the result of the shah's dilatory tactics which in the end left him no room for manœuvre. A con-stitutional representative government was probably what the mod-ernizers and westernizers really desired, and they skilfully exploited the shah's weakness and impolicy. The Fundamental Laws of 30 December 1906, and their Supplement of 7 October 1907, provide examples of two incompatible outlooks within the opposition— the Muslim traditionalist and the European modernist, and show that it is the modernist outlook which clearly prevailed. The traditional strain is exemplified in article 1 of the Supplementary Laws, which enacts that Islam according to the Ja'fari sect (i.e. Twelver Shi'ism) is the religion of the State, 'which faith the Shah of Persia must profess and promote'. Article 2 is yet more unambiguously traditionalist. It states: 'At no time must any legal enactment of the Sacred National Consultative Assembly, established by the favour and assistance of His Holiness the Imam of the Age (may God hasten his glad Advent!), the favour of His Majesty the Shahinshah of Islam (may God immortalize his reign!), the care of the Proofs of Islam [i.e. the *mujtahids*] (may God multiply the like of them!) and the whole people of the Persian nation, be at variance with the sacred principles of Islam or the laws established by His Holiness the Best of Mankind [i.e. the Prophet Muhammed] (on whom and on whose household be the Blessings of God and His Peace!)'. The article went on to require the establishment of a committee of five *mujtahids* to whom proposed legislation would be submitted and who had the power to 'reject and repudiate, wholly or in part, any such proposal which is at variance with the Sacred Laws of Islam, so that it shall not obtain the title of legality. In such matters', the article went on, 'the decision of this Ecclesiastical Committee shall be followed and obeyed, and this article shall continue unchanged until the appearance of His Holiness the Proof of the Age [i.e. the Hidden Imam whose reappearance will inaugurate the reign of justice] (may God hasten his glad Advent!).'

In contrast with this article, which from the outset remained inoperative, the constitution abounded in provisions unmistakably European in provenance which clearly showed the influence of the westernizers. The second paragraph of the preamble to the Fundamental Laws, for instance, spoke of the right the shah was conferring on 'each individual of the people of our realm' to participate in choosing by popular election the members of the national consultative assembly. Article 2 of these Fundamental Laws asserted that the assembly represented 'the whole of the people of Iran, who thus participate in the economic and political affairs of the country'; article 8 of the Supplementary Laws, again, affirms; 'The people of the Iranian Empire are to enjoy equal rights before the Law'; article 26: 'The powers of the realm are all derived from the people' and article 35: 'The Sovereignty is a trust confided (as a Divine gift) by the people to the person of the Shah'. This notion of a state composed of 'individuals' each of whom is endowed with 'rights', who are the source of public authority and who bestow 'sovereignty' on the ruler, is of course utterly at variance with the traditional Islamic theory of government. Equally at variance with both practice and theory was the separation of legislative, judicial and executive power which the constitution enjoined, and the responsibility of ministers to the assembly which it also prescribed.

As the sequel showed, it was hardly to be expected that a constitution of this character, promulgated in such circumstances, would operate in a country like Iran in a manner even remotely resembling the intentions and hopes of its authors. Muzaffar al-Din opened the Assembly on 7 October 1906. He died the following January and his son Muhammad Ali Shah (1907–9) succeeded him. From the start it was clear that he and his ministers were utterly opposed to the assembly and that Russia was taking his part in the dispute. The authority of the shah having been seriously shaken and that of the assembly hardly established, the maintenance of law and order became very difficult. Disorder broke out in the provinces and the authority of government disappeared. In August, the prime minister, pro-Russian and opposed to the constitution, was murdered by a member of a secret society. In December the shah, by arresting the new prime minister and other ministers who were in favour of the assembly, tried to reassert his own unfettered power. Popular clamour in Tehran and the provinces foiled him for the time being. In February 1908, a bomb was thrown at his motor car, but the shah escaped. In June the cossack brigade bombarded and cleared the assembly. Prominent popular leaders were arrested and two of them strangled without trial. On 27 June the shah dissolved the assembly and abolished the constitution as being contrary to Islamic law. Thereupon the *anjumans* of Tabriz, the capital of Azerbaijan, rose in rebellion, ousted the shah's men and held the town for some nine months, keeping a besieging force at bay. Other movements against the shah were organized from Rasht and from Isfahan. From the latter city, a force of Bakhtiari tribesmen marched on the capital and, effecting a junction with a force from Rasht, entered Tehran on 13 July 1909. On 16 July, Muhammad Ali, having taken refuge in the Russian legation, abdicated. He was formally deposed at a meeting of the assembly that same evening and his twelve-year old son Ahmad Shah (1909–25) proclaimed his successor.

Towards the end of 1909, elections for the second legislative session were held and the assembly met on 5 December 1909. Its record was quite as chequered as that of the first session. The Bakhtiari chieftains who were now preponderant in the government did not exactly have constitutionalism at heart; the country was in turmoil and the Russians ready to exploit the opportunity in order to establish and extend their position in the country. Some eighteen months after the inauguration of the second legislative session, in June 1911, matters came to a head. The ex-shah attempted to regain his throne by landing in Iran and fomenting a rebellion in which he was joined by Lur and Turkoman tribes whom he had tempted to his side. The rebellion was put down and the ex-shah forced to flee. But these events caused more disorder and anarchy in the country. To safeguard their interests in the south, the British landed troops in Bushire. The Russians took the opportunity to reinforce the troops they had stationed in the north ever since the summer of 1909. In May 1911, an American, Morgan Shuster, had been appointed treasurer-general of Iran. This displeased the Russians who began applying pressure on the Iranian government. This culminated in a forty-eight hours' ultimatum delivered on 29 November 1911, which demanded Shuster's dismissal. The government, knowing itself powerless to resist the Russians, wished to comply but the assembly wanted to resist. The government which had issued from the Bakhtiari march on Tehran in 1909, the object of which had been to re-establish the constitution, now broke the deadlock by forcibly disbanding the assembly and suspending the constitution. This was practically the end of constitutionalism in Iran. Ahmad Shah attained his majority in July 1914; the opportunity was taken to resume parliamentary government. But the third legislative session met in the shadow of the first world war which affected Iran in various disagreeable ways. The Germans and their Ottoman allies naturally did what they could to arouse opposition to the Russians and the British. Their task was made easy among the official and intellectual classes by Russian and British unpopularity, which stemmed from the constant intervention of these powers in Iranian politics during the past decade. German activities naturally elicited a Russian reaction. In November 1915, Russian troops seemed to be advancing on Tehran; the assembly therefore broke up and most of its members fled to Qum. The assembly was not to meet again until 1921. By then, the war and its aftermath had wreaked havoc on the government of Iran and had thrown up various contenders for power whose instincts and methods were certainly not constitutional. One of these contenders, Riza Khan, an officer of the cossack brigade, made himself master of the country by a military *coup d'état* and had himself proclaimed shah in 1925. Riza Shah ruled from 1925 to 1941 as an unchallenged despot. During his reign the assembly met regularly, but it was no more than a decorative appendage of the régime. Nothing that has happened under his successor has served to make constitutionalism and representative government of any significance in Iranian political life.

The record to the two other constitutional régimes in the Middle East during this period was hardly more brilliant. Constitutionalism in the Ottoman empire and in Iran was the outcome of a native movement of opinion, of a local reaction to the European challenge. In these two states constitutionalism may have been helped or hindered by the policies of the European powers. In Egypt and in Iraq, however, constitutional government was introduced and advocated by a European Power, Great Britain. The aftermath of war saw Egypt plunged in an agitation against the British occupant, who had proclaimed Egypt a Protectorate in 1914. The British government eventually gave way to this agitation, and by the declaration of 28 February 1922 recognized Egyptian independence. Egypt, as the authors of the declaration envisaged, would become a constitutional kingdom endowed with representative institutions and a responsible government. In April 1922 a committee was appointed to draft a constitution, and in October it submitted a draft which affirmed that sovereignty belonged to the Egyptian people and which provided for elections and a parliament to which ministers would be responsible. King Fu'ad, who had unexpectedly succeeded his brother in 1917 and whose autocratic proclivities were well-known, objected strenuously to the draft constitution. He succeeded in making numerous changes which increased his own powers, and it was only after much pressure by Allenby, the British high commissioner, that he approved the constitution in its emasculated form in April 1923.[11] Whether this or any other constitution would have been promulgated without British pressure is mere speculation, but it remains true that the British thought it necessary and desirable to press Fu'ad to grant a constitution. We may therefore conclude that they believed it feasible for an independent Egypt to become a constitutional monarchy with a representative and responsible government. The political history of Egypt under the monarchical constitution in fact continuously and systematically belied these expectations. The reason was the very same which accounted for the ill-success of Ottoman and Iranian constitutionalism, namely that western-style elections and representative institutions were incapable of representativeness, and therefore incapable of providing constitutional and responsible government. Elections in Egypt under the monarchy, far from determining the character of the government in Cairo, were themselves determined by whichever faction happened to dominate the Cairo political scene. In 1923, the elections were overwhelmingly won by the Wafd, a populist movement created and controlled by Sa'd Zaghlul who, inspired and instigated by Fu'ad in 1918, had challenged the British protectorate. In 1923, he had the benefit of the king's support because his rivals had Allenby's support; it was indeed on behalf of these rivals that Allenby had pressed an unwilling Fu'ad to approve the constitution. Zaghlul formed a government and during his period of office tried, by means of demonstrations and similar stratagems, to intimidate Fu'ad into conceding him the primacy in the state. But his government lasted barely a year. The British governor-general of the Sudan was murdered in November 1924 by terrorists connected with the Wafd. Zaghlul resigned and Fu'ad dissolved the parliament. He appointed a non-Wafdist ministry which immediately proceeded to conduct new elections. These resulted in a draw between Zaghlul's supporters and the government's men. This was the only election under the constitutional monarchy the results of which did not correspond perfectly with the desires of whichever party happened to be dominant at Cairo. The reasons for this undoubtedly was that the new government did not have enough time to destroy or neutralize Wafdist organization in the provinces which Zaghlul had been able to consolidate during his period in power. The new parliament met once in March 1925 and was immediately dissolved. The government dispensed with a parliament for more than a year and the king's influence was supreme. The British high commissioner who succeeded Allenby, Lord Lloyd, judged this to be undesirable. He used his influence and power which was still great—since the declaration of 28 February 1922, while conceding Egyptian independence, had reserved to the British government the defence of Egypt, the security of British imperial communications, the protection of foreigners and the Anglo-Egyptian Sudan—in order to persuade the Egyptian government to carry out elections. Lloyd's intervention was a defeat for Fu'ad and the elections of May 1926 duly registered the fact by returning a Wafdist majority. The logic of constitutional responsible government would have therefore required Zaghlul to form an administration, but he was unacceptable to Lloyd and a non-Wafdist became prime minister. The following year Zaghlul having died, his successor Nahhas made use of his parliamentary majority to compel his own appointment as prime minister. Shortly afterwards he fell foul of the British and, notwithstanding his large majority, Fu'ad dismissed him, dissolved the parliament and appointed as prime minister Muhammad Mahmud, the leader of the Liberal Constitutional Party. The new prime minister suspended the constitution and ruled for a year without a parliament. In 1929 a Labour government came to power in Great Britain and wished to conclude an Anglo-Egyptian treaty. Such a treaty could not, in its view, possibly be negotiated and concluded except with a government which had the right to speak on behalf of the Egyptian people, and only a government enjoying a parliamentary majority, the Labour ministers believed, had this right. Great Britain's position in Egypt lent great weight to such a view. Muhammad Mahmud's position thus became untenable. The subsequent elections ratified Muhammad Mahmud's—and Fu'ad's—setback by returning a large Wafdist majority. The Wafd formed an administration which failed to conclude a Treaty with the British. The king dismissed it, and appointed Isma'il Sidqi, a non-Wafdist, as prime minister. Sidqi dissolved the parliament, promulgated a new constitution which gave greater powers to the executive and held new elections. The electors returned a very large anti-Wafdist majority. This parliament lasted from 1931 to 1936, a period during which Egypt was in effect governed by Fu'ad through a series of king's men. In 1936, the British once again wished to conclude a treaty with Egypt; once again they made it clear that they would negotiate only with an Egyptian government which could claim to represent Egypt; and it was again clear that they believed the Wafd to speak for the Egyptian people, or at any rate for a large majority of it. It became therefore clear that the royal policy had sustained a setback, which the electors duly ratified by returning a very large Wafdist majority. Nahhas formed a Wafdist administration which signed the Anglo-Egyptian Treaty of 1936. Fu'ad died the same year, and was succeeded by his son Faruq, who was then a minor. He assumed his powers on attaining his majority in July 1937. He was as antagonistic to the Wafd as his father had been, and in December dismissed Nahhas and appointed in his place Muhammad Mahmud who dissolved the parliament elected in 1936. The Wafd thus sustained a defeat which the electorate ratified by returning a large anti-Wafdist majority in 1938. This parliament lasted until 1942, when the British, fearing the king's pro-Axis sympathies, forced him by a *coup d'état* to appoint Nahhas prime minister. He held new elections at which a large Wafdist majority was returned. The second world war being nearly over in 1945, Faruq was able to dismiss Nahhas. His successor dissolved the 1942 parliament and a large anti-Wafdist majority was returned. The 1945 parliament was the only one to run its full course under the constitutional monarchy. The 1950 elections returned a Wafdist majority, an outcome which may have been the result of an understanding between the king and the Wafd. The military *coup d'état* of July 1952 put an end both to monarchy and to parliamentary government.

In Iraq too, constitutionalism introduced and established by the British, proved—albeit for different reasons—a fiasco. Iraq was formed out of three ex-Ottoman provinces—Mosul, Baghdad and Basra—which the British conquered and occupied during the first world war. Conditions in these three provinces differed widely. The overwhelming majority in the south was composed of a Shi'ite semi-settled agricultural population accustomed to defer to its tribal leaders and to the *mujtahids* of Najaf and Karbala; the north had a majority of Kurds; the west and north-west contained a large agglomeration of Sunni Arab nomads. These and other disparate elements the British government forced in 1921 into one centralized state controlled from Baghdad over which they placed as king, Faysal, the third son of the Sharif of Mecca. Power in this overwhelmingly Shi'ite and Kurdish state was exercised by politicians and bureaucrats drawn from the Sunni Arab minority whose model and inspiration was the centralized absolutism of the Ottoman empire whose servants they had hitherto been. This centralizing absolutism these men wished to use on behalf of an ideology, that of Arab nationalism, which they wanted to impose on this heterogeneous and apolitical population. To all these complexities and potential conflicts, the British added the further complication of constitutionalism and responsible parliamentary government. A constitution setting up a parliament to which ministers were responsible was promulgated in 1925. Iraq was then not an independent state but a mandated territory, and the British high commissioner had a supervisory, restraining and moderating influence. But even during this period it was apparent that elections went as the administration wanted them to go. After the mandate was terminated in 1932, elections and parliaments were only counters in the political game as it was played by the handful of politicians in Baghdad. Iraqi politics had a very narrow base and hence were highly unstable. In the period of the constitutional monarchy from 1921 to 1958, there was a total of 58 cabinets. This narrowness and instability tempted politicians to gain and hold power by extra-constitutional means. In 1934–6 they made use of tribal dissidence in the imperfectly policed south in order to force changes of government in Baghdad. These tribal rebellions were put down by the Iraqi army. The officers, seeing how indispensable they were to the politicians, themselves started to intervene in politics in combination with this or that faction of politicians. The period 1936–41 therefore saw a succession of military *coups d'état*. The last one, in April 1941, brought into power a pro-Axis government. This led the British to intervene and until 1945, Iraqi politics were under British supervision. After 1945, owing to the increase in centralization the tribal uprisings of the 1930s were no longer possible and by continuous purges and strict control the army was prevented from interference in politics; but eventually such measures proved useless and a military *coup d'état* in July 1958 made a bloody end of the constitutional monarchy. Between

1945 and 1958, the same narrowly-based political game went on being played in the capital between a handful of politicians who manipulated elections and manœuvred and intrigued each other out of office.

The exception to this common fate which overtook constitutionalism in all middle-eastern countries is found in the Lebanon. Today's Lebanon is the direct heir of the autonomous *sanjaq* of Mount Lebanon. Its area is, to be sure, more extensive and what had been in the *sanjaq* a Druze-Maronite dialogue has become in the Lebanon as enlarged by the French mandatory a complex, subtle, and occasionally perhaps a precarious Christian-Muslim conversation. Mount Lebanon between 1830 and 1860 underwent many vicissitudes and catastrophes which issued in a compromise dictated, enforced and supervised by the powers. The essence of this compromise was that neither of the two communities should be able to dominate or threaten the other. It is this which, regardless of the actual power and influence of the administrative council of the *sanjaq*, enables us to affirm that here is a state of affairs in which the checks and balances of constitutionalism have a chance to operate. The principles of the settlement of 1861 were carried over into the Lebanese constitution of 1926 which in its article 95 enshrines the principle of 'confessionalism': 'As a provisional measure and for the sake of justice and concord' reads the article, 'the communities shall be equitably represented in public employment and in the composition of the Cabinet, such measure, however, not to cause prejudice to the general welfare of the State.'[12] This provision itself has been powerfully reinforced by the various electoral laws which have been successively in force in the Lebanese Republic. Thus article 3 of the electoral law of 10 August 1950 enacts that in every (multi-member) constituency the seats shall be distributed according to an attached schedule which faithfully mirrors the communal pattern of the district. To take Beirut as an example, the law provides that it shall have 4 Sunnis, 1 Shi'ite, 1 Maronite, 1 Greek Catholic, 1 Greek Orthodox, 1 Protestant, 1 Armenian Catholic, 2 Armenian Gregorians, and 1 member to represent the Minorities. In the Lebanon therefore, constitutionalism rests on 'confessionalism' and is inseparable from it. The *rationale* of this situation was described by Shibl Dammus, the rapporteur of the (Lebanese) Commission which drafted the constitution of 1926. He wrote:

1. The Lebanese people is composed of a multitude of communities, each having its own religious beliefs, mentality, customs and peculiar traditions. To reject the system of confessional representation disrupts the equilibrium and gives preponderance to certain communities at the expense of others. Jealousy, resentment, and even continuous disorder may be the outcome.

2. Representation in parliament must reflect the character of the country; and as the country is divided into several communities, it is necessary for these communities to be represented; otherwise the representation will not be faithful.
3. The country is still imbued with the spirit of confessionalism; the time has not come for these prejudices to be given up and we cannot abandon in a day a mentality which is several centuries old.
4. Confessional representation safeguards minority rights and allows no scope for recriminations.
5. Solidarity between the various communities is not yet so perfect as to enable us to disregard confessional politics.
6. The Lebanese people is not yet accustomed to give the primacy to patriotic solidarity over confessional solidarity.
7. The [religious] communities of the Lebanon are the equivalent of political parties.[13]

In no other middle-eastern country were the various interests in society fortunate enough to be given their due, both in form and in substance, within the political scheme. With the exception of the Lebanon, therefore, the countries of the middle east have known constitutionalism only as a mere device which various factions within the official classes have used in order to prosecute their rivalries. Finally, in our own day, as the absolutism of an earlier day has become somewhat tinged with totalitarianism elections and representative assemblies so-called have been used to indoctrinate the population and to elicit, organize and sustain enthusiasm for the ruling group and its policies.

NOTES

1. On the significance of the *sened-i ittifaq*, I follow the argument of B. Lewis; see article 'Dustur' in *Encyclopaedia of Islam*, 2nd ed., vol. II, p. 640.
2. Campenon's letter is reproduced in Pierre Grandchamp, *Etudes d'histoire tunisienne*, Paris 1966, pp. 144–9. The extracts translated above are at pp. 146–7.
3. Grandchamp, *op. cit.*, p. 152.
4. Text of rescript in Muhammad Khalil Subhi *Tarikh al-hayat al-niyabiyya fi Misr* (Parliamentary History of Egypt), vol. V, Cairo, 1939, p. 79.
5. Subhi, *op. cit.*, pp. 84 and 93.
6. *Modern Egypt*, vol. I, pp. 83–6. See also pp. 105–9 which are also highly relevant.
7. The relevant documents are in Subhi, *op. cit.*, pp. 151–246.
8. I leave aside here the Legislative Council and the Legislative Assembly, established in 1883. Their inspiration was entirely British and they are best understood in the context of British traditions and practices relating to legislative and representative institutions in India and in colonial territories. The functions of these bodies, from 1883 until they were suspended in 1914, were almost purely consultative, and were rigidly governed by the fact that

the last word in everything which mattered lay with the British agent and consul-general.

9. Bernard Lewis, *The Emergence of Modern Turkey*, 1961, pp. 174–5.
10. See David Farhi, 'The Şeriat as Political Slogan—or the "Incident of the 31st *Mart*"' in *Middle Eastern Studies*, vol. 7, no. 3, and Victor R. Swenson, 'The Military Rising in Istanbul 1909' in *Journal of Contemporary History*, vol. V, no. 4 (October 1970).
11. See E. Kedourie, 'The Genesis of the Egyptian Constitution of 1923' in *The Chatham House Version and other Middle-Eastern Studies*, 1970.
12. This is the text as amended in 1943, when a reference to the French mandate was removed.
13. Passage cited in Pierre Rondot, *Les Institutions politiques du Liban*, Paris, 1947, p. 80.

2. Political Parties in the Arab World

The Arabic word for political party is *hizb*. The word primarily means a group, faction, or the supporters of a man who share his ideas and are ready to defend him. It is therefore by a natural extension that the word has come to denote political parties in the modern European sense of the word. But this usage is very recent, as may be seen from an examination of nineteenth century dictionaries. Thus Kazimirski's *Dictionnaire* (1860) defined *hizb* as a '*troupe d'hommes*'; Lane's *Lexicon* (1863 *et seq*.), as a 'party or company of men, assembling themselves on account of an event that has befallen them'. Bustani's *Muhit* explains that a *hizb* is a *ta'ifa*, i.e. a group. Dozy's *Supplément* (1881) records an interesting variant, where it lists among the meanings of the word 'ordre religieux'. Later dictionaries begin to record the political connotation which the word was beginning to acquire: Badger's *English-Arabic Lexicon* (1881) translates 'party' as *hizb* and Hava's *Arabic-English Dictionary* (1899) translates *hizb* as 'party of men, confederacy, division'.

Literary evidence, in support of the lexicographical, does tend to show that in the last two decades of the nineteenth century, *hizb*, though it was not yet a fully recognized part of the political vocabulary, was coming, albeit slowly and hesitatingly, to have a certain political connotation. An excellent illustration of this ambiguous and fluctuating usage occurs in the minutes of Ahmad 'Urabi's trial at Cairo in 1882. 'Urabi was asked how he allowed himself to be described on a document as *ra'is al-hizb al-watani*; he replied that it was well-known that Egypt was inhabited by different races (*ajnas*) and that every one of these races may be considered a *hizb*, 'and further, the natives of the country are a *hizb* on their own, denominated *fallahin* in order to humble them (*kama inna ahl al-bilad hizb qa'im bi-dhatihi yutlaq 'alayhi lafz fallahin idhlal^an lahum*)'. But 'Urabi went on to say that every people had *ahzab* engaged in preserving their liberty and defending their rights.[1] It is clear that in this passage *hizb* stands in 'Urabi's mind for two different meanings, which he cannot clearly distinguish, viz. the older and general one of a group, and the later and specific one of a political party. A saying attributed to 'Urabi's contemporary Jamal al-Din al-Afghani during his sojourn at Istanbul (1892–7) indicates a use of the word *hizb* more definitely in the sense of a political party. He is reported as saying that there should be nothing to prevent the oriental from joining one party after another (*al-hizb ba'd al-hizb*) until individuals appeared in the east—as they have in the west—who would consider death for the sake of their *watan* (i.e. birthplace) a gain.[2] Finally an illustration drawn from the first decade of the twentieth century shows how *hizb* has come to be stabilized in meaning and to signify unambiguously a political party. In an article of 1906, discussing whether a nationalist party can be said to exist in Egypt, Farah Antun states that a *hizb* signifies in politics 'the organized struggle of one group against another owing to a difference of opinions and interests between the two sides (*ta'allub jama'a 'ala jama'a ukhra li'khtilaf ara' al-fariqayn wa masalihihim*)', and he goes on to say that by *ta'allub* he means that the group would become a single, solidary entity working to attain its aim, '*ijtima'uha 'isba wahida wa ta'aduduha tawassul^{an} ila bulugh muradiha*'.[3]

In the article just cited, Farah Antun came to the conclusion that, on his definition, there was no nationalist party in Egypt for the reason that the crucial element of organization was lacking. His conclusions may be considered to apply generally to the Arabic-speaking areas for the greater part of the period in which people became accustomed to think of parties as a usual political phenomenon. There is no doubt that they came so to think as a result of contact and familiarity with European politics, in which parliaments and estates, having continuously existed since mediaeval times, provided a natural context and an indispensable setting for parties and party organization. Such representative institutions were absent in the Muslim world, and it is therefore not surprising that only contact with Europe made organization into parties for political action familiar and attractive. Familiar and attractive, that is, to the small minority which was open to European influences, and which was therefore critical of native and traditional institutions. Parties were therefore at first usually organized or inspired by radicals who were intent on drastic reforms; and, because such parties had, in the absence of representative institutions, little scope to manœuvre, their radicalism became intensified; this very radicalism alienated the authorities who, often trying to suppress these parties, forced them underground. In short, all these factors meant that parties in the Arabic-speaking areas were, at the outset, small groups of people, influenced by European ideas, who were or affected to be dissatisfied with existing political conditions, whose organization was loose and ephemeral, and whose action was usually clandestine.

One of the earliest of such groupings in Egypt—calling itself, however, not a *hizb* but a *jam'iyya*, i.e. society—was *jam'iyyat ittihad Misr al-fatat*, the society of the Union of Young Egypt which existed in Alexandria in 1879 at the beginning of the reign of Khedive Tawfiq. It would seem to have been the outcome of Afghani's political teachings and to have been formed by his followers. A letter to Afghani from his follower Ibrahim al-Laqqani, dated Beirut 15 February 1883, explains that the Young Egypt Society consisted of members of the Sursuk, Qitta, Zughayb and Mukhalla' families—all Syrian Christians—who had induced some Muslims to join them and published an Arabic-French newspaper preaching Afghani's views and calling on the Khedive to institute political reforms. Mustafa Riyad Pasha, then chief minister, banned the newspaper; the Group tried to publish a second one, but the Muslim members seceded and, according to Laqqani, even tried to harm the Syrian Christians who thereupon gave up in disgust, saying that they had no personal interest in the matter—since they were all protected by European powers—but had merely wished to serve the Egyptians.[4]

Another early grouping in Egypt was that known as *al-hizb al-watani*, (the National Party) which also seems to have been organized in 1879 after Tawfiq's accession. This group was also opposed to the Khedive and his minister Mustafa Riyad, but seems to have had no connexion with the Young Egypt Society. Its members were ex-ministers, like Muhammad Sharif Pasha, who were Mustafa Riyad's rivals and who disliked his administrative reforms; some of them worked for the restoration of the ex-Khedive Isma'il, and some to advance the claims of 'Abd al-Halim Pasha, the last surviving son of Muhammad 'Ali Pasha, to the Khediviate which he had long desired. This group became connected with the officers who under Ahmad 'Urabi's leadership, and moved by military grievances, carried out a *coup d'état* against Tawfiq and his government on 9 September 1881. The ostensible aims of this *hizb* were a constitutional and parliamentary régime for Egypt and the cessation of foreign interference. These aims were taken over by 'Urabi and his followers when, the *coup d'état* having demonstrated their power, they supplanted Sharif Pasha and the other notables in political leadership. These officers in fact became *al-hizb al watani*, and with their defeat by the British army in 1882 the party ceased to exist.

There is no trace of party activity in Egypt until after the accession of the Khedive 'Abbas Hilmi in 1892. 'Abbas tried in the early years of his reign to break loose from British control, and one of his methods was to inspire political agitation by young Egyptians, graduates of European universities or European-type schools in Egypt. Ahmad Lutfi al-Sayyid has recorded that in 1896, when he had just graduated from the Law School, 'Abbas saw him in audience, and he was afterwards enrolled in a secret society of which the Khedive was the president and the members of which included Mustafa Kamil and Muhammad Farid; this group, according to

Lutfi al-Sayyid, was the nucleus of what came to be later known as *al-hizb al-watani*.[5] Of this group, the most prominent was Mustafa Kamil (1874–1907). As his letters to the Khedive's Arabic Secretary (published in 1962 by M. Anis) show, his political activities at the outset of his career were directed and financed by 'Abbas. From a letter cited by 'Abd al-Rahman al-Rafi'i in his biography of Mustafa Kamil, it appears that relations between him and the Khedive remained very close until 1904. Thereafter Mustafa Kamil seems to have worked on his own, and increasingly in opposition to 'Abbas. In 1907 he formally launched a party which was called *al-hizb al-watani*, dedicated to securing the British evacuation of Egypt. At the first annual conference of the party he was elected president for life, but he died soon afterwards. His successor was Muhammad Farid (1868–1919), who in 1912 left Egypt to avoid imprisonment for alleged subversion against the Khedive's government. It is difficult to see that the Nationalist Party had much influence on Egyptian politics. When it was founded in 1907, the influence of Mustafa Kamil, after his parting with the Khedive, was already on the wane. The party, after his death, had some reputation and influence based on the newspapers which Mustafa Kamil had started in the days when he had the Khedive's support, namely *al-Liwa'*, *The Egyptian Standard* and *L'Etendard Egyptien*; the party also attracted many sympathizers among the intellectual and official classes: 'Abd al-Rahman al-Rafi'i gives a long list of Mustafa Kamil's sympathizers and disciples;[6] of these the majority cannot have been actual members of the party, while the best known of those who were, e.g. Mustafa al-Nahhas, Hafiz 'Afifi, Isma'il Sidqi, had, in their active political careers after the first world war, nothing at all to do with the Nationalists. It is quite symbolic of the party's fortunes that a statue of Mustafa Kamil which it had made after his death remained shut up in a school until 1938, because no Egyptian government could be induced to offer a public site for its erection.[7] The party's rôle in Egyptian parliamentary life under the Monarchy (1923–52) was insignificant. The party were occasionally allotted a handful of seats in the preliminary bargaining between politicians in Cairo which often determined the exact composition of Egyptian parliaments. This handful of seats represented such influence and power as the party still had and which it exercised in coalition with other parties against the Wafd. Nationalists very rarely exercised political office. Hafiz Ramadan, the president of the party, was a minister in Muhammad Mahmud's second ministry (30 December 1937 to 5 April 1940), in Hasan Sabri's ministry (27 June 1940 to 14 November 1940), in Ahmad Mahir's first and second ministries (5 October 1944 to 24 February 1945), and in Mahmud Fahmi al-Nuqrashi's first ministry (25 February

1945 to 26 November 1945); but in holding office in these administrations, Hafiz Ramadan was acting against the wishes of his party
colleagues, and may therefore be considered more as an Independent
than as a Nationalist representative. In 1946, the breach between him
and his colleagues was healed, and three Nationalists accepted
office in two subsequent administrations as the avowed representatives of their party: Muhammad Zaki 'Ali and 'Abd al-'Aziz al-
Sufani in Ibrahim 'Abd al-Hadi's ministry (28 December 1948 to
25 July 1949), and 'Abd al-Rahman al-Rafi'i together with Muhammad Zaki 'Ali in Husayn Sirri's third ministry (26 July 1949 to 3
November 1949). The Nationalist Party, in common with all other
Egyptian political parties, was dissolved and its assets confiscated by
decree of the Revolutionary Command on 18 January 1953.

Mustafa Kamil's foundation of the Nationalist Party in 1907 was
followed in the same year by the foundation of other groups, calling
themselves parties, which proved to be more ephemeral and to be
even less organized than *al-hizb al-watani*. The first which falls to be
mentioned in *hizb al-umma* (the People's Party), which was founded
in September–October 1907, and which consisted of a group of
notables and landowners, who promoted the publication of the
newspaper *al-Jarida*. The common denominator of the group, as
'Abbas Mahmud al-'Aqqad put it, was that they were under the
Khedive's displeasure (*maghdub 'alayhim*) and that they could hope
therefore to curry favour with the British Residency. Whether this
was so or not, the fact is that the British presence enabled them to
express opposition to the Khedive's ambitions. Some of the prominent members of this party became associated with *hizb al-ahrar
al-dusturiyyin* (the Liberal Constitutionalist Party), which was
founded in 1922. The name of another party to be recorded is that
of *hizb al-islah 'ala 'l-mabadi' al-dusturiyya* (the Party of Reform
according to Constitutional Principles), which again came to be
spoken of in 1907. It is difficult to say that it was more than a label
invented by the Khedive's men to counteract the effect of Mustafa
Kamil's founding of the Nationalist Party; it seems, in fact, possible
to associate only one name with it, namely that of 'Ali Yusuf, the
editor of *al-Mu'ayyad*, which, after Mustafa Kamil's defection,
became the Khedive's main newspaper organ.

The end of the first world war inaugurated a new chapter in the
history of Egyptian political parties. Widespread agitation in Egypt
for some three years was finally successful in persuading the British
government to abolish the Protectorate which it had assumed over
Egypt in 1914. This was done by the unilateral declaration of 28
February 1922, one of the consequences of which was the transformation of the Sultanate into a constitutional Monarchy and the setting

up of a parliament composed of a house of representatives elected by indirect suffrage and a senate partly elected and partly appointed. The general scheme of the Egyptian constitution—promulgated by a Royal Rescript in 1923—was that a cabinet drawn from the majority in parliament would hold office so long as it retained the confidence of this majority. Such a state of affairs gave obvious scope for the creation and the functioning of parties on the European model. The first of these parties which must be considered is the *Wafd*, which has its origin in the struggle which led to the abolition of the Protectorate. In this struggle Sa'd Zaghlul (1857–1926), who came to lead and embody the *Wafd*, had taken, by the play of circumstance and his own considerable shrewdness, a leading part. The appellation *Wafd* originated in a demand which Zaghlul, together with 'Abd al-'Aziz Fahmi and 'Ali Sha'rawi, put before the British high commissioner on 13 November 1918, to be allowed to proceed in a delegation (*wafd*) to Great Britain to discuss Egypt's relations with the protecting power and her constitutional future. This demand was made with the knowledge and approval of Sultan Fu'ad and his ministers, but the three personalities who lent their names to it came inevitably to be the focus of the political agitation which followed its rejection and the repressive action taken by the British authorities. Between 1919 and 1923 many Egyptian public men were associated with Zaghlul in the political movement which came to be known as the *Wafd*, but Zaghlul managed to capture the public sentiment and to be exclusively identified with the successful struggle against Great Britain. His earliest and most prominent associates broke with him and became his fierce opponents. Of the three personalities who saw the British high commissioner in November 1918, 'Ali Sha'rawi resigned formally from the *Wafd* in 1921 and played no further part in politics, and 'Abd al-'Aziz Fahmi became a Liberal Constitutionalist and later entirely forsook politics. Others, such as Muhammad Mahmud, Isma'il Sidqi, 'Ali Mahir, Muhammad 'Ali 'Alluba, became declared opponents of the *Wafd*. By 1923, Zaghlul was surrounded by younger men who were little known and newcomers to Egyptian politics, necessarily very much under his domination: his nephew Muhammad Fath Allah Barakat, Mustafa al-Nahhas, who had been a magistrate in Tanta and who had been delegated by the Nationalist Party to represent them in the original *Wafd*, William Makram 'Ubayd, who had been a civil servant, Muhammad Nadjib al-Gharabli, Ahmad Mahir, Mahmud Fahmi al-Nukrashi, 'Ali al-Shamsi, all of whom came to be prominent in the Wafdist movement at one time or another between 1924 and 1952. The *Wafd* as a formal body was organized in 1919 at the inception of the anti-British agitation. It took the form of a central committee of public men, the ostensible business of which was to direct from Cairo the collection by provincial committees of signatures to a petition praying the British authorities to allow an Egyptian delegation to proceed to London. It is not known how effective such a coutry-wide organization was, and there is a suspicion that the *Wafd* committees benefited, at the outset at any rate, from the support of the Sultan and his government. After 1921, the prominent members of the original *Wafd* left it and Zaghlul became the undisputed leader of those who remained, the committee being his creature and instrument. But Zaghlul then and later refused to be considered as the leader of a mere faction, holding that he was the sole authorized delegate of the Egyptian people, and that it was his opponents who were guilty of factionalism. A characteristic claim of his, made in a speech of 2 July 1924, was 'I am not the president of a party, but the delegate of a nation (*wakil umma*)'.[8] His followers indeed acclaimed him as the *za'im*, the Leader (a title which devolved on his successor Mustafa al-Nahhas), his house came to be called *bayt al-umma*, (The House of the Nation) and his wife Safiyya *umm al-misriyyin* (the Mother of the Egyptians).

Zaghlul won the elections held in December 1923 under the new constitution, and his followers constituted the overwhelming majority of the House of Representatives. He formed a government almost half the members of which—it is interesting to note—were non-Wafdists. This is not how the constitution was supposed to work, and it is generally explained by the fact that the king's and the administration's influence had been exerted on Zaghlul's behalf during the elections, because the king did not wish the latter's rivals, the Liberal Constitutionalists, to win, and that one of the conditions of his cooperation was the appointment of a number of his nominees to ministerial posts in Zaghlul's cabinet. The importance of this incident is to underline what henceforth became a feature of Egyptian politics under the monarchy, namely that the decisive struggles for power occurred outside parliament, the composition and working of which merely ratified decisions reached elsewhere. This meant that Egyptian parties could not have the same character or function in the same way as those found in the normal kind of representative and constitutional régimes. The subsequent history of the *Wafd* shows this clearly. Zaghlul's overwhelming majority did not prevent him from resigning when assassins, who were later shown to be Wafdist sympathizers, murdered Sir Lee Stack in Cairo in November 1924. The parliament elected at the beginning of the year was dissolved by royal rescript in December. New elections were held in March 1925, but, the Wafdists being in the majority in the new parliament, Ahmad Ziwar Pasha, the prime minister, dissolved it.

This election was perhaps the only one in the political history of Egypt under the constitutional monarchy when an election went against the wishes of the effective authority in the country. The reason is not absolutely clear, but it would seem that Ahmad Ziwar's administration had had little time to dismantle the network of Wafdist committees in the country-side which Zaghlul in his year of power must have overhauled and strengthened. Ziwar dispensed with a parliament until the British high commissioner, fearing unfettered palace rule, which Ziwar's ministry in effect signified, pressed for new elections. The palace being checkmated, the electorate ratified its defeat by electing a Wafdist parliament in May 1926. But since Zaghlul, the leader of the *Wafd*, was not acceptable to the British authorities as prime minister, the normal play of party politics in a constitutional and representative régime was again frustrated, and 'Adli Yakan, the Liberal Constitutional leader, took office at the head of a coalition of Wafdists and Liberal Constitutionalists. The coalition subsisted until March 1928, when the Liberal Constitutionalist 'Abd al-Khaliq Tharwat, who succeeded 'Adli in April 1927, having failed to negotiate a treaty with Great Britain, found his position untenable and yielded his place to Mustafa al-Nahhas—on whom had fallen Zaghlul's mantle—who formed the first wholly Wafdist administration. Al-Nahhas soon found himself at loggerheads with both the king and the British authorities; in June 1928 the king dismissed al-Nahhas, dissolved parliament, and called on Muhammad Mahmud, now president of the Liberal Constitutionalist Party, to form a government. The new prime minister obtained from the king authority to suspend elections and parliamentary government for a period of three years. But in 1929, a new government in London having made clear that it would negotiate only with a Wafdist government (whom it regarded as the only legitimate representative of Egypt), Muhammad Mahmud resigned and new elections took place; they ratified the decision of the British government and returned a Wafdist government, which took office on 1 January 1930. Negotiations between Nahhas and the British government having failed, and the king disliking a Wafdist government, he dismissed it in June of the same year, commissioned Isma'il Sidqi to form an administration, dissolved the parliament and promulgated a new constitution and a new electoral law. Elections under the new dispensation were held on 1 June 1931, and a new parliament was returned with a satisfactory governmental majority. A complicated series of events in 1935–6 forced the king to seek an accommodation with the Wafdists. He re-established the constitution which he had abrogated in 1930. This was a victory for the Wafdists, and the elections which were held in May 1936 ratified it by returning a parliament with an overwhelming Wafdist majority. King Fu'ad died in April 1936, to be succeeded by his son Faruq, who attained his majority in July 1937. A clash between him and the *Wafd* was not long in coming. In December 1937 he dismissed Nahhas and shortly afterwards dissolved the parliament. The new parliament had an insignificant Wafdist minority, thus ratifying the victory of the king. This parliament itself was also dissolved as a result of an extra-parliamentary clash of power. By the *coup d'état* of 2 February 1942, the British authorities forced a Wafdist government on the king. This government dissolved the parliament of 1938 and obtained an overwhelming majority at the subsequent elections. It ruled until October 1944, when the king found the power to dismiss it and dissolve its parliament. The ensuing elections were boycotted by the *Wafd*, and the parliament elected in January 1945 was wholly anti-Wafdist. This parliament was dissolved in November 1949, and the election of January 1950 gave an overwhelming Wafdist majority; the course of events which led to this result is still very imperfectly known, but there is reason to suppose that it was the outcome of a reconciliation between the king and the *Wafd*. The Wafdist government lasted until January 1952, when it was dismissed by the king. Its parliament, the last under the constitutional monarchy, was dissolved shortly thereafter.

The course of events here briefly set out indicates that in the Egyptian parliamentary régime, contrary to the intentions of its founders, and indeed to its normal working elsewhere, it was the government—or rather the actual effective authority in the country at any given time—which determined the character and composition of a parliament, and not the other way round. This had a fundamental bearing on the character and functions of the political parties. These could not function as coherent parliamentary and electoral organizations dedicated to the acquisition of popular support and the exercise of political power within a legislative assembly. These so-called parties could rather more intelligibly be described as either movements or factions. The *Wafd* was clearly a movement; Zaghlul claimed to be above all parties and interests, to be the representative and leader of the nation; he thus inaugurated a new style of politics of which appeal to the mass was the most significant characteristic. This new style, which depends on a leader with a hypnotic popular appeal, who is the ultimate depositary of unfettered power, was made possible by the disintegration of traditional society, the erosion of traditional authority, the increase of literacy, the improvement in communications, and the existence of a new urban amorphous mass of recent migrants from the country-side, leading lives of material poverty and spiritual disorientation. All these created new conditions of political action, new possibilities of canalizing hitherto untapped sources of political power by organizing the passive and malleable mass into a formidable phalanx round a leader and his slogans. It is evident that the *Wafd* under Zaghlul and Nahhas attempted this. They were only intermittently successful, and they ultimately failed. The reasons for their failure may possibly have been an imperfect grasp of the new techniques, the presence of British power and influence as a check and a disturbing factor, the existence of other, more traditional forms of authority which still had some life in them and, of course, sheer accident. But the *Wafd* again and again tried to create various organizations for the recruitment and control of their supporters. Foremost among these, and the least known in their detailed working, are the *Wafd* committees which spread over the whole country. When the *Wafd* was either expecting or exercising power, it attempted to create specialized organizations to cater for different sections of the population, particularly students, industrial labour, etc. The example of Fascists and Nazis no doubt stimulated the creation of a Wafdist para-military group, *al-qimsan al-zarqa'*, i.e. the Blueshirts, which functioned in 1936–7 and which had some analogy in both name and function with Blackshirts and Brownshirts. The *Wafd* were not the only ones to experiment with these new possibilities; one writer has indeed claimed that the Nationalist Party was the first to organize Blueshirts, and that the *Wafd* filched the idea from it.[9] Be this as it may, the Nationalist Party never succeeded in becoming a movement, and remained what may be called a faction. One organization which from the outset attempted to be a movement was *Misr al fatat*, founded by Ahmad Husayn in 1933, it is claimed at the inspiration of King Fu'ad.[10] Its slogan was *Allah, al-watan, al-malik*, i.e. God, the Fatherland, the King, and it attempted to organize its adherents into Greenshirts (*al-qimsan al-khadra'*), which frequently clashed with the Blueshirts. Another organization which became a political movement had, at its inception, quite a different character. *Al-Ikhwan al-muslimun* (the Muslim Brethren), founded in 1928 by Hasan al-Banna was at the outset dedicated to a renewal of the religious life, to the fight against laxity, scepticism and unbelief prevalent among Muslims as a consequence of European influence. Some ten years later, the Brotherhood was an extensive organization covering a large part of Egypt. Because Islam is *din wa-dawla*, i.e. a religion and a political authority, and because the circumstances after 1940 became propitious, the Brotherhood under its *murshid*, i.e. Guide, came to play an increasingly political role. Al-Banna's political transactions are still quite obscure, but the Brotherhood was a formidable weapon which he and his successor Hasan al-Hudaybi could use in pursuance of their aims in the troubled years between the end of the second world war and the dissolution of the Brotherhood by the Egyptian Revolutionary Command in January 1954. The tight organization of the Brotherhood enabled al-Banna and his collaborators to set on foot a secret terrorist apparatus (*al-jihaz al-sirri*) which was used to enforce the wishes of those who controlled it until an attempt on the life of Colonel Jamal 'Abd al-Nasir in October 1954 resulted in the arrest and trial of the most prominent Brethren—al-Hudaybi included—the execution of six of them, and presumably the final destruction of the apparatus.

In contrast to these organizations which may be called political movements, other groupings in Egyptian politics under the constitutional monarchy may be termed factions. They consisted of people who, by virtue of their educational attainments or an inherited position, were members of the official classes and therefore had the necessary knowledge and connexions for filling political office and exercising power. Such men were loosely grouped under party labels which they acquired by accident at some point or another. They may be called factions rather than movements, because they seldom or never sought to involve the masses in politics in the manner of the *Wafd* or the Muslim Brethren, and yet were not strictly parties, since the constitutional régime in Egypt worked in such a fashion that parties could not function, let alone flourish. These groupings may not therefore all be dismissed as a mere collection of placemen eager for office and ready to do the bidding of whoever gave them office; but whatever their original aims and motives were, the situation was such that if they desired to take part in politics they had to acquiesce in measures and combinations quite remote from their proclaimed principles. A good case in point is the Nationalist Party, which started with an articulate ideology, but the activity of whose leaders under the constitutional monarchy had, as has been seen, little to do with this ideology. Another party between whose activities and principles a great gap opened was the Liberal Constitutionalist Party. The party was formed in October 1922 as an answer to Zaghlul and the *Wafd* by some of the most prominent of Egyptian statesmen who earlier that year, in collaboration with Allenby and his British advisers, had induced the British government to issue the declaration of 28 February. The president was 'Adli Yakan and the main leaders were 'Abd al-Khaliq Tharwat, Hasan 'Abd al-Raziq, 'Abd al-'Aziz Fahmi, Isma'il Zuhdi and Muhammad Mahmud. Some of them had belonged to the pre-war Umma Party, and some had, from the end of 1918 to the end of 1921, formed themselves into a group, *al-hizb al-dimuqrati* (The Democratic Party), which included Muhammad Husayn Haykal, Mustafa 'Abd al-Raziq,

Mansur Fahmi, Mahmud 'Azmi and 'Aziz Merhom. This small group of educated men looked forward to an Egypt where the rule of law would be supreme, and where political liberty and economic equity would be assured. Most of this group passed into the Liberal Constitutionalist Party and greatly influenced the formulation of its objectives and policies. But we find that, in fact, sheer political expediency very frequently determined the *ministrables* of the party in taking office, and that this opportunism was on the increase as time went on. Liberal Constitutionalists took part in Ziwar's second ministry of 1925–6, but when 'Abd al-'Aziz Fahmi was dismissed as minister of justice following the 'Ali 'Abd al-Raziq affair,[11] his two Liberal Constitutionalist colleagues resigned in protest. But it was a Liberal Constitutionalist, Muhammad Mahmud, who took office when King Fu'ad dismissed Nahhas in 1928 and who, regardless of his Party's principles, governed without a parliament for fifteen months. Again, it was Muhammad Mahmud who took office when King Faruq dismissed Nahhas in 1937 and for some eighteen months, until the king dismissed him, presided over a government which, whatever its exact label, was in fact purely one of the king's men. The further history of the Liberal Constitutionalists until their extinction in 1952 is that of a faction enjoying office and power as and when they could. Five other such factions remain to be enumerated, two specifically set up as organizations providing support for governments chosen and inspired by the king, and three formed out of seceders from the *Wafd*. The first two were *hizb al-ittihad* (the Unionist Party) set up in 1925 as an organization of king's men during Ziwar's administration, and *hizb al-sha'b* (The People's Party) a similar organization created in 1931 during Isma'il Sidki's administration. Both parties effectively disappeared from the scene as political circumstances changed. The three organizations of seceders from the *Wafd* were *al-hizb al-sa'di* (the Sa'dist Party), formed when Hamid al-Basil seceded from the *Wafd* in 1930, which proved quite ephemeral; *al-hay'a al-sa'diyya* (the Sa'dist Organization), formed when Mahmud Fahmi al-Nuqrashi and Ahmad Mahir fell out with the *Wafd* in 1937, which went on as a political grouping until 1952 and which provided three prime ministers and other ministers in anti-Wafdist governments; and *al-kutla al-wafdiyya al-mustaqilla* (the Independent Wafdist Bloc), formed when Makram 'Ubayd was expelled from the *Wafd* in 1943 and which consisted of his own personal following, and provided two or three ministers in three coalition governments which succeeded the *Wafd* government of 1942–4.

The Ottoman empire. The earliest parties in the Arabic-speaking areas of the Ottoman empire were in their origin and character somewhat similar to the earliest Egyptian parties. They were groups of young men touched by western influences and discontented with what they considered to be the constricting and stagnant conditions of the empire under 'Abd al-Hamid II. In those years there was little scope for overt political action, nor were the generality of the subjects much inclined to question the established and traditional order. Such groups were small, clandestine and ephemeral. One of the earliest of these groups was one formed by some Christian students at the Syrian Protestant College at Beirut in the early 1880's; they had fallen under the influence of a Maronite who taught French at the College and who was imbued with French libertarian and revolutionary ideas. These young men conceived the project of fomenting a movement to end Ottoman supremacy in the Lebanon. They went so far as to write and surreptitiously post up in public places placards in this sense, but as no response was forthcoming the group dissolved itself in 1882–3. Another group was the one which came into being at Damascus in the early years of the twentieth century. It was composed of young Muslims who were disciples of Shaykh Tahir al-Jaza'iri, who was Inspector of Education in the Damascus *vilayet* and who lived in Damasucs from 1880 to 1905. The group is known as *halaqat Dimashq al-saghira* (the Small Damascus Circle) and it included Shaykh Jamal al-Din al-Qasimi, Shaykh 'Abd al-Razzaq-al-Bitar and Shaykh Salim al-Bukhari. These were among the original members, who were joined by younger men including Muhibb al-Din al-Khatib, Salah al-Din al-Qasimi, 'Abd al-Hamid al-Zahrawi, Shukri al-'Asali, 'Abd al-Rahman al-Shabandar, Muhammad Kurd 'Ali, Faris al-Khuri and Salim al-Jaza'iri. The circle apparently discussed literary, religious, and increasingly, when the younger men joined it, political questions. Muhibb al-Din al-Khatib was apparently the mainspring of this later development. Some of the younger members of the circle went to Istanbul in about 1905, and in 1906 Muhibb al-Din al-Khatib and his friend 'Arif al-Shihabi founded there a secret society, *jam'iyyat al-nahda* (The Renaissance Society), and asked two friends still in Damascus, Salah al-Din al-Qasimi and Lutfi al-Haffar, to found a branch in the city. The *jam'iyya* consisted entirely of a small group of young educated Damascenes, and in spite of its foundation at Istanbul, Damascus was its centre. After the Young Turk Revolution, the *jam'iyya* applied for permission to function openly, and interested itself for a few years thereafter in spreading knowledge of Arab history and Arabic literature and in providing a local forum for discussing such political issues as it was safe to raise publicly. Another group, or at any rate the name of a group which existed at the beginning of the twentieth century falls also to be recorded. It is the *Ligue de la patrie arabe,* founded by Najib 'Azuri, a Syrian Christian who had studied in Paris and then become an official in the Jerusalem *vilayet*; this post he left in apparently suspicious circumstances and he was condemned to death *in absentia* by an Ottoman court in 1904 for treasonable activities in Paris. Who, apart from the French retired official E. Jung (who has chronicled his activities) collaborated with him, is obscure. The programme of his *Ligue* was the creation of an Arab empire extending over Mesopotamia, Arabia and the Levant and the creation of a 'spiritual' Caliphate. But the *Ligue* seems to have been of little consequence and to have sunk into obscurity when his periodical, *L'Indépendence Arabe,* of which eighteen numbers came out in 1907–8, ceased publication.

It was only after the restoration of the Ottoman constitution in 1908 that many Arab parties were formed, and became quite active for a time. Because of the vicissitudes of the Ottoman parliamentary régime of 1908–14, these parties could not function as normal parliamentary parties, nor could they, owing to the state of society then obtaining, aspire to enlist mass support. They were small, ephemeral factions made up of members of the official classes and such others as had access to European ideas. It is commonly agreed that the first of these groupings was *jam'iyyat al-ikha' al-'arabi* (the Society of Arab Brotherhood), founded by the Damascene Shafiq al-Mu'ayyad and others, mainly Syrian, officials and notables in Istanbul in 1908. A report in *The Arab Bulletin* (24 May 1918) records that the group came into being as a consequence of the 1908 Parliament refusing to accept Yusuf Shitwan as member for Benghazi and Shafiq al-Mu'ayyad as member for Damascus. The group seems to have lasted for a few months and then to have been dissolved in April 1909. In this year in Istanbul *al-muntada al-adabi* (The Literary Club) was founded, which was ostensibly a cultural club for Arab youth in Istanbul, but many of its activities were political. It was shut down by the Ottoman authorities in 1915, at which time its secretary, the Syrian 'Abd al-Karim Qasim al-Khalil, was accused of treason and executed. Two groupings dating from this period, among Syrians and Lebanese living in Egypt, may be noticed. The first is an ephemeral group called *jam'iyyat al-ikha-al-'uthmani* (the Society of Ottoman Brotherhood), which apparently lasted for only a few weeks, among the members of which were Rafiq al'Azm, Rashid Rida, Ya'qub Saruf, Jurji Zaydan, Na'um Shuqayr and Da'ud 'Ammun. The second grouping was *al-ittihad al-lubnani* (*l'Alliance libanaise*) formed by Maronite notables in Cairo in November 1909. It was founded by Iskandar 'Ammun, Antun al-Jumayyil and Da'ud Barakat. Before the war its programme consisted in demanding better commercial facilities within the empire for Mount Lebanon, widening the suffrage for its assembly, increasing the number of its members and widening its powers, and annexing the Biqa‘, Tripoli and Beirut to Mount Lebanon, to form what came to be known under the French mandate as the Grand Liban. This last point came to form the main issue for which the *ittihad* worked after the outbreak of war, when the partition of the Ottoman empire became a possibility. The *ittihad*—the president of which from 1917 was Auguste Adib—lost its *raison d'être* with the French occupation of the Lebanon. Apart from these groups which functioned publicly, a number of secret groupings are also recorded. Towards the end of 1909, there was formed in Istanbul a secret group composed of officers and university students mainly from Syria, *al-jam‘iyya al-Qahtaniyya* (the Qahtan Society). The group was dedicated to the encouragement of Arab nationalism, and among its prominent members were the two officers Amin Lutfi Hafiz and Salim al-Djaza’iri, nephew of Shaykh Tahir, ‘Abd al-Karim al-Khalil and ‘Arif al-Shihabi, all of whom were executed for treason by the Ottomans in 1915–16. Another secret grouping was one founded by students, again mainly Syrian, in Paris in 1909. This was *jam‘iyyat al-umma al-‘arabiyya al-fatat* (the Young Arab Society), which was founded by Ahmad Qadri, ‘Awni ‘Abd al-Hadi and Rustum Haydar. The aim of the society was Arab independence. It is of course difficult to know the extent and effectiveness of the operations of a secret society, but the members of *al-fatat* seem to have carried on conspiratorial activities against the Ottomans in the Levant until the end of the first world war; many of them became prominent later on in Syria, Palestinian and Iraqi politics. Another secret society was *al-‘alam al-akhdar* (the Green Flag). It was founded by students in Istanbul in September 1912, but seems to have been more ephemeral than most and there is no record of any activity for which it was responsible.

The internal and external vicissitudes to which the Ottoman empire was subject in the years immediately preceding the first world war created fears and tensions and afforded occasions for political action and openings for political ambition, so that in 1912 and 1913 new Arab political groupings came into being. Of these new groups, the best-known was *hizb al-lamarkaziyya al-idariyya al-‘uthmani* (The Administrative Decentralization Party), which was founded in Cairo in December 1912, and which, as its name showed, was dedicated to the achievement of administrative decentralization and provincial self-government in the Ottoman empire. The founders were again Syrians, the most prominent among them being Muhammad Rashid Rida Rafiq al-‘Azm, Shibli Shumayyil, Iskandar ‘Ammun and Muhibb al-Din al-Khatib. The programme of the party was obviously akin to the ideas of Prince Sabah al-Din and the *Hürriyet ve i'tilaf firkasi* in Istanbul, which was opposed to the Committee of Union and Progress. It may well be that the activities of *hizb al-lamarkaziyya* are to be understood not so much in terms of its formal programme, as of the complicated struggles of Istanbul politics, which eventually led to the complete hegemony of the Committee of Union and Progress. Again, the programme cannot explain, rather it contradicts, their activities at the beginning of the 1914–18 war when they seem to have organized spying in Syria and Mesopotamia on behalf of the British authorities in Egypt.[12] The same political struggle between I'tilafists and Unionists would seem to account for a similar development in Beirut, where a number of notables, both Christian and Muslim, were encouraged by Kamil Pasha's government towards the end of 1912 to form a group, *al-jam'iyya al-'umumiyya al-islahiyya* (the General Reform Society), to work for decentralization and provincial self-government; but when the Committee of Union and Progress took power at the beginning of 1913, it set itself to eradicate any influence its opponents might have, and the Unionist *vali* of Beirut, who had replaced the I'tilafist one, declared the Society illegal and dissolved it on 4 April 1913. Kamil Pasha's government attempted to organize support for itself in Damascus as well, but Unionist influence there was strong enough to prevent the formation of a *jam'iyya* like the Beirut one. The same attempt was made at Basra, where the I'tilafist leader was Sayyid Talib al-Rifa'i al-Naqib. Sayyid Talib had attempted, without success, to be recognized as the Unionist boss in Basra; he was merely returned as deputy for Basra in the Istanbul parliament, and there earned the gratitude of Kamil Pasha by his attacks on the Committee of Union and Progress.[13] At the beginning of 1913 the same conjunction of events which led to the creation of *hizb al-lamarkaziyya* and the Beirut *jam'iyya* led also to the formation by Sayyid Talib of a similar group in Basra, which he also called *al-jam'iyya al-islahiyya*, ostensibly dedicated to the same objects. He attempted to extend his activities to Baghdad and Mosul; in the former a group of his followers led by Muzahim Amin al-Pačaji formed *al-nadi al-watani al-'ilmi* (The National Scientific Club), which, in spite of its name, was a mere adjunct of the Basra group; to the latter he sent his follower Sulayman Faydi in an attempt to drum up support for the I'tilafists. In neither city was the attempt very successful, and the Unionist government found very little difficulty in snuffing it out. It was otherwise in Basra, where Sayyid Talib's family was powerful and influential and where he himself was acquainted with local men and issues, and moreover had no hesitation in employing hired assassins to enforce his desires. But the Unionists eventually succeeded in gaining him over, and at the outbreak of the first world war he and they were friends.

The period between the Italian conquest of Tripoli and the outbreak of the first world war saw also the creation of two secret Arab groups. The first of these was *jam'iyyat al-'ahd* (The Society of the Covenant), which was founded on 28 October 1913 by Binbashi 'Aziz al-Misri. Its members were army officers and included Salim al-Djaza'iri, Nuri al-Sa'id, Yasin al-Hashimi, his brother Taha, Jamil al-Midfa'i, Tashin 'Ali, Mawlud Mukhlis, Amin Lutfi, 'Ali Jawdat al-Ayyubi and 'Abdullah al-Dulaymi. Its official programme was to promote autonomy for the Arabic-speaking countries of the Ottoman empire, and to transform the empire into a dual monarchy on the lines of the Austro-Hungarian monarchy. But the fact that it was a secret society composed of army officers ready to take action in support of their political views and that many of the members deserted from the Ottoman army before and during the first world war is at least as important as the tenor of the official programme. The other secret grouping was that formed by Rashid Rida under the name of *jam'iyyat al-jami'a al-'arabiyya* (the Society of Arab Union). Rashid Rida has stated that the group was founded following the Ottoman defeat in the Balkan wars when 'the founders decided that the strength would be useless unless the rulers of the peninsula were united in an alliance'.[14] Rashid Rida seems to have enrolled various potentates of the peninsula in this Society, but apart from a long and fearsome oath,[15] no activity by the group is recorded.

When the Ottoman empire entered the war in November 1914, political activity by Arab groups and parties, such as it had been in the six years from 1908, virtually came to a stop. It was only at the end of the war, in 1918, that a new grouping came into being in Cairo known as *al-ittihad al-suri* (the Syrian Union). This comprised a number of Syrians who had become opposed to Husayn, Sharif of Mecca and King of the Hijaz, whose ambitions in Syria they mistrusted. Their views are to be gathered from the memorial they addressed to the British government in the summer of 1918, which elicited the reply known as the Declaration to Seven Syrians.[16] The group included Michel Lutfallah as president, Rashid Rida as vice-president, 'Abd al-Rahman al-Shabandar and Salim Sarkis as joint secretaries. When eventually Sharif Faysal was installed in Damascus at the head of an Arab government, the conditions in Syria became such that the grouping had no longer a *raison d'être* and, in fact, its members are later found adopting a variety of positions in Syrian politics.

The short-lived Sharifian régime in Syria (November 1918 to July 1920) was characterized by an active, not to say turbulent, political life. The *fatat* society was reconstituted with some of the most prominent Sharifians, such as 'Ali Rida al-Rikabi, Yasin al-Hashimi, Ahmad Qadri and Nasib al-Bakri as leaders. But the *Fatat* never seems to have made its existence or membership public; instead, a political party was organized to work in public for the aims of the secret society: this was *hizb al-istiqlal al-'arabi* (the Party of Arab Independence), the declared purpose of which was the liberation of all Arab countries from foreign domination. The pan-Arab inclinations of the leaders of the *istiqlal* and the *fatat*, many of whom were then young, unknown, and with no local standing in Damascus, evoked some opposition among Damascene notables, who organized *al-hizb al-watani al-suri* (the National Syrian Party), the secretary of which was Muhammad al-Shariqi and the declared aim of which was to work for a Syria 'independent within its natural frontiers'. Another group concerned with the political future of Syria was one organized by some Syrian Christians in Cairo in 1919 to work for a United States mandate in Syria. The group was called *al-hizb al-suri al-mu'tadil* (the Moderate Syrian Party), and its members included Faris Nimr, Sa'id Shuqayr, Ya'qub Sarruf and Ilyas 'Isawi. The group delegated two of its members, Faris Nimr and Khalil Khayyat, to put its views before Charles Crane of the King-Crane Commission which visited the Levant in the summer of 1919. When it became clear that there was no possibility of the U.S.A. accepting such a mandate, nothing more was heard of the group.

The aftermath of war saw Mesopotamia, which was under British occupation, in an unsettled condition. The tribes and cities of the Middle and Lower Euphrates, predominantly Shi'i, were in effervescence, as were the Kurdish areas; Baghdad was full of disgruntled ex-Ottoman officials and officers, and the Sharifian régime in Syria encouraged warlike activities against the British authorities. The Sharifian officers in Syria who had been members of the pre-war *'ahd* sent emissaries to Baghdad, and secretly constituted a group of their sympathizers under the name of *jam'iyyat al-'ahd al-'iraki* (the Iraqi Covenant Society). This was a predominantly Sunni group. Some Shi'i leaders of Baghdad and Kazimayn formed their own secret political society to protect Shi'i interests in the anti-British struggle. The society was known as *jam'iyyat haras al-istiqlal* (the Guardians of Independence Society). Its founders included 'Ali al-Bazirgan, Shaykh Muhammad Baqir al-Shabibi, Hadi Zwayn, Muhammad Dja'far Abu'l-Timman and Sayyid Muhammad al-Sadr. With the installations of Faysal as King of Iraq in 1921, new issues and new groupings led to the disappearance of both the *'ahd* and the *haras*.

Iraq. The Kingdom of Iraq was supposed to be a constitutional, parliamentary monarchy. But as in Egypt, though here the circumstances and reasons were quite different, parliament never functioned in a normal or representative fashion but was rather the instrument of whatever effective authority existed in the country at any moment. Parties therefore during the monarchical régime (1922–58) may be described as more or less factions composed of politicians manœuvring on the restricted and artificial political scene of the capital. The first parties to be formed under the monarchy were *hizb al-nahda al-ʿiraqiyya* (The Iraq Renaissance Party) and *al-hizb al-watani* (The National Party), both founded in August 1922. They were composed of public men who were dissatisfied with the second ministry of Sayyid ʿAbd al-Rahman al-Naqib and who were prepared to adopt an intransigent stance towards the mandatory power. The leaders of the *nahda* group included Hamdi al-Pačaji and Naji al-Suwaydi, whilst *al-hizb al-watani* was, and remained until the mid-thirties when it disappeared from view, identified with Muhammad Jaʿfar Abu'l-Timman whose following it in fact constituted. Al-Naqib's government also organized its supporters in a party known as *al-hizb al-hurr* (The Liberal Party), which disappeared from view when al-Naqib finally relinquished power in November 1922. The *nahda* seems to have disintegrated some time between 1924 and 1925. The next party to be recorded is *hizb al-taqaddum* (The Progressive Party), formed in June 1925, which was in fact the following of ʿAbd al-Muhsin al-Saʿdun who formed his second administration at that time; the party disappeared when this ministry fell in November 1926. Another party, even more ephemeral, dating from this period, was *hizb al-shaʿb* (The People's Party), which Yasin al-Hashimi formed in November 1925 in order to muster opposition to the government. Parties are no more heard of until 1930 when an Anglo-Iraqi treaty was being negotiated, and political rivalries and passions were at a high pitch. Nuri al-Saʿid was Prime Minister—in his first administration—and in order to muster support for his policies formed *hizb al-ʿahd* (The Party of the Covenant)—appropriating the name of the secret society of which he had been a member in Ottoman times; this party stayed in being until Nuri al-Saʿid relinquished power in October 1932. The chief opponent of the administration, Yasin al-Hashimi, also formed a party in 1930, which was known as *hizb al-ikhaʾ al-watani* (The National Brotherhood Party). The *ikhaʾ* group included Rashid ʿAli al-Gaylani, Hikmat Sulayman, Naji al-Suwaydi, ʿAli Jawdat al-Ayyubi, Kamil al-Čadirji and ʿAbd al-Ilah Hafiz. The group remained in being until April 1935 when it voluntarily dissolved itself, its leader Yasin al-Hashimi having just then formed his second administration. The group played an important role in Iraqi politics, organizing conspiracies and fomenting tribal rebellions in the Euphrates against the governments then in power. During the brief administration of Naji Shawkat (November 1932 to March 1933) an ephemeral parliamentary group, *al-kutla al-barlamaniyya* (The Parliamentary Bloc), was formed in order to support the government, and the group went out of existence when it fell. A similar group, similarly ephemeral, was *hizb al-wahda al-wataniyya* (The Party of National Unity), which was formed to support the first administration of 'Ali Jawdat al-Ayyubi (August 1934 to February 1935). From the *coup d'état* of General Bakir Sidqi al-'Askari (October 1936) until April 1946, Iraqi politicians did not seem to find it necessary or feasible to group themselves into parties, but in this period two political groups deserve mention because they embody ideological trends which were to reappear after the second world war. The first of these groups was *jam'iyyat al-islah al-sha'bi* (the Popular Reform Society), formed in November 1936, the founders of which were Kamil al-Čadirji, Yusuf Ibrahim, Naji al-Asil, and Muhammad Dja'far Abu 'l-Timman. The tone of the group was set not by its founders but by a younger group of members who held socialist views and who had been informally associated since 1931 round the newspaper *al-Ahali*, and who were therefore known as *jama'at al-Ahali* (the Ahali Group); this younger group included Husayn Jamil, 'Abd al-Qadir Isma'il and his relative 'Abd al-Fattah Ibrahim, Muhammad Hadid and Khalil Kanna, all of whom had some role to play in Iraqi politics after 1945 and all of whom, except for the last-named, remained faithful to the socialist ideology. This younger group in *jam'iyyat al-islah al-sha'bi* seem to have been in hopes that their ideas would be adopted as the official programme of the government, but the resignation of three of their founders from the Hikmat Sulayman administration in June 1937, and the fall of Hikmat Sulayman shortly thereafter, spelt in fact the end of the society and its activities. The other group worth mentioning in the period 1936–46 is *nadi al-Muthanna* (the Muthanna Club), which existed from about 1937 to the collapse of Rashid 'Ali al-Gaylani's *coup d'état* in May 1941. The club was dedicated to the spread of pan-Arabism; its ideas were influential at the time and many of its members participated in Iraqi politics after 1945, notably in *hizb al-istiqlal*.

After the second world war, the Regent 'Abd al-Ilah in a speech of December 1945 gave an impulsion to the formation of political parties, and in April 1946 five parties were licensed: *hizb al-ahrar* (the Liberal Party), *hizb al-istiqlal* (the Independence Party), *al hizb al-watani al-dimuqrati* (the National Socialist Party), *hizb al-sha'b* (the People's Party) and *hizb al-ittihad al-watani* (the National Unity

Party). *Hizb al-ahrar* was founded by eight men, none of whom was prominent in politics; it does not seem to have had any noticeable political activity, and it decided to 'freeze' itself in December 1948, after which date nothing more was heard of it. *Hizb al-istiqlal* was formed by a group which included Muhammad Mahdi Kubba, Khalil Kanna and 'Abd al-Razzaq al-Zahir; it was pan-Arab in its views and included many of those who had followed or sympathized with Rashid 'Ali al-Gaylani's *coup d'état* of 1941. The party remained active in opposition to successive governments until it went out of existence in September 1954, when a decree was issued at the beginning of Nuri al-Sa'id's twelfth administration dissolving all existing associations and clubs in Iraq. *Al-hizb al-watani al-dimuqrati* was formed by some of the old members of *jam'iyyat al-islah al-sha'bi*; the founders included Kamil al-Čadirji, Muhammad Hadid, Husayn Jamil, 'Abd al-Wahhab Mirjan and Sadiq Kammuna; it declared itself dedicated to the reform of land tenure, equality, social welfare and economic planning. The Party was active in opposition to successive governments, but it decided to suspend activities between December 1948 and March 1950 when it considered that the repressive policy of the authorities allowed it no scope to function; the government dissolved it in September 1954. The founders of *hizb al-sha'b* included 'Aziz Sharif, Tawfiq Munir and 'Abd al-Amir Abu Trab; the Party was socialist and more to the left than *al-hizb al-watani al-dimuqrati*; it was banned for subversion in September 1947. The founders of *hizb al-ittihad al-watani* included 'Abd al-Fattah Ibrahim and Muhammad Mahdi al-Jawahiri; it too, was leftist in sympathies and was also banned for subversion in September 1947. It will be observed that contrary to the pattern of Iraqi political parties in the 1920s and 30s, these parties were not combinations of politicians competing among themselves for power, but were rather—except for *hizb al-ahrar*—ideological groups who remained strangers to political power, and whose weapons—mostly ineffectual—were the public speech, the newspaper article and the occasional demonstration.

But the more usual kind of Iraqi political party is also met with after 1945. Sami Shawkat and a few of his associates formed a party, *hizb al-islah* (the Reform Party), in November 1949; this group was not successful in attaining office and amalgamated in July 1951 with *hizb al-umma al-ishtiraki* (the People's Socialist Party), which Salih Jabir and his associates had formed the previous month to act as a rival grouping to Nuri al-Sa'id and his associates. The latter had himself formed a party in November 1949 (which he voluntarily dissolved in August 1954) and gave it the name of *hizb al-ittihad al-dusturi* (the Constitutional Unionist Party). It remains finally to notice a hybrid group of politicians and ideologists which was formed in May 1951 under the name of *al-jabha al-sha'biyya al-muttahida* (the United Popular Front). The founders included Taha al-Hashimi, Muzahim al-Pačaji, Muhammad Rida al-Shabibi, Nasrat al-Farisi, Sadiq al-Bassam, Burhan al-Din Basha'yan, Mahmud al-Durra, Najib al-Sayigh and 'Abd al-Razzaq al-Shaykhli. The *jabha* was dedicated to the principle of neutralism in foreign policy; it therefore opposed the Anglo-Iraqi Treaty of Alliance and the governments who were in favour of upholding it. It was not a homogeneous group, being composed of politicians hoping for office and using the front as a lever for their ambitions, and of ideologists whose hopes of office were remote; rifts between members appeared, and in August 1954 the front ceased all activity.

Syria. The early years of the French mandate in Syria show little party political activity. Syrian nationalists protested now and again at French rule in Syria, but until 1925 such protest was little organized. In May of that year, the Syrian leader 'Abd al-Rahman al-Shabandar founded, together with other Syrian nationalists, including Hasan al-Hakim, Lutfi al-Haffar and Faris al-Khuri, *hizb al-sha'b* (the People's Party); but this Party was short-lived, since the French authorities banned it the following August on suspicion of involvement in the Druze rebellion which had just started. In the anti-French troubles, which followed, Shabandar took a prominent part, and when the French were successful in pacifying the country, he went into exile and remained absent from Syria until 1937. The next Syrian political grouping was *al-kutla al-wataniyya* (the National Bloc), formed about 1929, which was organized formally at a meeting in Homs in November 1932. The National Bloc was dedicated to the attainment of Syrian independence and Arab unity; it was led by Ibrahim Hananu and Hashim al-Atasi, and among its prominent members were Sa'dullah al-Jabiri, Jamil Mardam, Shukri al-Quwwatli, 'Abd al-Rahman al-Kayyali, Lutfi al-Haffar, Edmond Rabbath, Fakhri al-Barudi and Mikha'il Ilyan. The Bloc was the main political grouping in Syria in the 1930s. Its leaders were influential in the country and frequently enjoyed a considerable following in their localities; the Bloc was essentially a coalition of notables united by struggle against the French, but here and there, now and again, they succeeded in mobilizing the mass and organizing it in towns like Damascus, Hama and Aleppo, but only by fits and starts. Their success in this enterprise was greater between 1936 and 1939 when they exercised power with French help and consent, dominating the legislature and dispensing administrative patronage; in this period, they organized a para-military youth movement, *al-shabab al-watani* (the National Youth), the uniform of which was an iron-grey shirt. Along with the *kutla*, there were in the 1930s a variety of evanescent political groups which came and went depending on French encouragement, political rivalries or foreign (whether European or Iraqi) inspiration. Of the groups, the best known are *'usbat al-'amal al-qawmi* (the league of National Action), *hizb al-wahda al-arabiyya* (the Party of Arab Unity), *hizb al inqadh* (the Party of Rescue), *al-jabha al-wataniyya al-muttahida* (the United National Front), and *al-hay'a al-sha'biyya* (The Popular Bloc), which constituted Shahbandar's own political following when, on his return to Damascus in 1937, he fell out with his colleagues of the National Bloc. Overt political activity in Syria ceased between the outbreak of the second world war and 1943, when parliamentary elections were held, but in 1941 a small political group dedicated to the support of Rashid Ali al-Gaylani in Iraq was formed by two Damascus school teachers, Michel Aflaq and Salah al-Din al-Bitar; the group was known as *jama'at nusrat al-Iraq* (the Aid Iraq Group); it was a nucleus of what later became *hizb al-ba'th al-arabi* (the Arab Resurrection Party). In 1953 this Party amalgamated with a group founded in the late 1940s by Akram al-Hawrani, *al-hizb al-arabi al-ishtiraki* (the Arab Socialist Party), in order to become *hizb al-ba'th al-arabi al-ishtiraki* (the Arab Socialist Resurrection Party), dedicated to pan-Arabism and socialism and operating not only in Syria but also in the Lebanon, Jordan and Iraq as well, and, with the support of sympathetic army officers, actually exercising power in both Syria and Iraq. The elections of 1943 resulted in an overwhelming majority for the National Bloc, which took power and, with British support, succeeded in securing French departure from Syria. The Bloc, a coalition of politicians, suffered from fissiparous tendencies; this was the case in 1936–9, when jealousy and dissensions between different leaders and areas were already visible, and also after 1943, when the very extent of its victory aroused jealousies and cupidities. In 1947 some politicians seceded from the Bloc and formed *hizb al-sha'b* (the People's Party). Another group of politicians, constituting the following of Khalid al-'Azm, was formed in 1955 under the name of *al-kutla al-dimuqratiyya* (the Democratic Bloc). But political factions such as the National Bloc, the People's Party and the Democratic Bloc, became of little importance when after 1949 army officers constantly intervened in politics. It was these officers who increasingly determined the character of political life in Syria after 1949.

The Lebanon. Political activity in the Greater Lebanon, which the French authorities constituted in 1920, was somewhat different in character from that obtaining in the autonomous *mutasarrifiyya* of Mount Lebanon. In Mount Lebanon the main political problem arose out of the rivalries and mutual fears of Druzes and Maronites; whereas in Greater Lebanon, the presence of a sizeable Muslim population, predominantly Sunni, meant that political rivalries and combinations were more complex, but the parliamentary institutions as devised by the mandatory government ensured that the political divisions between parties did not reproduce, reflect and hence exacerbate religious differences. An early political grouping which was more like a discussion group than a political party proper was *hizb al-taraqqi* (the Progress Party), which existed for a few years after 1920. It was headed by the Marquis de Freij and included among its members Emile Edde, Bishara al-Khuri, Yusuf al-Jumayyil and Michel Shiha. It was, however, not until the early 1930s that a stable and relatively long-lived political grouping came into being. This was *al-kutla al-dusturiyya* (the Constitutional Bloc), which was a grouping of deputies in the chamber elected at the beginning of 1934 headed by Bishara al-Khuri who, for the next decade, was to contend for office and power with his fellow Maronite Emile Edde. *Al-kutla al-dusturiyya* was so called because one of its members had asked before the elections of 1934 for the restoration of constitutional and parliamentary government. Emile Edde's supporters were grouped in *al-kutla al-wataniyya* (the National Bloc), which in 1945 changed its name to *hizb al-sha'b* (the People's Party). Other factions composed of politicians and their clients appeared after the withdrawal of French authority in 1943; they were all ephemeral, coming into being under particular circumstances and disappearing with their disappearance: thus a group calling itself *hizb al-istiklal* (the Independence Party) came into being in 1944 to oppose Riyad al-Sulh, then in office; it included 'Abd al-Hamid Karame, Sa'ib Slam, 'Abdullah al-Yafi and Henry Pharaon; in 1946 another such group, calling itself *kutlat al-islah* (the Reform Bloc), was formed by 'Abd al-Hamid Karame, Yusuf Karam, Kamal Junblat, 'Umar Bayhum and 'Umar al-Da'uq to oppose Sami al-Sulh, then in office; 1947 saw still another group, *kutlat al-taharrur al-watani* (the National Liberation Bloc), similar in aim and slightly different in composition. Besides these political factions, the Lebanon has seen other political groupings. In 1932, Antun Sa'ada formed *al-hizb al-suri al-qawmi al-ijtima'i* (the National Social Syrian Party, commonly known as the Parti populaire syrien); this was an ideological movement dedicated to the formation of a political entity embracing the Lebanon, Syria, Transjordan, Palestine, Iraq and Cyprus, this area being, according to the founder, the homeland of the Syrian nation. Antun Sa'ada attempted—with some success—to create a mass movement in Syria and the Lebanon which inclined to violence and conspiracy in politics; the party had many ups and downs both in Syria and the Lebanon before and after Antun Sa'ada's execution in July 1949 when he was convicted by a Lebanese military court for taking part in armed rebellion. 1936–7 saw the formation of two movements with paramilitary features: *hizb al-najjada*, which grew out of the Muslim Boy Scout movement, and *hizb al-kata'ib al-lubnaniyya* (*les Phalanges libanaises*) founded by Pierre Jumayyil for the protection of Maronite interests. Finally, in 1949, Kamal Junblat founded *al-hizb al-taqaddumi al-ishtiraki* (the Socialist Progressive Party), which advertised a socialist ideology, but which remained, by and large, a group consisting of the founder's personal following.

Palestine. Zionism was the main issue against which the Arabic-speaking population of Palestine had to define its political divisions and rivalries. Leadership in this struggle was disputed by two leading families, the Husaynis and the Nashashibis. A member of the former, Muhammad Amin al-Husayni, became early in the 1920s *mufti* of Jerusalem and president of the Supreme Muslim Council (set up by the mandatory authorities to administer Muslim religious endowments and establishments); from the latter, Raghib al-Nashashibi became mayor of Jerusalem. These two personalities became the focus round which their respective followers were gathered, and in the 1920s Arabic-speaking Palestine was divided between two factions, the *majlisiyyun* (i.e. pro-Council men) who constituted the Husayni following, and the *mu'aridun* (i.e. Oppositionists) who opposed them. In 1931, a number of politicians who believed in Pan-Arabism formed *hizb al-istiqlal*; (the Independence Party); the group included Akram Zu'aytar, Subhi al-Khadra, 'Awni 'Abd al-Hadi, Muhammad 'Izzat Darwaza, Mu'in al-Madi and 'Ajjaj Nuwayhid; in December 1934, the Nashashibi faction was formally constituted into a party, *hizb al-difa' al-watani* (the Party of National Defence), and in April of the following year the Husayni faction also constituted itself into a party, *al-hizb al-'arabi al-filastini* (the Arab Palestine Party), the president of which was Jamal al-Husayni. In June of the same year Dr. Husayn al-Khalidi (hitherto in opposition to the *mufti*) organized his following into *hizb al-islah* (the Reform Party), and, opposing the Nashashibi faction, captured the office of mayor of Jerusalem. In October 1935 a Nablus group formed itself into *hizb al-kutla al-wataniyya* (the National Bloc Party). All these different groupings proved quite ephemeral, for in April 1936, at the beginning of the long drawn-out Palestine troubles, they agreed to form a body, *al-lajna al-'arabiyya al-'ulya* (the Supreme Arab

Committee), in which they were all represented, in order to coordinate the struggle against the mandatory power. The subsequent events in Palestine between 1936 and 1948 allowed no further opportunity for the formation of party groups. But some of the parties formed earlier, notably *hizb al-istiqlal* and *al-hizb al-'arabi*, resumed their activities between 1943 and the end of the Mandate.

The Sudan. Political parties in the Sudan were quite late in making an appearance and when they did, their activities were governed by their connexion with the heads of the two leading *tariqas*, the Khatmiyya and the Ansar, and the attitude they adopted towards union with or separation from Egypt. In March 1938 the formation of a group, *mu'tamar al-khirrijin al-'amm* (the General Graduates' Congress), was announced, the aim of which was to promote the general welfare of the country and its graduates (by the term 'graduate' was meant someone who had finished school at the intermediate grade or above). The group wished for a greater share in government to be given to the Sudanese. A split in the ranks of the Congress led after 1942 to the formation of another group, the *ashiqqa'* (the Brethren), led by Isma'il al-Azhari, which was allied with the Khatmiyya *tariqa* and dedicated to unity with Egypt. Opposing them was *hizb al-umma* (the People's Party), which called for the complete independence of the Sudan, and was backed by the Ansar. In August 1949 another group, *al-djabha al-wataniyya* (the National Front), was formed which aimed at Dominion status for the Sudan under the Egyptian crown. To this group Khatmiyya support was given for a time. In 1951 a group dedicated to the formation of a Sudanese republic immune from Mahdist influence was formed: it was called *al-hizb al-jumhuri al-ishtiraki* (the Republican Socialist Party); it never had much influence. In 1952 the *ashiqqa'* and the *jabha* combined to form *al-hizb al-watani al-ittihadi* (the National Unionist Party) which, led by Isma'il al-Azhari, proclaimed unity with Egypt as its objective. This group came to power in January 1954 and remained in office until the *coup d'état* of 1958 put an end to party political activity. In spite of its professed aims, the Party, when in power, found that it had to acquiesce in separation from Egypt.

Tunisia. The French Protectorate of Tunisia, dating from 1881, was the framework within which organized Tunisian political activity took place. This Protectorate facilitated the settlement of Frenchmen and other Europeans in the country and slowly led to increasing French control over Tunisian administration. Such a situation led a small number of educated Tunisians to form a group in 1907 known as the *Parti jeune tunisien*, whose aim was to work for a constitution and a greater scope for Tunisians in public affairs. The group included 'Ali Bash Hamba and 'Abd al-'Aziz al-Tha'alibi. At the end of the first world war, the group came to be known as the *Parti tunisien*. It presented a memorandum to President Wilson in April 1919 and published a book in Paris in 1920, *La Tunisie martyre*, which was written by Tha'alibi and Ahmad Saqqa and which set out Tunisian grievances. In June of the same year, the *Parti tunisien* changed its name to *Parti libéral constitutionnel* (*al-hizb al-hurr al-dusturi*), commonly known thereafter as the Destour. Towards the end of the 1920s the party became revitalized through the efforts of a younger generation of members, including Habib Bourguiba, al-Shadhili Khayrallah and Mahmud Matiri. The younger men led by Bourguiba soon clashed with their elders, and at the party congress of Qasr Hilal in March 1934 Bourguiba captured the organization, which he continued henceforth to lead in spite of many challenges and vicissitudes. The party came henceforth to be known as the néo-Destour to indicate the rejection by the new leaders of the ideas of those whom they called '*archéos*'. Under Bourguiba's leadership, the neo-Destour stood for Tunisian independence. Bourguiba also transformed the party into a mass movement with a country-wide organization and a pyramidal chain of command with himself at the apex. The party was composed of branches (*shu'ab*) of two kinds: territorial (*shu'ba turabiyya*) and non-territorial (*shu'ba ghayr turabiyya*), the latter being found in a large city like Tunis, and comprising members from the same hometown or locality. The party also organized the youth in special formations, *al-shabiba al-dusturiyya* (the Constitutionalist Youth) and controlled the Tunisian trade union movement. The new technique of canalizing mass emotions for political ends is described in a remarkable passage by one of Bourguiba's prominent followers, in which he says that when Bourguiba made speeches orator and audience became as one flesh, the mass responding to the inflexions of the speaker's voice 'being moved by his emotion, angered by his anger, and reflecting if he compelled it to think'.[17] After the attainment of Tunisian independence, the néo-Destour consolidated its position in the country, and is today the only political organization in Tunisia.

Algeria. It is only after the first world war that purely Algerian organized political activity emerges. And it emerges not in Algeria itself, but among the Algerian proletariat in France. In 1926, the French Communist Party tried to organize Algerian workers into a grouping known as the *Etoile nord-africaine*; in 1927 this grouping came to be led by the Algerian Messali al-Haj who had served in the French army and been demobilized in France. The *Etoile* was a left-wing anti-colonial proletarian organization which operated in France, not in Algeria. It had many ups and downs, its leaders were repeatedly prosecuted and the association itself banned for alleged subversion. In 1936 Messali al-Haj, having fled to Switzerland to escape the police, met there the Amir Shakib Arslan and, under his influence, gave up his Communist sympathies and began to work for an Arab Islamic Algeria. In 1937 he founded the *Parti du peuple algérien* which recruited its members and organized them in cells in Algeria itself, and worked for Algerian independence. On the outbreak of the second world war, the authorities banned the party and imprisoned its leader. In 1946, having been allowed to return to Algeria, he organized his followers into a new party, the *Mouvement pour le triomphe des libertés démocratiques*, which called for a sovereign Algerian republic and for the unity of the Maghrib. The *Mouvement* was the public and legal front of the *Parti du peuple algérien*, which had worked underground since its banning in 1939. An even more secret grouping which was set up by Messali al-Haj and his colleagues was the paramilitary *Organisation spéciale*, the head of which was Ahmad bin Bella. In April 1954, he and eight of his colleagues set up in Cairo the *Comité révolutionnaire d'unité et d'action* which organized insurrection against the French authorities in Algeria. The *Comité* launched the *Front de libération nationale*, to whom the French government eventually conceded Algerian independence. The Front has become the only political movement in the Algerian Republic.

Other political groupings appeared on the Algerian scene in the 1930s and 40s. In 1934, Muhammad Salah bin Jilul organized the Muslim local representatives of the *département* of Constantine into a *Fédération des élus musulmans du département de Constantine*. Other *fédérations* were also set up and these groups, loosely organized as they were, did attempt to adopt a common line of policy towards the authorities. What they desired was a lessening of Algerian disabilities and a greater share in the government. Algerian independence was not an objective of theirs; neither was it the objective of the *Rassemblement franco-musulman algérien*, which Bin Jilul organized in 1938, or of the *Union populaire algerienne* which Farhat 'Abbas set up in the same year. Neither of these groups was destined to have a long life. In March 1943 Farhat 'Abbas addressed a manifesto to the governor-general of Algeria entitled *L'Algérie devant le conflit mondial: Manifeste du peuple algérien*, asking for justice for the Algerian Muslims and Algerian autonomy. In 1944 Farhat 'Abbas organized *Les Amis du manifeste et de la liberté*, which he designed as a mass movement to take the place of the *Parti du peuple algérien*. Whether or not his methods in 1944–5 contributed to the rising of

May 1945 in the Constantinois, the authorities did arrest him and dissolved his organization. On his release in 1946 he organized the *Union démocratique du manifeste algérien*, forsaking mass agitation, his watchword being: 'Ni assimilation, ni nouveaux maîtres, ni séparatisme.' In April 1956, he joined the National Liberation Front.

Morocco. Organized political party activity in Morocco dates from the 1930s. Its origin lies in the protest organized by some young Moroccans in 1930 against the Berber dahir and French policy, which they took to aim at separating the Berbers from the Moroccan polity. A group of these young men produced in 1934 a *Plan de réformes marocaines*, and organized themselves into a *Comité d'action marocaine*. The group included Muhammad Hasan al-Wazzani and 'Allal al-Fasi, who were the two most prominent members, 'Umar 'Abd al-Jalil, Muhammad al-Makki al-Nasiri, Mahmud al-Yazidi and Muhammad Duyuri. The *Comité* was banned in March 1937 and reconstituted the following month as the *Parti national pour la réalisation du plan de réforme*, which also was banned the following October. In April 1937 Muhammad Hasan al-Wazzani, who had fallen out with his fellow-members of the *Comité*, organized a political group under the name of *Action nationale marocaine*, which was likewise banned in October 1937. These early political groupings were much influenced by the political ideas of Shakib Arslan, who had visited Tetuan in 1930 and to whom Muhammad al-Wazzani had for some time acted as secretary; they were also encouraged in their activities by the sympathy of some French socialists, notably Robert-Jean Longuet who had started the periodical *Maghreb* in Paris in 1932.

Between October 1937 and 1943 there was little political party activity in the French zone of Morocco. In the Spanish zone, the Spanish civil war starting in 1936 had a direct and important influence on the character of political party activities. The Spanish Nationalist authorities, who speedily came to control the zone, wished to secure political support among the Moroccans and encouraged the formation in June 1936 of a party led by 'Abd al-Khaliq al-Turays (Torres) under the name of *hizb al-islah al-watani* (National Reform Party). In February 1937 Makki al-Nasiri was encouraged to form a rival group, *hizb al-wahda al-maghribiyya* (the Party of Moroccan Unity). The two groups remained in existence until the end of the Protectorate, intermittently enjoying the favour and support of the authorities.

Towards the end of 1943, conditions inside and outside Morocco making political activity in the French zone once more possible, the *Istiqlal* party was formed. It was led by the same group who had formed the *Comité d'action marocaine* and the *Parti national*; its most prominent members were Ahmad Balafrij, 'Abd al-Rahim bu 'Abid, Muhammad al-Yazidi and 'Umar 'Abd al-Jalil. But the *Istiqlal* party differed from earlier groupings by the fact that it succeeded in organizing from 1945 onwards a countrywide network of cells (*djama'at*, sing. *djama'a*) with a pyramidal chain of command; it could thus mobilize the masses in the struggle against the French Protectorate which ended successfully in 1956. The *Istiqlal* party during the period 1945–56 thus functioned as a movement. Alongside it there were a number of groupings which were more in the nature of factions: Muhammad Hasan al-Wazzani organized in 1946 the *Parti démocratique de l'indépendance* (which after independence became the *Parti démocratique constitutionnel*); the Sharif Mulay Idris organized in 1947 the *Parti démocratique marocain des hommes libres*, and in 1948 Bashir Zimrani formed the *Parti du peuple marocain*. These two latter parties supported the Protectorate and in turn enjoyed official protection.

After independence the *Istiqlal* party emerged as the most powerful political organization in the country, but in 1959 there was a split in its ranks, and two of its leaders, Mahdi bin Barka and 'Abd Allah Ibrahim, led a new party with leftist leanings, the *Union nationale des forces populaires*, which was suppressed speedily. When King Hasan took the reins of government in his own hands, Moroccan political parties became no more than marginal groups occasionally expressing their opposition to the régime.

This survey of political parties in the Arab world during the first five decades or so of the twentieth century throws light from another angle on the crisis in which most middle-eastern polities find themselves. These political parties have on the whole neither succeeded in representing the classes or groups or interests of Arab society, nor have they been able to make parliamentary, constitutional government work. In the last decade or two they have been succeeded by government-sponsored monopolistic single parties (an expression which is a contradiction in terms), the purpose of which is to mobilize the population and control it on behalf of rulers, whose power derives from military *coups d'état*. These organizations seem to have no autonomous life, and to be an emanation of the government. In this of course they differ from such a body as the Communist Party of the Soviet Union which does itself effectively control both government and army. But the example of the Soviet Union has no doubt served to make the military régimes aware of the possibilities and methods of totalitarian control. This is perhaps the most significant impact of Communism on the political life of the Arab world. As for the local Communist parties their action and influence during the period covered by this survey—and indeed afterwards—have been minimal. Small, fissiparous, clandestine groups, founded or inspired by emissaries of the Third International, or by Jewish Communists in Palestine, or by Armenian refugees of leftist sympathies, wedded to an ideology which made no sense of any kind in middle-eastern conditions, they were in no position to take part in the politics of the Arab states. Because of this, and because, in any case, there is an abundant literature on them[18]—and its very abundance can mislead as to their importance—they have been omitted from this survey.

NOTES

1. Salim Khalil al-Naqqash, *Misr li'l-misriyyin* (Egypt for the Egyptians), vii, Alexandria, 1884, 44–5.
2. Muhammad al-Makhzumi, *Khatirat Jamal al-Din al-Afghani al-Husayni* (Memoirs of Djamal al-Din al-Afghani), Beirut, 1931, 86–7.
3. *Hizb al-nasyunalist fi Misr* ('The Nationalist Party in Egypt') in *al-Djami'a*, New York, v/6 (1906), 224.
4. Iraj Afshar and Asghar Mahdavi, eds., *Documents inédits concernant Seyyed Jamal-al-Din Afghani*, Tehran, 1963, plates 106–17.
5. *Qissat hayati* (The Story of My Life), Cairo, 1962, 36.
6. *Mustafa Kamil*, Cairo, 1939, 364–8.
7. *Mustafa Kamil*, 301–2.
8. Muhammad Ibrahim al-Jaziri, ed., *Athar al-za'im Sa'd Zaghlul* (Literary Remains of the Leader Sa'd Zaghlul), i, Cairo, 1927, 211.
9. Mustafa al-Hifnawi, *al-Sifr al-khalid* (The Everlasting Record), Cairo n.d. [after 1936], 5–6.
10. P. Graves, 'The story of the Egyptian crisis,' in *The nineteenth century and after*, March 1938.
11. See Kedourie, 'Egypt and the Caliphate 1915–1952' in *The Chatham House Version*.
12. See Kedourie, *England and the Middle East*, 1956, 47 and 62.
13. *The Arab Bulletin*, no. 17.
14. *Athar Rafiq al-'Azm*, (Literary Remains of Rafiq al-'Azm), Cairo, 1926, i, p. viii.
15. Reproduced in Amin Sa'id, *al-Thawra al-'arabiyya al-kubra* (the Great Arab Revolt), Cairo, 1934, i, 49–50.
16. Kedourie, *England and the Middle East*, 113–15.
17. 'Ali al-Bahlawan, *Tunis al-tha'ira* (Tunisia in Revolt), Cairo, 1954, 73.
18. W. Z. Laqueur, *Communism and Nationalism in the Middle East*, 1956; John Batatu, 'Some Preliminary Observations on the Beginnings of Communism in the Arab East' in J. Pennar, ed., *Islam and Communism*, Munich 1960; Robert Rezette, *Les partis politiques marocains*, Paris, 1955; M. W. Suleiman 'The Lebanese Communist Party', *Middle Eastern Studies*, 1967; R. le Tourneau, *Evolution politique de l'Afrique du Nord musulmane 1920–1961*, Paris 1962; and various chapters in M. Confino and S. Shamir, eds. *The U.S.S.R. and the Middle East*, 1973.

3. The American University of Beirut

> Alike in the life of mankind and in the development of the
> individual, the deed comes first, and later the reflection; and it
> is with the question, 'What have I done?' that we awake to facts
> accomplished and never intended, and to existences we do not
> recognize, while we own them as the creation of ourselves.
>
> F. H. Bradley

The American University of Beirut celebrated its centenary in 1966.
A hundred years is a substantial period in the life of any institution
and to have survived, and thrived, for a whole century is something
worth celebrating. But our habit of reckoning in centuries, useful and
convenient as it is, can also be highly misleading; for to adapt a well-
known aphorism, though all centuries are equal, yet some centuries
are more equal than others. The century which has elapsed since the
foundation of the university is broken up by so many revolutionary
upheavals in the conditions of middle-eastern life that the centuries
preceding it seem to us by comparison a flat and monotonous expanse
in which the interval say between 1566 and 1666 is no more than a
mere arithmetical fact. This last century saw the tempo of middle-
eastern history accelerating prodigiously. Institutions like the
American University, which helped to give its impetus to this radical
change, and in the process saw themselves altered beyond recognition, are eminently worthy of the historian's attention; and it is very
much to be hoped that an able historian will be encouraged soon to
study the abundant materials which have no doubt survived and to do
justice to this important, indeed gripping subject.

It may be objected that the American University of Beirut has not
remained unchronicled until now. This is quite true, but the two
works which have so far been devoted to it are in their various ways
unsatisfactory. Bayard Dodge, who served between 1923 and 1948 as
the third president of the university and who was himself the son-in-
law of the second president, published in 1958 a slight sketch entitled
The American University of Beirut which was no more than a brief
recital of salient dates and events. A more substantial work, *That
They May Have Life*, was published by the trustees in 1941 on the
seventy-fifth anniversary of the university. It was written by Stephen
B. L. Penrose Jr. who later served as the fourth president, between
1948 and 1954. Owing to the war the author was unable to consult the
Beirut archives, and the book, though long and detailed, suffered

besides from other defects. Large parts of it are a mere recital of 'facts and figures', and welcome as are the many documents which the author cites or reproduces, the discussion of them remains on the whole superficial and undistinguished. To supplement these two works, we now have a volume of documents relating to the history of the university in the nineteenth century. This volume, for the publication of which we must be grateful to the university, brings together the *Annual Reports* of the president of the Syrian Protestant College (as the University was known until 1920) to its board of managers in Beirut.* These *Reports* deal with the academic years from 1866/7 to 1901/2, with the exception of 1892/6 and 1897/8, which are missing. These *Reports*, then, cover exactly the tenure of Daniel Bliss (1823–1916) whose term of office thus extended over thirty-six years, more than a third of the university's life so far.

The Syrian Protestant College was an off-shoot of American missionary enterprise in the Levant which began in the third decade of the nineteenth century under the aegis of the American Board of Commissioners for Foreign Missions, which was jointly conducted by Presbyterians and Congregationalists until 1870—after which the Presbyterian Board of Missions took charge of the work in Syria. The college, incorporated with a board of trustees under the laws of New York State, was until 1903 administered by the president and faculty under the supervision of a local board of managers responsible to the trustees and composed mainly of missionaries together with the British and American consuls. On the retirement of Daniel Bliss, who was succeeded by his son Howard S. Bliss (1860–1920) the local board decided to dissolve itself.

The college had very small beginnings. As the *Report* for 1877 (p. 34) puts it: 'We commenced with our first class in a hired dwelling house of six or seven rooms, badly situated and poorly ventilated, where we continued for two years suffering many inconveniences and subject to the derisions of our enemies.' The teaching staff then consisted of the president, a French instructor for one hour a day and one native tutor; the students were sixteen in number. Twenty-five years later, the teaching staff consisted of thirteen Americans, one French instructor and four Syrians. 'Now,' stated the president in his *Report* for 1891 (p. 126), 'we have from twenty-five to thirty acres of land, six buildings the flooring of which will measure about 76,000 square feet, or over one and three-fourths acres, a library of about 5,000 volumes, a fair amount of apparatus, also geological, botanical, zoological and archaeological collections.' That year the students in

* *Annual Reports, Board of Managers, Syrian Protestant College, 1866–7/1901–2.*

the preparatory, collegiate and medical departments numbered together two hundred. Since then, of course, the college has gone from strength to strength and it is today rightly considered as a leading university in the Arab east. There can be no doubt that, judged by any mundane standard, the university is a success.

But would the founders of the college, we may ask, have been pleased to see their work judged by such a standard? To this question there is, as it happens, a fairly conclusive answer supplied by a member of the board of managers who was present at the foundation of the college. Writing in 1893, the Reverend Henry Jessup, an American Missionary of long standing in the Levant, and an exact contemporary of Daniel Bliss, wrote: 'Education is only a means to an end in Christian missions, and that end is to lead men to Christ and teach them to become Christian peoples and nations. When it goes beyond this and claims to be in itself an end; that mere intellectual and scientific eminence are objects worthy of the Christian missionary, that it is worth while for consecrated missionaries and missionary societies to aim to have the best astronomers, geologists, botanists, surgeons and physicians in the realm for the sake of the scientific prestige and the world-wide reputation; then we do not hesitate to say that such a mission has stepped out of the Christian and missionary sphere into one purely secular, scientific and worldly. Such a work', he concluded, 'might be done by a Heidelberg or a Cambridge, a Harvard or a Sheffield, but not by a missionary society labouring for spiritual ends.' (Henry Harris Jessup, D.D., *Fifty-Three Years in Syria*, New York 1910, vol. II, p. 592.) We take it that the American University today does aspire to 'mere intellectual and scientific eminence', that it is ambitious to be judged by the same standard by which we judge 'a Heidelberg or a Cambridge, a Harvard or a Sheffield'. This, in the eyes of its founders, must be accounted utter failure, but whether it represents success or failure this difference between expectations and their fulfilment must be one of the main themes of a proper history of the American University. Such a history would have to exhibit in detail how this great change came about, how the middle-eastern environment Cleopatra-like subverted an initial distaste and often an active dislike for the area, its inhabitants and its religions, what part was played by the very human instinct to preserve what had been so painfully built up, and what the share was of debate within American Protestantism itself as it confronted an increasingly secular society and a hitherto unsuspected diversity of religious experience. Only someone with access to the documents can possibly do justice to this subject. What can be done here is to indicate the kind of picture emerging from published accounts.

The Reminiscences of Daniel Bliss, edited and supplemented by his eldest son (New York, 1920) have preserved for posterity Daniel Bliss's graduation address when he was on the threshold of his missionary career. 'Tyrant, Despot, Pope and Priest', exclaimed the ardent young graduate, 'are ever the enemies of agitation, and when in their domains a master spirit arises and disseminates freedom and truth, the rack and inquisition claim another victim. There can be no quiet,' he affirmed, 'when antagonistic principles meet. The great model Agitator brought not peace to human society but a sword.' His contemporary Jessup after nearly three decades of missionary endeavour in Syria still retained the same burning conviction in the superiority and the eventual triumph of his religion. 'The Christian Church,' we read in his *Mohammedan Missionary Problem* (Philadelphia 1879, pp. 134–5), 'cannot regard with indifference the welfare of one hundred and seventy-five millions of our race. The moral degradation, the spiritual blindness, the deep religious needs of so many men, the pitiful condition of Moslem women, the want of all that we hold dear and sacred in the Christian home, and the utter lack of anything like a provision for human redemption, should awaken our deepest sympathies and enkindle new zeal in every Christian breast.' Muslims as they are now and as they have ever been 'have no conception of a holy God nor of holiness of life. The moral standard of Mohammed himself was so low that we cannot expect true ideas of holiness among his followers.' In Jessup's philosophy of history two events were 'providentially related': 'one was the rise of the Mohammedan religion—the other the christianization of the Saxon race in Britain'; and the hidden significance of these two events was manifested only in these latter times when 'widely extended as is the Mohammedan religion, it is completely encircled by Anglo-Saxon Christian political and civil power'; when therefore the time comes for the conversion of Muslims to Christianity, 'as it *must* come, it will not be to Latin or Greek Christianity, but to the simpler and purer form of the Protestant evangelical faith.' (*Op. cit.*, pp. 13, 61, 73 and 72.)

A great gulf appears between this implicit trust in the ways of Providence, this utter confidence that the missionaries' religion was the only true one, and the words of Daniel Bliss when in 1904 he was president emeritus. 'We do not aim,' he said in a speech at the unveiling of his statue in Beirut, 'to make Maronites, or Greeks, or Catholics, or Protestants, or Jews, or Moslems, but we do aim to make perfect men, ideal men, God-like men, after the model of Jesus against whose moral character no man ever has said or can say aught.' (*Reminiscences*, pp. 220–3.) The implications which this kind of language carries come out clearly in the outlook and the statements of Daniel Bliss' son and successor, Howard Bliss. He was, writes his own successor and son-in-law, 'very modern in his ideas. Although he was deeply religious, he accepted the implications of Higher Criticism and tried to make the students good members of their own sects rather than Protestants.' (Dodge, *op. cit.*, p. 35.) Shortly before his death he wrote for the *Atlantic Monthly* an article on 'The Modern Missionary' (reproduced in Penrose, pp. 178–96) which according to Latourette, a leading historian of Christian missions, was reprinted by the American Board of Commissioners for Foreign Missions 'with the commendatory imprimatur of James L. Barton, the senior secretary of that body,' which showed that 'it obviously represented the policy of more than one group.' Latourette describes the article as 'a very persuasive and widely read and approved presentation' of the position of those missionaries who, 'moulded by the liberalism which prevailed in some ecclesiastical circles in the Occident', gave up the idea of making formal converts and 'sought, rather, to permeate existing communities with ideals of Christian origin without effecting a change in outward religious affiliation' (K. S. Latourette, *A History of the Expansion of Christianity*, vol. VI, p. 64.)

The liberalism of which Latourette speaks may be illustrated by a book which Dr. James Barton published in 1912 and which he revealingly entitled *Human Progress Through Missions*. This work displayed the missions as agents of industrial, commercial, scientific, philological and lexicographical progress. Of missionary education in the Ottoman empire the author had this to say: 'The schools in Turkey eighty years ago were all connected with the Oriental churches and mosques, and the curriculum consisted largely in teaching pupils to read an ancient ecclesiastical literature in an unknown tongue of the meaning of which they understood little or nothing. Into these conditions the missionary brought the modern school with modern text-books . . . Persistently the missionaries have adhered to the idea that the future of the Turkish Empire required the modern school . . .' (pp. 36–7).

Howard Bliss' language in this article coming as it does from a minister of religion, is indeed remarkable. To illustrate the religious *ambience* of the college, he states that 'missionary and Christian as it is,' yet it joins every year in the celebration of Mohammed's birthday. 'In the closing address, given by a responsible officer of the College, the speaker makes it clear that, as a representative of the Christian religion, he is glad to have a sympathetic share in all efforts to strengthen the forces of righteousness in the world. Praising the splendid democracy that obtained in early times among the Moselms themselves—no rights withheld because of colour, poverty or social status—. . . he pleads that this spirit should not only be maintained among Moslems today, but extended by them so as to embrace all mankind.' On this showing, the modern missionary's religion is in large measure one of social service and political endeavour. The modern missionary's success, thought Howard Bliss, was not to be measured by 'ecclesiastical statistics' but rather by his pervasive and enduring influence. He should account his mission successful if the graduate of his institution 'makes it easier to foster education, to overturn tyranny, to soften fanaticism, to promote freedom in state and church. The story of Bulgaria and Turkey and China and Japan and India amply attests this.'

Howard Bliss' successor had exactly the same attitude: 'To us,' he said in his inaugural address of June 1923, 'Protestantism means religious freedom, and as a Protestant institution we wish to give our students freedom of worship and freedom of belief . . . It is for the mosque, synagogue or church to provide the practical formalities of organized religion . . . Our University does not champion the cause of any one sect, but she does bind on her armour to champion the cause of the spiritual; of working with God. We wish every student to be religious.' (Penrose, *op. cit.*, pp. 292–3.) A sympathetic visitor to the university in 1937 described it as 'a non-denominational, scientific exponent of practical Christianity' and he went on: 'The University does not believe in scientific truth apart from Christian ethics. At the same time it is conscious of the dangers entailed in all religious matters in Lebanon, and is non-denominational. Such an attitude can be translated into reality only through a practical application of the basic truths contained in Christianity. The University tries to infuse into its students a new sense of social responsibility and service.' (Rom Landau, *Search for To-morrow*, 1938, p. 126.)

The gospel of social service, of democracy and progress, is not the same as the gospel of salvation; spiritual warfare is not the same as petty and miserable human strife, and there are dangers in the latter from which are immune those who joyfully wrestle with the Prince of Darkness. Confusion between spiritual and worldly causes, and the absurdity into which such confusion leads is aptly shown in a passage from the pen of Daniel Bliss' eldest son. Frederick Bliss, archaeologist and student of oriental religions, shared with his father's generation their belief in the superiority of Protestantism over all other religions, and in the uniform beneficence of its influence over the middle east. In his book, *The Religions of Modern Syria and Palestine*, published in 1912, Frederick Bliss seemed to confuse the tidings of Christian liberty which the Protestant missionaries brought from their western home, with the western appetite for political activism with which the east was also then being fast infected; witness the following passage (pp. 313–14) where western and missionary influence is discussed: 'How powerfully it has worked during the last third of a century can be accurately gauged by comparing the attitude of the common people when a constitution was promulgated in 1877 with their attitude when precisely the same constitution was proclaimed in 1908. At the earlier period the people, ignorant and apathetic, were as little affected by the granting of rights as they were the next year by their withdrawal. When, thirty years later, Abd-el-Hamid was forced by the Young Turks to declare once more for constitutional rule, the whole empire went mad with joy . . . It is quite legitimate to find an important factor of this preparedness of the common people in the spread of schools of all kinds through the empire. The paramount influence of the American mission schools, where principles of true liberty were not only taught but incarnated, cannot,' Frederick Bliss asserted, 'be overestimated.'

The same confusion between spiritual causes and human ambitions may perhaps be discerned in the intervention by his brother, the second president, at the Paris Peace Conference. As is well known, his proposal for a commission of enquiry into political conditions in the Levant was at the origin of the King-Crane Commission and its curious Report. His influence with President Wilson was exerted in an anti-French sense: 'I believe,' he wrote to him in a memorandum of January 1919, 'that French guardianship [in Syria] would be rejected for three reasons: serious-minded men in Syria fear that the people of Syria would imitate France's less desirable qualities; they do not consider the French to be good administrators; they believe that France would exploit the country for her own material and political advantage. They do not trust her.' (Quoted in H. N. Howard, *The King-Crane Commission*, Beirut 1963, p. 25.) Sincere and well-meant as this was, yet it was a political intervention: that is to say, an anti-French was *ipso facto* a pro-British or a pro-Faysal posture, and surely to the spiritual eye there should be little to prefer between such powers and principalities, or their small and vain ambitions.

Another facet of this dogma-free religion of social service is held up for us to see in Rom Landau's report of his visit to the university in 1937. He asked the president how they managed to develop in Arab students an interest in 'social service' and was told that it was done through 'nationalism': 'Nowadays,' the president said, 'nationalism is the fashion. All our students want to see their country strong and prosperous. But they begin to realize that this cannot be achieved unless they, with their greater knowledge and better opportunities, set out to improve the conditions of their less fortunate fellows. I guess this is the most productive way of using Syrian nationalism.' The atmosphere of the university in those years

—it may be different today—the ethos of 'nationalism' and 'social service' which it fostered, is evoked by a report of the president in 1938 that 'for some reason few Muslim students enjoy Mosque services,' that on Muslim fast days 'the Arabian students attend [college] prayers wearing their Arab costumes,' that when the Muslim Society celebrated the Prophet's birthday 'a Greek Orthodox leader mounted the rostrum and presented to the Moslem Society a beautifully ornamented copy of the Koran together with a flag of green silk on which appeared, side by side, the cross and the crescent.' (Penrose, *op. cit.*, pp. 295–6.) 'Social service through nationalism', 'nationalism through social service': the propositions are interchangeable and neither has much to do with the idea of a university.

The idea of a university in the western world today—and the American University is of course an offshoot and a creation of the western genius—is equally removed from the founders' missionary zeal and from their successors' preoccupation with social service. A university's business is to increase, to safeguard and to transmit learning. This has not been so in the past and it may change in the future. But for the last few generations this has been the ideal and the tendency, and with this ideal and tendency religious tests and political preoccupations are alike incompatible. It is interesting to see how the university, whether consciously or not, has followed this tendency and conformed to this ideal. The name by which the university is known is significant in this respect. From its foundation until 1920, it was called the Syrian Protestant College—an accurate and informative title. The *Annual Reports* tell us (p. 200) that the board of managers voted to ask the trustees to change it to Syrian Protestant University; on Daniel Bliss' retirement the board of managers affirmed: 'It is a Christian College founded as a Missionary Institution in the fear of God and on the work of God'; and Penrose tells us (p. 172) that another suggestion was to call it Beirut Christian University. Yet both titles were in the end turned down: 'It was inadvisable,' writes Penrose, 'to continue the term Protestant because students and faculty now represented nearly every religious form in the Near East and there was no point in needlessly emphasizing sectarian distinctions. Likewise', he continued, 'although there was never any intention to weaken in any way the original principles of the founders, the term "Christian" in the title seemed to provide unnecessary emphasis on religious differences which might prove unfortunate.'

The change of name is of great significance. It symbolizes the abandonment of compulsory religion for the students and of religious tests for the teachers. The original regulations of the Syrian Protestant College required all boarders to attend prayers morning and evening, to be present at the Protestant Church twice every Sabbath and to assist at the regular Bible lesson on every Wednesday. The *Report* for 1887 mentions that Muslims and Jews had requested the college to provide dietary facilities for them and to modify the rule regarding prayers: 'When the Mohammedans and the Jews are fully convinced (as they soon will be),' the *Report* however observed, 'that we are far more anxious to establish a Christian College both in principle and in form, than we are to increase the number of our students, they will patronize the Institution.' Until the end of the century the trustees remained adamant in their refusal to relax the rules concerning attendance at prayers and at Sunday School or to allow separate catering facilities for non-Christians. After the Young Turk Revolution, in 1909, Muslim and Jewish students went on strike against compulsory church attendance, and the trustees again affirmed: 'The College was not established merely for higher secular education, or the inculcation of morality. One of its chief objects is to teach the great truths of Scripture; to be a centre of Christian light and influence; and to lead its students to understand and accept a pure Christianity, and go out to profess and commend it in every walk of life.' In 1914 the Ottoman government passed a law which forbade the college from giving religious instruction to any except Protestants; the faculty then ruled that every religious exercise should be paralleled by a non-religious one and the students had to attend the one or the other. Developments since 1915 have made reversion to compulsory religion out of the question. (*Annual Reports*, pp. 3 and 102, and Penrose, *op. cit.*, pp. 52 and 134ff.)

A similar fate overtook religious tests for the faculty. At the start of their operations the missionaries entertained the belief that, in Jessup's words, 'the advance of education and popular knowledge will expose the absurdities of many parts of Mohammedan doctrine and practice' (*The Mohammedan Missionary Problem*, p. 95). The *Annual Reports* again and again show the confident assumption that 'the spirit of enquiry' must inevitably result in conversion to Protestantism. 'Mental and moral science,' we read in the *Report* for 1871, 'is so intimately connected with man's spiritual nature that opportunities are continually occurring in the class room to enforce the great fact upon the mind of the student that a pure morality and a rational religious faith are in accordance with the constitution of the human mind, and a necessity to its highest well-being.' The same *Report* ends by affirming that 'steady progress is being made in educating the minds of the students by leading them to investigate for themselves and to rely upon arguments founded upon facts instead of blindly following the opinion of others.' (*Annual Reports*, pp. 18 and 22.) But it was speedily shown that to follow the argument withersoever it leads—and this is certainly implied in the idea of a modern university—did not necessarily serve to confirm the truths of Protestantism. At the commencement for 1882 Dr. Edwin Lewis, Professor of Chemistry and Geology, delivered to the graduating class an address on 'Knowledge, Science and Wisdom', the text of which is now printed as an Appendix to the *Annual Reports* (pp. 247–56). Professor Lewis discussed Darwinism and made the point that the truths of science were quite distinct from the truths of religion: 'if it is established by science that the body of man had gradually evolved from lower animal forms until it reached its present state, that will not have any relation with the origin of the first man and will not nullify his being a man nor will it waive the responsibility imposed on him by God. Do not fear facts . . .' In the words of Daniel Bliss this address created 'discord and rebellion'. It was criticized as inappropriate and the president of the trustees asked for a copy of the address. Thereupon Dr. Lewis resigned, and his resignation was followed by that of the eminent Dr. Cornelius Van Dyck, the Professor of Pathology and of his son William, who was also a teacher in the medical department. These events led the trustees to require the permanent members of the faculty to subscribe to a declaration of principles which included ten articles which in the words of the tenth of them may be taken as representing 'the consensus of Protestant creeds, as opposed to the erroneous teachings and practices of the Romish and Eastern Churches.' The signatories were further to declare their 'hearty sympathy' with, and to pledge their 'active cooperation' in advancing the 'chief aim' of, the college, 'which as a missionary agency is to train up young men in the knowledge of Christian truth'; the teachers were also to pledge themselves 'to the inculcation of sound and reverent views of the relation of God to the natural universe as its Creator and supreme Ruler, and to give instruction in the special department assigned us, in the spirit and method best calculated to conserve the teachings of revealed truth and demonstrate the essential harmony between the Bible and all true science and philosophy.' The trustees also asked that all non-permanent teachers should, if possible, be 'not merely members of Evangelical Churches, but in full sympathy with the spiritual and missionary aims of the College.' The policy of the trustees remained in force for twenty years until Howard Bliss succeeded his father in 1902 and stated that the declaration was against his 'conscientious convictions', and the trustees then agreed that it should no longer be required (*Annual Reports*, pp. 69–75 and 80; Penrose, pp. 47–9). Everything which has happened since then makes inconceivable the re-imposition of religious tests in the university.

The Lewis affair deserves further scrutiny. On his resignation, the medical students and the two upper classes of the literary department absented themselves from their classes and protested to the authorities against the 'suspension' of Dr. Lewis who, as their petition puts it, 'has been charged with setting forth Darwin's infidel opinions.' Other exchanges between faculty and students followed, and the board of managers finally decided to suspend a number of students for a month and to demand their repentance before they were allowed to return. Some of the suspended students did apologize and were allowed to return, but the 'rebellion', as the president called it, must have been quite widespread in the college, and those students who by their return showed that they disavowed the earlier protest were subjected to the contempt and attacks of their fellow-students: 'Soon,' Daniel Bliss tells us in his account of the affair, 'disrespect passed into annoyance, and annoyance into abuse. The animosity seemed to be increased when one of the Seniors of the Medical class returned and made his submission . . . This state of things culminated at night on the 24th of May [1883], when several Literary students, armed with clubs, made a sudden attack upon five or six medical students, beat and wounded them severely. The assault was so wanton and brutal that the police, being informed, took the culprits to prison.' These few dry lines in their brevity show us vividly the impact, the often violent and disruptive impact, of western ideas on the middle-eastern mind. The intellectual history of the middle east has of late been treated at great length by a multitude of authors, some competent, others pedestrian, and yet others plainly boring. Most of these works have been the dutiful summaries of the dull thoughts of second-rate minds, and they have failed to communicate to us the violent excitement and strains which Darwin's 'infidel opinions' and other subversive notions—whether infidel or not—must have generated in this traditional and hitherto quite isolated society. The fracas of 24 May 1883 is a tantalizingly brief episode in that intellectual history of the modern east which yet remains to be written.

Such an intellectual history would have to devote a chapter to the contribution of the American missionaries to the creation of a modern literary Arabic. As is well known, they initiated and carried through a complete new translation of the Bible. Neither the vocabulary and style of this translation, nor the extent of its diffusion, nor the character of its influence have yet been properly examined. Instead a fiction has gained wide acceptance, one of the many fashioned or sometimes only intimated by the consummate artifice of George Antonius. 'The educational activities of the American missionaries,' we read in *The Arab Awakening* (p. 43), 'had, among many virtues, one outstanding merit; they gave pride of place to Arabic, and, once they had committed themselves to teaching in it, put their shoulders with vigour to the task of providing an adequate literature. In that they were pioneers; and because of that, the intellectual effervescence which marked the first stirrings of the Arab revival owes most to their labours.' This mystificatory account—fanciful enough in what it conveys and implies—becomes even more fanciful in Penrose's history. Penrose, who seems to have shared the political sympathies which *The Arab Awakening* exemplified and propagated (see, for instance, an article of his, 'Building up the Voltage' in the magazine of the Anglo-Arab Association, *The Arab World*, January 1954: 'Besides the Zionists, who are ever present, another sinister force has appeared against the new Administration, etc. . . . .'), but who was distinctly more artless, and therefore more downright, than Antonius has this to write about the Arabic language and the missionaries: 'The language of the people was Arabic and it seemed only natural to the Americans to teach in Arabic. Having no desire, as others had, to 'frankify' the natives for imperialistic purposes, and realizing the untold wealth of the rapidly vanishing Arab culture, it seemed wiser to them to make use of it.' (*That They May Have Life*, p. 6.) What are we to say of this picture which presents the missionaries as the pioneers of the 'Arab revival', as the anti-colonialist restorers of linguistic treasure? We shall say that it does not tally with the record, which is more complicated and less glamorous than we have been given to understand.

Whether to use English or the vernacular in missionary schools and colleges had long been a subject of debate in the American Board of Commissioners for Foreign Missions. When the foundation of the Syrian Protestant College was being mooted the senior secretary of the board was Rufus Anderson, who about that time published a history of the first fifty years of the board. This work records the views of missionaries in India and Ceylon on the teaching of English in their establishments. The missionaries working among the Mahrattas believed that English was not suited to their purposes: 'The English language,' they observed, 'is made to too great an extent the medium of communicating instruction. Experience has seemed to show that such schools are not the most efficient instruments in forwarding the great work of the missions—that of making known the gospel to the heathen, and saving souls. The vernacular of any people,' they concluded, 'is believed to be the most suitable language in which to communicate truth, and through which to affect the heart.' This particular objection to the use of English is reinforced by another, perhaps weightier one, brought forward by the missionaries in Ceylon: 'The English language as acquired by the Tamil young man,' they stated, 'found no market in his native village, nor within the territory occupied by the mission, except as the mission became the purchaser by giving him a salary that would meet his own views. The consequence was, that it was needful to give larger salaries than the village churches would be able to pay; and too often the graduate went into the more lucrative service of the government, or of some merchant or planter, and thus his labours and influence were lost to the mission and to his native village. Were our object merely to educate and civilize the people,' they went on to observe, 'this might do; but the churches cannot afford to prosecute their work in this manner.' (*Memorial Volume of the First Fifty Years of the American Board of Commissioners for Foreign Missions*, Boston 1861, pp. 317 and 325.)

Very similar considerations arose in the Levant field. In 1836 the missionaries had opened a high school in Beirut which provided teaching in English. 'This school,' we learn from Dr. Barton, 'was apparently a great success, but four years later the pupils, because of their practical knowledge of English, became so useful to the English officers, then quartered in Beirut on account of the political troubles, that the school was broken up. No doubt,' Dr. Barton observes, 'this unfortunate experience had much influence in leading the Board to endeavour to exclude English from mission schools.' (James L. Barton, *Daybreak in Turkey*, New York 1908, p. 184.) When the Abeih Seminary was reopened in 1848, English and French were removed from the curriculum, 'owing', Dr. Jessup tells us, 'to the strictly vernacular policy enjoined by the American Board of Missions'; and this policy, it would seem, was very much that favoured by the senior secretary: Jessup goes so far as to speak of 'the edict of Dr. Anderson excluding English from all mission schools of the American Board'. In Jessup's view, this policy was a decisive failure: by 1858 'prominent families' in the Lebanon were withdrawing their children from the American establishments, because these were teaching only Arabic, and sending them instead to the Lazarists and Jesuits. The Abeih Seminary 'which had stood at the head of Syrian high schools now shrank to a third or fourth place.' 'Steam,' says Dr. Jessup, 'had brought Europe face to face with Syria, and the Syrians demanded French and English.' Who should supply this demand? 'Was it to be left to the Jesuits, those enemies of a pure Gospel, those masters of intrigue and duplicity and perverters of the human conscience? This must not be.' And to prevent this, the Syrian mission decided to ask the American board to sanction the foundation of a college. The Syrian Protestant College was far from being founded to 'give pride of place to Arabic,' to use Antonius' words, or to develop 'the untold wealth of the rapidly vanishing Arab culture,' as Penrose suggests; it was rather to repair the consequences of Anderson's 'strictly vernacular policy' which was sending the Syrians to the Jesuits; Jessup goes so far as to say that it was Anderson's policy which was 'largely the occasion of the founding of the Syrian Protestant College'. (*Fifty-Three Years* . . . pp. 222 and 298ff.)

We do not know in any detail the discussions between the Syria mission and the American board which preceded the foundation of the college. Jessup remarks that the board 'gave their approval of the plan, but with evident misgiving,' and adds that 'their letter was a masterly statement of the objections to high grade English teaching institutions on the mission field.' This letter, which, we learn, was written by Dr. Anderson, urged that 'Asiatics acquiring civilized habits will be unfitted to live at home in their native region, and do good to their own people,' that 'a smattering of English fills men with conceit, makes them unwilling to labour in the villages, and that they will be dissatisfied and heartless grumblers, were we to offer them less than double or treble the sum cheerfully accepted by those educated in a vernacular course.' (*Fifty-Three Years* . . . , p. 301.) It is difficult to resist the inference from all this that Daniel Bliss and his colleagues in the Syria mission wished the new college to teach in English but that they were overruled by Anderson and his committee in Boston. They were not for long. When in 1872 the preparatory department was started, it was found that to teach in Arabic was impracticable; in 1880 the literary department changed over to English, and in 1882 it was found necessary to conduct the teaching in the medical department in English. (Penrose, *op. cit.* pp. 30 and 45.) The 'vernacular' policy, if persisted in, would have spelt stagnation and failure. Though this may now be forgotten or ignored, the essential condition of survival and expansion was in fact to teach in English, thus ensuring for the university a vital and continuous link with civilization.

4. The *Alliance Israélite Universelle*, 1860–1960

The title of M. Chouraqui's copious and important study* calls to mind Narcisse Leven's earlier history of the *Alliance israélite universelle, Cinquante ans d'histoire* (2 vols., Paris, 1911–20), and immediately invites comparison between the two books. The earlier work devotes over one thousand pages to the first fifty years of the *Alliance*, while the later work, roughly half the size of its predecessor (even when allowance is made for the somewhat smaller type in which it is set), deals with a period which is longer by fifty crowded, difficult and generally catastrophic years. A re-reading of Narcisse Leven's work confirms one's first impression that of the two it is the more spacious and leisurely, and that its unhurried exposition and patient marshalling of detail allow the reader a more satisfactory glimpse into the political transactions of the *Alliance* and its remarkable educational enterprise. Again, the present work devotes much space to a quick and potted review of recent Jewish history; it would have been perhaps preferable for the author to assume his readers' familiarity with the main lines of modern Jewish history and to devote this space to a more detailed history of the *Alliance* itself. Lastly, the scheme of the book may also perhaps be queried. Of its five parts the first gives an account of the foundation of the *Alliance*, the second is entitled 'Adolphe Crémieux and Political Emancipation', the third 'Narcisse Leven and Salvation through the School', the fourth 'Sylvain Lévi and the Crisis of European Judaism', and the fifth 'René Cassin and the Promotion of the Rights of Man'. There is, of course, no gainsaying the prominence of these personalities in the life and fortunes of the *Alliance*, but it is doubtful whether the history of such an organization is best periodized in terms of personalities.

In the first part of his work, M. Chouraqui describes the circumstances, the outlooks and the motives of those French Jews who came together to found the *Alliance* in 1860. They belonged to the first and second generations which followed the emancipation proclaimed by the French Revolution. They were liberals in politics and religion, and believed that it was necessary for French Jews, who enjoyed civic and political equality with their Christian compatriots, to take the initiative in defending and advancing Jewish rights everywhere. The well-known statesman Adolphe Crémieux (1796–1880), who himself served as president of the *Alliance* shortly after its

---

* André Chouraqui, *Cent ans d'histoire: L'alliance israélite universelle et la renaissance juive contemporaine (1860–1960).*

73

foundation, was their exemplar and inspiration. M. Chouraqui sketches the portraits of some of his collaborators, and the details he provides give us some idea of the problems they faced and how they reacted to them. One of the founding members was Isidore Cahen (1826–1902); he was a graduate of the Ecole Normale Supérieure who in 1849 was appointed to teach philosophy at the lycée of Napoléon-Vendée and rejoiced that he, a Jew, would be able to teach philosophy to Christian youths. But the Bishop of Luçon took exception to the appointment and, in a charge to his parishioners, wondered how 'wise and prudent statesmen could have conceived and executed the project of sending to one of the most religious and believing areas of France a Jewish professor, and one moreover given to the teaching of philosophy'. The Bishop demanded his replacement by one 'imbued with truly Christian sentiments, and a sincere Catholic'. The minister of education gave in to this pressure and transferred Cahen to Tours where, moreover, he was to teach literature and not philosophy. Cahen refused to accept the transfer, resigned his post, and devoted himself to journalism in the *Archives israélites*, of which he became the editor.

M. Chouraqui quotes passages from Cahen's editorials (p. 32) which show his views on Judaism and Jewry in the modern world. 'In the French polity', he writes in 1857, 'there are only Frenchmen; the Jews no longer form either a nation or a race or a freemasonry, or even a commercial association; they are no longer anything but believers . . . when they believe.' 'We have become the scattered links of a religious community', he writes again, 'and we are no longer the dispersed members of a dissolved nationality; since the misfortunes to which they are collectively subject and the extortions which they suffer bring the Jews together, they have the right to consolidate their community by developing a solidarity to confront injustice.' Another founding member was Elie-Aristide Astruc (1831–1905), a rabbi of Sephardi origin who advocated a rationalist and reformist theology of a kind which a fellow-rabbi denounced as '*le rationalisme vulgaire et brutal*'. Yet another was Jules Carvallo (1819–1915), a distinguished engineer who was placed first of his year when graduating from the Ecole des Ponts et Chaussées; he was a Saint-Simonian and considered, remarks M. Chouraqui, perhaps too favourable to Christianity since he entertained the idea of Jesus having a providential mission. Finally we may mention another of these founding members, the poet Eugène Manuel (1823–1901), who drafted the first manifesto of the new society; his latitudinarian point of view may be gathered from the following lines (p. 33):

> Trois peuples m'ont donné ce qu'il me faut pour vivre,
> Les Romains et les Grecs et mon peuple hébreu.

Rome m'apprit le droit dans son code et le livre,
Athènes la beauté,
Jérusalem son Dieu.

The immediate occasion which precipitated the foundation of the *Alliance* was the Mortara Affair of 1858, when papal gendarmes in Bologna forced their way into a Jewish household and abducted a child six years old on the pretext that he was a Christian. A Catholic servant in the Mortara household had secretly baptized the boy when he was gravely ill in the hope that, should he come to die, his soul would be saved. The child survived, but later on her own death-bed the servant confessed the deed to a priest. The ecclesiastical authorities then proceeded to abduct the child. Many, including Napoleon III and Francis Joseph, appealed to the Pope to release the child, but the Church would not give him up. He was brought up a Christian, ordained as a priest, and died a canon. These events, it would seem, led this intelligent and public-spirited group of French Jews to found the *Alliance* as a world-wide association for the defence of Jewish interests. The name of the new society was inspired by the Universal Evangelical Alliance which had been founded in London in 1855 and which had actually invited Jews to its membership in the belief that they were necessary to the divine economy of salvation.

The objects of the society are succinctly and precisely described in the first article of its statutes. These objects are:

1. To work everywhere for the emancipation and the moral progress of the Jews.
2. To provide efficacious aid for those who suffer because of being Jews.
3. To encourage the publication of works contributing to these ends.

As M. Chouraqui's work makes amply clear, very soon after its foundation the *Alliance* began to take action and make representations to governments wherever Jewish rights and interests were involved; its example encouraged the setting-up of affiliated or similar bodies in Great Britain, Germany and Austria-Hungary. That the *Alliance* was able to accomplish so much, in the first fifty years of its existence at any rate, was clearly a consequence of European dominance in the world, and of the willingness of European statesmen to use their influence in the cause of civic and political emancipation. The political climate in which the *Alliance* operated before 1914 and the unstated assumptions which its officers and those to whom they appealed took for granted may be illustrated by a letter from Crémieux to Beaconsfield at the time of the Congress of Berlin

(p. 85): 'You are going', he wrote on 21 June 1878, 'to ensure for the Christians, against persecution by the Muslim, the freedom of Christian worship, security for their persons, for their families, for their property. . . . What I, president of the *Alliance israélite universelle*, ask in the name of the Jews of the world, is that you would ensure for the Jews, by a similar decision, against persecution by the Christian, the freedom of Jewish worship, security for their persons, for their families, for their property.'

It is, of course, idle to suppose that the European powers who lent a favourable ear to the pleas of the *Alliance* were moved by pure altruism. It is more accurate to say that they saw in the protection of Jewish communities in the middle east, north Africa and elsewhere a profitable, as well as a legitimate, exercise of their power and influence. At the very beginning of its history, the *Alliance*, as M. Chouraqui remarks (p. 152), attempted to persuade the French government to place all Jews in Muslim lands, and particularly those of north Africa, under French protection. This kind of approach, whatever its advantages, necessarily made the *Alliance* a supporter of French interests abroad. M. Chouraqui allows as much when he remarks (p. 58) that 'the close and, so to speak, organic relations' of the *Alliance* with the Quai d'Orsay were a secret for nobody. It would have added much to the interest of this history, let it be said in passing, if M. Chouraqui had expanded somewhat this cryptic and suggestive remark. There was, of course, nothing wrong in French citizens promoting French influence in the world, but the *Alliance* had in fact set out to be a supra-national organization, and 'close and, so to speak, organic relations' with the Quai d'Orsay, as the German Jews repeatedly complained, somewhat detracted from this claim.

Consideration of the official activities of the *Alliance* also reveals something painfully paradoxical in its situation. The *Alliance* could do so much for Jews in the Balkans, the middle east and north Africa because it could persuade the French and other European governments to give it help and support. And yet, these European countries and very frequently their official and ruling classes spread in the non-European world the traditional perniciously systematic anti-Judaism so characteristic of European thought, and its no less characteristic modish successor, the so-called 'scientific' antisemitism. France is a case in point. Some twenty years before the foundation of the *Alliance* it was the French consul in Damascus who, in 1840, fabricated the blood libel against the local Jewish community. No argument or pressure would make him abandon his murderous campaign, and he was throughout supported by his government. (See the full discussion of the Damascus Affair by A. M. Hyamson in the *Transactions of the Jewish Historical Society of England*, vol. XVI (1952), pp. 47–71.)

Some fifty years later the Dreyfus Affair showed the fragility of official goodwill towards the Jews, and fifty years after that the Vichy régime (which can be looked upon as a delayed eruption of all the malevolence and rancour spread and accumulated during the *Affaire* and its aftermath) actually decreed that the French Jews of France and north Africa were aliens in their own country. To rehearse these episodes is useful because, as has been said, they serve to underline the paradoxical situation in which the *Alliance* had to act. M. Chouraqui himself is perhaps not sufficiently struck by this paradox, and at times he gives the impression of being quite unaware of it. Thus he says (p. 240) that the French presence in north Africa 'has not always been sufficient to prevent antisemitic disturbances, particularly in Tunisia and Algeria.' The fact is of course that antisemitism in north Africa was introduced and propagated by French settlers and officials.

Until the advent of Nazism the *Alliance* was resolutely non-Zionist, not to say anti-Zionist. Indeed Professor Sylvain Lévi (1863–1935), president of the *Alliance* from 1920 until his death, is a familiar figure in Zionist demonology. M. Chouraqui quotes copiously from his letters and from his famous address to the Peace Conference in order to clarify and illustrate his attitude (pp. 223ff. and *passim*). He also reproduces in an appendix (pp. 470–2) a letter from Jacques Bigart (1855–1934), secretary of the *Alliance* from 1881, written to a correspondent in Salonica in May 1918. Lucid, shrewd, and far-sighted, the letter shows that the objections of the *Alliance* to Zionism were generally neither frivolous nor malicious nor—as the Zionists have usually alleged—instigated by French ambitions in Palestine. The objections were, on the contrary, reasoned and reasonable, and some of them are still valid today. 'Palestine', he observed, 'has fewer than 100,000 Jews and 500,000 Arabs. The governments of the Entente pride themselves on allowing national self-determination. Is it allowable, under these conditions, to have the majority governed by a small minority?' 'They also say:' he continued, 'today we are a minority, but in x years by means of immigration we shall be a majority. Having regard to the Arab awakening to which the Entente gives support, and which tomorrow perhaps will play an important rôle in the Asiatic provinces of Turkey, is there not a great danger in confronting it with a politico-national "Judaism" the followers of which are recruited *abroad* (and in what circles!)? This is the point of view of many Frenchmen who are very favourable towards the Jewish element but who, having studied the Arab problem, observe an incompatibility between Zionist demands and the ambitions of the prominent leaders of re-awakened Arabia.' In view of this attitude, consistent and held over a long period, it is curious to see

M. Chouraqui, in describing the educational activities of the *Alliance* in Palestine before 1914, remark (p. 365) that it was preparing the native Jewish population 'to receive the new spirit which the great movement of the Return was to breathe into the whole country'! We may here also take up another curious remark of M. Chouraqui's which again seems irreconcilable not only with the assumptions and policies of the *Alliance*, but with the actual facts themselves. This is when he refers (p. 339) to a so-called law whereby the attainment of sovereignty by a Muslim state is accompanied by the disappearance of its Jewish community! How do the cases of Turkey and Iran, or of Morocco and Tunisia fit this law? Egypt attained full independence in 1936, but its Jewish community continued until the 1950s; Iraq became fully independent in 1931, and it was only in 1951 that the Iraqi Jews were pressured into leaving for Israel. Is it not more accurate to say that it was the existence of Israel which put Jewish communities in Arab (not Muslim) countries at risk?

We have not yet mentioned that for which the *Alliance* is best known, namely its justly-renowned educational network, principally in the middle east and north Africa. The first school under the auspices of the *Alliance* was opened at Tetuan at the end of 1862. By 1900 the network comprised 100 schools in which some 26,000 pupils were being educated; by 1914 there were 188 schools with some 48,000 pupils. The catastrophes which engulfed Jewish life after the first world war arrested this progress, and in 1960 there were 131 schools with 45,000 pupils. According to M. Chouraqui, some 600,000 pupils have passed through the *Alliance* schools in the last hundred years.

What adds further lustre to this great achievement is that the education which these schools provided was remarkably thorough and solid. As early as 1867, the *Alliance* founded its own teachers' training college, the *Ecole Normale Israélite Orientale*, which has produced a continuous supply of high quality teachers—themselves for the most part recruited from the middle east, the Balkans and north Africa—who, with uncanny and economical skill, managed to impart to pupils, through the medium of a foreign language (French) the ability to think with precision and to express themselves with clarity. One such teacher, M. Elie Capon, by whom I had the good fortune to be taught, exemplifies in my mind the methods and achievements of the *Alliance*. Rigour and clarity of thought, and a spare and elegant style in which to express it: these were the hallmarks of his teaching, and its beneficient influence is always apparent to me whenever I have occasion to put pen to paper. There is little doubt that this exemplary achievement was in some way linked to the fact that French was the language of instruction, that French textbooks could be used, and traditional French pedagogical methods—

with their emphasis on solid academic achievement—could be applied. Since the end of the second world war, political pressures in the countries where the *Alliance* operates have forced the abandonment of French as a language of instruction, and the *Ecole Normale Israélite Orientale* must now concentrate, as M. Chouraqui observes (p. 195), not on training French schoolteachers as hitherto, but rather teachers of French in foreign countries (*non plus des instituteurs français, mais plutôt des professeurs de français à l'étranger*). M. Chouraqui does not tell us how this radical modification of tested pedagogical methods affects the quality of education in *Alliance* schools.

The educational activities of the *Alliance* raise the fundamental issue of western influence in non-western lands and the reactions which this influence provoked. In the eyes of the founders and administrators of the *Alliance*, it was a wholly beneficent enterprise. They had no doubt that a good western education would liberate the energies of their eastern coreligionists and ameliorate their conditions. At the same time, they were also aware—or perhaps they were made aware by the opposition which their schools evoked in some communities—that there was incompatibility between the new outlook they were introducing and the norms and beliefs of these traditional societies. M. Chouraqui has a passage (p. 157) in which he contrasts the traditional *Talmud Torah* teacher with the product of the *Ecole Normale Israélite Orientale*. 'The one'. writes the author 'was the heir of two millennia of Israel's exile trained in the Talmudic disciplines which had impressed on the depth of his soul the lessons of Israel's wisdom which is entirely given over to the worship of God and the knowledge of His law. He was the product of a sacral world in which the dominant preoccupation was the incarnation of the Torah in everyday life, whilst waiting for the coming reign of a transcendent God, who is present in the mind and heart of His children. In this life of usually ascetic renunciation, one hope shone, that of the triumph of the Messiah who will deliver Israel from the slavery of exile and restore Jerusalem in glory. On the other hand, the *Alliance* schoolmaster had already in the depth of his being broken with the traditional legacy of the synagogue. He was a product of the dominant European culture. Voltaire and Rousseau, the Encyclopaedists and the Romantics nourished his thought more than did the Prophets and the Talmudists. He believed more in the light of reason than in God's salvation, in the benefits of progress more than in the Messiah's redemption, more in man's creativity than in God's providence. The traditional teacher could not but see in the *Alliance* schoolmaster the product of a foreign world. On his side, the schoolmaster could not help being shocked by the appearance of the

Talmudic teacher, whose heir he was setting himself up to be, and who lived in a world so different from his own.' The archives of the *Alliance* must be full of material bearing on this crucial issue, and it is somewhat regrettable that M. Chouraqui has not utilized them more fully in order to illustrate with specific and concrete instances the clash which he so eloquently describes. Here too, it would seem, his predecessor's account has virtues which we miss from this work. Leven's second volume in particular abounds in descriptions of clashes within Oriental communities between traditionalists and innovators in the nineteenth century, clashes which were the direct consequence of the activities of the *Alliance*. His full account of communal strife in Istanbul and Adrianople, in Jerusalem, Baghdad and Damascus, throws much welcome light on these communities, whose history in modern times is still largely unknown. The historian who will write it will no doubt find the archives of the *Alliance* one of his most precious sources.

5. The Death of Adib Ishaq

The intellectual history of the middle east in the nineteenth and twentieth centuries includes a chapter, long hidden, and as yet still very imperfectly known. It concerns the spread of religious heterodoxy, unbelief or scepticism among Muslims, Christians and Jews alike. The traces of such revolt against the traditional faiths are now both faint and fragmentary. This is because those involved, or their friends and relatives, have been anxious, for a variety of reasons, to disguise or suppress the evidence of dissent and deviation. The history of Afghani and his circle is a case in point. He and his disciples successfully propagated the notion that far from being a free thinker and a sceptic, Afghani defended, indeed embodied, orthodoxy.[1] That concealment and deception should have been resorted to indicates the strain and perhaps the danger to which were exposed those who might be considered guilty of religious deviation. Another case in point is that of the Maronite As'ad al-Shidyaq who converted to Protestantism in the 1820s and in consequence died a prisoner of the Maronite patriarch, and that of his brother Faris who had to flee Beirut for the same reason.[2]

Other fragmentary evidence which has survived occasionally provides a vivid glimpse of the strain under which laboured those who dared to question traditional orthodoxy, and such evidence obliges us to see in quite a new light their career and their writings. For instance, Butrus al-Bustani (1819–83), the eminent lexicographer, *savant* and journalist, propagated in some of his writings a kind of ideal natural religion which ought to unite men divided by the warring dogmas of their actual religions. Does not this somewhat colourless and insipid view attain for us a greater and more moving significance if we keep in mind Bustani's own religious history? A Maronite and a seminarist, at about the age of twenty-one while reading the Syriac Testament, he suddenly 'found', we are told, the doctrine of justification by faith, and 'leaving his monastic retreat, fled to Beirut, where he entered the house of Dr. Eli Smith [an American Presbyterian missionary] for protection. For two years he was a prisoner, not venturing outside the gates, lest he be shot by spies of the Maronite patriarch.'[3] Whether Bustani's life was really in danger we do not know. But this report gives us an idea of the pressures and tensions to which Bustani became subject, when he was converted to the doctrine of justification by grace: it meant who knows what personal distress, what painful contentions with, what hurtful estrangements from, community family and friends. His rather dull thoughts on politics and society take on thereby more significance, are invested with more interest than their strictly derivative character would normally give them.

Religious indifferentism and scepticism, not to speak of anti-clericalism would have occasioned, if openly avowed, as much tension in the community as conversion to another religion. We can clearly see this from the history of Adib Ishaq. A Greek Catholic from Damascus, born in 1856, he was educated at the Lazarist school in that city where he learnt French, as well as Arabic. He seems to have been a precocious boy. By the age of eighteen he was editing a newspaper in Beirut, writing poetry, translating plays, among which Racine's *Andromaque*, and mixing on an equality with the local men of letters. It was his interest in plays and play-acting which seems to have led to his departure for Alexandria, where he went in 1876 to collaborate with his fellow-countryman Salim al-Naqqash (d. 1884), a pioneer of the Arabic-speaking theatre.[4] The theatrical venture not having prospered, he went the following year to Cairo. With him he had a letter of introduction to Afghani whom he thus came to know at an early and impressionable age. Very soon he obtained, it seems with Afghani's help, a licence to edit two newspapers which became, in effect, Afghani's mouthpiece, where the Sage of the East was celebrated in extravagant terms, and articles of his published.[5]

Adib Ishaq's connexion with Afghani and his involvement in Egyptian politics made him, as may be seen from those articles of his which have been reprinted, into a radical activist, glib and confident in laying down first principles and quite ready to denounce those rulers and ministers guilty of contravening them. But as the two successive editors of his literary remains were careful to exclude what they considered extreme or intemperate in his writings, we cannot appreciate to the full Adib Ishaq's particular style of ideological politics—a style which he must have been one of the first to practise in the middle east.[6]

Along with this ideological style of politics, Adib Ishaq showed remarkable elasticity in changing sides and patrons, and great ability in justifying each turn and twist with elevated reasons and lofty principles.[7] His private life seems to have left somewhat to be desired: he was a habitual drunkard, and a discreet obituary declared that his health was impaired and his death hastened by his promiscuous behaviour (*tasāhuluhu fī ṭuruq mu'āsharatihi*) and indulging youthful passion (*iṭlāq hawā al-nafs fīma tasūq ilayhi-al-shabība*).[8]

It would therefore be surprising if Adib Ishaq's attitude to religion were not somehow consonant with his political and private behaviour; the more so as he was a fervent disciple of the heterodox and esoteric

Afghani. He himself wrote a biographical notice of Afghani about 1880 which is as interesting for what it guardedly hints, as for what it openly declares.[9]

It is perhaps significant that the notice is at its most allusive when dealing with Afghani's beliefs. Adib Ishaq says that in his youth Afghani investigated both the traditional and the rational sciences, 'the beliefs of the old philosophers (*hukama*) predominated with him, and he became tinctured with somewhat of sufism'; he went into retirement—being then less than twenty years of age—and emerged 'firmly convinced of the sway of reason, and the principles of rational philosophy (*mustaqirr al-ra'yy 'ala hukm al-'aql wa uṣūl al-falsafa al-qiyāsiyya*). Adib Ishaq then describes how Afghani fell out with al-Azhar and formed his own circle of followers and disciples 'to some of whom he divulged his liberal opinions, taking the path of salvation from superstition and ignorance'. Among those who were thus saved from superstition and ignorance Adib Ishaq was no doubt included. The editors of his remains were discreet in their selection of his political writings; they may have had equal reason to censor Adib Ishaq's discussion of religious topics. What has been preserved in the literary remains does indicate that Adib Ishaq had the usual 'enlightened' view of the course of European history, in which the intolerant priestly power is contrasted with the tolerance introduced by the French Revolution.[10]

When it became clear that a Christian such as Adib Ishaq really had no place in 'Urabi's movement, Adib went back to Beirut, and once more became the editor of a newspaper, *al-Taqqadum*, which he had edited before his departure for Egypt. He was soon involved in a controversy with the Jesuit newspaper *al-Bashir* on the subject of compulsory secular state-provided free education which the French government was then introducing, and which was strenuously opposed by the Roman Catholic Church. The editors of Adib Ishaq's remains have not reprinted the text of his articles on this subject, but he himself stated in the preface of a treatise on compulsory education (which he was unable to finish) that his controversy with the Jesuits on this topic was acrimonious.[11] We take it that the acrimony was mutual, the Jesuits being no doubt particularly incensed by the fact that Adib Ishaq was a member of their community. It is most probable that they gave as good as they got. But what they got may perhaps be appreciated from the one specimen of Adib Ishaq's polemical style which has been preserved in his literary remains. This is an abusive attack on the French publicist Gabriel Charmes, entitled 'A guest of little shame'. Charmes had visited the Levant and published what Adib Ishaq considered to be disobliging remarks about the native clergy.

You pretend [wrote Adib Ishaq in a characteristic piece of invective] that [our] religious leaders are greediest for money, and most careful of it; that their morals are the worst, that they are most given to [low] desires, and most prone to behave dishonourably; in all this unlike the religious heads of your people. Are you blind, or do you think men blind? Or were you not told by the muleteers and pimps whose company you kept, that it has not occurred to any of us to think ill of [our] religious leaders, or to incline to [religious] doubt, being of all men most attached to what they preach, until our country was infested with the foreigner's corruptions, until we saw the activities of those whom you praise, and had reports of them sufficient to render one blind and deaf, and until it seemed to us that the corruption has become general in the country?[12]

Some two years following his controversy with *al-Bashir*, Adib Ishaq died at the early age of twenty-eight, on 12 June 1884.[13] His death was the occasion of an incident which his brother described briefly in his notice of 1909. Awni Ishaq wrote:

An event took place on the day of his death which was a relic from the Dark Ages, and which almost resulted in untoward effects. The priest who was charged by his relations to pray over him and to discharge his religious duties refused to accompany the body or to introduce it into the church, unless our father would write in his own hand and sign a letter affirming that his son was a Catholic and had died a Catholic. This was because some of his colleagues (*zumala'*) whom he had relentlessly attacked in his lifetime were full of hate against him. They exploited the priest's ignorance and persuaded him to do what he did, in order to assuage their vengeful feelings over [Adib's] dead body. They showed no respect for the deceased, nor did they pity his sorrowing parents. Rather, their cruelty led them to this behaviour which almost brought about a clash between the friends of the departed and some of their ignorant partisans. Following this *fracas*, and the concern to prevent what was going on, in order to avoid [the worse] which might happen, some traitors succeeded in hiding much of [Adib's] literary remains, the writings, speeches and compositions mentioned above which he—God's mercy upon him—had been resolved to revise and publish.[14]

The passage, as may be seen, is reticent to the point of obscurity, and raises more questions than it answers. What we are to understand from it is that the ecclesiastical authorities raised difficulties over Adib Ishaq's burial in consecrated ground and with the proper rites; and that this was the doing of 'colleagues' of Adib's who wanted to take revenge on him. The 'colleagues' were most probably the editors of the Jesuit periodical with whom the dead man had been so recently involved in an acrimonious polemic. In the absence of further evidence, we would have had to confine ourselves to this bare supposition. But, as it happens, we have at our disposal a very full report of the events which took place at Adib Ishaq's death. This is found in a despatch sent by Patrimonio, the French consul general at Beirut, on 6 September 1884.[15]

Patrimonio wrote that Adib had fled from Egypt to Beirut having quickly realized that there was no place for a Christian in 'Urabi's movement. In Beirut, he edited *al-Taqaddum* which was marked by 'a real liberalism' both in politics and religion; and this led to his being in the bad books (*vu d'un mauvais œil*) of the religious authorities. Two other material points are mentioned in the despatch. Adib Ishaq, Patrimonio indicates, was a freemason. It is most probable that this was so. Adib Ishaq was the first to reveal, in his notice of Afghani, that the latter had founded a masonic lodge in Egypt attached (*tābi'*) to the Grand Orient of France,[16] and it is to be expected that so close a disciple of the Sage would have been inducted into the lodge. The fact of his being a freemason must have served to exacerbate ecclesiastical disapproval, for it was only shortly before Adib's death, on April 20, 1884, that Leo XIII had condemned freemasonry in his encyclical 'Humanum Genus'.

In the second place, Patrimonio asserts bluntly that Adiq Ishaq was a freethinker. This was proved, according to Patrimonio, when on his death-bed Adib vehemently refused the ministrations of a priest. If this was the case, then the behaviour of the ecclesiastical authorities following his death becomes entirely comprehensible. Though his brother is silent on the point, it would seem that the family 'not caring to seem to share the views of the deceased', did make the declaration required by the ecclesiastical authorities, namely that Adib had died 'in communion with the Church'.

The burial could now go forward at the small parish church of Hadath where Adib had died. But it seems that his friends were determined to make of his burial an occasion for demonstrating against the Catholic church, and its obscurantism and tyranny. An obituary in *Lisan al-Hal* indicates that they thought first of burying him in Beirut,[17] where the funeral procession would be more numerous and a demonstration more effective. But the ecclesiastical authorities were not taking any chances. Not only was the burial to take place at Hadath, but also the parish priest was instructed to expedite (*brusquer*) the ceremony, and particularly to prevent speeches being made. The priest, Patrimonio reports, applied these instructions 'not without some brutality' and was said to have taken the precaution of getting some of his parishioners to be present in the church in order to lend him their help should the need arise. It is presumably to this that Awni Ishaq refers when he remarks obscurely that a clash took place between his brother's friends and the 'ignorant partisans' of his enemies. The priest at any rate was so far successful that Adib's friends could not make their speeches until after the end of the religious ceremony.

A few days after the funeral, *al-Bashir* published the declaration made by Adib Ishaq's father. This occasioned the outbreak of a furious polemic against the Jesuits, which was further fed by the publication of Leo's encyclical. Adib Ishaq's friends, Patrimonio states, were themselves freemasons, and they were naturally concerned to defend his reputation and theirs from the accusations which the Catholic church made against freemasonry. It seems that they went so far as to summon the superior of the Jesuit order in Syria to appear before the criminal court. He refused, alleging French protection. The controversy became so envenomed that the civil authorities were forced to take notice, and the governor told Patrimonio that he was going to take action against *al-Bashir* and its opponent *al-Muqtataf*. The latter periodical, edited by Ya'qub Sarruf, Faris Nimr and Shahin Makarius, it is interesting to remember, had taken a prominent part in a slightly earlier controversy which had shaken the Syrian Protestant College, where Sarruf and Nimr were employed. In that controversy it had espoused Darwinism to the great distress of the Presbyterian missionaries who ran the College.[18] The editors of *al-Muqtataf*, we may also remember, had radical political views which they derived from a teacher of French at the Syrian Protestant College—views similar to those of Adib Ishaq.[19] In early September, then, the governor addressed warnings to both *al-Bashir* and *al-Muqtataf*. The former was told that polemics and personal attacks were being published on its pages, and that in one number in particular an article condemning Voltaire had cited 'among others a seditious sentence the publication of which was forbidden.' One wonders if the Ottoman authorities appreciated the irony of rebuking a Jesuit newspaper for spreading Voltairean sedition. A similar warning went to *al-Muqtataf* which was told that its polemical articles had gone beyond the permissible limits, and that to persist in them would perturb public opinion and occasion conflict; to continue in the controversy was therefore forbidden.[20]

The death of Adib Ishaq also resulted in the publication of an anonymous pamphlet in French attacking the Jesuits and defending his memory, a copy of which Patrimonio sent home with his despatch. It is the only document relating to this controversy which is available so far, and is reproduced below. It is of interest in giving us an idea of the terms in which the controversy was conducted, and of the charges which the Jesuits were making against Adib Ishaq. The quarrel between them, the pamphlet declares, was one between the 'apostle of tolerance' and the 'delegate of fanaticism'. The publication of the declaration made by Adib Ishaq's father, it goes on to say, was meant to be a warning addressed by the Jesuits to all unbelievers and freemasons. Their grievance against Adib Ishaq was that he was a member of the literary society, *Zahrat al-adāb* which they falsely declare to be a centre of impiety, and a preparatory school for freemasonry, to which he is accused of belonging. But all their accusations against the freemasons are palpable calumnies which will rebound to the benefit of freemasonry itself. This is because everyone knows what freemasons are like, and that there is nothing sinister or frightening about them. In any case is it for the Society of Jesus, itself a secret society, to reproach another organization for its secrecy? The Jesuits have accused the freemasons of plotting against the lawful government of the country. Have they forgotten that it was they who recently refused to divulge their statutes to the French government? Is there a country in Europe from which they have not been expelled because of their ceaseless plotting, their dangerous teaching, their claim to form a state within a state?

The pamphlet may also be considered as a landmark. As Patrimonio wrote, this was the first time that freethinking had been given public expression in the Levant. What is certain, he went on, is that slowly there was being formed in Beirut an educated public, and that every year a large number of Christian graduates who no longer find employment in Egypt, stay in Syria. They read, make comparisons, and desire change. The first-fruits of this development may be seen in this anonymous pamphlet.

Two or three decades later the effects of this increasing secularism were to be much more clearly seen in the politics of the Sanjaq and in wider issues alike. Thus, when Muzaffar Pasha was governor-general of the Lebanon, he deliberately encouraged the freemasons, and tried to use them as a weapon in his quarrel with the Maronite Patriarch. Frederick Bliss, writing in 1912, noted that under Muzaffar the Maronite hierarchy was 'threatened by the activity of the societies of Freemasons and other popular benevolent associations which have sprung up in the Lebanon since the beginning of the century in consequence of the liberal ideas brought back from the New World by returned emigrants'. These societies carried on an anti-clerical propaganda which the hierarchy naturally tried to counter: a bitter pamphlet and newspaper war was waged, and the Maronite patriarch put the freemasons under the ban.[21]

The character of these free-thinking attacks on traditional religion and the Maronite church may be gathered from the writings of the Maronite Jabran Khalil Jabran (1883–1931), who is best known to western readers as the author of *The Prophet*. In 1908 he published a collection of short stories, *al-Arwah al-mutamarrida* (Rebellious Spirits) which attacked the hypocrisy and cruelty of traditional

society, and called for the liberation of the individual from oppressive
legal and social institutions. The last story in the collection, *Khalil
al-kafir* (Khalil the Blasphemer), is the account of a monk in a prosperous monastery in Mount Lebanon who rebels against the shame-
less exploitation of the peasants in the name of religion by the monks
who preach virtue and practise vice, and the alliance at the expense of
the people between the priest and the landlord. Khalil proclaims
publicly the tenets of true religion which are summed up in the statement that 'the will of the people is the will of God'. This true religion
is the religion of freedom which Khalil invokes in this litany: 'Hear
us, O Freedom; have pity on us, O Daughter of Athena; save us, O
Sister of Rome; deliver us, O Companion of Moses; give us succour, O
Loved One of Muhammad; teach us, O Bride of Jesus; strengthen our
hearts so that we may live; or else strengthen the arms of our enemies
against us so that we may die and disappear, and thus have repose.'

But the most prominent anti-clerical publicist in the later controversy was another Maronite, Amin al-Rayhani (1876–1940), who
made a sustained assault on the Maronite hierarchy and on Catholic
'superstitions'. His most daring attack on the church occurs in the
parable, *al-Muhalafa al-thulathiyya fi'l-mamlaka al-hayawaniyya*
(The Triple Alliance in the Animal Kingdom) which he published in
1903, and which is said to have been publicly burnt more than once,
so strong were the emotions which it aroused. The hero of the parable
is a fox, a journalist by profession, who defies the priestly power
represented by a horse, a mule and a donkey. They find his defiance
so intolerable that they condemn him to death, and he is publicly
burnt at the stake (a martyr to free thought) by the ox (who represents
the civil power). At the end of the trial the horse sums up, as president of the ecclesiastical court, the charges against the accused. The
fox, he states, had confessed that he did not believe in holy scripture,
or in God, or in the divinity of the Lion (i.e. Jesus), or in holy images,
or that the Lioness (i.e. Mary) had conceived without sin and,
finally, that he did not believe in divine miracles. This verdict, in fact,
sums up the comprehensive attack which Rayhani mounts against
the Christian creeds. The audacity of his attack may be appreciated
from the passage in which the fox is interrogated by one of his judges,
the donkey, about the Virgin Birth:

DONKEY: Did you not say that virginity is incompatible with giving
birth, i.e. that a pure female cannot be a mother?
Fox: I only said that giving birth is incompatible with virginity.
DONKEY: What do you understand by virginity?
Fox: I ask to be excused from answering. I am not a doctor. All that I
know is that fire is generated only through friction, and the same is the
case with children.

DONKEY: Do you except no one from this principle?

FOX: Do you by this mean the story of the Lioness and the Lion?

DONKEY: Yes. Do you not believe that the Lioness conceived without the animal copulation to which you refer?

FOX: How can this be, when natural laws teach us that it is only by friction can two things give birth to a third?

DONKEY: But this conception took place by the will of the Holy Spirit which descended on the Lioness as appears in Holy Scripture.

FOX: This is only your delusion. If it is true that the Holy Spirit had descended on the Lioness, then her legal spouse would have had the right to divorce her according to the law. If he did not do so, then this was a kind of tolerance and forbearance for which he deserves great thanks and praise. But who knows, maybe he had no witness . . .

Mockery of this kind naturally asked for retaliation. Rayhani was savagely attacked by Father Louis Cheikho on the pages of *al-Mashriq* as a false would-be philosopher who scoffed at the mysteries of the religion in which he had been brought up, mysteries such as the Trinity, the Incarnation and the Virgin Birth. And many years later Cheikho, who remained very hostile to Rayhani, published a report that he had become a Muslim under the name of Muhammad Amin al-Rayhani. The report was, literally speaking, false. Free-thinkers like Rayhani were past believing in any traditional religion. But belief Rayhani still seemed to need and, as is well-known, from belief in Christianity he fell into a belief in Arabism.[22]

APPENDIX

C'est au Liban, à l'ombre de ses bois et dans le silence de ses vallées, que j'ai reçu la nouvelle de la mort de mon pauvre ami ADIB; ce coup fatal je m'y attendais comme tous ceux de ses amis qui continuaient à aller lui porter un peu d'encouragement et de consolation dans la dernière période de sa maladie. Personne de ceux qui l'entouraient de leur affection ne conservait d'illusion sur l'issue de la maladie qui le minait insensiblement; lui seul restait fort calme et nous entretenait rarement de la mort, soit qu'il se fit illusion sur son état, soit que, dans nos entretiens, il ne voulât pas nous mettre sur un sujet mutuellement pénible.

Sa mort n'a donc été une surprise pour personne, et encore moins pour moi qui savais lui dire le dernier adieu quand, obligé de quitter la ville, je fus lui serrer la main quinze jours avant qu'il eût fini de respirer; mais quoique longtemps avant sa mort nous eussions tous porté dans le cœur le deuil de notre pauvre ami, je n'en ai pas moins pleuré à chaudes larmes le jour où j'ai appris que tout était fini.

J'ai pleuré dans le recueillement et le silence, j'ai pleuré tout seul, mais je savais fort bien que je n'étais pas le seul à pleurer cet ami sincère et dévoué, ce cœur ardemment généreux, cette figure si franche et si sympathique, cette intelligence si grande et si ouverte. Je savais bien qu'il laissait une douleur cuisante à tous ceux qui l'avaient connu de près de vifs regrets à tous ceux qui avaient entendu l'orateur, lu l'écrivain et compris le penseur.

En descendant de ma retraite au Liban, où j'étais un peu inaccessible aux échos de la ville, j'ai su, comme je m'y étais au reste attendu, que la mort de notre pauvre ami avait eu un grand retentissement in Syrie et en Egypte mais j'ai appris également les tristes incidents qui ont marqué le jour de ses funérailles; j'ai lu tous les panégyriques émus auxquels a donné lieu cette grande perte, mais j'ai lu également les articles du «BÉCHIRE» et les bras m'en sont tombés!

Je suis sorti cette dernière lecture atterré, navré, écœuré, indigné!

Le «BÉCHIRE», avis à ceux qui peuvent encore l'ignorer, est ici le journal des pères Jésuites, l'organe attitré de la gent moutonnière, cléricale et fanatique.

Mais savez-vous d'abord quels sont les tristes incidents, les tiraillements pénibles qui se sont produits à l'enterrement de notre pauvre ami?

Je ne veux pas les rappeler ici pour soulever de nouveau le dégoût chez ceux qui ont été les témoins écœurés et résignés de ces scènes déplorables, mais je tiens à les faire connaître à tous les absents qui, comme moi, n'ont pu rendre le dernier devoir, l'hommage suprême, à l'ami qui s'en allait, au talent qui disparaissait pour toujours.

Il est également bon que tout le monde sache que le fanatisme bête est sans pitié, sans entrailles et que rien ne peut trouver grâces à ses yeux, ni l'éclat du nom et du talent, ni le deuil de toute une foule, ni la douleur paternelle, ni le respect que l'on doit aux morts!

C'est le curé de la paroisse à Beyrouth qui a eu les tristes honneurs de cette journée doublement triste; il faut avouer cependant un peu à sa décharge, qu'il n'a été que l'exécuteur fidèle d'un plan de campagne conçu apparement par l'état major du camp clérical.

Si l'on ne peut donc lui reporter l'honneur de la conception, encore faut-il rendre pleinement justice à son talent d'exécuteur: Il a été intraitable, il n'a pas bronché, il n'a pas transigé, cet homme est apparement fait de l'étoffe des bourreaux!

On l'appelait pour enterrer un mort, pour faire son métier de prêtre, et rien ne lui aurait été plus facile que de trouver dans le dédale infini de la casuistique un biais quelconque pour faire à notre ami, en tout repos de conscience, les honneurs de la religion malgré tous les griefs que les fanatiques pouvaient invoquer contre lui.

Mais non, ce n'est pas un acquit de conscience qu'il cherchait, ce ne sont pas des apparences qu'il voulait sauver, c'était une vengeance que le fanatisme avait méditée sur un apôtre de la tolérance, et l'occasion était vraiement trop belle pour la laisser échapper.

La grande douleur de la famille, le peur du scandale tout avait admirablement servi le projet misérable, aussi le délégué du fanatisme n'y est-il pas allé par quatre chemins. En arrivant il a dicté carrément ses conditions, il a mis le concours de son ministère au prix d'une déclaration écrite, explicite que le défunt était mort catholique.

C'est en vain que le pauvre père de notre ami s'est récrié contre ce précédent inusité, c'est en vain qu'il a protesté contre cette prétention extraordinaire, rien n'a pu faire broncher le bourreau, ni protestations, ni prières ni déclarations orales, il tenait absolument à sa déclaration écrite, il avait apparement l'ordre de l'extorquer à tout prix, et il n'a été content que quand il a pu serrer soigneusement dans sa poche cette fameuse déclaration que vous connaissez; je ne vous en parlerai donc pas, mes amis, mais prenez bien note de ce précédent créé, de cette jurisprudence établie: On peut fort bien désormais mourir catholique par procuration.

Eh bien, quand cette déclaration a été carottée croyez vous que notre bon curé se soit tenu pour satisfait? Non, une fois sa déclaration en poche, il a exigé que les funérailles se fissent immédiatement.

En vain lui représentait-on que l'heure était encore trop matinale, que les amis et les connaissances n'avaient pas encore eu le temps d'arriver de la ville; les prières et les observations ne faisaient que l'exaspérer et l'irriter d'avantage, et s'il n'eût tenu qu'à lui, notre pauvre ami eût été conduit à sa dernière demeure, sans pompe, sans bière, sans compagnons, absolument comme un criminel.

Les démonstrations de regrets, la pompe, la vue des amis se pressant derrière le cercueil mornes et abbattus, tous ces témoignages de respect et de douleur devaient sans doute offusquer énormément de délégué du fanatisme.

Ces gens là, s'ils le pouvaient voudraient réserver le monopole des pompes funèbres rien que pour leurs adeptes et leurs amis; ils n'entendent pas que l'on puisse mourir respecté, regretté, et pleuré si l'on ne meurt pas dans leurs bonnes grâces et ne croyez pas qu'ils se gênent pour le dire ou qu'ils biaisent pour l'imposer quand ils peuvent; non, non le triste héros de cette journée, après toutes les humiliations, toutes les avanies dont il a abreuvé une famille malheureuse et ses amis éplorés, n'a pas craint d'apostropher bien haut une personne fort honorable qui annonçait dans la maison mortuaire, au milieu d'un petit cercle d'amis, son intention de prononcer au cimetière quelques paroles de regrets.

Il a également imposé silence au premier orateur qui avait commencé au cimetière la série des discours, et il n'a pas craint de pousser l'impudence, l'oubli de toute réserve, et de toute convenance jusqu'à déclarer anathèmes toutes les personnes qui étaient restées au cimetière pour entendre les adieux émus, qui étaient prononcés sur la tombe de notre pauvre ami.

Je vous vois d'ici, mes amis hausser les épaules, mon récit vous parait incroyable et tout au moins énormément suspect d'exagération; mais non, je vous le jure, ce que je vous rapporte n'est que la stricte vérité; ce n'est pas une blague, ce n'est pas une invention, ce n'est pas non plus, ni une histoire de moyen âge, ni une épisode de l'inquisition, encore une fois, c'est la vérité toute nue, attestée par toutes les personnes qui ont suivi le convoi funèbre de notre pauvre ami.

Et maintenant, comparez s'il vous plait l'attitude pleine de fougue, de morgue, et de provocation de ce ministre d'une religion de paix, avec l'attitude pleine de réserve, de résignation, et de conciliation de nos amis, et de tous ceux qui ont assisté la malheureuse famille dans cette grande journée d'épreuve! De quel côté était le calme, la dignité, la sagesse, le respect de la douleur, l'entente vraie de l'esprit évangélique?

Je félicite sincèrement mes amis d'être restés impassibles devant les provocations et les défis; ils se sont ainsi noblement vengés, et ont grandement honoré la mémoire de celui qui était parmi nous, le grand apôtre de la tolérance et de la conciliation!

La déclaration dont je vous parlais tout à l'heure, cette déclaration arrachée à la faiblesse d'un père éplorée, vous savez tous l'usage qui en a été fait.

Elle a été immédiatement publiée, à grand fracas dans le «BÉCHIRE», l'organe que je vous ai présenté. J'avais donc raison de vous dire qu'en l'exigeant, le curé de la paroisse n'était que l'instrument de volontés supérieures; j'avais donc raison de vous dire qu'en faisant une condition sine quâ non de son concours, il ne cherchait ni à se mettre en règle avec sa conscience, ni à sauver les apparences aux yeux du monde catholique. C'était, il n'y a pas à en douter, une tactique méditée d'avance, pour avoir l'occasion et le prétexte de lancer de haut, un avis et une menace à l'adresse de tous les mécréants, de tous les suspects d'irréligion, de tous les francs-maçons, et en un mot, de quiconque croirait pouvoir frustrer impunément les jésuites d'hériter légitimement de son cadavre.

Eh bien! Il faut que cette pauvre tactique soit dénoncée; il faut que l'on sache que ces ministres d'une religion divine ne reculent pas, pour les besoins de leur cause, pour les besoins de leurs intérêts, devant les moyens les plus petits et les plus mesquins.

Ou vous avez cherché à vous mettre en repos avec votre conscience, en règle avec votre religion, ou non. Si c'est un légitime acquit de conscience que vous avez voulu, pourquoi ne vous êtes-vous pas contentés d'une déclaration orale? Et, ayant exigé et obtenu une déclaration écrite, pourquoi vous êtes-vous empressés de la publier immédiatement?

C'est donc un avis que vous avez voulu donner et une intimidation que vous avez entendu faire.

Je vous plains sincèrement si vous en êtes réduits aujourd'hui à mettre au service de votre cause le scandale, la brutalité et l'intimidation!

Vous trahissez Jésus-Christ, vous allez contre l'enseignement de l'évangile, et vous donnez une triste idée de votre cause et de votre apostolat, car la violence, l'intimidation, et l'injure ne doivent jamais marcher au service des bonnes causes: celles–ci s'imposent exclusivement par la raison, la douceur et la persuasion.

Oui, rien n'a manqué à la mémoire de notre pauvre ami, de la part de ceux auxquels Jésus-Christ a expressément recommandé: Aimez ceux qui vous haïssent, bénissez ceux qui vous maudissent.

Ils ont déployé, comme vous l'avez vu, le jour de l'enterrement, toute la morgue, toute la brutalité possible et sur une tombe à peine fermée, sur de la terre encore fraîche, ils ont versé à grands flots l'injure et l'outrage; ils nous ont défiés dans notre douleur, ils nous ont blessés dans le vif de notre deuil, ils nous ont insultés dans notre mort. Ils ont déchiqueté un corps inanimé, ils y ont mordu à belles dents, ils s'y sont abattus comme des vautours, ils ont, comme des sauvages, assouvi sur un cadavre leur soif de vengeance!

Entre gens civilisés, quand la retraite est sonnée, quand les combattants se sont séparés, il y a la trève des morts; on recueillit ses blessés, on ramasse ses morts et on les enterre religieusement. Vous autres, vous avez attendu précisément que notre ami fût dans la tombe, que sa grande voix se fût éteinte, que sa belle main se fût à jamais paralysée, pour commencer une lutte déloyale, pour entamer une campagne dégoûtante, abominable.

Vous avez pensé que lui parti, sa mémoire vous échouerait entre les mains comme une proie facile; vous avez spéculé sur la faiblesse et la douleur de ses amis, vous avez pensé que cette grande perte nous démoraliserait, romprait nos rangs, et nous jetterait dans la prostration.

Vous vous êtes trompés.

Si c'est une lâcheté de s'attaquer aux morts, il est encore infiniment plus lâche de ne pas les défendre; nous ne faillirons pas plus à nos morts, que nous ne faillirons à notre devoir et à notre honneur!

Mais d'abord qu'avez-vous reproché à notre cher ADIB?

Son premier crime à vos yeux, est d'avoir été un des membres les plus actifs, les plus zélés, les plus influents de notre chère société «ZAHRET-el ADABE».

C'est vrai, pour une fois vos reproches sont pleinement fondés; mais ce sont précisément ses titres à notre reconnaissance et à notre admiration!

Les meilleurs souvenirs que nous garderons de celui qui a été prématurément enlevé à notre affection, ce sont les souvenirs de ces soirées intimes, à l'ombre de notre société, où la grande âme de notre ami s'épanchait sans gêne, où sa parole ample, claire, scintillante, coulait comme les flots limpides d'un fleuve majestueux.

Je ne puis me rappeler sans émotion ces longues heures, durant lesquelles notre pauvre ami nous tenait collés à ses lèvres, nous surprenant par la sûreté de ses jugements, nous étonnant par sa grande érudition, nous subjugant par sa mâle éloquence; ses accents harmonieux et cadencés, son élocution facile, lumineuse, coquette à force de correction, nous transportaient d'admiration et quand à la fin de ses chaleureuses improvisations, il nous lançait sa dernière période, quand il nous jetait son bon mot de la fin, les applaudissements de nos confrères crépitaient comme la grêle!

Et vous voulez que cet homme n'ait pas eu toute notre admiration et toute notre affection?

Certes nous n'avons pas la prétention de donner notre ami pour quelque demi-dieu, pour quelque saint anachorète, pour un homme rigoureusement parfait et sans reproche, pour un esprit extraordinaire.

Non, ses titres qu'il s'est faits lui-même à l'admiration de tous, sont assez beaux et assez nombreux pour que nous n'ayons guère besoin de lui en forger.

Nous ne vous demanderons point de le canoniser; nous savons fort bien que c'était un homme, et que comme homme, il devait avoir ses qualités et ses défauts, mais c'est pour ses qualités et malgré ses défauts que nous l'aimions, que c'était l'orgueil de notre société; mais, mille fois pardon, j'oubliai que notre société n'a pas eu la bonne fortune de trouver grâce à vos yeux.

Pourquoi?

Un mot d'explication pour tous les braves gens qui seraient tentés de prendre toutes vos paroles pour des paroles d'évangile.

Et d'abord qu'est-ce que c'est que notre société?

C'est une société purement littéraire reconnue par un «Iradé Sénié».

L'objet de notre société est de servir de trait d'union entre tous les jeunes gens qui ont le culte des belles et bonnes choses; notre but est de nous instruire les uns les autres, de nous y délasser des labeurs physiques dans la culture des choses de l'esprit.

La politique et la religion sont chez nous tout à fait hors de question.

Notre société se recrute indifférement dans toutes les communautés, sans aucune préoccupation ni politique, ni religieuse.

Nous ne demandons à ceux qui veulent bien venir à nous, à part une certaine culture intellectuelle, que d'être des hommes honnêtes, tolérants, d'un caractère sociable et aimable.

Et voilà pourquoi toutes les opinions, toutes les convictions religieuses peuvent se coudoyer chez nous: elles se croisent sans jamais se heurter. Nous n'avons jamais chez nous des querelles de théologiens, nous gardons nos convictions dans notre poche et notre religion dans notre cœur!

Les gens qui promènent la religion partout, pour promener partout leur masque et le prétexte de leur domination, ces gens, qui veulent que l'église soit dans tous les coins et la théologie de toutes les discussions, ne peuvent pas, ne veulent pas comprendre que l'on puisse, quoique pour un moment, laisser dormir en paix ses convictions religieuses.

Ils ne veulent pas comprendre que l'on puisse se rencontrer sur un terrain neutre, tel que celui de la morale, de la science et de la littérature.

Eh bien, n'en déplaise à ces gens là, notre société compte parmi ses membres des libres-penseurs, des indifférents, comme elle compte des hommes profondément et sincèrement religieux; eh bien malgré cette diversité d'opinions, nous vivons ensemble dans les meilleurs termes, dans la plus parfaite harmonie, sur un terrain soigneusement neutralisé.

Mais ça se pratique ainsi partout, mais cela se voit partout et pour ne citer qu'un exemple célèbre, un exemple d'hier, Monseigneur Perraud l'évêque français d'Autun ne siège-t-il pas fort bien à côté de Monsieur Renan à l'Académie française?

Vous ne pouvez pas croire à cet accord, vous ne voulez pas y croire, comme vous ne voulez pas reconnaître que l'on puisse être honnête homme, sans avoir en perspective le ciel pour récompense, comme vous ne voulez pas admettre que l'on ne puisse voler dans la poche du voisin, si l'on n'a point dans le ventre la peur de l'enfer.

Au nom de la dignité humaine, nous protestons contre votre doctrine!

Et cependant vous savez la faire sonner bien haut cette dignité humaine, quand vous vous indignez contre les savants et les naturalistes qui donnent une origine fort modeste à notre espèce humaine!

Étrange manière de comprendre cette dignité!

Vous vous récriez en son nom, contre ceux qui font procéder l'homme de l'orang-outang et vous n'avez garde de la maltraiter cette pauvre dignité, quand vous faites naître tous les hommes avec des penchants naturels, innés pour le mal et des instincts pervers!

Eh bien quel est l'homme qui ne préférerait cent fois descendre des plus humbles artisans, mais d'artisans honnêtes, que de venir dans le monde avec un sang noble dans les veines, mais de ce sang vicié et vicieux?

Mais me voici bien loin de mon sujet, revenons à notre société que vous avez présentée au public comme un foyer d'impiété, comme une école préparatoire à la franc-maçonnerie.

C'est faux, absolument faux.

Des francs-maçons, tout en restant francs-maçons, sont peut-être venus à nous, quelques-uns de nos confrères peuvent être allés à la franc-maçonnerie, tout en restant assidus à nos séances, tout ça est fort possible, tout ça est très probable; mais de là à faire de notre société une antichambre et une succursale de la maçonnerie, il y a un abîme et vous l'avez franchi sans scrupules, dans votre excellente logique.

Eh bien sachez que nous sommes une association absolument libre, absolument indépendante; nous ne sommes inféodés à personne, nous ne recevons le mot d'ordre de personne, nous ne servons absolument que les intérêts de notre société qui sont les nôtres; mais sachez également que nos confrères n'aliènent pas en entrant chez nous leur liberté de faire; ils ne font aucun vœu d'exclusivisme, ils sont libres d'aller partout où bon leur semble, partout où il y a un peu de bien à faire et une bonne cause à défendre!

Passons au second crime!

Mes bonnes commères signez-vous, notre cher ADIB était ... un ... un ... franc-maçon!

Ne vous est-il donc jamais arrivé de remarquer la nuit des fantômes rasant les murs en silence, évitant les grands chemins, se glissant dans les rues tortueuses, se dérobant soigneusement aux regards des indiscrets, débouchant presque à la même heure de plusieurs directions sur un point central?

Eh bien, laissez moi vous le dire à l'oreille, ce sont des francs-maçons, la bête noire des Jésuites, ils s'en vont à la faveur de l'obscurité armés ... de cannes et de parapluies, pour croquer des prêtres, et manger des gouvernements!

Ah les monstres, et dire que c'est le soir après avoir copieusement diné qu'ils s'en régalent!

Leur appétit monstre ferait envie à plus d'un, car vous savez qu'en général les prêtres et les gouvernements ne sont pas faits de chair tendre!

Je n'ai pas l'honneur d'appartenir à la franc-maçonnerie, mais si j'en étais, je serais humblement d'avis que l'on restât constamment impassible et indifférent devant le débordement d'injures, de mensonges, de balivernes dont le «BÉCHIR» s'est fait depuis longtemps déjà, une spécialité contre les francs-maçons.

Je ne plaindrais sincèrement que les pauvres abonnés du «BÉCHIRE» qui doivent avoir déjà leur plein dos de ces philippiques endormantes, toujours répétées sur le même thème et sur le même ton, mais il me semble que tous les francs-maçons de bons sens, de sens rassis, devraient rire sous cape de toutes ces exagérations ridicules, de toutes ces colères affectées; ils devraient s'en frotter les mains d'aise car au fond ça doit fort bien arranger leurs affaires.

Toutes ces sornettes que les jésuites, trop intelligents pour y croire eux-mêmes, débitent d'un ton trop sérieux contre les francs-maçons, il n'y a plus que les bonnes vieilles femmes et les galopins de 2 à 15 ans pour les avaler. Ceux qui connaissent ce que c'est que la maçonnerie, qui entre parenthèses se laisse aisément pénétrer, ceux-là ne se laissent pas prendre naturellement à ces grossières calomnies, et tous les hommes de bon sens, sans aucun parti pris, finissent par se demander si ces attaques virulentes, incessantes ne sont pas des manœuvres, et si ces sorties enflammées ne sont point des colères de commande.

Je suis certain que ces exagérations, bêtes à force d'être ridicules, finissent par faire gagner plus d'un à la franc-maçonnerie, absolument comme les exagérations et les innovations superstitieuses des Jésuites sur le domaine de la religion jettent tous les jours une masse de dégoutés dans les bras de l'indifférence et de la libre pensée.

Je ne comprends pas que les Jésuites, qui ont la réputation d'être des habiles, continuent à rééditer contre les francs-maçons, en les amplifiant, des accusations vieilles comme Hérode qui pouvaient passer jadis dans le bon vieux temps pour de l'argent comptant, mais qui sont aujourd'hui complétement démonétisées.

Qui ne sait cependant que quand on dégringole, le secret de se sauver quelques fois, de se soutenir encore un peu, de ne pas trop mal tomber, est dans l'à-propos avec lequel on se débarrasse de son lest?...

Comment voulez-vous croire plutôt à l'opinion des Jésuites sur la franc-maçonnerie qu'ils continuent à regarder à travers leurs intérêts, à travers leurs traditions, à travers leur haine de famille, et ne pas croire plutôt à ses propres yeux et à son expérience de chaque jour?

Les francs-maçons, du moins ici, ne vivent point dans le désert, ils n'habitent ni des rochers, ni des antres, ils ne se renferment ni dans des couvents ni dans des cloîtres, ils vivent parfaitement et paisiblement au milieu de nous et, pour la plupart, ils ne nous cachent point leur qualité de francs-maçons; nous les coudoyons tous les jours dans les rues, nous nous frottons à eux dans les affaires, nous nous rencontrons avec eux dans les familles, nous nous croisons enfin dans toutes les relations de la vie; eh bien j'ai eu beau écarquiller les yeux, j'ai eu beau me mettre à l'àffût, ces gens ne m'ont pas paru ce que le BÉCHIRE et ses amis, se sont plu à nous les dépeindre.

Pour moi la qualité de franc-maçon n'est certainement pas un certificat infaillible de civisme et d'honnêteté. Les francs-maçons n'ont pas plus que d'autres le monopole de la vertu et de la verité, mais s'ils ne sont pas des anges, s'ils ne sont certainement pas pétris d'une pâte différente à celle de tous les hommes, ce sont pour la plupart, il ne faut pas craindre de le crier bien haut, de fort honnêtes gens, d'excellents pères de famille, de braves garçons, des amis bien serviables et avec ça ni sots ni bêtes pour la plupart du temps.

Ils peuvent de plus se flatter de compter dans leurs rangs, par tout le monde, autant et plus que toute société, des célèbrités et des illustrations dans le monde de la science et de la politique.

Et vous voulez, mes révérends pères, que nous ayons des yeux pour ne pas voir, des oreilles pour ne pas entendre, que nous démentions notre expérience de chaque jour pour croire à vos diatribes enflammées, à des absurdités que vous semblez répéter comme par la force d'inertie et pour ne pas en perdre l'habitude?

C'est trop demander franchement à notre naïveté et notre bonne foi!

Vous avez reproché à la Maçonnerie ce que vous avez reproché à notre société, d'être une société secrète, un foyer d'impiété et de révolution.

Je ne me charge sans doute pas de relever en détail vos accusations contre la franc-maçonnerie, ce n'est pas mon affaire; mais franchement vous sied-il, à vous la compagnie de Jésus, de jeter la pierre aux sociétés secrètes, vous la société secrète par excellence?

Nous ne sommes point, bien s'en faut, une société secrète mais si dans notre société «ZAHRET-el-ADABE» nous préférons de garder l'incognito, si nous aimons la vie et l'intimité de famille, si nous avons horreur de faire recette sur un théâtre, dans un cercle, ou dans un amphithéâtre, c'est que le bruit n'est point notre affaire, c'est que dans un égoisme tout à fait humain, nous demandons spécialement à notre société, un délassement intellectuel de nos fatigues et une diversion utile et agréable aux soucis des affaires.

Nous n'aimons point de jeter de la poudre aux yeux du public, nous ne courons pas après une vaine popularité; nous nous plaisons à rester chez nous, comme d'honnêtes bourgeois, nous aimons de vivre tranquillement en famille. Nous n'avons ni le désir ni les moyens de faire autrement.

Nous sommes un petit groupe d'amis, de bonnes connaissances qui prélevons une faible cotisation sur l'argent que nous arons pour pourvoir au modeste entretien de notre société.

Le piété des fidèles ne nous fait ni des loisirs ni des rentes, nous ne vendons ni des messes ni des indulgences, nous ne faisons point de quêtes, nous ne sollicitons pas de subventions, voilà pourquoi nous ne tenons pas salles ouvertes comme ceux qui entre autres vœux ont fait celui de la pauvreté!

Vous nous avez accusé avec la franc-maçonnerie de comploter contre le gouvernement légal de notre pays.

Avant de lancer une accusation aussi perfide, en avez-vous mesuré toute la gravité, toutes les conséquences?

Mais à qui croyez vous pouvoir donner le change?

Vous supposez sans doute à nos gouvernants une forte dose de naïveté?

Comment se défiraient-ils d'une société, aujourd'hui universellement répandue, qui de notoriété publique compte dans ses rangs des empereurs des rois, des princes de sang, des présidents de république, des ministres et une masse de fonctionnaires d'état de tout rang et de tout grade? Une société qui compte dans son sein une telle masse d'autorités, ne peut être un danger pour l'autorité!

Se défiera-t-on donc de notre pauvre petite société qui jouit d'une existence officielle, dont les statuts sont approuvés par le gouvernement, et dont les portes sont constamment à la merci de son représentant?

Si vous avez cru par un zèle indiscret, suspect et hypocrite donner le change sur vos propres menées, vos insinuations plus infâmes que ridicules, plus ridicules qu'infâmes, nous obligent à vous rappeler que dernièrement en France vous avez refusé de soumettre vos statuts à l'examen de l'autorité civile, de votre gouvernement légitime.

Est-ce que l'on ne ferait pas aujourd'hui le tour de l'Europe si l'on voulait vous citer tous les pays dont vous avez été chassés et proscrits à cause de vos menées incessantes, de votre enseignement dangereux, de votre prétention de former un état dans l'état?

Ces noirs desseins que vous nous prêtez à grands cris, cette tactique plutôt, me remet involontairement en mémoire une délicieuse fin de lettre de votre bon ami Paul Bert dans la dédicace de son livre, la morale des Jésuites, à Monseigneur Freppel; il lui disait:

«Qui n'a vu dans quelque rue de nos grandes villes fuyant devant un groupe «acharné à sa poursuite, un homme éffaré, criant plus haut que tous:

«Au voleur! au voleur!

«Quel est il?

«Les naifs seuls s'y trompent.»

Ne serait-ce pas là votre jeu?

Je ne me charge pas d'y répondre, mais on ne ferait pas mal quelque part de méditer sur ce point d'interrogation!

Et maintenant, mes bons amis, ce n'est pas ma faute si ces pages écrites sous l'empire d'une bien légitime émotion sont fumantes de colère et d'indignation.

Celui qui sème le vent récolte la tempête!

Ces gens là ont semé à pleines mains l'injure et l'outrage contre une mémoire justement chère et illustre, la calomnie et la diffamation contre des sociétés respectables et justement respectées, le mépris et le dénigrement contre des personnes justement marquantes, justement considérées au milieu de nous.

Qu'ils récoltent la tempête de nos colères et de notre indignation!

Il nous ont provoqués, ils nous ont défiés dans notre douleur, dans nos amitiés, dans nos convictions, dans tout ce que nous avons de plus cher; ce n'est donc pas ma faute s'ils m'ont obligé à prendre la plume et à sortir d'une réserve tout à fait naturelle à mon caractère!

Un mot encore pour rassurer ceux de nos amis que le déchaînement du fanatisme jésuitique a pu émouvoir:

Les sociétés calomniées ne seront ni moins fréquentées ni moins courues, au contraire:

Nos amis insultés dénigrés ne s'en porteront pas plus mal et n'en resteront pas moins légitimement respectés;

La mémoire outragé de notre illustre ami ne s'en conservera pas moins parmi nous chère et grandement honorée, et un jour viendra sans doute où sur cette tombe, sur laquelle le fanatisme a versé des injures, au lieu des prières, s'élèvera un monument pour venger l'injure et consacrer la légitime admiration de nos concitoyens pour celui qui a été à la fois un cœur généreux, un écrivain de race, un bel orateur et un profond penseur!

NOTES

1. See Elie Kedourie, *Afghani and 'Abduh: An Essay on Religious Unbelief and Political Activism in Modern Islam*, 1966.
2. Kedourie, *The Chatham House Version*, pp. 320–1.
3. H. H. Jessup, *Fifty-Three Years in Syria*, New York, 1910, vol. II, pp. 483–4.
4. See a biographical notice of Naqqash in Niqula Yusef, *A'lam min al-Iskandariyya* (Notables from Alexandria), Alexandria, 1969, pp. 464–9.
5. Kedourie, *Afghani and 'Abduh*, p. 23 and Salim al-Anhuri, *Sihr Harut* (Harut's Magic) Damascus, 1885, pp. 179–80.
6. A selection of Adib Ishaq's writings was first published at Alexandria in 1886, under the title *al-Durar* (The Gems). It was edited by one of his Syrian friends, Jirjis Mikha'il Nahhas. A fourth, much enlarged, edition appeared in Beirut in 1909, edited by his brother Awni Ishaq. Nahhas' introduction is included in the later edition. Awni Ishaq's principle of selection is stated on p. 8, and Nahhas' similar principle on p. 18.
7. The details are in Kedourie, *Afghani and 'Abduh*, pp. 32 and 36.
8. The drunkenness is mentioned in Abd al-Latif Hamza, *Adab al-maqala al-suhufiyya fi Misr* (The Art of the Newspaper Article in Egypt), vol. II, Cairo, 1950, p. 15. The obituary was published in the periodical *al-Hilal* and reproduced in The Gems, 4th ed.; the passage cited above is at p. 31.
9. It is printed in The Gems, 4th ed., pp. 220–3.
10. The Gems, 4th ed., a speech on 'Fanaticism and Toleration', pp. 50–8, and an article on 'Freedom', pp. 187–9, where the second estate in France prior to the Revolution are declared to have infringed the rules of religion 'through their meddling in temporal affairs until they established a kingdom within the kingdom'.
11. The Gems, 4th ed., p. 246; the fragment of the treatise is at pp. 244–68.
12. The Gems, 4th ed., p. 329.
13. Most reference works record Adib Ishaq's death as having taken place in 1885. But this is a mistake, which originates in a notice which appeared in *al-Hilal* and which is reproduced in The Gems, 4th ed., pp. 30–1. The correct date is undoubtedly 1884. This is what Anhuri, his friend, states in Harut's Magic, p. 145. It is confirmed by the fact that Afghani and Abduh reported his death briefly in *al-Urwa al-wuthqa* (Beirut ed., 1933, p. 464); as is well known *al-Urwa* was no longer appearing in June 1885 (it may be said in passing that such a perfunctory report of the death of so close a collaborator of Afghani's lends credence to the view that Afghani and Abduh considered Adib Ishaq a turncoat; see Kedourie, *Afghani and Abduh*, p. 32). Lastly a despatch from the French consul at Beirut reporting Adib Ishaq's death (which will be discussed below) is dated 6 September 1884 and thus conclusively establishes the correct date.
14. The Gems, 4th ed., pp. 10–11.
15. Archives du Ministère des A[ffaires] E[trangères], correspondance politique des consuls, Beyrouth vol. 27, Patrimonio's despatch no. 210, Beirut, 6 September 1884.
16. The Gems, p. 221.
17. The Gems, p. 28.

18. Nadia Farag, 'The Lewis Affair and the Fortunes of al-Muqtataf', *Middle Eastern Studies*, vol. 8, no. 1. (January 1972); 'The American University of Beirut', above.
19. Reminiscences of Faris Nimr as recorded in Zeine N. Zeine, *The Emergence of Arab Nationalism*, Beirut, 1966, p. 59n.
20. Text of letters from the press director of the vilayet as published in *Hadiqat al-akhbar*, Beirut, 4 September 1884, enclosed in Patrimonio's despatch cited above.
21. F. Bliss, *The Religions of Modern Syria and Palestine*, p. 112. See also two despatches on Muzuffar's encouragement of the freemasons and their campaign against the patriarch from the French consul general at Beirut A.E., Nouvelle Série, vol. 110, no. 17 of 17 March and no. 26 of 3 May 1907.
22. Rayhani, *al-Muhalafa al-thulathiyya* . . . 2nd ed., Beirut, 1972. The quotations are from pp. 119–20 and 110–11; Kedourie, *The Chatham House Version*, pp. 322–5; see also *al-Mashriq* vol 1 (1909), pp. 639 and 717, vol. 13 (1910), pp. 140ff., 390ff. and 477–8 for Cheikho's attacks on Rayhani; and vol. 21 (1923), pp. 478–9 for the report of his conversion to Islam.

6. Mr. Memmi on Jewishness and the Jews

Mr. Albert Memmi is a Tunisian Jew born in 1920, the son of a saddle-maker in the Jewish quarter of Tunis. Like so many Oriental Jews he was given an entrance into western, and more particularly, French culture through one of the excellent schools founded and maintained for the last century all over the Muslim world by the Alliance Israélite Universelle. Mr. Memmi is the author of two interesting novels, *La Statue de Sel* and *Agar* in which autobiography looms very large, and of a short essay, *Portrait du Colonisé précédé du Portrait du Colonisateur*, which contain reflections of a 'progressive' kind on what is known as imperialism and colonial liberation. *Portrait of a Jew* was first published in French in 1962, the English translation coming out a year later. Like the novels, the *Portrait* contains a large element of autobiography, and it is perhaps this which largely makes for its interest; like the essay, it is full of 'philosophical' speculations which arouse a great many objections, and make the work somewhat less readable than it might have been. The book is divided into four parts: The misfortune of being a Jew, The mythical Jew, The shadowy figure and The heritage. Of these, the second part is devoted to the discussion of various European racial and economic myths about the Jews; it is not only a showing-up of these popular idiocies for what they are (something which has been done many times), but also an incisive discussion of the role of myth in the structure of the psyche, a role which in no way depends on its truth or falsehood, however these terms may be understood. Chapter 21 in the fourth part also calls for special mention. It is a *locus classicus* of sociological religion, an account of what being Jewish means to someone of Jewish parentage who continues to consider himself a Jew without believing in or practising Judaism as usually and traditionally understood.

Mr. Memmi begins by asserting that there is 'a universal Jewish fate', that 'precisely the same situation exists everywhere'; towards the end of his book, he states that the portrait he has painted is a portrait of himself, but also by extension a portrait of other Jews; and other Jews describing their various experiences would, he feels confident, paint essentially the same portrait. To write of his own destiny —and by implication of the destiny of all Jews—seems to Mr. Memmi a necessary enterprise; necessary to him personally: 'I refuse', he writes, 'to spend my life brooding over my situation as a Jew. Since the issue cannot be dodged, it seemed to me preferable to

see it through, at least once.' Brooding is indeed the right word, and
the book is full of an obsessive self-pity and self-depreciation which
make of it yet another highly interesting example of the destructive
effect of Europe on Jews and Judaism. His attitude can be easily
illustrated from the abundance of statements which litter his book;
p. 21: 'I know scarcely any Jew who rejoices in being one'; p. 26,
quoting from a book by a certain Clara Malraux: 'You cannot explain to others what it is to be a Jew nowadays. It is as though you
suddenly discovered you had syphilis, as it was to have syphilis in
other times when there was no known treatment for it'; p. 27:
Judaism is a neurosis, an inescapable fatality; p. 28: no Jew is natural
or sure of himself; p. 31: Jews cannot peacefully lie still in the sun;
p. 32: Jews are always on the move; p. 38: 'The misfortune of the
Jew concerns all Jews, who are called Jews largely because of that
gloomy peculiarity'; p. 40: it is not easy for a Jew to be an explorer or
a world traveller; p. 54: 'I say in short, that I am a problem'; p. 57:
to be a Jew is first and foremost to find oneself called to account; p.
59: to be a Jew is to be set apart from other men; it is also to be set
apart from oneself; p. 60: a Jew cannot help looking at himself with
astonishment and suspicion; p. 80: the Jew 'is truly insolvent in his
private life both as a citizen and as an historical man'; etc., etc.
These statements, be it noted, are cast in the universal mode, pur-
porting to apply to all Jews at all times and everywhere; but this
universality is of course spurious, and what is supposed to describe a
universal and inescapable Jewish fate refers in reality, but in an
eccentric and mystificatory manner, to the sombre history of
European Jewry, when, after 1789, it tried to make its way into a
European society which seemed increasingly incapable of accommo-
dating religious or linguistic diversity. This foreshortened and inade-
quate view of Jewish history leads the author to try and force the
diversity of Jewish experience into his one mould. Thus, when he
comes to speak, as he rarely does, of his own Tunisian community in
relation to its Muslim overlord, he gives the impression that Jewish
disabilities under Muslim rule were of the same kind as Jewish disabilities under Christian rule; again, in order to show that the Jewish
fate is the same everywhere, he discovers a hitherto unknown catastrophe involving Ottoman Jewry, writing p. 44: '1908 to 1925:
15,000 Levantine Jews flee the revolt of the Young Turks'; finally, a
significant linguistic confusion is worth noting: the author has so
imbibed a certain modern European version of Jewish history that in
referring to the Jewish quarter of Tunis he call it a ghetto, thus
assuming a similarity in the situation of the Jews under Christian and
under Muslim rule.

The author also indulges in these dubious universalities when discussing other than Jewish matters. He writes, p. 238, that it is the desire of Jews to belong which makes them adhere in Italy to Fascism, in Germany to Nazism, and in France to Gaullism! We wonder whether this is sober truth or rhetoric which, in order to persuade, finds it convenient to speak of Jewish Nazis and to equate Fascism, Nazism and Gaullism in their attitude to politics in general and to Jews in particular. Or consider the following passage (pp. 51–2): 'Society as a whole calls the Jew to account, insistently and contin-uously; with bitter incidents to be sure, but on a chronic basis. There is no rupture, no real break between the anti-Semite and his people, but a gradation, an exasperation, a systematization. Just as there is a simple gradation and not a difference in nature between the good employer and the bad, and perhaps, ultimately, the slave-trader.' In this passage it is not so much the assertion about antisemitism as the analogy by which it is buttressed which is so arresting. In Mr. Memmi's book it is the employer as such who is the carrier of evil, and it must follow that the good employer is as bad as the slave-trader, is *perhaps* (to emulate the author's caution) responsible for the slave-trader. How convenient.

This work, then, must not be considered a treatise conveying infor-mation and wisdom about the world, but rather an exhibit which illustrates a state of mind, an experience, a prevalent illusion. We have to ask not whether what the author says is true, bur rather why exactly he should be saying the curious things he does say. And here we must put first, but perhaps not foremost the literary influence. The book is dedicated to Jean-Paul Sartre and bears many traces of the philosophical style associated with him, both in its strong points, such as the discussion on myth, and in its weak, such as the equation of a good employer with a slave-trader. But there is an even more direct influence, namely Sartre's own views not so much on Judaism as on Jewishness. Sartre's views may be summed up in a sentence which Mr. Memmi quotes towards the end of his book (p. 262): 'The Jew', writes Sartre, 'is a man whom other men consider a Jew and who is obliged to make decisions starting from the situation in which he is placed.' Mr. Memmi criticizes this view for making the Jew mere negativity, a creation of what others think of him; but if he criticizes it, he is nevertheless profoundly influenced by it as the quotations about the misfortune of being a Jew amply show. But it would be mistaken to think that Mr. Memmi speaks in this way only because he is Sartre's disciple. He says (p. 186) that he is neither a believer nor scarcely ever a practising Jew. Since therefore he has shed the only characteristics which have traditionally defined a Jew, it is no wonder that he is perplexed as to his own identity, that Sartre's definition of a Jew should attract him so much, and that he should exert himself to prove the falsity of the antisemitic vulgarities which popular science and universal education have spread in Europe in modern times, and which must loom very large in the horizon of one who is unsure of his own identity. What makes Mr. Memmi's case interesting is that, by origin, he belongs to Oriental Jewry, which has nestled for so long in the benign shadow of Islam and which Europe and Zionism have contributed so powerfully to dislodge and pulverize. Since neither popular science nor democracy, nor the theological odium which has so mercilessly pursued European Jewries, had any hold on the Muslim world, it would never have occurred to an Oriental Jew to take seriously those calumnies so familiar in Europe or to think them worth discussing. That Mr. Memmi should exert himself so much in this matter is an indication not merely of literary influence, but of the presence and influence of European anti-semitism in north Africa, which was introduced and propagated by the French settlers. This is common knowledge, but Mr. Memmi's own work, in particular *La Statue de Sel*, powerfully illustrates the corrosive effect of this anti-semitism on a young Jew who had grown up sheltered within the ancient communal institutions sanctioned by Islamic practice.

The autobiographical passages in the *Portrait* (which are much the most interesting part of the work) also strikingly illustrate this point. In a passage which occurs towards the beginning of the work (p. 37) the author writes: 'I do not know what other young men in the world discussed around campfires or during long winter nights, but the subject that interested us, the one we argued passionately was the nature of anti-Semitism.' One hopes for the author's sake that this is hyperbole, but if he did use his leisure in so dismal a fashion, the impulse surely cannot have arisen from the circumstances of indigenous society, must rather have been generated by contact with Europeans. Another passage in the book indicates that this was in fact so: 'I did not really understand', he writes (p. 61), 'what anti-Semitism was; only little by little did I become aware of it and, not until later, when I went to Europe where outsiders mingled freely with the Jewish community and I came in contact with non-Jews, did I fully realize their rejection of us.' In another passage (p. 83) he describes the shock which he sustained when he found that European writers whom he admired hated or despised Jews; writers like Shakespeare, Molière, Voltaire and Gide ('Gide! Gide whom I admired so much ... Gide of all men ...'). Finally, there was an experience beside which literary abuse and the settlers' malice was of little import, namely the short German occupation of Tunis and the Nazi terrorism which the author personally experienced. We may then fairly say that the book is a quite typical reaction to European culture and to its persistent anti-Judaism which, when the author was growing up, was in an acute and murderous phase. Typical also in a sadder and deeper sense, in that like so many European Jews in the modern period, whether 'assimilationist' or 'Zionist' he has taken over the assumptions and attitudes of the enemies of the Jews. A personal experience here comes to mind. As an adolescent in Baghdad during the second world war, I came to know an Italian Jew, Enzo Sereni, a Zionist long settled in Palestine who, under cover of war work, had been sent by the Palestine Zionists to preach their creed to the Jews of Iraq, whom they could not otherwise have hoped to reach. Sereni was in many ways an attractive figure with a gift for gaining the confidence and devotion of the young. I was much attracted by his stimulating and varied discourse—for he was not the usual narrow and dim-witted ideologue. But I still vividly remember the occasion when he started discussing what he called 'Jewish self-hate', and how incomprehensible and repulsive the whole notion was to me. What I suppose he meant—though this, of course, I only appreciated much later—was the state of mind of European Jews who, being introduced to a seemingly superior European culture in the eighteenth century and finding some of the foremost representatives of this culture, people like Voltaire, Kant, Lichtenberg, profoundly and eloquently anti-Jewish, believed that this too was a necessary part of Enlightenment. Some such attitude, or some variant of it, has been widely prevalent among European Jews and has led either to 'self-hate', or an apologetic, defensive attitude, or a radical rejection of Jewish life as it is, in favour of some bronzed, heroic future exaltation. This last variant is of course the corollary of Zionism, and the mythic way by which it rejoins anti-semitism. This attitude Mr. Memmi has imbibed, as may be seen from the quotations given above. He has imbibed it in a specifically Zionist form, and we find him exhibiting that strand of populist demagoguery which east European conditions wove into Zionism. Thus, as a young man, he disliked rich Jews because they were rich; he records (p. 124) how he and his young Zionist comrades 'were so furiously angry at the rich German Jews that we received the announcement of their early tragedies rather coldly and, I must confess, almost with satisfaction: these powerful communities had always refused to receive our comrades, whether as propagandists or fund-raisers'. Again (p. 130): 'I had no doubt that the real Jew was the poor Jew, for I myself was the real Jew. Perhaps, as luck would have it, the ghetto [he means the Jewish quarter of Tunis] may have saved me from a little of that torturing Judeophobia so common among Jews themselves.' Common as Mr. Memmi may think such sentiments, at least among his own forbears they must have been highly uncommon.

Along with so many other commonplaces of European culture, Mr. Memmi has also acquired a taste for political salvation, and developed a need for being absorbed in a mass. Religion for him is strictly civic in character, a social cement, something like the rite of a kin-group, or the ceremonial union between a polis and its tutelary god. Thus he complains that as a Jew in France, he cannot take part in Christmas, that he cannot identify himself with Clovis, and goes so far in confounding Jewish history with his own yearnings that he speaks (p. 216) of 'the persistence of my people in seeking to be admitted into the confraternity of their fellow men, something they have sought so humbly for centuries'! The assumption here is that the relation between citizens is and ought to be like the relation between brothers. For Mr. Memmi this seems the obvious truth. He does not appear to realize that in fact this is a very recent (and catastrophic) notion spawned by the *sans-culottes* of European political thought, or that (with the notable exception of ancient Greece) all that men, including 'my people', generally wanted out of politics, before the last hundred and fifty years or so, was only to secure to them a mere modicum of law and order.

Far then from being an account of the universal Jewish fate, this book is so much a product purely of its time and place that it is unable to master and explain even the author's own particular experience. It is a book to sadden a reader, but not so much in the sense intended by the author; sadden him not at the recital of Jewish sufferings in modern times (which many others have rehearsed more eloquently than Mr. Memmi); but at a reaction to these sufferings so uncritical, so sentimental and lacking in fortitude, so much the unconscious victim of current slogans, so passively immersed in the turgid flow of words and events, that it becomes a prime example of that spiritual subversion by which modern Europe has given so refined a twist to the ancient oppression.

7. The Politics of Political Literature: Kawakabi, Azoury and Jung

It is now generally agreed that Abd al-Rahman al-Kawakibi and Negib Azoury are the first to have formulated in books the view that the Arabs were entitled to secede from the Ottoman empire and to have the Caliphate transferred back to them. The arguments by which such a demand was supported are certainly worth examining; but since these arguments are not academic or scientific, but political or practical, it becomes equally interesting to examine the circumstances in which they were published, and the political and other purposes which they furthered. So far as Kawakibi is concerned, Sylvia G. Haim has drawn attention to certain evidence tending to show that *Umm al-qura*, in which Kawakibi advanced a claim on behalf of the Arab caliphate, was probably a piece of Khedivial propaganda, a weapon which may have been of some use in furthering the Khedive Abbas' various ambitions.[1]

It is possible to adduce further evidence in support of the view that about the time of the appearance of Kawakibi's pamphlet, the Khedive was engaged in manœuvres and intrigues against the Ottoman sultan and the caliphate. It is well-known that the Young Turk Murad al-Daghistani (1853–1912), the editor of *Mizan*, fled to Cairo in 1896 and that he was there in touch not only with other Young Turks but also with the Khedive. In a letter to Salisbury of June 1896, Cromer described Murad as 'an impecunious scamp' and declared that the Khedive's association with the Young Turks was 'rather a curious local development'.[2] Murad seems to have concocted, together with his Young Turk friends and with the Khedive's help, a plot for terrorizing Abd al-Hamid by spreading propaganda in favour of an Arab caliphate. The caliphate was indeed at that time a main theme of anti-Hamidian Young Turk propaganda in Constantinople itself. In the latter half of 1896 a pamphlet was circulating in religious circles of the capital arguing the lawfulness of deposing a Caliph 'who causes a state of things injurious to the Moslems and subversive of religion', or who is 'disastrous to the nation', or if 'the Mussulman world or part of it' objects to him, and even the lawfulness of killing him if he 'leaves the straight road and turns aside to violence and tyranny'. Again, at the beginning of 1897 a proclamation was disseminated in Constantinople describing the parlous condition of the empire and declaring that the cause of all this was Abd al-Hamid 'unjustly called the Khalif'.[3]

As for Abbas himself, it would seem that his interest in the caliphate dated from a visit to Constantinople in 1895. There, as Cromer later reported, he met Jamal al-Din al-Afghani who 'appears to have dropped some vague hints that the Khedive might advantageously place himself at the head of the Moslems in Egypt and Arabia and acquire a position independent of the Sultan'. Cromer thought that Abbas was 'coquetting' with ideas of this sort. He had tried, in 1896, to abolish the usual prayers for the sultan in the mosques of Cairo, but the ulemas opposed this attempt so strongly that it was dropped, though it seems that the change was effected in the Khedive's private mosque. Abbas also sent a strong partisan of his as an emissary to Medina, whose object remained mysterious, 'but', Cromer observed, 'he has manifestly something to conceal, as I hear that he denies having undertaken the journey'. Again, the Khedive wanted to send a German-Swiss convert to Islam, Dr. Hess, who posed 'as an extreme partisan of the Khedive', on a mission to Ibn al-Rashid.[4] The reports of the French representative at Cairo add more details to this picture. Writing at the end of 1897 of Murad bey's visit to Cairo the previous year, he asks: 'Who can go so far as to assert that the dream of an Arab caliphate was not [then] agitated, since the replacement of the Sultan was at that time the essence of Young Turk policy?

'Do I have to recall', he went on, 'that during the same period, some Turkish journalists who were writing in support of Abdul Hamid's policy, were beaten up and abused by some young men belonging to His Highness' palace? These young men would surely not have acted in this way had they not been more or less directly authorized.' The poet Wali al-Din Yakan (1873–1921) happened—as he records in his memoirs—to be one of those who were beaten up on this occasion, and confirms the French diplomat's assertion that his assailants were members of Abbas' entourage.[5]

These activities of the Khedive's did not remain hidden from Abd al-Hamid. As an informant of Cromer's reported in October 1897, the journey of Abbas' emissary to Medina became known at Constantinople, where it was also learnt that a manifesto attacking the sultan's right to the caliphate had been distributed in Arabia. Also, Murad bey, who had been enticed back to Constantinople from Europe in August 1897,[6] revealed the Khedive's ambitions, it seems, to Abd al-Hamid.[7] It is interesting to observe that at about that time the Ottoman authorities in Syria received orders to expel all Egyptians from the country. Both Cromer and the French representative agree that this expulsion was connected with the Khedive's activities.[8]

But it is evident that in pursuing these intrigues the Khedive was not executing a long-term policy, that the Young Turks and the propaganda for an Arab caliphate were for him a weapon, a lever, to force the sultan to give him more consideration, or to get favourable treatment for his financial interests in the empire. Thus, after having supported Murad and the Young Turks, he broke with them and tried to mend his relations with Abd al-Hamid by buying up at considerable cost Young Turk newspapers. 'I understand', wrote Cromer in December 1897, 'that the latter propose to accept the money and then begin their attack in some other form in the hope of getting more. Further, Princess Nazli [niece of Isma'il Pasha and thus second cousin to Abbas] recently translated Schiller's "William Tell" into Turkish. It was intimated to her by the Khedive that the work had a revolutionary tendency. She at once expressed her willingness to sell the whole issue at 4 shillings a copy—an offer which was accepted.'[9] But the sultan seems to have remained alert and suspicious of his vassal. Thus in February 1898 the Mufti of Gaza, his son and his brother were arrested and deported: 'A reason that has been given to me privately', wrote a correspondent to the British consul at Jerusalem, 'is that the Khedive hopes to come to El Arish on the 15th of Shawal, and for fear of intrigue they were sent out of the way, as the Mufti has influence over a large section of the Arabs', while his son was 'the head of the thieves'. Again, at the other end of the Arabic-speaking provinces, in Basra, the British vice-consul cabled on 27 November 1899, that the sultan had personally telegraphed to the vali to use every endeavour to arrest emissaries whom the Amir of Najd was sending to the Khedive with valuable presents and 'dangerous advice concerning, I believe, Mecka'; the vice-consul added that the sultan was evidently very uneasy about the Arab coast of the Persian Gulf.[10]

The sultan was perhaps right to be so wary. For it was about then that Kawakibi appeared in Cairo, where his activities were to show that Abbas may have decided to resume his earlier anti-Hamidian activities. Kawakibi is said to have appeared in Cairo in 1898, having left his native Aleppo in obscure circumstances. In Cairo he came to be known to Abbas, and there is little doubt that the journey to Arabia and to Somaliland which he made some time between his arrival in Cairo and his death in 1902 was undertaken for political purposes on behalf of Abbas and perhaps also of Italy, or perhaps on their joint behalf. This is what is hinted by the discreet Rashid Rida, and strongly affirmed by the Lebanese journalist Ibrahim Salim al-Najjar (d. 1957) who knew Kawakibi in Cairo: 'He went to Aden', writes Najjar, 'to persuade the Arabs to recognize the Khedive of Egypt as caliph, a mission which I believe need and necessity compelled him to undertake.'[11]

In September 1899 the sultan sent a message to the British ambassador, to complain that certain 'ill-disposed and wicked persons' had formed a secret committee in Egypt in order to plot against him as caliph, and to send emissaries to the Hijaz to further their intrigues.[12] The complaint was possibly based on some report of Kawakibi's journey—if the journey took place that year—or it may have referred to Kawakibi's book *Umm al-qura*. The book, it will be recalled, is couched in the form of proceedings of a secret society of that name meeting in Mecca. *Umm al-qura* became generally known when Rashid Rida serialized it in the fifth volume of *al-Manar* between April 1902 and February 1903. But this was not, it seems, its first publication. In his doctoral dissertation, 'The Relations between Abbas Hilmi and Lord Cromer', Dr. Mohamad El-Mesady describes what must be the first edition of *Umm al-qura*, a copy of which he examined in the library of the Oriental Institute at Oxford.[13] Dr. Mesady writes: 'The title-page shows the place and the year of publication: Port Said, 1316 A.H. The year was engraved with the title, which was used in its original form for later editions. . . . The date 1316, suggests that the book was published before June 1899.'[14] It is not likely that this first edition was published commercially. Rather, it must have been printed for clandestine distribution in the Ottoman empire, and carefully designed to mislead its readers into the belief that here were the actual minutes of a secret society meeting clandestinely at Mecca. The fiction was reinforced by Port Said being shown as the place of publication, thus confirming the statement in the 'minutes' that Port Said or Kuwayt would become the secret headquarters of the society.[15] And it does seem to be the case that many readers were misled into believing that the society of *Umm al-qura* really existed. Thus the French representative at Cairo went so far as to send home in 1902 a note on this society. The note, which is unsigned, declares that the society had been founded 20 years previously with the aim of deposing the Ottoman caliph in favour of the Khedive Tawfiq, that it had then a branch in Mecca which was dissolved when Tawfiq died, and that its members were the allies of the Young Turks.[16] And as late as 1932, Professor H. A. R. Gibb could refer to the 'meeting held at Mecca in 1898 behind closed doors'[17] as though it had really taken place.

When this first edition of *Umm al-qura* appeared in 1899, Kawakibi had been only a year or so in Egypt; he was not particularly rich (indeed, there is a story that he was a paid monthly salary of £50 by Abbas),[18] and it is highly unlikely that he would have been able to produce on his own and distribute without the help of a publisher this long and elaborate document. A passage towards the end of *Umm al-qura* indicates who was most likely to benefit from its propagation.

In this passage the president invokes Abbas' protection for the society, and his help for those who are engaged in 'upholding religion', 'and no wonder for he is a goodly young prince brought up to be solicitous for religion and zealous for '*arabiyya*'.[19] That Abbas was behind *Umm al-qura* is a probability that amounts to a moral certainty. What was his purpose? No doubt the same as in 1895–6. The note sent by the French representative in 1902 gives us a clue. The only aim of the society, this note states, 'is to frighten the Sultan and to make him believe that the old society is still in existence and that it still has followers who plot against him in Syria'.

II

A few years after the launching of the imaginary society of *Umm al-qura*, another society, scarcely less imaginary was announced to the world. This was the *Ligue de la patrie arabe* with which the names of Negib Azoury and his co-adjutor Eugène Jung are associated. What then were their objects? The received account has it that Azoury, an Ottoman official in Jerusalem, after a disagreement with the governor, leaves his post for Cairo, and proceeds thence to Paris where he publishes a book, *le Réveil de la nation arabe*, establishes the *Ligue*, and for a year or so in 1907–8 in collaboration with Eugène Jung publishes a monthly, *l'Indépendance arabe*, which is supposed to be the organ of this society. The book, the society and the periodical advocated the Arab cause and called for the secession of the Arab provinces from the Ottoman empire and their constitution into an independent Arab kingdom. But so far as is known no one, except Azoury and Jung, was active in the *Ligue* or indeed belonged to it. How and why did they come to act as they did?

Azoury seems to have been a Maronite or a Uniate Catholic who graduated from the *Mülkiye* in Constantinople and followed for a period the lectures at the Ecole des sciences politiques in Paris. In 1898, when he was about 25 years of age, he was appointed assistant to the governor of Jerusalem. According to A. Boppe, the French diplomat who was, as his despatches show, very well informed on Ottoman affairs and who was consul-general at Jerusalem while Azoury was there, this provincial appointment was a sinecure rewarding Azoury for giving up Young Turk activities and declaring his loyalty to the sultan; such an appointment, he stated, was known in the Ottoman administration as that of an *icamete memour* or *chargé de résider*. While in Jerusalem he married the daughter of the local sub-agent of the *Messageries maritimes* and thus became the brother-in-law of the governor's dragoman Bechara Habib. About 1904, he seems to have fallen out both with the governor, Kiazim bey, and with his brother-in-law. F. Wiet, Boppe's successor at Jerusalem, suggests that Azoury wanted his brother-in-law's post for himself, then aspired to be made director of the *Régie des tabacs* at Jaffa, and that on being disappointed in both ambitions he quarrelled with the governor and started a campaign against him. The director of the trades school run by the *Alliance israélite* in Jerusalem, Albert Antébi, also suggests that Azoury in some way blackmailed his wife's family by threatening to denounce them to the authorities.[20]

Azoury himself later on declared that his conflict with Kiazim bey was personal and that it was 'The pretext for which I was waiting to put in hand the schemes by which I had been haunted since childhood'. In fact, *le Réveil de la nation arabe* contains a great deal of invective against Kiazim and Azoury's brother-in-law, both of whose photographs are reproduced in it. Kiazim and Bechara Habib are accused of having made immense fortunes out of bribes, and Kiazim of having attempted to assassinate Azoury.[21] In any event, Azoury finding himself at odds with the governor, thought it expedient to leave for Egypt, in the first half of 1904. In Cairo he began a campaign against Kiazim in an obscure newspaper, *al-Ikhlas*, accusing him of corruption, and taking care that the relevant issues should be sent, through foreign post offices, to notables and officials in Jerusalem. Reporting on these attacks before the identity of their author had become known, Boppe wrote that it was difficult to know whether this was an attempt to blackmail an able administrator who believed that the end justified the means, or whether this was a product of real hatred, the secret revenge of an official in disgrace.[22] I have not been able to consult *al-Ikhlas* so as to determine the character of Azoury's campaign, but the accusations he makes in *le Réveil de la nation arabe* probably indicate its main lines. Antébi's letter gives other details. He declares that Azoury denounced Palestinian Jewry, the *Alliance israélite* and its agricultural school, Mikveh Israel, represented Kiazim as someone sold to the Jews, and the native Muslims and Christians as enslaved to them, for all of which Antébi was responsible.[23] Again, what Azoury wrote in *le Réveil* seems to confirm Antébi's statement. This book Azoury announces as the complement of another work then in preparation to be entitled *The Universal Jewish Peril*. The latter book was to bring proof of what the Jews really are from the Bible itself which, as interpreted by them, is 'a dangerous and immoral' book, constituting the most terrible indictment of this people. Readers might ask, Why speak of Jews in a work dealing with the Arabs? The answer is that 'exactly at the moment when Israel is so near to success, our movement comes in order to destroy its projects of universal domination', and that the Arab nation and the Jews who want to reconstitute 'on a very large scale' the ancient kingdom of Israel have to fight until one side is victorious over the other, and that the 'fate of the whole world' will depend on the outcome of this clash.[24] *The Universal Jewish Peril* was never published and the rest of *le Réveil* apart from a passage on the immense, centralized power of the Jews and on the dangers of Zionism hardly mentions Jews or even Zionist enterprise, though here and there Azoury refers to the power of the Jews in having innocent people arrested, etc. It is clear that whatever he may have seen of Jews in Palestine, and whatever their activities, he was not concerned with a local issue or specific grievances. What was taking place in Palestine was part of a world-wide conspiracy which if it were to succeed, would have fateful, disastrous consequences; but which the Arab awakening will now fortunately foil in time. Azoury, in other words, voices the anti-Judaism and anti-semitism fashionable among the *bien-pensants* in France at the turn of the century and with which no one who, like Azoury, was in Paris in the late 1890s could have failed to be acquainted. Mr. A. Hourani writes that the name, *Ligue de la patrie arabe* clearly echoes that of the anti-Dreyfusard *Ligue de la patrie française*. If we remember that this Ligue was at its apogee precisely in the late 1890s, then Mr. Hourani's suggestion will also throw a welcome light on the probable sources of Azoury's preoccupation with the Jewish peril.[25]

Azoury's campaign in *al-Ikhlas* meant that he had burnt his boats in Jerusalem. It would seem that as a result of it, charges of treason were brought against him at Constantinople, that he was tried and condemned to death *in absentia*. This is what he himself asserts, and what the French consul-general at Jerusalem also states.[26] What the exact charges were is not now known, but the fact is that he left Cairo for Paris probably towards the end of 1904; and whether his departure was connected with this sentence is also obscure. He declares in *le Réveil* that there was an attempt to extradite him from Egypt.[27] In any case, he had hardly arrived in Paris when he began printing proclamations, both in French and Arabic, in the name of the *Ligue de la patrie arabe*. These proclamations attacked Turkish domination and exploitation of the Arabs, and called for the secession of the Arab provinces from the Ottoman empire. The *Ligue*, Azoury declared, had made 'immense progress in only a few months. We already have committees in all the large cities of Palestine, Syria and Mesopotamia, as well as in Egypt and Syria; all the enlightened Great Powers are unanimous in approving our movement, and we can be sure of their sympathies.' He also advised 'our fellow-citizens, to obey confidently the Arab governors who will take the place of the Turkish valis and mutassarifs'. The arguments of the proclamation were taken up and amplified in *le Réveil de la nation arabe* which the well-known publisher, Plon, brought out, at the beginning of 1905. In his book, as in his proclamations, Azoury spoke of the Arab, Kurdish and Armenian national movements and argued that they would help one another in destroying Turkish domination. In the book he went so far as to say that the three revolutions, Arab, Kurdish and Armenian, would be accomplished in the space of twelve days and without any bloodshed.[28] This fancifulness is also evident in his discussion of the caliphate: 'Last year', he wrote, 'a committee composed of some ulemas met in Mecca in order to discuss the establishment there of a purely religious Arab caliphate: this committee decided to entrust this important dignity to a Christian foreigner rather than abandon it to the loathsome Abdul-Hamid.'![28]

The bulk of Azoury's book is, however, taken up with a discussion of the interests of the great powers in the Ottoman empire. He is very anti-Russian. If Russia gets established at the Dardanelles, he warns, 'we Easterners must renounce all hope of national independence'. Britain is also afraid of Russian penetration in the Ottoman empire, and this fear is so great that she would not mind any power taking over the Levant, provided it was not Russia. This leads him to argue in favour of a French protectorate: 'France is the nation which has more rights and more interests than anyone else in the Ottoman Empire'; France must not renounce her religious protectorate in the Levant: 'domination of the Mediterranean may be found under the paving stones of the Holy Sepulchre'; 'No one will have the right to govern us but France, and no Power will be so heartily acclaimed when landing in the Arab countries on the day when the dismemberment of the Turkish Empire will have been decided.'[29] It was this anti-Russian stance and this advocacy of the use by France of her traditional right to protect Catholics in the Ottoman empire which must have led Wiet, in his despatch of 8 February 1905, cited above, to state that Azoury's proclamation and his book were inspired, in part at least, by the writings of the 'sieur Alphonse Alonzo dont ce Consulat Général a eu, à diverses reprises, l'occasion de s'occuper', and that Azoury's writings were 'des compilations qui n'ont pas le mérite de la nouveauté.' And it is a fact that Alonzo, who seems to have been a resident of Jerusalem, and to have been in the 1870s (until he was dismissed in 1878) an attaché at the French consulate-general there, did publish three pamphlets in 1901, 1902 and 1904, in which he denounced Russian ambitions in the Levant, and the neglect by the governments of the Third Republic of the French right to protect Catholic clergy and establishments in the Ottoman empire.[30] Wiet's hint of Alonzo's influence over Azoury also suggests another channel through which anti-semitism could have come to the latter, since as is well-known, anti-semitic themes were then current in Catholic circles in the Levant.[31]

Using the French post offices in the Ottoman empire, Azoury set about distributing his proclamations to officials and notables. Wiet's despatch of 8 February 1905, was occasioned by the arrival of copies of these proclamations in Jerusalem and the request of the governor that the French post office should refrain from distributing them. With his despatch, Wiet included a French and an Arabic version of a manifesto addressed to all the '*Citoyens de la Patrie Arabe asservie aux Turcs*'. Writing on 1 February of the same year, Captain A. F. Townshend, British vice-consul at Adana, also forwarded a copy of the same proclamation in French together with another one, also in French, addressed to the '*Nations éclairées et humanitaires de l'Europe et de l'Amérique du Nord*'. The circulars, the vice-consul stated, had been sent to most of the consuls at Adana, to hotels and to several prominent residents, and had caused quite a stir amongst the officials, written as they were in a 'confident and ambitious tone'.[32] From Beirut, again, the French acting consul-general reported shortly afterwards the arrival of Azoury's manifesto, He too declared that it had caused a stir in official circles 'which its author, a certain Négib Azoury, ex-secretary of the Governor of Jerusalem, a most suspect and disreputable person [*personnage des plus suspects et des moins recommandables*] intends, no doubt, to exploit.'[33]

But in the Levant, there was precious little for Azoury to exploit. The arrival of his manifesto coincided with a flare-up of fighting in the Yemen and desertion there by Ottoman troops originating from Syria. This conjunction must have worried the Ottoman government which, in the summer of 1905 sent an investigatory commission to Beirut and elsewhere to find out whether there was any truth in the rumours of an Arab nationalist movement. The French consul in Damascus, reporting the arrival of the commission, wrote that he himself had looked into these rumours and was convinced that they were without foundation. The desertions in the Yemen were chiefly the result of privations and bad treatment, and it was an error to attribute them to a political movement. A movement of this kind was more likely to be found among the Damascene notables, but nothing in their attitudes or the language they held, or their antecedents indicated that they were ready to run the risks of conspiring for the benefit of a pretender who was anyway yet to be found. It was only some young men, most of them government officials, who had sometimes expressed themselves in an imprudent manner.[34]

His colleague in Beirut reported that the commission had had the governor of Acre dismissed for being too complaisant in his attitude to the local notables and that one of these, Shaykh As'ad Shuqayr was exiled from Acre to a place near Tyre. We may recall that As'ad Shuqayr was, between 1908 and 1918, one of the pillars of the Young Turk movement in the Levant, and this will serve to emphasize the point that subversive attitudes in the Arabic-speaking provinces during Abd al-Hamid's reign, were not necessarily, or even frequently, connected with Arab nationalism.[35]

The British consul-general in Beirut for his part reported about the same time house searches by the police who were looking for treasonable documents. These, he thought, were instigated by spies taking advantage of the disorders in the Yemen by forwarding mendacious reports. 'The Arabs', he wrote,' have always been a more or less discontented race under Turkish rule, and there is no doubt that they are affected by the revolutionary condition of many other parts of the Empire and especially that of the Yemen, but I am not aware,' he concluded, 'of the formation of any revolutionary league by Syrians.'[36]

The last word on Azoury's manifestos and their effect in the Levant may be left to the sagacious Boppe. In his despatch of 26 September 1905 from Constantinople quoted above, Boppe declared that the Arab national movement so much agitated in the French press existed only in the imagination of some journalists, and the reports from the consuls confirmed this. For instance, the consul at Aleppo had reported the existence there of a 'secret committee of Arab independence', but the declarations made to the consul by those who were alleged to be its two principal leaders were no more worthy of confidence than the allegations spread in Paris by the author of the *Réveil de la nation arabe*. It was the reviews of this book in the French press, Boppe affirmed, which had ended by creating an Arab question.

Boppe concluded his despatch by suggesting that the ministry might like to find out how Azoury, 'this adventurer' as he described him, was able to finance himself in Paris, and who had helped him to get a publisher like Plon to bring out his book. The records of the ministry do indeed throw some light on the manner in which Azoury acquired at least one official patron in the French official world who may have been of some help in smoothing the newcomer's path and opening useful doors for him. In 1905 it so happened that a small commercial printer approached the Imprimerie nationale in Paris and explained that he had been asked by clients to print an Arabic text. As he did not have Arabic type himself, he was enquiring whether the Imprimerie nationale would undertake the work for him. Something about the inquiry aroused the suspicion of the director, M. Christian, and he wished to have the Arabic text translated. For some unknown reason it was Azoury who was called upon to do the translation. The text turned out to have nothing commercial about it, but to be rather a call to Muslims to support the Ottoman caliphate and to oppose British and French intrigues in the Muslim world. The authorities suspected that a north African whose long-standing anti-French activities were known to them, was the author of this document, and that the Germans were somehow behind it. It would seem that Azoury became for Christian more than a mere translator, that he began purveying 'information' about pan-Arab intrigues which so impressed the director that we find him writing to the ministry of Foreign Affairs to ask that it should give Azoury his fare to Egypt, whither he wanted to go. Whether the ministry complied with this request is unknown, but in January 1906 we find Azoury in Cairo writing to Christian offering to organize an insurrection in Syria in favour of France, for a sum of 100,000 francs. If the French government were to pay this sum, declared Azoury, this might decide groups of businessmen and nationalists with whom he was in touch to provide the funds needed. Some six weeks later, Azoury wrote again to say that he was on the trail of a frightful intrigue against France details of which he could not possibly disclose by letter. Would the French authorities, therefore, give him, his wife and child return passages and a month's expenses in Paris so that he might disclose in person what he had learnt? Also, in return for this precious information, would the French give him the 100,000 francs so that he might start the movement he had sketched in his earlier letter?[37] It is not known with what response Azoury's proposition met, but for the next ten years or so he was to try, in partnership with Eugène Jung, to extract from various governments large sums of money by promising to start, on their behalf, rebellions in the Ottoman empire.

Azoury's partnership with Jung was another fruit of his visit to Paris in 1905. Jung, who described himself as a former 'Vice-Résident de France' in Tonkin, declares that he met Azoury following an article on Mascat he had written in the *Revue libre*, and that they then organized a press campaign, presumably when Azoury's book was published, in favour of Arab independence. In 1906 Jung himself published a book, *Les Puissances devant la révolte arabe*, which he dedicated to Azoury and in which the latter was described as '*le chef et le créateur du mouvement arabe en Syrie*'. In this book, Jung took the line, later to be made popular by Antonius in his book, *The Arab Awakening*, that it was Muhammad ibn Abd al-Wahhab who had begun in Najd the Arab national movement and that his movement was at once national and religious. We may note that Azoury and Jung were Antonius' precursors in another respect. The periodical, *l'Indépendance arabe*, of which Azoury was *directeur* and Jung *rédacteur en chef*, and which appeared in Paris between April

1907 and September 1908, printed in Arabic on the cover of each of its issues from July 1907 to June 1908 in letters of gold a large extract from Ibrahim al-Yaziji's well-known poem which begins: 'Arise and awaken O ye Arabs'. This first half of the first verse figures, as is common knowledge, as an epigraph on the title-page of Antonius' book. It is somewhat curious to see Antonius none the less sourly dismissing Azoury in two curt paragraphs as one of those advocates of the Arab revolt who, as result of foreign education' 'had strayed from the sources of its inspiration'[38]

Azoury's ten-year partnership with Jung was based on an essentially simple gambit: by means of books, periodicals which they published, or articles which they succeeded in planting in newspapers and magazines, they would create the impression that a powerful 'Arab movement' existed in the Ottoman empire; they would then claim that Azoury was the head of this movement and able to control it; and they would then offer its use to this or that government against large quantities of money and arms. No government was in fact taken in, but Azoury and Jung never tired from pursuing the same manœuvre again and again. Azoury's movements between 1906 and the Young Turk revolution in July 1908 are not certain, but he seems to have divided his time between Paris and Cairo. In a despatch of 29 January 1908, Chavandier de Valdrome, the French representative at Cairo, described Azoury as the Paris correspondent of a French-language periodical, *l'Egypte*. This despatch referred to an earlier one, written the previous May (which is not in the file) when Azoury had 'sollicité une mission de notre gouvernement', and the French representative had been asked to report on him. The *mission* is unspecified but it may well have been of the same kind as that he had proposed to Christian at the beginning of 1906. In that earlier despatch Chavandier had referred to 'the campaign conducted by this Syrian who had offered his services to various diplomatic missions and who has tried very adroitly to make use of his connections with each of them in order to set intrigues on foot and retail interested information.'[39]

Azoury seems to have used again shortly afterwards the same tactic of referring to alleged connexions in high places in order to impress an official interlocutor. As is well known, after the Young Turk revolution in July 1908, elections were ordered to be held in the Ottoman empire. Azoury appeared in Jerusalem and according to the French consul-general put himself forward as a '*candidat arabe*'. He visited the consul-general and 'producing a letter addressed to himself by Mr. Pouliat, Senator, seemed very disappointed that I had not received from Your Excellency or the [Constantinople] Embassy a recommendation in his favour or the Croix de Chevalier of the

Légion d'Honneur which, so he alleged with a wealth of details, had been promised to him with a view to helping him getting elected'. Azoury also asked the consul-general to put in a word for him with the Latin Patriarchate, but the consul-general excused himself from intervening, without specific instructions, in party quarrels. He expressed his regret, but, he added, '*J'avoue que ce ne fut guère que par devoir de courtoisie*'.[40]

Azoury did not succeed in getting himself elected. He seems thereafter to have established himself at Cairo. Among his various enterprises there, was to become 'Foreign Secretary' of a Young Egypt Party promoted by a certain Idris Raghib who was also proprietor of *l'Egypte* for which, as has been seen, Azoury had acted as Paris correspondent before 1908. In this capacity Azoury had been, according to the January 1908 despatch of the French representative at Cairo cited above, quite hostile to the Egyptian nationalists. But a writer observed in 1911 that *l'Egypte* had by then a 'singular and marked sympathy with the Extremist cause' and was 'belived to be subsidized by the Extremist Party'. *L'Egypte* would seem to have been published in both an English and French edition which 'offered entirely different policies to their readers, the former being pro-English, while the latter was furiously Anglophobe in its tendencies'.[41]

That this was the line taken by *l'Egypte* Azoury himself confirms in a letter to Jung dated 17 November 1912, in which he tells him that France must not repeat the mistake of 1882 by leaving the British with a free hand in the east: '*As for ourselves,*' he declares '*we shall always be loyal to France and it will not be our fault if we have no success. We must have help, and we must be told what we are required to do; we will then accomplish what is expected of us.*' Azoury goes on to say that they were not asking for a support which might look compromising, or for some extraordinary aid: all that was wanted was 600,000 francs 'to calm down the impatient, win over the discontented and perfect the organization of our action in such a way as to remain in control of it until the end'.[42]

Jung transmitted this letter to the ministry of foreign affairs, and followed it up with other letters asking for money, arms and the *légion d'honneur* for himself and Azoury. He was interviewed several times by an official and told in the end that his schemes were not acceptable. Presumably to get rid of his importunities, he was given a small sum of money (an *allocation*) to reward him for his services as Paris correspondent of *l'Egypte*.[43] In giving, over ten years later, a public—and abbreviated—account of his negotiations with the ministry, Jung records that while asking for a sum of 600,000 francs, 4,000 rifles and 2 million bullets, he also told the authorities that a banker would immediately advance the money if he could have the oral approval of the French government for this scheme. The banker, hints Jung, was a Jew, for he said that 'this was the result of interesting negotiations between the Jews and the *Comité arabe*.' These negotiations are probably on a par with Azoury's and Jung's other negotiations which were no more than attempts to embroil a party in their intrigues by alleging that some other, very powerful, party was supporting them, or was controlled by them. But, in view of what Azoury had to write about the Jewish peril, it is interesting to see here the help of the Jews invoked and made use of.[44]

Shortly before Jung made his approach to the French ministry of foreign affairs, Azoury in Cairo was trying to get Italy to back his schemes. On the occasion of the Tripoli war, he approached the Italian representative at Cairo, and offered to raise a revolt in Syria in the Italian interest, if the Italians would supply him with 10,000 rifles, with 200 bullets each. Eventually he came down to 2,000 rifles, but the Italians would not bite.[45]

The outbreak of war in the summer of 1914 must have seemed to Azoury and Jung a heaven-sent opportunity. Jung lost no time in approaching the French foreign office with plans for raising the Levant against the Ottomans. 'I must tell you', he wrote to Jules Cambon, the director-general of the ministry of foreign affairs, 'that one of the principal leaders of the Arab National Party is M. Négib Azoury bey ... now director of the newspaper *l'Egypte* in Cairo, and is preparing himself for action there.' It was, of course, of the highest importance to the partners that Azoury should be recognized as the leader of Arab nationalism. In *la Révolte arabe* Jung is quite sarcastic about the Arab congress which met in Paris in June 1913, pointing out that it consisted of twelve members, and an audience of forty-eight, 'among whom were numerous young students, a little girl, and two French missionaries'. All the same, his claims on behalf of his partner were not successful. On his visiting card which accompanied his letter to Cambon, someone noted: '*n'est pas connu de M. Cambon.*'[46]

Rebuffed by the French, Jung turned to the British embassy at Paris with the same proposals. He obtained an interview with a member of the embassy, Percy Loraine, and declared that he had been advised by the *cabinet* of the French foreign minister 'to explain the proposals which he had in mind to me personally at His Majesty's Embassy, and had added, so Monsieur Jung said, that they regarded the proposals as serious and important and thought that if Great Britain were to take any initiative on the lines which he suggested, as being the Power mainly interested in the Arab portions of the Ottoman Empire, the French government would fall in with the suggestions of His Majesty's Government'. Jung again paraded

Azoury as 'one of the leaders of the Independent Arab movement' which had 'a regular network of lodges all over Syria, Palestine and Mesopotamia' of which Azoury was the organizer. Jung proposed that the Entente Powers should proclaim Arab independence under their joint protection and cause an Arab caliphate to be proclaimed. If this were done, the Arab provinces and the Arab soldiers would become disaffected towards the Ottoman empire. Pressed to explain how these things would come to pass, Jung explained that 'Nedjib-Azuri Bey and his associates had got plans and could mention the name of a person who would, they believe, be most acceptable as Caliph, and best justified for that position by lineage'.

Loraine prudently asked the Quai d'Orsay which official had sent Jung to him, and was told that 'he had not been recommended to come to His Majesty's Embassy and that my name had not been mentioned to him. I asked whether Monsieur Jung was a serious person and was informed that he was not, and that considerable caution should be used in dealing with him: that he has been discarded from the French service for reasons on which it was unnecessary to insist, and that he was not altogether free from suspicion.' When Jung telephoned later, Lorraine told him that the ambassador did not authorize him to take any action on the former's proposals: 'Monsieur Jung said: "Et alors, quoi?" I replied "Alors—l'affaire en reste là."'[47]

We too may at this point take our leave of Monsieur Jung. But not before recording one of the first casualties of the Arab revolt which broke out in the summer of 1916: in Cairo, on June 28 of that year Azoury, 'the great friend of France', his associate announced in a letter to the president of the Republic, 'died of joy on seeing his efforts come to fruition'.[48]

NOTES

1. Sylvia G. Haim, *Arab Nationalism*, Berkeley, 1962, pp. 27–9.
2. Cromer Papers, F.O. 633/6, no. 260, Cromer to Salisbury, 30 June 1896.
3. F.O. 424/189, no. 27, Currie to Salisbury, Constantinople, 1 October 1896; and F.O. 424/191, no. 138, Currie to Salisbury, Constantinople, 16 February 1897.
4. F.O. 78/4864, Cromer to Salisbury no. 132 Secret, 12 October 1897.
5. Archives du Ministère des A[ffaires] E[trangères], Paris, Egypte N[ouvelle] S[érie], vol. 14, Cogordan's despatch no. 312, Cairo 26 December 1897. Cogordan refers to another desptach of his, no. 297 (not in the file) with which he had enclosed a pamphlet accusing the Khedive of aspiring to the Caliphate. Wali al-Din Yakan, *al-Ma'lum wa al-majhul* (The Known and the Unknown), vol. I, Cairo, 1909, p. 108.

6. Murad left Egypt for Europe perhaps towards the end of 1896. It may be that Cromer was instrumental in his departure from Cairo. In his letter of 30 June 1896, cited above, Cromer writes of Murad: 'Most of what he says about the Sultan is quite true, but that is beside the point. I have sent for him, and I dare say he will do what I tell him. We must not have any press prosecutions.' In his despatch no. 132 Secret, of 12 October 1897, Cromer strongly expresses his concern lest Abd al-Hamid should believe that the British had a hand in these intrigues. On Murad's stay in Europe see E. E. Ramsaur, Jr. *The Young Turks*, Princeton 1957, pp. 37–51. Murad's return to Constantinople is reported in Currie's despatch no. 572, Constantinople, 26 August 1897, F.O. 424/192, no. 95.

7. The informant's report is enclosed in Cromer's despatch no. 135 Secret, Cairo, 23 October 1897, F.O. 78/4864.

8. Cromer's no. 132 of 12 October 1897 cited above; Boutiron's no. 274, Cairo, 27 October 1897, A. E., Egypte, N.S. vol. 14.

9. Cromer Papers, F.O. 633/6, no. 290, Cromer to Salisbury, 11 December 1897.

10. F.O. 195/2028, Dickson's no. 10, Jerusalem, 1 March 1898, enclosing extract from private letter Gaza 26 February. F.O. 195/2055, Wratislaw's telegram Secret and Confidential no. 9, Basra, 27 November 1899.

11. Article by Najjar in his own periodical *al-Liwa*, Beirut, reproduced in *al-Hadith*, Aleppo, January 1940, p. 7. The article promises a sequel with more details, which I have been unable to trace. See also Sylvia G. Haim, 'The Ideas of a Precursor', unpublished Ph.D. dissertation, Edinburgh University, 1953, pp. 10–12, and Kedourie, *The Chatham House Version*, p. 195.

12. F.O. 78/4995, O'Conor's no. 439 Confidential, Therapia, 13 September 1899. There had been another complaint, the previous March, about Young Turks in Egypt being encouraged by the Khedive, F.O. 78/4992 O'Conor's no. 159, Constantinople, 30 March 1899.

13. I myself saw this copy many years ago when the Oriental Institute collection was housed in the Griffith Institute at the Ashmolean Museum, Oxford. I understand that it is now not to be traced.

14. Mohamad Gamal-El-Din Ali Hussein El-Mesady, 'The Relations between Abbas Hilmi and Lord Cromer', unpublished Ph.D. dissertation, University of London, 1966, p. 270, f. 2.

15. *Al-A'mal al-kamila li-Abd al-Rahman al-Kawakibi* (The Complete Works of Abd al-Rahman al-Kawakibi) ed. Muhammad 'Umara, Cairo, 1970, p. 295.

16. A.E. Egypte, N.S. vol. 14, Cogordan's no. 55, 12 April 1902. The despatch refers to an earlier one (no. 42 of 24 March) in which reports in European newspapers regarding the society of *Umm al-qura* and the Khedive's connexion with it were discussed. It will be remembered that Rashid Rida had just started serializing the book in al-Manar.

17. H. A. R. Gibb in *Whither Islam*, 1932, p. 355, f. 1.

18. Haim, *Arab Nationalism*, p. 28.

19. Complete Works, pp. 295–6. To translate *''arabiyya'* as Arabism would be to give Kawakibi's language a very modern sound, but there is no doubt that by this word he means the Arabs and all the cultural and religious values associated with them.

20. A.E. Turquie, N.S. vol. 177, Boppe's no. 165, Constantinople, 26 September 1905; Turquie, N.S. 109, Wiet's no. 109, Jerusalem, 8 February 1905; Archives de l'Alliance israélite universelle, Paris, VII. E. 18. Antébi's letter no. 45, 16 February 1905.

21. *Indépendance Arabe*, no. 7–8, October–November 1907, leading article by Azoury; *Le Réveil de la nation arabe*, Paris, 1905, pp. 29–30, 191–3, 203–4.

22. A.E. Turquie, N.S. 131, Boppe's no. 39, Jerusalem, 30 June 1904.
23. Antébi's letter of 16 February 1905, cited above.
24. *Le Réveil* . . . , pp. III–VIII.
25. Albert Hourani, *Arabic Thought in the Liberal Age 1798–1939*, 1962, p. 277.
26. Wiet's no. 14 of 8 February 1905, cited above.
27. *Le Réveil* . . . , pp. 191–2.
28. *Le Réveil* . . . , p. 229. Azoury, it will be remembered, had been a Young Turk precisely at the time when it was a Young Turk ploy to threaten an Arab caliphate.
29. *Le Réveil* . . . , books II–IV passim, and particularly pp. 108, 115 and 128.
30. Alphonse d'Alonzo, *La Russie en Palestine*, Paris 1901; *Cardinal et ministre général*, Jerusalem 1902; *Les Allemands en orient*, Brussels 1904. In the first of these pamphlets Alonzo declares (p. 108f.) that his family 'a travaillé pendant plus de trois siècles à défendre la cause des catholiques en Terre Sainte'.
31. See e.g. Kedourie, *The Chatham House Version*, p. 336.
32. F.O. 195/2187, Townshend's no. 5, Adana, 1 February 1905.
33. A.E. Turquie, N.S. vol. 177, despatch no. 8, 14 February 1905.
34. A.E. Turquie, N.S. vol. 109, despatch no. 7, 20 July 1905.
35. A.E. Turquie, N.S. vol. 109, despatch no. 37, 31 July 1905. On As'ad Shuqayr's hostile attitude towards Arab nationalism before and after 1918 see the memoirs of his son Ahmad al-Shuqayri, *Arba'un 'amm fi'l-hayat al-arabiyya wa'l-duwaliyya* (Forty Years in Arab and International Life), Beirut, 1969, p. 10. Ahmad himself was born at his father's place of exile.
36. F.O. 195/2190, Drummond Hay's despatch no. 50, Beirut, 5 August 1905.
37. A.E. Turquie, N.S. vol. 177, where all the documents relating to the Arabic leaflet are collected, together with Azoury's two letters to Christian from Cairo, dated 8 January and 22 February 1906.
38. Antonius, p. 99.
39. A.E. Turquie, N.S. vol. 179, despatch no. 29 confidential, 29 January 1908.
40. A.E. Turquie, N.S. vol. 132, Gueyraud's despatch no. 17, Jerusalem, 8 October 1908. Azoury's electoral manifesto is printed in *l'Indépendance arabe*, nos. 16-17-18 (July–August–September 1908), the last number of this periodical to appear.
41. J. Alexander, *The Truth about Egypt*, 1911, pp. 281 and 363–4.
42. A.E. Turquie, N.S. vol. 117, copy, in Jung's handwriting of letter from Azoury, Port Said, 17 November 1912. The passage in italics is underlined in this copy.
43. Jung's letters are in A.E. Turquie, N.S., vol. 117; reports of interviews with him by a member of the minister's *cabinet*, E. Daeschner, are in volume 118; and a note in volume 119, initialled by Daeschner, 19 January 1913, records the payment to Jung, '*pour clôture*'.
44. Eugène Jung, *la Révolte arabe*, vol. I, Paris, 1924, p. 49.
45. Jung, *la Révolte arabe*, vol. I, pp. 39–40.
46. A.E., Guerre 1914–18, vol. 852; Jung, *la Révolte arabe*, vol. I, p. 68.
47. F.O. 371/2147, 87764/W44, memorandum by P. Loraine, Paris, 15 December 1914, enclosed with letter of December 16 from Lord Granville to G. Clerk.
48. A.E., Guerre 1914–18, volume 874, Jung's letter of 20 August 1916.

8. The Impact of the Young Turk Revolution on the Arabic-speaking Provinces of the Ottoman Empire

The *coup d'état* of July 1908, known as the Young Turk Revolution, has an archetypal significance in subsequent Arab politics, and its consequences and reverberations are, even today, far from being exhausted. It is thus of some interest to know what the immediate impact of this *coup d'état* was in the Arabic-speaking provinces of the Ottoman empire. The most cursory investigation will immediately serve to increase our interest for—as is shown below—the reaction in these provinces to the events in Macedonia and Constantinople are intriguingly similar. The similarity is intriguing because it could not have been manufactured or evoked by a 'communications industry' which did not exist then, and because these provinces were anyway more or less isolated from one another.

At the accession of Abd al-Hamid, the Arabic-speaking provinces, particularly Syria and Palestine like so many other parts of the Ottoman empire, were in a state of disorder and discontent which made them almost ripe for rebellion. There were many reasons for this state of affairs, the remote ones having to do with the very character and functioning of the *Tanzimat*, while the proximate ones were related to the war of 1876–8, and the scarcities, and the burdens of taxation and conscription which were its consequence. But the end of the emergency brought an immediate amelioration and in the years following the Treaty of Berlin Abd al-Hamid seems to have effectively re-established the authority of his government in the provinces. In Syria, as the perspicacious and learned Hogarth observed, Abd al-Hamid 'took in hand, in the early eighties, the public insecurity of northern Syria and southern Palestine, multiplying guards and increasing garrisons, and paying particular attention then and later to both the Kurds of Amanus and the robber Armenians of Zeitun. Improved communications, however, he knew, or soon learned, would provide the most effective means to his end. In the year 1885, when the Jaffa—Jerusalem track was improved into a metal chaussee, began an era of road-building throughout Syria, and in 1886 it was followed by one of railway construction. This was destined, in the course of the next thirty years to give Syria through-connection with Constantinople, a railway from Aleppo to Bir es-Seba linked to five ports, and trunk

lines to Arabia on the one hand and Mesopotamia on the other.
When it is remembered, further, that such harbour structures as
exist in Syria, and the equipment of principal cities like Aleppo,
Damascus, Beirut and Jerusalem with broad ways, modern buildings,
electric lighting, tramways, and other convenient apparatus, are
also of Abdul Hamid's time, one is bound to admit that a good
deal of beneficent construction—almost all in fact, that makes Syria
as a whole the most civilized province of Turkey at this day—
stands to the credit of a Sultan whose energies are popularly supposed to have been uniformly destructive and sinister.' Hogarth
goes on to point out that all these activities were supplemented by a
deliberate effort to diminish nomadism, by means of free or favourable grants of land, by opening local markets, increasing the number
of police stations, garrisons and administrative posts in areas like
Trans-Jordan, hitherto very imperfectly policed.[1] Thus, by the end
of the first decade of Hamidian rule, the Arabic-speaking provinces
became tranquil and contented, not to say docile, and must be
presumed to have known that happiness which is said to be the lot
of countries with no history.

Four regions are an exception to this state of affairs, namely the
Hauran, southern Kurdistan, lower Mesopotamia and the Yemen.
In all these regions, roads were poor or non-existent, and large
groups of nomads and semi-nomads were able to resist control by
the central government. But this state of affairs was, so to speak,
traditional and endemic, and by no means indicated new or increasing disaffection towards the government. On the contrary, the settled
population themselves generally considered these turbulent nomads
a threat to their property and sometimes to their very existence,
and were not sorry to see the authorities mount successive expedi-
tions against these predatory hordes.

But the very success of Hamidian policies: the more orderly
administration, the improved communications, the increasing
number of schools, the slowly rising and spreading prosperity, itself
worked gradually to undermine Hamidian rule. Professor Bernard
Lewis has pointed out that it was in the field of educational reform
that the Hamidian régime made its first and greatest effort.[2] The
Young Turk conspirators were the outcome of Abd al-Hamid's
educational enterprise: so, in the Arabic-speaking provinces, the
civil and military high schools produced a steady, and a steadily
broadening, stream of young men with vaguely 'enlightened'
attitudes, who were secretly Young Turk in sympathy—and some
of whom came after 1913 (when the empire experienced disaster and
stress similar to that of 1876–8) to be in greater or lesser sympathy
with a more or less vague Arab nationalism. But these 'enlightened'

men could hardly be said to have posed a threat to the régime. If, perchance, their 'enlightenment' was overtly expressed, it took the form of a religious radicalism, inspired perhaps by Wahabism, and was generally *salafi* in character. A case in point is that relating to the well-known *'alim* Mahmud Shukri al-Alusi of Baghdad, who after 1908, was to show himself a fervent supporter of the Committee of Union and Progress. In 1905, while a teacher at the *madrasa* attached to the Haydarkhana mosque at Baghdad he, together with his cousin Thabit, who had been president of the municipality the previous year, Abd al-Razzaq efendi, a teacher at the A'zamiyya school and Hajj Hamad al-'Asafi, a wealthy Najdi merchant, were all, as the British consul-general then reported, arrested and deported. One reason seemed to be that the two Alusis and Abd al-Razzaq had written a book in praise of Wahabism which was to be printed in Egypt, the cost being defrayed by Hajj Hamad, and that they were suspected of corresponding with Ibn Sa'ud.[3]

A few years before, in 1901, 'no small stir' was caused in Damascus by the arrest and imprisonment of Abd al-Hamid al-Zahrawi. This *'alim* who came from Homs had published in his native city a clandestine newspaper, *al-Munir*, which, says his friend Rashid Rida, 'he used to print by means of gelatine and to distribute secretly all over the Syrian provinces, in order to serve the Committee of Union and Progress and to strive, in association with it, to save the state from the absolutist Hamidian administration. From that time,' adds Rashid Rida, 'he became attached to politics and remained involved in it all through his life.' Rashid Rida goes on to remark that he and his friend were both inclined to labour in the cause of religious and social reform, and adds, significantly: 'the relation of this to politics is obvious'. Zahrawi went from Homs to Constantinople where he worked the Arabic newspaper *Ma'lumat*. His opinions seem to have led the authorities to send him in semi-exile to Damascus, where he lived on an official pension of 700 piastres a month. He was now (in December 1901), according to the British consul who reported the occurrence, accused of having written a pamphlet printed in Egypt and privately circulated among his friends and acquaintances in Damascus 'in which the four sects ... of Islam ... are vigorously and unsparingly attacked, the author's religious views being, it appears, confined to a strict adherence to and compliance with the precepts of the Koran itself and that alone'. Zahrawi, Consul Richards also reported, was 'a well educated man with more than average intelligence and reflective powers who has made a thorough study of the Moslem faith and is convinced of the necessity of its reform more especially with reference to the traditions, glosses and other accretions which tend to sully and obscure the purity of his religion as set forth by the Prophet in the Koran.' Zahrawi, it seems, maintained 'that every Moslem who is mentally capable of understanding the Koran has an indefeasible right to interpret its precepts and dicta in accordance with the rules of grammar, logic and common sense: he is not bound to be guided in such matters by the Four Imams . . . or any other expositors.' This radical theology—the details of which Zahrawi conveyed to the consul when asking, through a friend, British intercession in his case—seems to have been accompanied by political radicalism. For, as Rashid Rida reports, when Zahrawi was arrested there was found on him the text of an article on the caliphate which had appeared in *al-Muqattam* newspaper over his initials. This article was described to the consul as 'containing a violent attack on the Sultan and a denial of his right to the Caliphate.' Through his friend, Zahrawi denied this and explained to the consul that it was not 'a denial of the Sultan's right to the Caliphate but an indictment of His Majesty as a person unfit to hold the August and Sacred office of Caliph'. The distinction seems very tenuous, and Zahrawi's explanation itself explains why the authorities sent him for trial in Constantinople. As for the pamphlet to which the consul refers, it includes three articles which were published in volume four of *al-Manar* under the title, *al-Fiqh al-islami*[4] (Islamic Jurisprudence). Zahrawi himself sums up his own view by declaring that in this writing he denies the utility of many sciences which the Muslims consider useful both in religious and mundane life.[5] Zahrawi attacked in this pamphlet, as is clear from the title, *al-Fiqh wa'l-tasawwuf* (Jurisprudence and Sufism), both traditional *fiqh* and sufism. When it was published in Egypt, Rashid Rida greatly disapproved of this publication. He declares that he had refused to publish Zahrawi's article on *tasawwuf* because discussion of this topic was useful only if it was carried on among the learned (*al-khawass*), and concludes by reiterating that Zahrawi's pamphlet, concerned as it was with abuses, should never have been printed, but that its matter should have been disclosed only to the learned.[6]

In the same volume of *al-Manar* Zahrawi published over his initials three other articles also attacking Sufism and traditional religion. These articles, significantly enough, also contain hints, albeit extremely oblique ones, of radical political views, as when Zahrawi declares that 'for example he whose mother calls him Sultan must not in effect become a Sultan', or when he declares that he and the group in whose name he speaks have interests which they are anxious to see protected by 'a sultanate with just laws and an acceptable head'. These articles were followed by a note from Rashid Rida which gives point to his remark quoted above about the relation between religion and politics. In this remark Rashid Rida hints at Zahrawi's sympathy with Wahabism, declaring that the latter believes that Wahabis are more entitled than others to the appellation *ahl al-sunna* and *ahl al-hadith* (followers of religious law and tradition).

Zahrawi and Alusi, then, have a common sympathy for Wahabism and hold the radical theological and political views which this sympathy seems to have entailed. Zahrawi, as his article of 1901 on 'Politicians and Politics' shows, shared the 'subversive' ideas of the Young Turks, and like Alusi became an open sympathizer with the Committee of Union and Progress after July 1908. These two cases are chiefly interesting because they give us an inkling of what went on in the minds of intellectuals in the first decade of the century, and of the kind of ideas which, with Abd al-Hamid's downfall, were to gain a numerous audience and a prodigious popularity. But they have also the interest of exceptions which prove the rule—the rule being that, as has been said, the Arabic-speaking countries under Abdul Hamid were quiet, if not lethargic. These two cases also show how vigilant and knowledgeable the authorities were in detecting theological deviation, and how shrewd they were in associating it with political radicalism. Even too vigilant, perhaps: in June 1905, again, as the British consul-general in Beirut reported, Hadj Mohiedinne Hamady, agent of the Khedivial Mail Steamship Company, was suddenly arrested on orders from Constantinople because, so the *vali* alleged, he was 'connected with an anti-Turkish party in Egypt and suspected of being in league with his relative Sheik Mohammed Abdo the Mufti of Cairo for the formation of a similar movement in Syria'. To support his contention, the *vali* declared that commentaries on the Koran by the Mufti were found among the arrested man's papers![8]

What evidence exists, then, shows that the Arabic-speaking provinces on the eve of the *coup d'état* of July 1908 were quiescent. Their reaction to this *coup d'état*, which will be discussed below, shows also that they were by no means dissatisfied with the Hamidian régime. It is commonly, and rightly, said that the Young Turk *coup d'état* came as a surprise in Constantinople itself. It was even more unexpected in the Arabic-speaking provinces. The evidence from the various centres is almost unanimous in this respect. A word on the character of this evidence is here apposite. As will be seen, it is mainly drawn from British consular reports. In many cases, perhaps in most, such reports provide the only readily accessible and coherent and continuous account of what went on in these areas; an account moreover, written by well-placed and privileged observers who, more often than not, knew intimately a consular district where they would have been stationed for many years. The value of these reports is further enhanced by the paucity of other evidence. European newspapers did not maintain regular correspondents even in the more important and populous of the Arabic-speaking centres, and local newspapers under Abd al-Hamid were generally timid and colourless, officially inspired or officially controlled. The newspapers of the post-Hamidian period, when available, are certainly a much more valuable source for the historian, but since they did not begin publication until some time after the *coup d'état*, there is a risk of their magnifying and embroidering upon events already dramatic enough in themselves; the more so that their contributors, from the nature of the case, were likely to be radical intellectuals swollen with triumph at the downfall of despotism. These writers have in fact succeeded in establishing and propagating their version of the events. Who does not now believe that the *coup d'état* of 1908 was greeted with popular rejoicings, and that mullas, popes and rabbis were perpetually embracing one another in the streets? Yet, as will be seen below, the immediate reaction to the *coup d'état*, in the Arabic-speaking provinces at any rate, was appreciably different.

The consular despatches are remarkably unanimous about these reactions. From Baghdad in the east, to Tripoli of Barbary in the west the story they tell is one and the same. In a despatch of 3 August, Ramsay writes from Baghdad: 'The announcement that Parliament is to be reassembled after a lapse of thirty years or so and that elections are to be held immediately, has been received with interest but without the smallest sign of enthusiasm.'[9] Writing on 11 August, the vice-consul at Mosul declares 'that all is quiet, and that people hesitate to commit themselves in the absence of knowledge of what is being done in other parts of Turkey'.[10] Longworth, writing from Aleppo on 20 August, reports: 'The Vizieral telegram announcing the revival of the Constitution was received here with astonishment bordering on incredulity. Such a sudden break with the past was wholly unexpected'.[11] His words are echoed by the U.S. consul at that place who writes that the announcement of the constitution 'at first stupefied the people'.[12] The impression of his colleague at Beirut was similar: 'In Syria,' he stated in a despatch of 4 August, 'the news of the promulgation of the Constitution was received with a certain amount of incredulity and scepticism . . . The acting Governor-General at Beirut waited for two days before he dared publish the important official telegram which he had received from Said Pasha, the Grand Vizier'.[13] The British vice-consul at Haifa— a local man—also reported a lukewarm reaction. When the inhabitants were sure of the news, he informed his superior at Beirut, they 'began some rejoicings though some of them were not really pleased with this change.'[14] The consul at Jerusalem adds his voice to this chorus. He writes on 6 August that the news of the re-establishment of the Constitution 'has so far had little effect here', and he adds: 'I lament that so little interest seems to be felt by the population at large in the great event which has taken place; the Christians indeed are mainly concerned with the apprehension that they will now be obliged to perform military service.'[15] Blech's language here deserves notice. He laments the lack of enthusiasm displayed by the population of his district for a change which he believed beneficial. In holding this opinion, he was quite typical of his fellow consuls. Their concordant reports concerning the negligible initial impact of the *coup d'état* become therefore all the more convincing.

This was the reaction in the Levant. It therefore causes no surprise to find that it was much more pronounced in other areas where European influences had not yet eroded traditional attitudes. Thus the acting consul at Jedda reported in a despatch of 25 August that up to 18 August the re-establishment of constitutional government had not yet been proclaimed by the authorities at Mecca and Ta'if and, he added 'at the latter place, some men who were found talking of Constitution and freedom were flogged by the order of the Grand Sharif'.[16] The consul at Benghazi had a similar story to tell: 'Among the Arabs', he wrote in a despatch of 20 August, 'the news that the Constitution was to be restored produced little or no impression. They seem indifferent as to the form of government and sceptical as to reform, tolerating Turkish rule as a Moslem rule and harbouring some veneration for the Sultan as religious Head of the Ottoman Empire.' The consul proceeded to give an instance of that salutary scepticism about the benevolence of power which life under traditional despotism (innocent as it is of brainwashing techniques) has—as one of its saving graces—always inculcated in its subjects. 'The fact that the people of Benghazi are able to elect a deputy to represent them at Constantinople', the consul observed 'appears to inspire the suspicion that whoever is elected is perhaps unlikely to return to Benghazi alive.'[17]

Tripoli of Barbary however seems, at first sight, exceptional in its behaviour. In a despatch of 27 July, the consul reported a great demonstration in which several thousands took part in a thanks-giving service at the mosque and then marched in a procession carrying inscriptions in praise of liberty, justice, etc.[18] But circum-stances in Tripoli were somewhat peculiar, and the events which shortly followed showed that reaction to the *coup d'état* in Tripoli was similar to, and even more pronounced than, reactions elsewhere in the Arabic-speaking provinces. For many years Abd al-Hamid had used Tripoli as a place of exile for political suspects who, by 1908, occupied a large number of official posts in the province. The *vali* of Tripoli since 1900 was Rejeb Pasha, appointed to this post because he also was politically suspect. Rightly so, it seems, for about 1904 he took part in a conspiracy whereby he would engineer a military rising at Tripoli, and proceed at the head of the rebels to Constantinople where he would force the sultan either to re-establish the Constitution or to abdicate.[19] A sympathetic obituary was to declare that 'in this province which was so little Turkish, but where the Turkish exiles were becoming more and more numerous, the *vali* could give free rein to his activity and to his liberal convictions', and that under his rule Tripolitania became a 'centre of Turkish liberalism, a spot where one could breathe freely and say aloud things for which people were hanged at Stamboul.'[20] It is this conjunction of a large number of opponents of the régime delighted at its downfall and a sympathetic and indulgent governor which must account for the rejoicings which the consul reported. Slousch, visiting Tripoli shortly afterwards seems nearer the mark when he writes that 'the grant of a Constitution had been first received by the Arabs of the city with a surprising indifference'.[21] The events which shortly followed the demonstration show decisively that the feelings which the *coup d'état* aroused were somewhat stronger than indifference. Owing, presumably, to his past, and to his known opinion, Rejeb Pasha was appointed minister of war in Kamil Pasha's cabinet and prepared to leave for Constantinople. To carry on the government pending the arrival of a new *vali*, Rejeb Pasha appointed Bekir Sami bey, mutasarrif of Jebel, and Young Turk in his sympathies. Immediately the appointment became known a tremendous agitation against it began. The largest meeting took place in the Karamanli mosque under the presidency of the mayor Hassuna Pasha, himself a descendant of the Karamanlis who had ruled Tripoli from 1711 to 1835. The meeting demanded that Bekir Sami's appointment should be revoked and all the Young Turks should leave Tripoli. Deputations besieged the *vali* with these demands as he was on the point of leaving for Constantinople; they insisted on them to such effect that Rejeb Pasha was compelled to cancel Bekir Sami's appointment, and to take aboard his ship 198 Young Turk exiles who left with him for Constantinople.[22]

The events of Tripoli show with particular clarity who were the immediate supporters of the *coup d'état*. They were a faction within the ruling institution, officials and officers who leaned more or less strongly towards Young Turk ideas. As has been seen, owing to peculiar circumstances this faction predominated in

Tripoli and had little difficulty in imposing official acceptance and ratification of the *coup d'état*. Even so, they did not have things entirely their own way. The dislike of the inhabitants of Tripoli for the Young Turks seems to have been shared by some of the officials who may have been reluctant to express open disapproval of the *coup d'état* at Constantinople. In his despatch of 9 August cited above, consul Alvarez reported that the governor of the fortress, clearly no sympathizer with the Young Turks, was summoned to a meeting of his officers and informed that he was deposed from his command. He expostulated, but was 'roughly' told: 'We don't want you'. His subordinates then took away his sword, cut off the tassel of his fez and conducted him to the castle in derision.[23] In Benghazi, too, the mutasarrif seemed lukewarm towards the constitution, and no festivities were held, as in Tripoli, in honour of the constitution. He was subjected, in consequence, to attacks in the Young Turk newspapers which now began to appear and denounced for corruption and treason. A new power now disputed his authority: 'Within the last three weeks', reported the consul in his despatch of 20 August, cited above, 'a secret "Committee of Young Turks" has been formed at Benghazi, the members of which are alleged to be the Public Prosecutor, the Presidents of the local Tribunals, the Cadi and a Jewish tradesman named Jacques Morens. The Cadi', Fontana added, 'is an old man, and much addicted to intoxicants, and his consenting to join the "committee" is probably mainly due to that fact.' There were now two rival authorities disputing the allegiance of the official classes, Salonica and Constantinople, and the former seemed increasingly to have the primacy over the latter: 'Red ribbons stamped with the word "Hurriyet" (Liberty)', Fontana also reported, 'were attached to school-boys' sleeves, and scarlet bands bearing the words "Liberty, Equality, Justice, Fraternity" received, apparently, from Salonica, were displayed in Turkish houses. An officer, the worse for liquor, who was making a speech in honour of the Constitution to a number of his fellow-officers in a café one evening, was politely requested by a Commissary of Police to make less noise or to retire from the café. The officer replied with insulting language, other policemen were called in and a struggle ensued between officers and police, ending in the forcible ejection of the latter.'[24] A fortnight later, Fontana signalizes the triumph of the new order by reporting that a ball in honour of the sultan's birthday was held in Benghazi, largely attended by both Christians and Turks. (Someone at the Constantinople embassy minuted: 'I wonder who they danced with at the ball.')[25]

The events of Tripoli and Benghazi are highly significant because they have their counterpart in the other centres of the Arabic-speaking provinces where the actions of Young Turk sympathizers show even more clearly that what took place there was a series of minuature *coups d'états* reproducing and supplementing the seizure of power at Constantinople. At Jerusalem, the governor in July 1908 was Ali Ekrem bey. He had been sent, as a vivid despatch from the U.S. consul Thomas A. Wallace rightly observed, 'in accordance with what had become a fixed policy of the Sultan, which for many years has been to give the position to one of his secretaries, it also being their first [administrative] appointment. So the incumbent has always represented the palace party and has brought with him its oppressive atmosphere.' Ali Ekrem bey was the son of the poet Namik Kemal, who himself had been involved in, and suffered for, a conspiracy against Abd al-Hamid in 1876. That his descendant should have held high office at Yildiz and had then been entrusted with this important and sensitive post tells us a great deal about Abd al-Hamid's character and methods, that he should now become the butt of a faction which claimed his father for one of its heroes partakes of the general irony of things. For, as Wallace proceeds to tell us, 'the overthrow of autocracy' took the governor by surprise and it was not until 8 August, a fortnight after the sultan had proclaimed the re-establishment of the constitution, that the sultan's rescript was read publicly at Jerusalem and official decorations and illuminations organized. In taking these actions, Ali Ekrem was clearly responding to the pressure of the Young Turk faction at Jerusalem, who were now taking their instructions from the Committee of Union and Progress at Salonica. For, as Wallace points out, the Committee had been able to lay hands on the telegraphic system 'and their numerous messages, calling for demonstrations, and encouraging the populace to assert their new legal rights, and not brook the interference of officials attached to the old régime, went free to the chief centres and were then repeated to smaller places. Thus, when Jerusalem wired its complaint of the then unsympathetic attitude of the governor, Ali Akrem bey, an answer by wire from Salonica, via Beyrout, came couched in terms that would have been treason a few days before. It was to the effect that any governor or official who put obstacles in the way of the people manifesting their joy were enemies to the liberty of the people and lawless in their actions, and that such were not worthy of being kept in their positions, and that it was for the people to boldly object and oppose such and permit nothing that was against the public peace to continue.' Not unnaturally, these incitements evoked a response at Jerusalem where, at the initiative of a 'Young Effendi' a local section of the C.U.P. was formed, who began organizing protests at the governor's tardiness in proclaiming the new constitutional era and who claimed the right to control the actions of officials and to remove those suspected of disloyalty to the new régime. The momentary fraternization between Muslims, Jews and Christians which now took place was no doubt the outcome of their inspiration and encouragement.[26]

The same kind of jollification inspired by the triumphant Young Turks was reported by the U.S. consul-general at Beirut. In a despatch of 4 August—quoted above—he wrote that 'we now observe, in the streets of Beirut, the Maronite priest four times kiss the Moslem Sheikh and the Moslem Sheikh responding by four times kissing the Maronite priest.' Here too, however, we observe the same assumption of power, which the regular authorities seemed unable to check, by the local Young Turk faction usually in direct and independent communication with Salonica, as Ravndal also reported: 'The military are the heroes of the day, beyond question. Kept in comparative obscurity and deliberately ignored are the Governor-General, the Mayor, the Chief of Police and other officials who still retain their functions although identified with the old style of rule.' These junior officers, Young Turk in sympathy, were, together with their civilian associates in 'unmistakable control'; the *vali* and the military commandant were compelled to submit completely to their wishes—such was also the impression of the British consul-general, reported in a despatch of 8 August. These Young Turk officers now made themselves responsible for order in Beirut, and set up a commission to investigate and recommend dismissal of officials. It was presumably as a result of its activities that, as Ravndal reported in a despatch of 14 August, the mayor resigned, that the chief of police, the commander of the gendarmerie, and the director of posts and telegraphs were arrested and sent to Salonica under guard.[27] At the end of August, the situation was still the same: the official representatives of the state still did not know where their authority stopped and where that of the committee began. The governor of Jerusalem, Ali Ekrem, had now been transferred to Beirut: 'He found the local atmosphere rather chilly and inhospitable and decided to resign and proceed to Constantinople in order to ascertain whether in the event of his re-appointment, he or Major Riza Bey, the local representative of the "Society of Union and Progress" would be in command.' His successor, Ravndal reported in a despatch of 2 September, functioned in an atmosphere of 'uncertainty and vacillation, in sharp contrast to the genuine enthusiasm, and lots of it' prevalent in the barracks.[2]

The evidence from Damascus and Aleppo provides the same picture of a forcible takeover by Young Turk officers, and of popular celebrations instigated by them, demonstrations which, it is interesting to note, are remarkably at variance with the spontaneous feelings of indifference and even sullenness which the population had originally evinced. 'The Union and Progress Society, whose individual members can only be conjectured vaguely here,' writes the British consul at Damascus on 12 August, 'is practically directing the Government gestation, military and administrative' and adds that officials suspected of being out of sympathy with them were being dismissed. And the U.S. consular agent reported the Damascenes to be shouting, under official patronage: 'Down with Tyranny! Long live Liberty?'[29] In Aleppo news of the *coup d'état* was speedily followed by the formation of a committee of twenty-one self-designated officers. We may suspect that their labours were responsible for the joyful demonstrations which followed the astonishment and the stupefaction with which the constitution was initially received.[30] The Committee of Union and Progress is thus seen establishing its own parallel government, which generally proved to be more powerful than the lawful government. The network seems to have perhaps extended down even to the less important centres. Thus the U.S. consular agent at Hodeida reported that on the initiative of the Young Turk committee, now acting in the open, the mutasarrif had been recently seized and sent out of the country on an Italian steamer, on the grounds that 'until now nothing was done for the election of members of the Parliament'.[31]

The Young Turk *coup d'état*, then, clearly administered a shock to the political institutions of the Ottoman empire, by reason of what happened not only in the capital, but also in the provinces. As has been seen, in the Arabic-speaking provinces—and surely elsewhere as well—the representatives of the lawful government were, in a great many cases, overborne, hustled, insulted, dismissed or even arrested by self-appointed secret committees of generally junior officers and officials, themselves secretly taking their instructions from an extra-legal secret committee sitting in Salonica. But the shock affected more than merely political institutions; its repercussions shook the traditional social hierarchies. Thus, in Haifa where, as elsewhere, the local authorities were 'not delighted' by the *coup d'état*, and only the officers were prompt to show their satisfaction, the *naqib al-ashraf*, an old man of eighty was accused of having cursed the constitution. He was brought to the *konak*. 'Many Musselmens were against him', reported the vice-consul, 'but when a young Christian, the prosecutor, began to insult him before the crowd calling him "traitor", the Mohammedans became exceedingly angry. The Sheikh was arrested and put in prison for three days but was acquitted by the court . . .

where more than a thousand Mohammedans were waiting for his acquittal. He was acclaimed by the crowd who cried "Long live the nation of Mohammed and the Sultan", The local authorities,' Abela concluded, 'are very weak and helpless and not in a position to calm the excitement of the people, if occasion should require.'[32] Similar humiliations were inflicted on a much more prominent traditional figure: the amir of Mecca. As has been seen, the sharif had received very unfavourably the news of the re-establishment of the constitution. Here, too, it was the junior officers who took matters in their own hands and proclaimed the constitution at Ta'if on 19 August. They brought the sharif to their barracks where he 'was made to stand by the side of three men picked out from the crowd (a slave, a bedouin and an ordinary soldier) and was asked whether he considered there was any difference before the law between him and the three men, who were standing with him. His reply was no.' The sharif was then made to swear on the Qur'an to follow the constitution, to stop illegal practices against the people of the Hijaz and the pilgrims, and to take immediate steps to secure the safety of the roads in the Hijaz. The measure of his fear and humiliation we may gauge by the fact that he threw all responsibility for the past corruption on to the shoulders of the *vali*, Ahmad Ratib who, he said, had compelled him to continue the abuses practised by his notorious predecessor, 'Awn.[33] A scarcely less prominent traditional figure, the *naqib* of Baghdad, descendant of Abd al-Qadir al-Gaylani and head of his *tariqa* was similarly held up to obloquy. The consul-general at Baghdad reported an inclination on the part of the Committee of Union and Progress (here as elsewhere the effective power) 'to show practical dislike to those who do not enthusiastically hail the Committee as the saviours of the country. Amongst these', he continued, 'are the Nakib and a good many others of good position.' The *naqib* was threatened with disagreeable things if he and his family did not join the committee, a demonstration against him was organized outside his house, and he was threatened with violence.[34]

Such attacks on traditional leaderships had for their—probably unintended—consequence a loosening of the social fabric and an erosion of the restraint and decorum inculcated in a traditional Muslim society. The Young Turk revolution seems in fact the first stage in a process which, over half a century or so, has led to a radical divorce in the Arab world between social position and political power, and to a conjunction between military might and demagogy. What happened in Damascus once it became clear that the Young Turks were in the ascendant may perhaps be seen as a first step on the fateful road which was to lead some obscure officer from, say, Bani Murr or Tikrit becoming, some decades later, as if by magic, the unchallenged and absolute master of a state and a society. The events in Damascus are the subject of an illuminating despatch of 10 August from the U.S. consular agent, Nasif Mashaka. He reported that the city was the scene of daily 'Aradat'. The term 'arada', he explained 'is a vulgar word, and it signifies that a big crowd from one and the same quarter is out celebrating, fully armed, and all the while shouting and rejoicing over some happy occurrence.' He went on: 'The numerous "Aradat" that are taking place daily are almost fearful. Imagine some five hundred illiterate young men, some with swords in their hands, others with revolvers and many with prohibited rifles stolen from the government, this whole crowd followed by a great multitude pass through the streets and the bazaars shooting and shouting ...' These crowds, declares Meshaka, are continuously harangued by Muslims and Christians delivering 'very liberal' orations: 'On the 8th instant, the orations in general were exceptionally liberal. A "Young Turk", having the grade of "Usbashy" stood on the platform, took out his sword and asked the people to stand up and repeat after him an oath to the meaning that if tyranny shall reign again, they would overthrow it no matter how dear it might cost them. They solemnly declared that they were ready to sacrifice for liberty their wives, their children and their blood! After this solemn oath three times three cheers were given for liberty, the Army and the sultan.

'A graduate of the American College in Beirut, Dr. Abdel Raham Shahbander, a very enthusiastic "Young Turk", before the audience asked the *vali*, the Mushir, Abdel Rahman Pasha [al-Yusuf] and some other Pashas to join in and deliver orations, and they, out of shame, I believe, promised to do so on Sunday; but after reflection it was found inconvenient for them to deliver public speeches and so it was postponed indefinitely.' The dislike of the notabilities for the new régime and its ways which is only hinted at here is explicitly asserted in a despatch from the British consul: 'There is,' wrote Devey on 12 August, 'some discontent on the part of the Ulemas and certain leaders of the town, for the Union and Progress Society is going forward in its own way and removing officials without consulting them.'[35]

This deliberate policy of humiliating and frightening the notabilities, however, risked getting out of hand, and the Young Turk officers who encouraged demonstrations and other outbursts of popular passion could not always keep them within bounds. What must have particularly alarmed Nasif Meshaka as a Christian was that, in spite of the 'very liberal' harangues with which they were regaled, the slogan which the 'aradat' were shouting was, as he reported in the despatch cited above, '"Dinna din el Islam, din Mohammad bel seif kam"—that means:' as he added, 'the Moslems' religion rose by the sword.' Such an outburst was an expression— but as will be seen below, by no means the only one—of powerful social tensions and fears which the *coup d'état* elicited. That the Muslim was supreme over the non-Muslim, which the Damascene mob affirmed by shouting that the religion of Mohammad rose by the sword, was the lesson which the Muslims of Jenin and Nablus also drew from the *coup d'état*: the popular interpretation in those places, wrote the British consul at Jerusalem was that 'now they could treat the Christians just as they wish.'[36] Communal tension does not seem to have been confined to the relations of Muslims and non-Muslims. In Jerusalem it rose between the Jews and the Greek Orthodox. In his despatch of 12 August cited above, Wallace, the U.S. consul at Jerusalem, had waxed enthusiastic about the cordial relations between the various communities which the *coup d'état* had brought about. But, in a postscript dated 14 August, he reported that the 'general amity' of which he had written, was marred 'by the action of some members of the Greek Church, notably the priests, in violently opposing the Jews, who, encouraged by the friendliness theretofore shown, attempted to pass along the street which borders the open quadrangle of the Church of the Holy Sepulchre.' Other incipient tensions and conflicts also made their appearance. The fellahin of the sanjaq of Jerusalem, reported Blech, were in September still enthusiastic about the Constitution, 'but it may be doubted whether they have a correct idea of its meaning. It will be a disappointment to some when they learn that liberty does not imply, as they seem to think, the general abolition of taxes.'[37] Miss Bell, who was travelling in 1909 in Mesopotamia, reports the reaction of the inhabitants of 'Ana on the upper Euphrates to the announcement of the constitution: 'When the telegram came last summer telling of liberty and equality,' she was told, 'the people assembled before the serayah, the government house, and bade the Kaimmakam begone, for they would govern themselves. Thereat came orders from Baghdad that the people must be dispersed; and the soldiers fired upon them, killing six men.'[38] And in the vilayet of Aleppo where large landowners had traditionally exercised extensive arbitrary powers over the peasants, the latter were, in some instances, showing an inclination to be 'refractory'.[39]

The attempt by the Committee of Union and Progress to elicit a—more or less artificial—popular support for the new régime elicited in turn a strong reaction from those notables who had supported the old régime and whom the Young Turks, in the first flush of victory, had wished to put down and humiliate. And as the evidence will be seen to indicate, these so-called reactionary supporters of Abd al-Hamid seem to have received a genuine and extensive popular backing. We are justified in regarding manifestations of popular support for the old régime as genuine precisely because such manifestations must have taken place against the will of the new authorities and in defiance of them. Nor is popular disapproval of the Young Turks difficult to explain. An Ottoman official who was serving at Ladhiqiyya at the time of the *coup d'état* declares in his memoirs that this city 'was no less patient than other Syrian centres in bearing the misdeeds of [Abd al-Hamid's] autocracy' and that one reason for this was 'the belief of the majority in the duty of obedience and submission to His Majesty the Sultan and the governors appointed by him whether upright or corrupt.'[40] A correspondent of the *Revue du monde musulman* in Cyrenaica writing in the latter half of 1908 reported that the 'natives of Barqa recognize no authority but that of the Sultan, and anything which does not emanate from the Commander of the faithful is for them a dead letter.' The Arabs of Cyrenaica, the correspondent went on, regarded Kamil Pasha's cabinet as having been formed without the sultan's assent, which has led to 'a certain weakening' of Ottoman authority in the province.[41]

At the time of the Italian attack on Tripoli, when enthusiasm for state and government was at a very high pitch among the Ottoman Muslims, the military commandant of Baghdad, Muhammad Fadil Pasha al-Daghistani made a speech in which he 'paid very high compliments to the people and troops of Iraq for their orderliness and obedience to constituted authority. He said that he had served Government in many places for about twenty-eight years, and that he had never seen better behaved people or more obedient soldiers than those of Iraq. He added that in the time of the *vali* Nazim Pasha, when first the Constitution was proclaimed in Turkey, he (the Wali) wrote to Constantinople that the people did not like the constitution, and he received instructions from headquarters to impose the Constitution by military force.'[42] Muhammad Fadil Pasha went on to say that he had reassured his headquarters concerning the loyalty of the people; his faith had not been misplaced 'and events had proved the truth of his assertion.' The situation in the autumn of 1911 no doubt made this kind of flattery desirable. But what is interesting is his reference to the *vali*'s warning that the province disliked the constitution. We can have no doubt that in so doing, he was merely reporting what in fact was the case.

The well-known Baghdadi chronicler, 'Abbas al-'Azzawi, who was twenty at the time of the *coup d'état*, has an illuminating passage in which he described the impression which the re-establishment of the constitution made among the Muslim population of Baghdad. The announcement of constitutional government was, he writes 'one of the greatest events, but people on the whole knew nothing about it, and gave it no other significance save that this freedom was putting them on an equality with the non-Muslims. This they looked upon as injustice; nay, they considered the repetition of the words: freedom, justice, equality, and fraternity an insult, particularly as the *khatt* of Gulkhana (the *tanzimat khayriyya*) aimed at the same object, and created at the time repugnance and a bad impression.' Some, he observes, knew the benefits of this new freedom owing to their acquaintance with the outside world, and their wider horizons; and they did attempt by means of articles and speeches to explain matters and make reform attractive, but 'the great majority was ignorant'. This majority, he goes on to say, however, 'was puzzled by what it kept on hearing about the great pressure and harshness being exerted in Istanbul and its environs [i.e. by the Young Turks] since it knew itself to have been immune from evils and from despotism. The majority kept on repeating that if the *shari'a* was in existence, what reason was there to rely on the constitution or on constitutional rights? The new administration was seen as merely a means for interference by foreigners.

'No wonder, since Iraq had experienced but little the ill effects of despotism, and that straitness had affected it but lightly, so that it was as if in a dream, and unaware of what was going on.'[43]

The events which took place at Baghdad in October 1908 reveal the popular temper and confirm 'Azzawi's account. To prepare for the forthcoming parliamentary elections, the Committee of Union and Progress sent a delegation to Baghdad composed of Hamdi Baban, a prominent CUP civilian at Istanbul who had Baghdadi connexions and two others to drum up support for the committee. The Young Turk supporters in Baghdad organized an ostentatious reception for Hamdi Baban and his colleagues. The day happening to be a Saturday, a large number of Jewish onlookers were, it seems, present. Shortly afterwards a meeting at which Jews were said to be present was organized at the Wazir mosque, which was attended by the local Young Turk committee including Mahmud Shukri al-Alusi and the poet Ma'ruf al-Risafi. The meeting heard a speech the gist of which was that members of parliament should be chosen more for their good qualities than for their local influence or wealth. Shortly before this meeting, the secretary of the *vilayet*, a prominent Young Turk, was seen smoking before sunset—and it happened to be Ramadan.

These events immediately elicited strong protests from a number of notables, including the *naqib*, Sayyid Abd al-Rahman and 'Isa al-Jamil, who had organized themselves into a committee which was locally known as the *Mashwar*. The *naqib*, as has been seen, had been the butt of agitations encouraged by the Young Turks; he had also been deprived of his seat on the administrative council of the province, while 'Isa al-Jumil had been revoked as head of the municipality.[44] The *Mashwar* now recorded in a memorandum that the mosque had been defiled by the presence of a large number of non-Muslims, and that three people had 'dishonoured' the Qur'an. 'It has been said', reported the British consul-general, 'that some of the *Mashwar* advised the people to collect the boys and youths and make a demonstration'. Whatever the truth of this allegation, the fact remains that a very large crowd of Muslims went to the *vali*'s house, who was informed that 'they did not appreciate the new Liberty' and that the secretary of the *vilayet* had to be dismissed. The *vali* bowed to their demands and either dismissed or suspended this official. The following day the *vali*, clearly intimidated by the *Mashwar* and the mob, arrested and imprisoned—without trial—Mahmud Shukri al-Alusi and Ma'ruf al-Risafi, who had been present at the Wazir mosque, and Abd al-Latif Thanayan, who may also have been present at this meeting, and who was also the editor of *al-Raqib*, a pro-Young Turk newspaper. Having been thus encouraged, the mob now proceeded to attack the Jews, a large and prosperous element in the city, who were accused of having desecrated the mosque by their presence, and who were suspected of sympathy for the Young Turks, having attended the reception for Hamdi Baban and his colleagues. 'In the forenoon [of 14 October]', reported the British consul-general, 'demonstrators arrived from the five quarters of the town and the large space in front of the Sarai was closely packed as well as the bazaars. The crowd attacked nearly every Jew who was seen and no-one seems to have interfered with them for many hours.' The reason for this inaction may have had to do with the fact, also reported by the consul-general, that while a large number of the officers were Young Turk in sympathy, the men were for a large part locally recruited, and might thus be unwilling to act against a local mob. Colonel Ramsay was also no doubt right in thinking that this demonstration 'probably went a good deal further than was intended by the promoters of it, who perhaps only wished, as they thought, to reduce the Jews to a respectful attitude and at the same time to give a lesson to the Young Turks.' But the significant thing is surely that the views of the *Mashwar* should have so readily evoked such a powerful popular resonance. Why this should have been so is again explained by Colonel Ramsay: 'Stories are told and believed', he wrote 'and it is more important that they were believed than that they were true, that Jews had abused Muhammadans and had even met violence with violence, and that in cases of altercation they had claimed absolute equality with Muhammadans. Such things were never dreamt of in Baghdad and it caused the more conservative people to think that the Muhammadan supremacy might be in danger from the Young Turks. This feeling was aggravated by the fact that some of the more active of the Young Turks are not very strict in the outward observances of the Muhammadan religion. There were many people who feared that the Young Turks thought more of their political ideas than of the injunctions of the Muhammadan religion, and that the Jews showed a tendency to think that they need no longer show any respect for the ruling race and the dominant religion.'[45] Ramsay's contemporary appreciation tallies exactly with 'Azzawi's retrospective account.

Mosul provides another striking example of the dislike which the Young Turks inspired in the Muslim population. As has been seen above, the reaction to the *coup d'état* in this city was at first non-committal, but the British vice-consul was soon reporting that the revival of the constitution was by no means welcome; indeed on the whole it was, he said, 'received with bad grace'. The immense majority of the inhabitants were Muslim and 'Far from being enthusiastic over the prospect of liberty, fraternity and a Parliament to redress their grievances this great majority are strongly opposed to a change in which they think they foresee a very real danger of Moslem supremacy.'[46] As they did elsewhere, the Committee of Union and Progress sent emissaries to Mosul to educate the population in the benefits of the constitution.[47] Their activities led to the exact opposite of what had been anticipated. In their speeches they seem to have gone out of their way to show disrespect to the sultan and 'the implied contempt for the Caliph', Wilkie Young reported, 'has evoked a good deal of unfavourable comment.' 'The Ulema', he also reported in a subsequent despatch, 'are in open opposition to them and signs are not wanting that mischievous persons are endeavouring to take advantage of the disturbed state of public feeling to excite religious animosity.'[48] This 'disturbed state of public feeling' shortly afterwards found vent in a formidable riot in which some seventy people perished. The riot was clearly the outcome of the widespread disaffection towards the authorities which the *coup d'état* created. Its victims were Kurds and, what is more serious from the government's point of view, largely men who wore the sultan's uniform. The Kurds predominated in the *vilayet* of Mosul, and were disliked by the predominantly Arab population of the city of Mosul. The riot seems to have been instigated by notables and ulamas in furtherance of obscure intrigues and tenebrous ambitions. Its immediate pretext was an allegation that a Kurdish employee of the tobacco *régie* at Mosul, strolling through the city on the second day of '*id al-adha*—4 January 1909—together with Muhammad and Mahmud, the sons of Shaykh Sa'id, the head of the Naqshabandi *tariqa* at Sulaymaniyya (who was then living in Mosul) molested or made improper advances to a local woman. An altercation ensued, and on that and the following two days, a mob led by a local bravo, Muhammad abu Jasim, attacked and murdered the eighty-year-old Shaykh Sa'id himself, his son Muhammad and sixteen others of his descendants, together with a large number of Kurdish gendarmes stationed in Mosul. In consequence of this riot, Wilkie Young wrote, 'the unfortunate impression' seemed to be gaining ground 'that the old landmarks of authority have disappeared and that as yet nothing stable has replaced them'.[49] As Miss Bell, who was then travelling in those parts, put it: 'If the leaders of the reactionary party had wished to embarrass the government and to show up its weakness, they were more than commonly successful. During the six weeks that elapsed before the arrival of troops from Diyarbekr and elsewhere, Mosul was in a state of complete anarchy. Christians were openly insulted in the streets, the civil and military authorities were helpless, and no less helpless was the local committee of Union and Progress.'[50]

The events of Baghdad and Mosul have their parallel in Damascus. As has been seen, the British consul reported in August that 'the Ulema and certain leaders in the town' were discontented, and though he did not expect any immediate trouble, yet Devey did express his apprehension of possible disorder, for the *coup d'état* had, in his view, much lowered the prestige of the government.[51] Events soon justified his fears. In a despatch of 1 October, he reported the formation of an Ulema Association. 'The Ulema', he explained 'through misapprehension and with uncalled for solicitude are anxious to conserve and uphold Islam against the liberal views of the Young Turks, while the latter have no intention at present to interfere with religious precepts. The first point of dispute was about women's wear which the Ulema wanted to be cut on a very simple mode, one piece enveloping the whole body; and the liberals denied them the right of interfering with this matter which should be regarded as pertaining to individual free choice. In this campaign,' Devey declares, 'the Ulema were defeated but not

without their rivals using threats of applying force.'[52] It may even
have actually come to the use of force. This is hinted at by Rashid
Rida, who visited Damascus at that time, when he writes, with his
usual discretion, that many disturbances took place when there was
shooting and people actually wounded 'as was told us by some,
and we do not like to go into details.'[53] But Rida discloses another
cause of tension at that time in Damascus, namely the elections and
the bitter enmity they brought to the surface between the notables
and the members of the Committee of Union and Progress, whom the
former considered as upstarts threatening their position. Two colonels
and a civilian roused their ire in particular, As'ad Bey and Salim Bey
al-Jaza'iri, and Dr. Haydar:[54] 'They hated the committee because it
created for those a position and influence in Damascus higher than
that of those disaffected notables who consider themselves the masters
of Damascus, and that influence should be confined to them and be
their exclusive monopoly.' Their methods—and those of their
opponents—are again hinted at by Rashid Rida, when he writes that
an armed gang excited by them erupted into the Umayyad Mosque
and attacked an 'alim for having induced some of the populace to
affix their seal to a petition nominating a—presumably Young
Turk—candidate, by pretending that the petition was asking for the
suppression of public dancing by women.[55]

Rashid Rida himself became the occasion of a serious disturbance.
At that point in his career, he was a fervent supporter of the Committee of Union and Progress. He was in Syria in the autumn of
1908. Towards the end of October he came on a visit to Damascus,
and was invited to preach in the Umayyad Mosque. He tells us
that his sermon dealt with the necessity of adopting European
scientific and industrial methods, and with showing that this in no
way infringed the teachings of Islam. The sermon was rudely
interrupted by an 'alim, himself a teacher at the Umayyad Mosque,
Salih Sharif al-Tunisi, whom Rashid Rida accuses of being a
follower of Abu'l-Huda al-Sayyadi. This 'alim, to quote the despatch
of the British consul, 'denounced him as "unbeliever" and his
teachings as heretical and aroused the public against him forcing
him to retire hurriedly from the Mosque.' Thereupon, As'ad Bey
who, as has been seen, was a pillar of the Committee of Union and
Progress at Damascus, arrested Shaykh Salih and took him to the
police station. When the people came out of the mosques after the
evening prayers and heard of the arrests they marched, 'in
thousands' according to Rashid Rida, to demonstrate and demand
the 'alim's release, shouting: Down with As'ad and the Committee
of Union and Progress! and, it is said, Down with the Constitution
and Long live the vali! This official was thus intimidated into

releasing Shaykh Salih and having him paraded in his own carriage to convince the populace that the 'alim was indeed free. The mob the British consul reported, then 'carried him in procession with insolent shouts back to the Mosque, in triumph, firing many shots as they went. The mob began to assemble an hour or so after sunset and were under no control nearly three hours.' As'ad had to hide in order to escape the fury of the mob. The incident, says Rashid Rida led to his having to leave Damascus, to the weakening of the Committee of Union and Progress and its defeat in the elections.[56] An eyewitness who published shortly afterwards an account of these events adds the significant detail that Rashid Rida was denounced by the mob for Wahabism.[57]

In the Hijaz, as has been seen, 'Ali, the amir of Mecca, had shown his dislike for the constitution and had been consequently humiliated in public. The vali, Ahmad Ratib, one of the Young Turk bêtes noires was also dismissed, accused of gross corruption and sent under arrest to Constantinople. His successor, Kazim, found the amir somewhat refractory, sulking in Ta'if and persistently refusing to come to Mecca. He therefore recommended his dismissal, and the fateful decision to replace him by his cousin Husayn was taken in November.[58] But it was not only the sharif 'Ali who was refractory; the Meccans too seemed to object to the Young Turks and their reforming zeal. In November 'serious disturbances' broke out in protest against a proposal by the Committee of Union and Progress to levy a cemetery tax; but the Meccans were also demonstrating against the Government's 'evident policy of curtailing the privileges and powers of the Grand Sharif.' 'The cry of "down with the red Tarboushes" (i.e. the Ottoman officials and soldiers)', the British consul also reported, 'was raised'.[59]

It will be remembered that the first local reactions to the Young Turk coup d'état at Benghazi and at Tripoli of Barbary were highly unfavourable. Passage of time does not seem to have induced a change of mind. Writing from the latter place at the end of September, the British consul reported that the attitude of the population towards the changes being introduced in the empire 'is, I regret to say, different from that of the Turkish population. Whereas the majority of the latter generally approve of the modifications that are being introduced into the administration even though they may not be aware of the width of their scope, the Arabs are much preoccupied about the reforms being in accordance with the principles of the Sacred Law.' What the Tripolitanians found most distasteful was the idea of the judicial and political equality of Muslims and non-Muslims.[60] The same dislike of the new order of things was manifest at Benghazi. Arabs of position, reported Fontana at the beginning of September, 'feel no great confidence in the stability of the constitution, consider a reversion to the former state of things not improbable, and regard with disapproval the licence of speech and tendency to insubordination to which the sudden and startling fall of an intensely autocratic form of government have not unnaturally given rise.'[61] The Committee of Union and Progress attempted to make their cause more popular. These efforts were in vain, both at Tripoli and Benghazi. In the latter place, in fact, opposition to the Young Turk delegate who visited the town in October, was vocal and unmistakable. The emissary, a major, called a meeting of notables in order to expound the programme of the committee. As soon as he concluded his speech, 'an elderly Arab rose and requested permission to speak. He said that the Arabs recognized three authorities, viz., God, the Prophet, and the sultan, or Khalif. And he asked whether the major or his colleagues had any letter of recommendation from the latter, or other credentials to show that his Imperial Majesty recognized and approved of their mission. The answer being in the negative, the Arab declared that he and his friends were unable to recognize that mission as a serious one, and the meeting was dissolved.' Not only was the Young Turk club shunned by the notables, where their presence, they feared, might later on be imputed to them as a crime, but it also seems to have conjured up a rival Arab club in opposition, whose members 'are not unswayed by reactionary inclination or ambition'. There was an exchange of visits between the members of the two clubs, 'the return visit paid by the Arabs culminating, purposely or otherwise, in high words and, it is said, the gleam of daggers.'[62]

This survey of conditions in the Arabic-speaking provinces during the months immediately following the *coup d'état* amply indicates the decline in governmental authority and the erosion of social stability which were its outcome. Men no longer took for granted the legitimacy of their government, and this, as it must always do, perilously increased social tension, and exacerbated the mutual fears and suspicions of Muslims and non-Muslims. The blow which the *coup d'état* administered to stable government also tempted local men of standing to try conclusions with the authorities in pursuit of greater profit and power. The events of Mosul, Baghdad, Damascus and Tripoli are clear and sufficient indication of the condition and temper of the country in the six months following the proclamation of the constitution. Two despatches from Basra, sent in February and March 1909, may be cited to show how the situation typically stood on the eve of the second *coup d'état*. Reporting an increase of disturbances by ruffians, and the murder of a rich Armenian, the British vice-consul wrote on 13 February: 'The state of the district is infinitely worse than it was before the Constitution was proclaimed, and I see no likelihood of any improvement under the very ineffectual administration of the present *vali*.' A month or so later, on 10 March, the vice-consul explains in another despatch that these disturbances are the work of a triumvirate consisting of the *naqib* of Basra, Shaykh Khaz'al of Muhammara and the Shaykh of Kuwayt who, in order to discredit the *vali*, combined to organize armed attacks on the city, and piracies in Shatt-al-'Arab.[63]

A despatch of 12 March 1909 from the consul at Jeddah may finally be quoted by a way of a verdict on this period not only in the Hijaz but also, by extension, elsewhere in the Arabic-speaking provinces. Through the change of amir and *vali*, Monahan observed, the pilgrims have been relieved of much extortion (though, we must add, they were not to enjoy this relief for long). But the country itself had gained nothing out of the constitution but 'some wooden boxes put up for the reception of dirt in some streets of Jeddah'. In any case, the fixed population of Jeddah was half negro, 'and does not, I think, taken in the mass, care for freedom or constitution or progress or sanitation'. Another benefit brought by the constitution was that two periodicals were published in Mecca. One, the *Hijaz*, published articles in praise of Islam and freedom, 'and, in one of its earlier numbers, a seemingly rather fanciful lucubration about the Prophet and the Arab race being the originators of Parliaments'. It may thus be seen that the Young Turks taught the Young Arabs more than the technique of the *coup d'état*. The other publication, *Shams al-haqiqa* appeared in both Turkish and Arabic. In Turkish it attacked the sharif Husayn for spending too much on banquets and too little on keeping the beduins in order, and for electoral jobbery in Mecca. And in Arabic it attacked Kamil Pasha as a slanderer who imputed to the Committee of Union and Progress a desire to dethrone the sultan.[64]

What *Shams al-haqiqa* denounced as slander soon proved to be the truth. The events of 13–27 April which began by a mutiny of troops at Constantinople, demanding the restoration of the *shari'a*, ended with the deposition of Abd al-Hamid, enforced by Young Turk officers in control of the third army in Macedonia, who marched on the capital from Salonika. The deposition may be seen as the outcome of the defeat of the Constantinople troops by the 'Operations Corps', or to be perhaps more accurate, of the defeat of non-westernized privates, corporals, sergeants and 'ranker' officers (who were to the fore in demanding the restoration of the *shari'a*) by the westernized Young Turk officers. Abd al-Hamid's deposition, in other words, was not the outcome of a popular movement. It would seem, rather, that in Constantinople, as in the Arabic-speaking provinces, the mass of the population was quite offended and alienated by the Frankish ways of Young Turks and their contempt for Islam and its traditional way of life. This it is which explains the popularity of the Muhammedan Union, whose propaganda, David Farhi writes, 'fell upon willing ears and released latent forces amongst the troops and the masses in the capital.'[65]

The Muhammedan Union, started in Constantinople, seems to have enjoyed great popularity in the Arabic-speaking provinces. '"Mohammedan Union" Societies', reported the U.S. consul-general at Beirut 'have been organized in Damascus, Homs, Hama and other typical Moslem strongholds, and may be counted on energetically to exert themselves directly, as well as through Bedouins, Circassians, Kurds and other professional marauders, to embarrass and oppose the constitutional party.'[66] The British consul at Damascus, in a despatch of 3 April 1909 wrote that thousands had already joined the union. A fortnight or so later, he wrote that during the previous three weeks some 20,000 had been signing a document in support of the union and of the shari'a, under the auspices of such notables as Abd al-Qadir al-'Ajlani, Amir 'Abdullah son of 'Abd al-Qadir al-Jaza'iri and Shaykh Badr al-din. Muhammad Kurd Ali later estimated the membership of the union in Damascus at 70,000.[67] When the news of the uprising by the first army corps reached Damascus, the inhabitants particularly of the Maydan quarter wanted to hold rejoicings, and the municipality was illuminated, though only in a small way.[68] The U.S. consular agent at Damascus, himself a Damascene, took the view that the Muhammedan Union had all the populace at its beck and call: 'Last Thursday [i.e. following the uprising at Constantinople], a few thousand of these met in the Midan armed to the teeth, and intended, it is said, to kill the Members of the Society of Union and Progress who they knew were assembled in the Grand Mosque. It appears they also contemplated destroying the various Government houses, as there was no need of them now that the Sheria or the Moslem precepts of religion was to govern the country.' A threat of military action by the commandant induced them to disperse, but there was nonetheless a panic among the Christians 'for the Moslems in their war songs mentioned that the Moslem religion was one of the sword and that being once again victorious, the Christian religion must give way.'[69]

From Aleppo, again, the U.S. consul sent an agitated despatch: 'Aleppo is in a panic, and as there are only 400 soldiers here, it looks bad should anything occur. The city is full of Beduin Arabs, Kurds and Circassians, and the Moslems are looking for trouble by taking mean advantage of the Christians in business deals in the shops, many of which are closed. There is not a weapon to be bought in Aleppo. Business is at a standstill, and there are grave fears of an outbreak at any moment.'[70] Even Beirut, where the reaction against the Young Turk *coup d'état* seemed to have been least strong, began to experience disorder in the first months of 1909. A despatch from the British consul-general of 12 April speaks of 'the continued existence of "mob rule" due to the prevailing mis-conception among the lower classes of the significance of the word "Liberty", tempered with a shrewd appreciation on the part of the populace of the weakness of the police and gendarmerie.' Cumberbatch went on to mention a case of mob-rule in which a Maronite newspaper editor was maltreated by a Muslim mob for an article he had written on the occasion of a visit by Sir Eldon Gorst to Syria which had taken place shortly before, in which the editor complained of the great disorder in the country and stated that they would be better off under European rule. Cumberbatch also gave an extract from a despatch by the vice-consul at Sidon who complained that murders and burglaries were on the increase, and declared: 'A general disenchantment is the main impression felt here by the people with regard to the new Constitution. All of them have already painfully ascertained that the new Regime has not conduced to any evident satisfactory result.'[71]

Mosul, where the great riots of January indicated the temper of the city, did not fall behind other localities in its enthusiasm for the Muhammedan Union. Early in April a notice was posted up, signed by a notable, Rashid al-'Umari, 'One of the most intriguing of notables', as the British vice-consul described him. The vali, however, took stern measures. Returning from a provincial tour just as the outbreak in Constantinople had taken place, he arrested Rashid al-'Umari together with Muhammad abu Jasim, the leader of the Mosul mob, and eleven others, thus maintaining the tranquillity of the city.[72] So that when Abd al-Hamid was deposed some ten days later 'not a voice', wrote Miss Bell, 'was raised against the second triumph of the new order. With the entire lack of initiative which characterizes the Asiatic provinces, men resigned themselves to a decree of Fate which was substantially backed by the army.'[73]

In fact, just as military power imposed the *coup d'état* of July 1908, so in April 1909 military power once more imposed the views and wishes of a handful of officers on a whole empire, again proving the truth of the maxim that in Muslim lands to him who has the power obedience is due. But it was not a ready obedience. 'In the large cities [of Mesopotamia] and especially in Baghdad' wrote the U.S. vice-consul when the triumph of the Young Turks was assured,

'I believe that a strong under-current of reactionary feeling has existed among the notables of the Mohammedan population, and, it is only due to the strength of the Young Turkish faction here— owing to many members of that party holding responsible and important positions among both the civil and military officials—that an outbreak of any disorder has been prevented.'[74] This judgement is echoed from the other end of the Arabic-speaking world by the British consul in Tripoli of Barbary. Reporting on a reception held to celebrate the accession of the new sultan, he declared that the attendance was very small, and the native element 'but sparsely represented'. 'In consequence of the reactionary sympathies of the mass of the population,' he went on to say, 'there was little or no animation and in comparison with previous occasions less interest was taken in the proceedings.'[75] His Benghazi colleague, Fontana, now in Aleppo made probably the same report which he woud have made had he not been transferred: 'The dethronement of Sultan Abd-al Hamid seemed to meet with very little approval among the majority of the local Moslem Arabs, who took very little part in the rejoicing otherwise so general.'[76] We may conclude this survey with a report which the consul in Jerusalem made some three months after Abd al-Hamid's downfall. 'I hear from different parts of the country', wrote Blech on 20 July, 'that the natives are believed to be but little in favour of the new régime—and that the League of Moslems numbers many adherents among them'. The Committee of Union and Progress, he went on, 'does its best to disseminate ideas of equality and constitutionalism, but it will take much time before these can bear fruit.'[77] The sixty odd years which have elapsed since the despatch was written throw a melancholy light on these hopes. We would now have to say that the very activity and example of the Committee of Union and Progress, by breaking the cake of custom, and by making attractive conspiracies and coups d'état, made constitutionalism virtually unattainable in these regions.

With his despatch of 20 July, Blech enclosed a despatch, dated the previous day, from the acting vice-consul at Jaffa, in which the latter reported that a Moor had gone berserk, shooting six persons, three of whom died. The Moor was apprehended. Admitting the deed, he used abusive language against the Constitution, the government and the new sultan, and declared that he was a partisan of Abd al-Hamid. May we not see in this poor, crazed, nameless and forgotten Moor the symbol of those disoriented multitudes whom the Young Turks, their self-appointed shepherds, were so blithely to lead into the shambles and the disasters of 1914–18?

APPENDIX

NOTES ON THE CITY OF MOSUL*

Mosul is situated on the right bank of the Tigris, roughly speaking equidistant from the Black Sea, the Mediterranean and the Persian Gulf, i.e. about 500 miles as the crow flies from Trebizond, Alexandretta and Basra. The journey from Alexandretta can be made by carriage, under favourable conditions, in fifteen days. Mule caravans take a few days longer and camel caravans anything up to six weeks according to the season. The journey from the Persian Gulf is generally of about the same duration, viz. four days by river-steamer from Basra to Baghdad, and from there to Mosul a caravan march of eight to twelve stages. From the north the approach is considerably longer, the most direct route being from Samsun to Diarbekir (19 stages) and from Diarbekir to Mosul down the Tigris by raft four to ten days according to the state of the river. Consequently it will be seen that, by whichever route, Mosul is the least accessible of the bigger cities in the Ottoman empire. This is the first obstacle to its progress.

Summer lasts from the end of April to the middle or end of October and is intensely hot, as much as 120 Fahrenheit being sometimes registered in the shade. A circumstance that makes the high temperature particularly trying is that, the houses being constructed of 'gess',† the walls absorb the heat during the day and give it out at night so that the early hours of evening in the stifling confinement of the city seem often to be as hot as any of the twenty-four. The writer has noticed 111 in the shade at sunset in August. Monsieur Thèvenot, visiting Mosul in 1664, wrote: 'Deux heures après le soleil levé il n'est plus possible d'aller dehors, jusqu'à qu'il y ait au moins une heure qu'il soit couché. Encore les murailles sont-elles si chaudes qu'à un demi-pied l'on en sent de la chaleur comme si c'était d'un fer chaud.' As an indication of the manner in which the walls retain the heat, the circumstance may be mentioned that eggs left in a closed room in the month of August hatch without any sort of attention.

Winter varies greatly in severity. The present has been so far exceptionally mild with only a few degrees of occasional frost. Three years ago the Tigris was frozen over and all the palms, oranges, olives and lemons were destroyed.

April and November, separating seasons of inevitable discomfort, are the pleasant months of the year; and they resemble each other in a manner which is perhaps not often to be noticed in other localities. The wonderful verdure of November following close upon half a year of blazing heat seems the more remarkable, and has given Mosul among the Arabs the name of Um-el-Rabiein, i.e. 'Mother of Two Springs'.

In the absence of European doctors it is difficult to obtain a reliable explanation of the deplorable condition of the city from the point of view

* Enclosed with despatch No. 4, Mosul, 28 January, 1909, in F.O. 195/2308.
† I.e. gypsum, which was used as cement. E.K.

of health. It is perhaps a platitude to say that the state of things would be very much less bad than it is under any other administration. The municipality do absolutely nothing—in fact natives declare they were better off before the era of municipalities, when each city-ward looked after its own affairs. There is no system of drainage. Refuse is thrown into the streets and even carcases are often left lying until trodden under foot. Each house has its well; but, the water being everywhere brackish, that required for drinking is brought in skins by mules or donkeys from the river. Incredible as it may appear, most of the drinking water is taken from a point on the river bank *below the city and barely 100 yards below the tannery*. The most prevalent diseases seem to be tuberculosis, typhoid and a peculiarly malignant form of malaria. An estimate furnished by the English dispensary gives the proportion of the entire population who suffer from tuberculosis in one form or another as 80 per cent, and it is said, on the same authority, that at least 10 per cent of the population suffer from ophthalmia or other diseases of the eye. Certainly the number of people one sees in the streets who are blind of one or both eyes or partially blind is appalling. The Mosul boil, a variety of that of Baghdad, seems to be universal and is often terrible in its ravages.

The city is built on two slopes of an eminence just sufficient to obstruct a general view of the whole from most points—a circumstance which has given it another Arabic name—that of the 'Hadba' Hunchback. It is surrounded by comparatively modern walls of no particular merit, built for protection against Arab raids. They are pierced by seven gates which are shut at sunset. For solidity and grandeur they cannot compare with those of Diarbekir which are entirely of basalt and of imposing regularity. Nor does Mosul present any other striking architectural feature. The mosques are poor and dilapidated, the streets are irregular, narrow and squalid and for the most part without any redeeming feature of picturesqueness. One might traverse it in half a dozen directions without coming upon any sign of art or even of skill. It is true that some of the houses of the Begs are vast and contain spacious courtyards; but to the street they only show high, windowless, dilapidated walls, pierced by a single gate-way heavily barred and studded with iron. Each house is in fact a fortress which could be defended by six or eight armed men against a mob almost indefinitely. One which was occupied last year by the British vice-consulate, is approached by a series of vaulted passages: and no less than five substantial gates would have to be demolished before the inner courtyard could be reached. The necessity for such defences is still insistent in a city where the wealthy keep their capital hidden in their houses, and murder and robbery are much less than a nine days' wonder.

The city is divided into 36 wards, each of which has its own traditions, animosities, customs and, to a certain extent, even dialect. The members of a great family always inhabit the same ward: and in several cases whole streets are inhabited by members and dependants of a single family. Feeling between the different wards is often strong and bitter and not infrequently gives rise to quarrels in which fifty or sixty take part on either side. Barricades are erected and the arms used are clubs, maces, revolvers, knives and stones. Only one such engagement took place last year, one man being killed and several wounded. Family feuds are common but less often lead to open hostilities, though in one case last summer an engagement to dine at one of the consulates was thrown over at the last moment on the ground that an attack was expected and the house was being placed in a state of defence.

Anything approaching an exact estimate is not obtainable, the population having hitherto successfully resisted all attempts to register their women: and, as usual in oriental cities but perhaps more so in Mosul than elsewhere, a very large proportion of the children not being entered at all. The total cannot, however, be far short of 100,000. Of these, nine-tenths are Moslems and the remainder Christians and Jews.

The only language spoken in the city (outside a Kurdish colony, numbering perhaps 3,000), is Arabic. It is hardly an exaggeration to say that among the Moslems there is practically no education at all. Even amongst the members of the great families there are very few indeed who can express themselves in Turkish: and, so far as I am aware, there is only one Moslem in the whole city who knows a European language, viz. Daud Chelebi, Dragoman to the German vice-consulate. This gentleman is also the only one who has visited Europe. Very few have been as far as Constantinople and hardly any among the upper classes have performed the pilgrimage. Even Baghdad and Aleppo, the nearest considerable cities (eight and ten days distant respectively), are known only by report to the majority of those who could afford to travel if they wished. Being on friendly terms with all the great Moslem families without exception, I have had opportunities of studying their habits during the past ten months. The very great, e.g. the Abdul-Jelils, do not visit their fellow citizens and in fact very rarely indeed leave their own houses. Three times a day, viz. morning, afternoon and evening, they sit in state in their Divan-Khanes and receive those who come to pay their respects. The remaining hours are spent in the harem. The houses of Mosul have no gardens and, for the most part, no view. Such is the life of nine out of ten of the Mosul Begs throughout the year, varied perhaps in one or two cases by a very occasional visit to some neighbouring village where they own property. Very few care for sport or appear to have any interest in life at all beyond, presumably, the delights of the harem. Most of them are said to drink excessively and, excepting the Abdul-Jelils, all are reputed to be grasping and avaricious. In their houses they wear their picturesque native clothes but latterly they have begun to don the usual travesty of European garments on the rare occasions when they go out. Their spacious, dilapidated courtyards have something noble about them and the crowd of armed servants in beautiful native costume are in keeping with the rather feudal aspect of the whole; but the rooms are for the most part mean and uninteresting, and seldom contain a fine carpet or a good piece of furniture.

It is probably the dullest and most self-satisfied society in the whole Ottoman empire. The impression that one receives is that it has been deadened and demoralized by generations of unhealthy, self-centred existence. Those who can afford to do nothing—and, their wants being few, such is the good or ill fortune of the majority—spend day after day, month after month, in absolute idleness with no interest and no purpose, the elder men sitting solemnly indoors, the young ones loafing and gossiping at the gate until it is their turn to succeed them. Probably there is no place which has been so little affected by movements in other parts of the empire. Mosul was conquered by the Turks in 1638: and, though there is less energy and intellect in its inhabitants today than three centuries ago, it is still *itself*, ruled in all essentials by its own Ulema and Begs and successfully opposing the *vis inertiae* of a somewhat brutish conservatism to all that approaches it from outside. Latterly knives and forks have been introduced but I am informed on excellent authority that there is no Moslem family in all Mosul that uses them unless guests of especial distinction happen to be present.

The attitude of the Moslems towards the Christians and Jews, to whom as stated above, they are in a majority of ten to one, is that of a master towards slaves whom he treats with a certain lordly tolerance so long as they keep their place. Any sign of pretension to equality is promptly repressed. It is often noticed in the street that almost any Christian submissively makes way even for a Moslem child. Only a few days ago the writer saw two respectable-looking, middle-aged Jews walking in a garden. A small Moslem boy, who could not have been more than eight years old, passed by and, as he did so, picked up a large stone and threw it at them—and then another—with the utmost nonchalance, just as a small boy elsewhere might aim at a dog or bird. The Jews stooped and avoided the aim, which was a good one, but made no further protest.

Some time ago a Moslem woman, having vainly disputed the price of some medicine sold her at the English dispensary, told the dispenser 'he would have cause to regret it'. Passing through the crowded market the following day he was very badly—almost fatally—stabbed by an individual who attacked him suddenly from behind and then disappeared in the crowd. No one intervened and it was subsequently impossible—as it always is—to obtain evidence: and the aggressor was never traced.

Some years ago a member of the leading Jacobite family in Mosul had the misfortune to offend a powerful Moslem family. Shortly afterwards he was surprised in the street, dragged into a courtyard and so severely beaten that he died of his wounds. Such instances might be multiplied; but the three cited will suffice to indicate the relations which unfortunately exist.

One other characteristic of Mosul Moslems may be noted. Their fanatical attitude towards other religions has been observed. It is a curious fact, however, that they are not at all exact in the observance of their own. Not half-per-cent of the population have performed the pilgrimage: and they seem to be equally careless of other essentials. Those who are sufficiently influential do not hesitate to seize 'Wakf' property or to build over cemeteries. Sabonji* is a notorious offender in this respect: and no one takes the trouble to oppose him. The murder of Sheikh Said (a

* A powerful notable whose intrigues constantly recur in Mosul despatches. E.K.

'member of the Family of the Prophet') and his entourage three weeks ago is another instance of the little respect in which traditions, which count for much elsewhere, are held by the 'fanatical' inhabitants of Mosul. These points are in such striking contrast with the attitude of pious Moslems in other districts that it would almost seem that the 'fanaticism' of this population is directed merely against what happens not to suit them and bears little relation to the tenets of their faith. It seems to be a perverse and demoralized race from which little good is to be expected and which only an impressive display of force will restrain from positive evil.

The recent disturbances offered a striking illustration of the traditional methods by which the Begs and local Ulema coerce and trifle with the Government: A plan of campaign is arranged at a 'mejliss' (assembly) in one of the great houses the night before; and Abu Jassim or some such ruffian is instructed to carry it out, being promised no doubt a new cloak or a few liras for his trouble. Needless to say, neither Ulema nor Notables show themselves when once the mischief has begun. When it is all over, they emerge and go in a body to visit the Vali—or perhaps to the Telegraph Office—with plausible expressions of regret for the occurrence and excuses for the mob, 'which', they say, 'is deplorably ignorant and unreasoning and will not be restrained when its feelings are strongly moved', sic, the fact being that the mob's 'feelings' are never moved unless by one of themselves. Successive Valis have learnt this and have compromised accordingly. It is said, however, that the government has never suffered ignominious defeat as on 6 January last.

As regards the lower classes of the Moslem population, ignorant and brutal though they are, I believe it would be found that there are none more submissive in the whole of Turkey. Their Ulema and Notables rule them like a flock of sheep: and given a sufficient display of force and determination and a few sharp examples, the central government would have no difficulty in establishing and maintaining its authority. It is an idle and easy-going population, working about three days of the seven and spending the remainder of its time gossiping in the coffee-houses or vacantly 'taking the air' on the city-walls. Like other idlers, however, the men of Mosul are always ready for mischief, more especially when it implies a prospect of plunder to be indulged in without much fear of the consequences. Their attitude on any given occasion will always depend upon a pretty shrewd estimate of the strength of parties and of the probable consequences of their action to themselves. If the present moment seems critical, it is due to the fact that in the last five years three weak Valis have been seen to succumb to local intrigues and that, though the latest disturbance was on a larger scale than any before, nearly a month has passed without a sign of life from the vaguely realized authority at Constantinople.

The total of the Christians in Mosul probably does not exceed 9,000. They are distributed among the following denominations: Chaldean Catholics, Syrian Catholics, Jacobites or old Syrians and a handful of Armenians, Protestants and Greeks.

The most important community are the Chaldean Catholics. These are Nestorians by origin who seceded from their old church and acknowledged the supremacy of the Pope about two hundred years ago. This movement towards Rome among the ancient and independent Churches of the East has continued intermittently ever since; and great efforts are made by the Dominican Mission in Mesopotamia to foster it. The Spiritual Head of all the Chaldean Catholics (in Persia as well as Turkey) is the Patriarch Emanuel who resides in Mosul. Their numbers in this city approximate 3,000. They have seven churches, twenty-one Priests and four schools which are attended by about 350 pupils. The rest of the children of this denomination attend the schools of the Dominican Mission.

This community [i.e. the Syrian Catholics] number in the city about 2,500. They are Jacobites by origin who, under French influence, have seceded from their ancient church and acknowledged Rome. Their Patriarch resides at Aleppo. In Mosul they have an archbishop, three churches, fifteen priests and three schools.

A Roman Catholic Mission was established here by Capucins in the seventeenth century and has been maintained continuously since. It is now in the hands of 13 Dominican Fathers and numerous Nuns. They have a very fine church and admirable schools giving instruction free to over a thousand pupils.

The Pope is represented in Mesopotamia by a delegate, Monseigneur Drure, who resides at Mosul. The funds by which the delegation is supported, with considerable state, were bequeathed for this express purpose by a French lady more than two centuries ago on condition that the Papal representative should always be a Frenchman.

The Old Syrians or Jacobites are one of the most ancient and interesting of the eastern churches. In spite of persecution and comparative poverty they have stoutly maintained their independence for sixteen centuries, steadily refusing to sacrifice their convictions and freedom for the advantages offered by Rome. When it is remembered that these advantages would include payment of their priests and bishops, free education for their children and, above all, the steady protection of their interests by the French government, this unbending attitude is the more remarkable in a comparatively small community. The 'distinctive doctrinal principle of the Jacobite Church is the Monophysite thesis'. Their head is the Patriarch Ignatius who lately had the honour of being received by his Majesty the King (v. 'Times' Dec.). He resides at the Monastery of Deir Zeforan near Mardin. There are several thousand Jacobites in India. In Mosul they number about 3,000. They have four churches in the city, four priests and three schools attended by about 200 children. The rest of them attend the School of the English Mission.

The Church Missionary Society maintains a school here which is attended by about 200 pupils, Protestant, Jacobite and a few Moslem. The most important branch of its work, however, is its medical mission. This has not yet been placed on a permanent basis, and the prolonged absence of the physician in charge—since the Autumn of 1907—has naturally impeded its progress. During two years' work previously to his departure for England, this mission seems to have earned the respect and gratitude of all classes of the population. It is superfluous to lay stress upon the value of medical work in such conditions as exist in Mosul. When it is remembered that at present there is no European doctor nearer than Baghdad (sixteen days' hard travelling, there and back), it is easy to understand the eagerness with which the return of the English doctor and the establishment of his proposed hospital are awaited.

The Armenians in Mosul number about forty families, the Protestants twenty-seven (27) families and the Greek Orthodox only seven or eight families. Each of these has its church.

Though, thanks to the efforts of the French and English missions, the Christians have made some progress, they are still lamentably backward. This is perhaps partly owing to the state of complete subordination to the dominant caste, in which they live and partly to certain inherent defects of character which they share with their Moslem fellow-citizens. Their houses are miserably poor: and the condition of their women is hardly better than those of the Moslems. No Christian woman dares cross the street without covering her face: they take their meals apart from their husbands, with whom, by the way, it would be considered 'disgraceful' for them to appear in public. In short, on most points, the customs of Christians and Moslems in Mosul closely resemble each other. Christian men generally marry at the age of thirty or thereabouts, girls at the age of twelve or thirteen.

The Jewish Colony is the oldest community in Mosul, having a continuous existence since the captivity. About a year ago the Alliance Israelite established a mission under the very able direction of Monsieur Maurice Sidi. It met at first with much opposition on the part of the ex-Vali, Mustapha Beg; but its position appears to have been officially recognized; and it is now doing excellent work in a quarter of the city which was perhaps more urgently in need of enlightened help than any other in Mosul—and this is saying a very great deal.

Mosul, Jan. 28. 1909   (sd.) H. E. WILKIE YOUNG

NOTES

1. U.K., Foreign Office, Historical Section, Peace Handbook no. 60, *Syria and Palestine*, 1920, pp. 41 and 42–3. The Handbook was anonymous, but Hogarth's authorship is ascertained from a list established by Professor Prothero, the general editor of the Handbooks, in F.O. 370/235, files L455 and L959/14/405.

2. *The Emergence of Modern Turkey*, 1961, p. 177.

3. F.O. 195/2188, consul-general Newmarch's no. 213/26, Baghdad 31 March 1905. The incident is described, with many interesting details by Alusi's disciple, Muhammad Bahjat al-Athari in *A'lam al-Iraq* (Iraq Notables), Cairo, 1345 A.H., pp. 99ff. Alusi had started out by being a follower of Abul-Huda and gained preferment as such, but by the age of thirty he had come under the influence of the writings of Ibn Taymiyya and Ibn al-Qayyim and became hostile to sufism and its tariqas. But for a long time he did not

dare disclose his beliefs: '*wa tasattara tahta sitar al-taqiyya*'. The work which aroused the suspicion of the authorities may have been *Tarikh Najd* (History of Najd) published by Athari after Alusi's death (1st ed. Cairo, 1343 A.D.) from a manuscript among the latter's papers. It is generally a fervent, not to say violent, defence of Wahabism against accusations which the Ottoman authorities had made at one time or another, and which, as Athari admits, were believed by the mass of the Muslims, *al-sawad al-jahil* (the ignorant mass) as he calls them.

4. In: no. 4, 20 April 1901, pp. 132–8; no. 10, 17 July, pp. 417–22; and no. 12, 31 August, pp. 453–61.

5. *al-Manar*, vol. IV at p. 418.

6. *Loc. cit.*, pp. 838–9. Muhammad Kurd 'Ali was instrumental in getting the pamphlet published in Egypt, and as a consequence was too afraid to go back to his native Damascus, and remained exiled in Egypt for a few years; see Jamal al-Din al-Alusi, *Muhammad Kurd Ali*, Baghdad 1966, p. 54. Kurd Ali is yet another one of these 'radical' intellectuals who seemed to proliferate in the last decade or so of Abd al-Hamid's reign.

7. Consul Richards' no. 80 and no. 82, Damascus, 30 and 31 December 1901, in F.O. 195/2097; Rashid Rida's obituary in *al-Manar*, vol. XIX, no. 3, 29 August 1916, at pp. 169–70; Zahrawi's articles entitled 'al-Siyasa wa'l-sasa' (Politics and Statesmen) *ibid.*, vol. IV, no. 18, pp. 728–31 and no. 20, 27 December 1901, pp. 761–7; the quotations above are at pp. 766 and 767. Rashid Rida's note on these articles, *ibid.*, vol. IV, no. 21, 26 January 1902, pp. 839–40.

8. F.O. 195/2190, Drummond Hay's no. 39 Confidential, Beirut 10 June 1905. Rashid Rida notices the incident in *al-Manar*, vol. VIII, no. 8, 19 June 1905, pp. 315–18.

9. F.O. 195/2275, file no 250, political diary of the Baghdad residency for week ending 3 August 1908, enclosed in Ramsay's no. 704/74 of 3 August.

10. F.O. 195/2275, despatch from Ramsay Baghdad no. 757/81 of 17 August.

11. F.O. 195/2272, file 70.

12. Department of State records, National Archives Washington, despatch no. 7 from J. S. Jackson, Aleppo, 5 August 1908. I am very grateful to the Warden and Fellows of St. Antony's College, Oxford, for making it possible for me to consult these records.

13. Department of State records, G. B. Ravndal's no. 171, Beirut, 4 August, 1908.

14. F.O. 195/2277, file 138, vice-consul Abela's despatch of 17 August enclosed with consul-general Cumberbatch's despatch no. 58, Beirut, 20 August.

15. F.O. 195/2287, file 59, Blech's no. 39 Confidential, Jerusalem, 6 August 1908.

16. F.O. 195/2286, file 72, acting consul Husain's no. 39.

17. F.O. 195/2271, Fontana's no. 16 Confidential, Benghazi 20 August. Fontana's report is confirmed by the French scholar N. Slousch who was then travelling in Tripolitania and who found the population of Benghazi showing 'symptoms of general discontent' immediately following the *coup d'état*. See N. Slousch, 'Le nouveau régime turc et Triploi', *Revue du monde musulman*, vol. VI (1908), p. 54.

18. F.O. 195/2271, Alvarez no. 48.

19. F.O. 195/2271, Alvarez unnumbered Confidential despatch, Tripoli 12 September 1908. The abortive conspiracy is related in Somerville Story, ed., *The Memoirs of Ismail Kemal Bey*, 1920.

20. N. S[lousch], 'Redjeb Pacha' in *Revue du Monde Musulman*, vol. VI at p. 156. Abd al-Hamid does not seem to have hanged people for expressing opinions, *vide* this multitude of exiles in Tripoli and elsewhere.

21. 'Le nouveau régime turc et Tripoli', *loc. cit.* at p. 54.
22. F.O. 195/2271, Alvarez no. 53 of 9 August, his no. 54 of 14 August and his no. 55 of 21 August. See also Slousch, 'Le nouveau regime turc . . .' *loc. cit.* at pp. 56–7. Slousch seems to have been an eyewitness of these events. He states that the meeting at the Karamanli mosque also resolved to demand the abolition of the Constitution.
23. F.O. 195/2271, Alvarez no. 53 cited above.
24. F.O. 195/2271, Fontana's no. 16 Confidential, cited above.
25. F.O. 195/2271, Fontana's no. 17 Confidential, 7 September.
26. U.S. National Archives, Department of State records, Wallace's despatch, Jerusalem, 12 August 1908.
27. Ravndal's no. 171, Beirut, 4 August; F.O. 195/2277, file 131, Cumberbatch's no. 55 Confidential, Beirut, 8 August; Ravndal's no. 182, Beirut, 14 August.
28. U.S. National Archives, Department of State records, Ravndal, Beirut to Leishman, Constantinople, no. 186, 26 August; and Ravndal, Beirut to Secretary of State, Washington, no. 176, 2 September.
29. F.O. 195/2277, file 137, Devey's no. 33, Damascus, 12 August; U.S. consular agent's despatch, Damascus 31 July, enclosed in Ravndal's no. 171 of 4 August cited above.
30. F.O. 195/2272, file 70, Longworth's despatch, Aleppo, 20 August; U.S. National Archives, Department of State records, Jackson's no. 7, Aleppo, 5 August; both cited above.
31. U.S. National Archives, Department of State records, Ravndal, Beirut to Leishman, Constantinople, no. 203, 23 November 1908, quoting report of consular agent at Hodeida.
32. F.O. 195/2277, file 139, vice-consul Abela's despatch of 17 August, cited above.
33. F.O. 195/2286, file 72, acting consul Husain's despatch no. 39, Jedda, 25 August, cited above.
34. F.O. 195/2275, file 291, Ramsay's no. 796/87 of 31 August.
35. U.S. National Archives, Department of State records, Nasif Meshaka's no. 105, to Ravndal, Damascus 10 August; F.O. 195/2277, file 137, Devey's no. 33, Damascus, 12 August, cited above.
36. F.O. 195/2287, file 68, Blech's no. 45, Jerusalem, 8 September.
37. F.O. 195/2287, file 68, Blech's no. 45, cited above.
38. Gertrude Bell, *Amurath to Amurath*, 1911, p. 95.
39. F.O. 195/2277, file 181, Cumberbatch's no. 74, Secret and Confidential, Beirut, 17 October. For a portrait of one such landowner see Gertrude Bell, *The Desert and the Sown*, 1907, pp. 313ff.
40. Yusuf al-Hakim, *Suriyya wa'l 'ahd al-'uthmani* (Syria and the Ottoman Era), Beirut, 1966, p. 159.
41. Revue du monde musulman, vol. VI (1908), p. 681.
42. F.O. 371/1528, file 346 Lorimer's no. 830/39, Baghdad, 9 October, 1911.
43. 'Abbas al-'Azzawi, *Tarikh al-'Iraq bayn ihtilalayn* (History of Iraq between Two Occupations), vol. VIII, Baghdad 1956, p. 160.
44. *Revue du monde musulman*, vol. VII (1909), p. 316.
45. F.O. 195/2275, file 340, Ramsay's no. 943–105, Baghdad, 19 October, 1908.
46. F.O. 195/2275, file 291, report from vice-consul Wilkie Young, Mosul, 19 August, enclosed with Ramsay's no. 796/87, Baghdad, 31 August, cited above.
47. Political education as practised by the Committee of Union and Progress sometimes seems a pure emanation of the spirit of comedy; thus in the vilayet of Damascus a commission composed of an *'alim*, Abd al-Razzaq al-Bitar,

a school-teacher, Quraysh efendi, a Muslim notable, Abd al-Rahman al-Yusuf, and a Christian notable, Mikha'il Sandah was sent out to Hauran 'in order to explain the meaning of liberty and of the Constitution to the Beduins, to enrol them under the Ottoman flag, and to spread among them the spirit of fraternity. They are expected to publish in the local newspapers their speeches and exhortations.' See *Revue du monde musulman*, vol. vi (1908), pp. 244–5.

48. F.O. 195/2275, files 333 and 363, Wilkie Young's Mosul diary for 14 October enclosed with Ramsay's no. 945/106, Baghdad, 19 October, and his diary for 20 October enclosed with Ramsay's no. 990/117, Baghdad, 2 November.

49. F.O. 195/2308, file 30, Wilkie Young's despatch no. 2, Mosul, 14 January 1909. The vice-consul also discusses the riot in the 'Notes on the City of Mosul' enclosed with his no. 4 of 28 January, *ibid*. (reproduced in an appendix below). The leader of the mob, Muhammad abu Jasim, led another mob a few years before which was successful in thwarting a plan by the Ottoman government to include women in a population census it was then conducting; see Khayri al-'Umari, *Hikayat siyasiyya min tarikh al-'Iraq al-hadith* (Political Episodes from the Modern History of Iraq), Cairo, 1969, pp. 96–8.

50. Gertrude Bell, *Amurath to Amurath*, p. 250.

51. F.O. 195/2277, file 137, Devey's no. 33, Damascus, 12 August, cited above.

52. F.O. 195/2277, file 174, Devey's no. 51, Damascus, 1 October.

53. *Al-Manar*, vol. XI, no. 12 (22 January 1909), p. 948.

54. Dr. Haydar may have been Salih Haydar who was condemned to death and executed in 1915, as was Salim al-Jaza'iri in 1916, both being accused of subversive activities as members of secret Arab nationalist societies.

55. *Al-Manar*, loc. cit.

56. *Al-Manar*, vol. XI, pp. 949–51; F.O. 195/2277, file 197, Devey's no. 58, Damascus, 27 October. Devey states that Amir Ali al-Jaza'iri was instrumental in getting Shaykh Salih released. In a later despatch (F.O. 195/2311, file 28, no. 5, Damascus, 19 January 1909) Devey declares that a new *vali* who had in the meantime been appointed to Damascus, carried out an investigation of the riot and found that a certain number of *ulama* 'were the real provokers of that unhappy incident'. Nazim Pasha made them acknowledge their mistake and promise to mend their behaviour.

57. A. J. B. Wavell, *A Modern Pilgrim in Mecca* [1912], 1918 ed., pp. 59–60.

58. There seems to be no basis for the frequent assertion that Husayn was appointed on the recommendation of the British Embassy at Constantinople.

59. F.O. 195/2286, files 107 and 113, Monahan's no. 60 and 62, Jeddah, 18 November and 2 December respectively.

60. F.O. 195/2271, Alvarez's no. 61, Tripoli, 30 September.

61. F.O. 195/2271, Fontana's no. 17 Confidential, Benghazi, 7 September 1908, cited above.

62. F.O. 195/2271, Fontana's no. 25 Confidential, Benghazi, 21 December. Alvarez's no. 63 and 65 of 9 and 17 October respectively (F.O. 195/2271) report on the visit of the Young Turk emissary to Tripoli, and describe the dissensions within the official and political class.

63. F.O. 195/2308, files 76 and 110, Crow's nos. 9 and 17 respectively.

64. F.O. 195/2320, file 25, Monahan's no. 12, Confidential, Jeddah, 12 March 1909.

65. David Farhi, 'The Şeriat as a Political Slogan—or the "Incident of the 31st *Mart*"' in *Middle Eastern Studies*, vol. VII, no. 3 (1971). See also Victor R. Swenson 'The Military Rising in Istanbul 1909' in *Journal of Contemporary History*, vol. V, no. 4 (October 1970).

66. U.S. National Archives, Dept. of State records, Ravndal's no. 249, Beirut, 25 April 1909.

67. F.O. 195/2311, files 84 and 97, Devey's nos. 18 and 22, Damascus, 3 and 19 April respectively; Muhammad Kurd Ali, quoted in Tawfiq Ali Baru, *al-Arab wal-Turk fi'l 'ahd al-dusturi al-uthmani* (Arabs and Turks during the Ottoman Constitutional Period), Cairo, 1960, p. 131.

68. F.O. 195/2311, file 97, Devey's no. 22 cited above.

69. U.S. National Archives, Dept. of State records, Meshaka to Ravndal, no. 148, Damascus, 22 April 1909.

70. U.S. National Archives, Dept. of State records, Jackson to Ravndal, no. 278, Aleppo, 20 April.

71. F.O. 195/2311, file 89, Cumberbatch's no. 30 Confidential, Beirut, 12 April 1909.

72. F.O. 195/2309, file 178, Wilkie Young's no. 12, Mosul, 9 April and his no. 13 of 16 April, both addressed to Ramsay, Baghdad.

73. *Amurath to Amurath*, p. 252.

74. U.S. National Archives, Dept. of State records, Bird to Ravndal, no. 614, Baghdad, 13 May 1909.

75. F.O. 195/2305, Alvarez's no. 18, Tripoli, 29 April 1909.

76. F.O. 195/2306, Fontana's no. 13, Aleppo, 27 May 1909.

77. F.O. 195/2321, file 78, Blech's no. 61.

9. Arabs Ancient and Modern

For quite some time now, the Arabs have been making a considerable noise in the world. Chanceries, academics and newspapers are
alike preoccupied with Arab grievances, demands and aspirations.
From small beginnings thirty or forty years ago, the Arab question
has become an industry similar to that of electronics or space
technology. But the Arabs have also become a bore. Fifty or a
hundred years ago an author who felt drawn to middle-eastern
subjects had a tremendous variety from which to choose: Barbary
corsairs, belly dancers, fanatical Mussulmans, sultans, pashas, moors,
muezzins, harems. Now, in a decidedly poor exchange, it has to be
the Arabs.

By Arabs of course we do not mean the lively and interesting
denizens of Cairo, Beirut, Damascus or Baghdad. We mean rather
the collective entity which writers of books manufacture and in
which they manage to smother the charm and variety of this ancient
and sophisticated society. This collective entity is a category of
European romantic historiography, and judged by its results, it is
not a felicitous invention; for as they are described by their inventors
the Arabs are a decidedly pitiable and unattractive lot; they erupt
from the Arabian desert; they topple two empires, while making
grandiloquent speeches in their rich and sonorous language; but
all too soon the rot sets in, materialism and greed erode their spirit,
and their caliphs change from lean puritans into fat voluptuaries.
After that, it is all up with them: they are engulfed and enslaved by
the Turks, hoodwinked by the British, colonized by the French,
humiliated by the Jews, until at last they rise up again to struggle
valiantly against Imperialism and Zionism under the banner of
Nationalism and Socialism.

The ultimate insult is that the victims of this European travesty
have accepted this caricature as a true picture of themselves, and as
nature is said to imitate art have, in the process, come in fact to
behave like it.

As may be gathered from the title of his book,* Mr. Carmichael
recognizes this story for the European concoction that it is. He
argues, in fact, that only now, because of the wide currency which
modern methods of propaganda and indoctrination have ensured
for this myth, has an Arab collective identity, shaped and sustained
by it, begun to emerge. He writes (p. 309):

* *The Shaping of the Arabs: A Study in Ethnic Identity* by Joel Carmichael.

It was in fact the Western habit of referring to Arabic-speaking Muslims, at least in the Middle East outside of Egypt, as 'Arabs' because of their language—on the analogy of German-speakers as Germans, French-speakers as French and so on—that imposed itself on an East that had never regarded language as a basic social classifier. It was natural for Europeans to use the word 'Arab' about a Muslim or even a Christian whose native language was Arabic; they were quite indifferent to the principles of classification in the East. The oddity is simply that this European habit became the very germ that the contemporary Arabs nationalist movement has sprung from.

Mr. Carmichael's purpose in this book is to show matters in a truer perspective. He begins by discussing the Arabs, i.e., the inhabitants of the Arabian peninsula, at the time of their eruption onto the stage of world history in the seventh century of the Christian era. He gives us an idea of their social and economic organization, describes the appearance of the Prophet Muhammad, the character of his message, the foundation of the Muslim polity in Medina, and the Muslim conquest of Mesopotamia, Syria and Egypt. These conquests meant the establishment of an Arab empire—an empire, that is, ruled by the Arabs of the Arabian Peninsula. But, as Mr. Carmichael argues, this Arab empire did not last for very long. With the conversion to Islam of the conquered populations, the Arab element speedily lost its dominance and became part of a new amalgam, the political institutions and the civilization of which we have come to identify as characteristically Islamic. In this new amalgam, from the start and until very recently, the dominant elements were the Persians and various kinds of Turks.

Toward the beginning of *The Shaping of the Arabs* Mr. Carmichael announces that his purpose is to 'extricate' their history from that of 'the far larger community of Islam'. The book is in fact a history of the Muslim world which draws on previous work in the field. The borrowing is somewhat uncritical, for we see the author drawing inspiration, on the one hand, from the works and theories of such eminent Orientalists as Brockelmann, Grunebaum, Lewis and Gibb, and, on the other, from writers like Antonius and Toynbee.

The author is not very successful in extricating Arab from Muslim history, and we may speculate on the character and legitimacy of the enterprise itself. Mr. Carmichael frequently states that very soon after the appearance of Islam Arab history proper becomes indistinguishable and inextricable from Muslim history. To try to extricate it from this history is to adopt the very perspective, invented and propagated by Europeans, which the author rightly finds so unsatisfactory. We may go further and say that to search for Arab elements in Muslim history is to be influenced by contemporary preoccupations and interests; it is to fall into anachronism, to show us the past tailored to present requirements. Consider, therefore, a passage such as the following (p. 58):

> In any case, the importance of Muhammad's role can scarcely be over-estimated. Though Islam began outwardly and inwardly as an Arab appendage, it soon overflowed the bounds of the people it had been born into and burst out of the Arabian Peninsula altogether. The paradox of Muhammad's life was that though he formed the Arabs into a people, he did so through a modality that was essentially self-contradictory, by laying the foundations of a universal religion.

Such a passage is heavy with the assumptions of a secular, 'sociological' culture, according to which religion is eminently an instrument or an appendage. It is safe to say that Muhammad and his contemporaries, and the successive generations of Muslims until almost yesterday, would have rejected utterly the notion of Islam as an appendage whether 'outward' or 'inward'. For them Islam was the central event of history which governed and coloured the whole of their lives. If this is so, then the paradox of which Mr. Carmichael speaks becomes somewhat artificial. Muhammad did not intend to form the Arabs into a people, nor did he in fact do so. Out of Arabs he made *Muslims*, and it is as Muslims that they went out of Arabia to make their conquests and establish their empire. Only modern Europeans and their middle-eastern imitators would look upon Muhammad as the founder of the Arab nation.

Thus it is Mr. Carmichael's undertaking rather than Muhammad's life which is paradoxical. He sees the radical failing of romantic European historiography, and yet exhibits, in many ways, the very same failing. When we come to the modern period, Mr. Carmichael also manages to present a romantic version of Arab history, no doubt because of the sources on which he seems to rely. Antonius, in his *Arab Awakening*, provided Arab nationalism with a mythical prehistory in the nineteenth century, and the mark of *The Arab Awakening* indeed lies heavy on Mr. Carmichael's account of the nineteenth and twentieth centuries. Like Antonius, Mr. Carmichael greatly exaggerates the role of the Syrian Christians as the precursors of Arab nationalism, and again like Antonius he attributes to the American Presbyterian missionaries an imaginary role as the mid-wives of this nationalism. He says, for example, (p. 288) that 'They took the view that if a nation is to be restored to an independent intellectual position, its primary tool must be its written language.' The fact is that they took no such view. The missionaries did for a time conduct classes in Arabic because they feared that were they to use English—which was in overwhelming demand—their catechumens would not long remain humble labourers in the vineyards of the Lord, but would begin to feel drawn to greener pastures.

Mr. Carmichael also helps to give further currency to the fiction long propagated by European publicists that 'Abd al-Hamid's régime, founded on corruption, espionage and oppression, was sadly unfit for a modern role.' There is much more to be said for the view that this Ottoman sultan was in fact, during much of the thirty-two years of his long reign, a powerful modernizer, and that his modernizing activities—by fostering a large group of European-educated, and therefore disaffected, officers—brought about the downfall of his régime in 1908. Again, Mr. Carmichael's account of the various wartime British commitments in the middle east and of Sharifian revolt is also unsatisfactory. He repeats the dubious but often-repeated contention that the Sykes-Picot Agreement of 1916—which he calls 'notorious' was irreconcilable with British promises to the Sharif of Mecca. In fact, far from being irreconcilable, the Sykes-Picot Agreement was designed to fit in with these promises. He also repeats the legend—first propagated by Colonel Lawrence—that Damascus was 'taken' in October 1918 by Faysal and Lawrence; he says that from the point of view of the Arabs, this was the 'first fruit of victory'. Indeed, to have got control of Damascus was a *coup*, but the city was not secured by Sharifian military prowess. Allenby forbade Damascus to the Australian and Indian troops who had borne the brunt of the fighting against the Ottomans, and allowed the Sharifians to enter it and to claim its capture.

Only after the first world war was Arab nationalism given its armour of doctrine, which was systematically spread through books, newspapers and the schools. This happened principally in Iraq, where under British auspices, Arab nationalists in control of the administration and of the educational system set out systematically to propagate their views and to indoctrinate the rising generation with it. According to this doctrine, by virtue of speaking one language, etc., the Arabs formed one nation and were therefore entitled to form one state. Like other nationalist doctrines, this one suffers from a simple logical defect, for there is really no way of showing that people who speak one language have to unite into one state. Mr. Carmichael, however, seems to take the doctrine at its face value, for he says (p. 383): 'What is artificial is not the concept of a unitary Arab state, which, regardless of the *material* obstacles to its realization, corresponds at any rate to a growing awareness of the Arabs of themselves as distinct from Europe, but the atomized states into which the Arabs are at present divided.' Two comments may be made: all states are artificial, and no state is natural; and however artificial the states calling themselves Arab may be, each has so far resisted all attempts to unite with another. These attempts at unity began in earnest in 1945 with the foundation of the Arab League under British auspices. From that day to this, the politics of Arab unity have consisted of one state seeking to gobble up another, and of the other states doing their best to stop this.

The Emir of Transjordan wanted to rule the whole of the Levant. The Syrians, the Lebanese, the Egyptians and the Saudis strenuously objected, and his ambitions came to naught. Iraq repeatedly tried to effect a union with Syria, and spent much money and effort on the project, but her rivals, Egypt and Saudi Arabia, proved more ingenious and succeeded in checkmating her. These events, which took place between 1945 and 1958, are the subject of Patrick Seale's excellent study, *The Struggle for Syria*. During the second world war the Syrians, with British help, shook off the French Mandate and became an independent republic. Their public men, like the public men of all the other Arab states, professed to believe in and to work for the ideal of Arab unity. Ostensibly to forward this unity they went to war in 1948 to prevent the partition of Palestine between the Zionist immigrants and its native inhabitants. It is doubtful whether they or their partners really desired this war, but Transjordan was bent on annexing as much as it could of Palestine, and Egypt could not passively watch such aggrandizement. With Transjordan and Egypt involved, the others could not remain un-involved. The 1948 war was fought by the Arab states perhaps more to foil one another than to prevent the establishment of Israel. The war ended disastrously for Syria and for the others. Syria's civilian rulers became discredited. The officers accused them of incompetence and corruption, and beginning in 1949 they mounted a series of *coups d'état*. Syria fell into the hands of the colonels. These colonels were from various factions and entertained various ideologies. Some—a few—were communists. Others were votaries of the PPS, a movement founded in the 1930s by a Lebanese who believed that a Syrian nation, not an Arab one, existed in the so-called Fertile Crescent, and that this Syrian nation had the right to form one state to include Cyprus, Lebanon, Palestine, Syria, Transjordan and Iraq.

The military followers of the PPS lost, not because their doctrine was more absurd than others, but because they proved less efficient than their rivals in parading their tanks and clobbering their enemies. These rivals happened to be devotees of the Ba'th—*anglice* the Arab Resurrection Party. This party was founded during the second world war by two schoolteachers in Damascus who were fervent believers in Arab unity and who insisted that this unity would come about only when the party mobilized all the masses and by catharsis drained all selfishness out of the Arabs, compelling them selflessly to love one another. The gospel of love did not make much headway among the sophisticated Syrians until some officers got taken with it. This coincided with a heightening of Iraqi–Egyptian rivalry in Syria; the Egyptian military régime, particularly after Suez, tremendously inflated its appeal as the foremost champion of Arab unity. The gospel of love became a hot gospel, and the Ba'thists believed that they had Colonel Nasser hooked. As it turned out it was he who had them hooked, but to this we shall come later. In February 1958 rivalries between the officers in Syria, combined with rivalries between Iraq and Egypt and between the U.S.S.R. and the U.S., precipitated a union between Syria and Egypt. The United Arab Republic, as the new state was called, was described by a writer in the London *Spectator* as an episode in the New Arabian Nights.

Mr. Seale weaves his way skilfully and gracefully through the mazes of this black comedy. Occasionally, however, he betrays a touch of earnestness out of keeping with the character of his story. He says, for example, that the Syro–Egyptian union remains the most important event in postwar Arab history. This is grossly to exaggerate the significance of the episode—admittedly one somewhat more bizarre than is usual for middle-eastern politics. He calls the founders of the Ba'th 'the most astute and the most principled men in Syrian public life': but their astuteness chiefly consists in their having indoctrinated a few officers who proceeded to carry out *coups d'état*—but who, by and by, turned on their mentors. As for their principles, they are perhaps more accurately called ideologists, and do we not know how unprincipled ideologues can be? What the leaders of the Ba'th did with their principles in the 1950s and 1960s would have done honour to a quick-change artist. Mr. Seale accurately describes the PPs as 'ex-officers, desperadoes, fanatical young men, dedicated cadres, bound by the rigid hierarchies of the party and the mumbo-jumbo of Sa'ada's ideas': Does this not fit the Ba'th to perfection? He also compliments the Soviet Union on its reappraisal of Arab nationalism in 1954–6, and declares that it was 'matched by no comparable intellectual and imaginative effort in the West': it is by no means clear that the Soviet Union's urge to replace Great Britain as the patron of Pan-Arabism has been more to her advantage than the earlier adventure was to Great Britain's.

But where in all this are the Syrians? Mr. Seale does not tell us what they, the *corpus vile* in all these experiments, think of it all. But perhaps it does not matter, for they have never been much accustomed to being asked their opinion about their rulers. For them the happy man has always been he who has a beautiful wife, a comfortable house, a lucrative occupation, who does not know government, and whom government does not know; in short, the private man. Resurrectionists of course do not respect privacy, and it has become more and more difficult to maintain it. Its only protection, such as it is, has been the anarchy of these short-lived régimes.

Mr. Seale stops at 1958. In *The Arab Cold War* Professor Kerr takes the story up to 1967.* It is a compact, cool and astringent essay, exemplary in every way. This is a second, expanded edition of a work which first appeared in 1965, and which originally covered the period between 1958–64. Professor Kerr's title describes precisely the state of Arab politics not only in the years with which he is concerned but ever since the foundation of the Arab League. His last paragraph, added after the June war, is a sound description of the origins of this particular episode, but with a few changes it can be made to apply to the first Palestine war of 1948. Professor Kerr writes:

> the Arabs paid for their quarrels by stumbling into war with Israel. The Egyptian ejection of the United Nations emergency force from Sinai, which triggered the explosion of June 5, clearly reflected the UAR's quest for prestige in other Arab capitals—a quest that had become reckless in consequence of events, described above, and particularly the November 1966 alliance which allowed the Syrian tail to wag the Egyptian dog. Once war began, other Arab governments lost control of their policies and were sucked in behind the UAR as hapless allies in a war to which their own rivalries had led them.

Egypt, or the United Arab Republic, as its rulers insisted on calling it even after the secession of Syria in 1961, has been, ever since the Suez affair of 1956, the pacemaker of Arab nationalism. It has used the potent slogans of this doctrine to subvert unfriendly Arab states and to create for its leader in all Arabic-speaking areas a strident and at times formidable following among the poverty-stricken, transistor-addicted masses. Yet when all is said and done, Egypt's Arab policy—which King Faruq invented for his own aggrandizement and which the officers who overthrew him in 1952 took up with such enthusiasm—has brought the Egyptians nothing but misfortunes and, in the six-day war of 1967, catastrophe. The ordinary Egyptian, a man of common sense, whose wits have been sharpened by life under a despotism, is probably asking himself and his fellows whether these hardships are really necessary. And if we are optimists, we will hope that one day his scepticism will communicate iteslf to his rulers. Faruq, however, must be held innocent of the other feature of Egypt's régime, its so-called 'social-

* *The Arab Cold War, 1958–1967: A Study of Ideology in Politics* (Second Edition) by Malcolm Kerr.

ism.' This in reality is no more than an oppressive and deadening étatism draining the country of all enterprise and initiative. An Egyptian joke has it that an economist, asked about the prospects of the Egyptian economy, replied that they were average; questioned further, he explained that he meant it was worse than the year before and better than the year to come.

Nineteen-fifty-eight, then, saw the union between Egypt and Syria. But if Damascus thought to captivate its virile and masterful captor, it had, as they say, another think coming. Nasser was the boss and he had no desire to become the evangelist of the new dispensation and preach the glad tidings of the coming Resurrection. He was boss in Egypt and meant to be boss in Syria. The Ba'th leaders gave him up for an unregenerate old Adam, and retired to pray and plot for the new heaven and the new earth which were surely coming. It is only through tribulation, we know, that believers reach the millennium, and Syria in 1958–61 went through such tribulation. The Egyptians proved incompetent colonial rulers, and Syrian officers conspired against the union and ousted the Egyptian viceroy from Damascus in September 1961. The Ba'th leaders supported the secession, but themselves split the following year. One faction wanted to take part in the predominantly non-Ba'th government which succeeded the Egyptians, while the other faction, sea-green incorruptibles, spurned and execrated such human weakness and corruption. Their day came in March 1963 when yet another *coup d'état* justly and providentially put them in power. They at once proclaimed their desire for a new and purer Arab unity and actually went to Cairo to talk it over. But the two partners, now bruised and world-weary, could not hit it off any more. In February 1966 a new and even stricter Ba'thist sect arose with a new *coup d'état*, the ninth in seventeen years. The two original apostles of the Ba'th were denounced by the schismatics, but fortunately had to suffer nothing worse than flight to Beirut. The tenth, an abortive one, took place six months later. And so it goes on. As the nursery rhyme has it:

Tourne, tourne, joli moulin

It will go on turning for a long time now.

10. The Apprentice Sorcerers

The author of this intriguing book* tells us that he went to Egypt in 1953 as an employee of the well-known Washington firm of management consultants, Booz, Allen and Hamilton. In 1955 his employers lent him to the U.S. Department of State where he was a member of a group called 'The Middle East Policy Planning Committee' the main purpose of which, he declares, was 'to work out ways of taking advantage of the friendship which was developing between ourselves and Nasser'. He left the State Department in May 1957 and in July of the same year set up in Beirut a 'government relations consulting office'. We also learn from his book that in 1947 he had been sent to Damascus—by whom is not stated—'to make unofficial contact' with Syrian leaders and 'to probe for means of persuading them, on their own, to liberalize the political system'.

As a result of his experiences Mr. Copeland is able to provide many curious details about the operation of what he calls crypto-diplomacy in the relations between the United States and the Arab world, particularly in the 1950s. When the diplomatic history of the period comes to be properly documented and written in detail, historians will no doubt find very useful the testimony which this book provides. But today the details recounted here can be no more than isolated—albeit piquant and entertaining—episodes.

The real value of this book today is that it documents and illustrates not so much transactions, quarrels and intrigues, as the state of mind of Americans at the centre or on the fringe of diplomacy who had to formulate during this period a policy towards the Arab world. After 1945 the United States found itself a great power with important political and strategic interests in the middle east. Hence the urgent necessity of adopting an attitude and formulating a policy towards the area. How did American officials look upon middle-eastern society and politics, and how did they think it could be approached and dealt with? The picture emerging from Mr. Copeland's book is detailed, consistent and rather extraordinary.

The ills of the Arab world, it would seem, were thought to stem from the fact that its political leaders were corrupt and unsuitable. The aim of the United States, it followed, was to ensure the disappearance of these and the rise of a new kind of leader. The commonly held view may be summed up by the words of a lecturer in a

---

* *The Game of Nations* by Miles Copeland.

joint State Department–Central Intelligence group orientation course who is quoted by Mr. Copeland as saying: 'Politicians in Syria, Lebanon, Iraq, and Egypt seem to have been elected into power, but what elections! The winners were all candidates of foreign powers, old landowners who tell their tenants and villages how to vote, or rich crooks who can buy their votes. But peoples of these countries are intelligent, and they have a natural bent for politics. If there is a part of the world which is crying for the democratic process the Arab world is it.' Thus to help the democratic process in Syria, the Americans

> did their part in intimidating those Syrians who had traditionally intimidated the citizens at election time and stood in the way of their voting according to their own inclinations. Landowners, employers, Ward bosses, and precinct police chiefs were all warned, directly and indirectly, that 'the people' must be allowed their complete freedom of choice.

The American oil companies provided posters to get out the vote, taxicab drivers were hired to take voters free to the polls, 'automatic tamper-proof voting machines, on the latest American pattern', were provided for the big cities, and the head of the Methodist mission extracted a promise from the Kurdish scribes that no advantage would be taken of the Kurdish voters' illiteracy to write in names of candidates of their own choosing. These stratagems availed nothing, and the elections were rigged in exactly the same way as before. Thereupon, the American minister at Damascus decided to encourage a military *coup d'état*, so that Syria might enjoy democracy.

> A 'political action team' under Major Meade [of the Legation] systematically developed a friendship with Za'im, then chief of staff of the Syrian Army, suggested to him the idea of a *coup d'état*, advised him how to go about it, and guided him through the intricate preparations in laying the groundwork for it.

Za'im turned out to be no more than an incompetent and short-lived military despot. The conclusion therefore was arrived at that what 'a genuine revolution' required

> was not a leader in isolation—some unprincipled colonel in the Chief of Staff position, or who would get into it long enough to order troops about—but an élite, inseparably bound to a sub-élite which, in turn, had roots in the populace.

The bizarre sequence of events, and the curious reasonings which led to them and to which they, in turn, led all had to do, we must remember, with U.S. foreign policy. Its executants, in other words, must have believed that the interests of the United States were not compatible with the existence of corrupt unrepresentative régimes, and that these interests moreover would be better served by their replacement with régimes which would be representative and not corrupt. Mr. Copeland insists that in acting as he did, the U.S. minister in Damascus was not behaving in an eccentric fashion: 'Later', he affirms, 'most of our other ambassadors and ministers in the Arab world were to tell me that had they been in [his] place they would have seen the situation as he saw it.'

Their search for 'genuine revolution' led these diplomats to ever more comprehensive theories and ever more ambitious schemes. As we have seen, their experience with Za'im made them sceptical of mere changes in governments or rulers. What was wanted was an élite to underpin the rulers, themselves in turn supported and buttressed by a population which presumably understood, approved and legitimated the aims of such an élite. Whoever knows the middle east will agree that such a quest was the political equivalent of the search for the philosophical stone. But, according to Mr. Copeland, American diplomats did in fact set out to seek the philosophical stone. It appears to have been decided that Egypt was the best place to start. In the early months of 1952, Mr. Kermit Roosevelt, a member of the Central Intelligence Agency, who was then in Egypt, met a number of officers who were involved in the conspiracy which led to the *coup d'état* of 22 July 1952. In these meetings it was understood that the Egyptian army would take control of the country with the aim of bringing about those conditions the lack of which led to corruption and discontent, and which in fact vitiated Za'im's *coup*. In other words, the new régime's task would be

> to bring about these conditions, which were (1) a literate populace; (2) a large and stable middle class; (3) a feeling by the people that 'this is *our* government' . . . (4) sufficient identification of local ideals and values so that truly indigenous democratic institutions could grow up . . .

Mr. Copeland states that the Americans believed that 'Nasser would as soon as practicably possible set about creating the conditions which Roosevelt and Nasser had agreed were prerequisite to genuine democratic government'. It will be noticed from this language that the American aim, as specified in the book under review, had become most ambitious and grandiose. It was no less than to create, by means of a government originating in a military *coup d'état*, the new kind of society in Egypt which would make corruption impossible and *coups d'état* unnecessary. An elementary question occurs to the mind, the answer to which is not to be found in Mr. Copeland.

It is whether a government controlled by conspiratorial officers was likely, even with the best will in the world, to promote the aims which Mr. Kermit Roosevelt agreed with Nasser's representatives were desirable, and whether it is not self-contradictory to hope for the creation, by government action, of 'a large and stable middle class', of 'indigenous democratic institutions' and of 'a feeling by the people that "this is *our* government"'. As for the fourth aim which Mr. Copeland lists, namely 'a literate populace', this can undoubtedly be achieved by a government disposing of large funds and extensive powers; but whether literacy is under all conditions politically an unmixed blessing one may take leave to doubt.

In any case, as we are told in this book, after his *coup d'état* Nasser was believed by U.S. officials to be 'the wave of the future'. To enable his regime to survive and realize the extraordinary aims described above, he was plied with all sorts of advice and help. Thus, for instance,

> Ambassador Caffery arranged with Nasser for the loan to the Egyptian government of perhaps the leading practitioner of 'black' and 'grey' propaganda in the Western world, Paul Linebarger, the former OSS propagandist who during the second world war had broadcast what were ostensibly German and pro-German newscasts but which were actually demoralizing to the Germans in effect. Linebarger showed the Egyptian propagandists how to damage hallowed figures (for example, General Naguib) while seeming to praise them—a technique which the Egyptians still use in Arab world politics.

Again, 'one James Eichelberger, a State Department political scientist' who had been an account executive for J. Walter Thompson, 'the world's largest advertising and public relations firm' was sent to Cairo where he talked with Nasser and his confidants and produced a series of papers identifying the new government's problems and recommending policies to deal with them. One of these papers, *Power Problems of a Revolutionary Government*, is printed as an appendix. It has a curious history. Eichelberger drafted it, it was translated into Arabic and commented upon by members of Nasser's staff, translated back into English for Eichelberger's benefit

> and so on back and forth between English and Arabic until a final version was produced. The final paper was passed off to the outside world as the work of Zakaria Mohieddin, Nasser's most thoughtful and (in Western eyes) reasonable deputy, and accepted at face value by intelligence analysts of the State Department, the CIA and, presumably, similar agencies of other governments.

This somewhat bizarre episode was by no means unique in the relations between Americans and Egyptians in those days. Mr.

Copeland, for instance, recounts the relations between General Naguib and another American, Leigh White who, it is true, had no official position. Mr. White came to Egypt when Naguib 'was becoming good copy in the international press'. Apparently it was he who really wrote Naguib's book which appeared under the title, *Egypt's Destiny*. When White

> talked about Naguib's philosophy he was talking pure Leigh White, a frustrated liberal who had not found such an outlet for his energies since the Spanish Civil War. White and the local CIA chief . . . loathed one another , . ., and many of the sensible and democratic utterances which Leigh attributed to Naguib first appeared as his own rejoinders in arguments with the CIA man—who, incidentally, was a Nasser man through and through!

Or, again, there was Professor Edward Mason who had been J. F. Kennedy's economics teacher at Harvard. Kennedy, who 'knew him to have no prejudices on the subject of socialism which would colour his judgment of Nasser's programme', sent him to Cairo to report on the régime.

> In his own meetings with Mason [writes Mr. Copeland], Nasser would ask, 'Are we doing anything differently than you would do if your were running the country?' The answer, more often than not, was 'No, Mr. President.'
> In July 1962 Mason returned to Washington to tell President Kennedy that he could not conscientiously find fault with any of Nasser's major actions. Nasser had forced him to admit that those actions which the United States Government found so objectionable—nationalisation of large segments of the Egyptian economy, various totalitarian measures such as censorship of the press and arrest of dissident politicians, and even the propaganda assaults on other Arab leaders whom Nasser believed to be friendly to the West—were actions which Nasser could logically be expected to take given his circumstances.

The paper by Eichelberger which was passed off as being by Zakaria Mohieddin and which Mr. Copeland prints in an appendix is an extraordinary document which repays some study. As its title indicates, the paper deals with the problems of a revolutionary government and the policies it has to adopt in order to cope with them. The idea of revolution which its author—whoever he is— entertains is that grandiose and romantic notion which has become current in Europe since the French Revolution. According to this view, a revolutionary upheaval properly speaking was one which totally refashioned man and society in all their aspects. Thus, the paper lays it down that a purpose of the revolution is to solve the pressing social and political problems which made the revolution necessary (and possible), thus ending abruptly the previous political system in which these problems had become unsolvable.

The paper never pauses to consider whether a 'solution' of social and political problems by any Egyptian government, whatever its complexion, is conceivable, or whether this way of speaking about politics and society is appropriate or indeed intelligible. The paper then proceeds to describe the means by which the revolutionary government is to achieve its objectives. Thus

> It is assumed that the judicial magistrature is under the control of the revolutionary government, and that all decisions in cases of violation of the security laws will not work against the convenience of the government.

Or thus:

> The police should be 'politicised', and should become, to whatever extent necessary, a partisan paramilitary arm of the revolutionary government.

Or, again, thus:

> The nerve centre of the whole security system of a revolutionary state (or of any state) lies in a secret body, the identity and very existence of which can be safely known only to the head of the revolutionary government and to the fewest possible number of the other key leaders . . . It is the duty of this body to be aware of all prejudicial activity, incipient or actual, whether outside of the government or within, whether it involves cabinet ministers or a captain in the armed forces.

Or, to give a last example, consider what is said about the 'mass organisation' which the revolutionary régime has to set up in order to mobilize the mass of private citizens and involve them in its own purpose. Its cadres may be found in the civil service, and its *modus operandi* is described as follows:

> Any government has many favours to bestow in the routine administration of its affairs, and in the enforcement of laws many citizens can find themselves in special difficulties. It should become apparent to all— although never officially declared—that the active support of the mass organization is the surest way of obtaining 'satisfaction' in such cases. In return for these services, the mass organization can expect the adherence of many people who otherwise might remain indifferent, and financial contributions or other types of active support should be much easier to solicit.

It is, of course, most doubtful whether Nasser and his fellow-conspirators had any need to call on the resources of American political science for such lessons in tyranny. What does remain most puzzling is why it was thought that the imparting of such lessons could advance the interests of the United States, or even contribute to the welfare of the Egyptian people. Now that Nasser is dead, and diplomatic relations between Egypt and the United States having been broken by his own action, it is clear that the U.S. policy of encouraging, befriending and helping Nasser as it is described, and to some extent defended, in this book, was a failure. It is of course impossible to give a proper account of U.S.–Egyptian relations in their highlights and vicissitudes during Nasser's rule until documents which are now confidential become freely available to students. For such an account this book is not, and does not pretend to be, a substitute. But if what it describes did take place, then one may say that U.S. policy during this period was dangerously doctrinaire and fanciful, and that these characteristics may perhaps account somewhat for its failures. Mr. Copeland himself speaks high words of praise for Nasser. His conduct, he says, 'has been almost entirely normal and predictable'; he is 'one of the most courageous, most incorruptible, most principled, and in his way most humanitarian leaders I have ever had the pleasure to meet'. Originally, he tells us, Nasser wanted arms for purely internal purposes and it was only the procrastination of the State Department which made him turn to the Soviets. Again, Nasser did not want to rule the Arab world: 'I believe it safe to say', affirms Mr. Copeland, 'that virtually all of us who have had prolonged personal contact with Nasser (Kermit Roosevelt, Robert Anderson, Eugene Black, and Charles Cremeans besides all our ambassadors to Egypt) would agree that he has no such ambition'. Mr. Copeland and all the eminent persons whom he mentions may, for all we know, be perfectly right about Nasser's intentions; but it is difficult to see what more he could have done, whether in Syria or Yemen, or Iraq or Jordan or Lebanon, if he had harboured such ambitions. In any case, the road to hell, as the adage tells us, is paved with good intentions: it is a piece of worldly wisdom which the agents of a great power should cherish more than ambitious and attractive theories about society or revolution.

11. Arabic Political Memoirs

Sex and power are perhaps the two most potent urges which can seize men and possess them. But the received wisdom of mankind has recognized that ecstatic and ineffable as are the pleasures they can procure, yet they must be approached with fear and circumspection, since they can also unleash chthonic forces and lead to terror and madness. Both Athens and Jerusalem taught this in their different ways, and their legacy was taken up and appropriated by both Muslims and Christians.

But in modern times large numbers of westerners have come to disbelieve in the horrors of love or politics, to forget that Venus can be a bird of prey *toute entière à sa proie attachée*, or that, for all our philosophy, the night can still 'sweat with terror', and we like weasels still be 'fighting in a hole'. Happiness through sexual satisfaction or through political action has been a dominant idea in Europe and America since Sade and St. Just, and it has naturally issued in the nihilism which is so widespread among western intellectual classes today. The prestige of the west has ensured the conversion of non-European intellectuals to these beliefs, which the techniques invented by Europe have helped to spread among them. They, too, have come to entertain delusive and exaggerated expectations about love and politics; and among them, too, nihilism is, in consequence, rampant.

Anyone surveying Arabic literary and political writing over the last few decades will find in it ample confirmation for these remarks. Young men growing up in the Arab middle east between the two world wars fervently believed that if only they could liberate themselves from the power of tradition, and control by foreigners, they would create for themselves *des lendemains qui chantent*, in which public happiness would be the crown and guarantee of private bliss.*

* As these lines were being written there reached me a small book by a well-known Syrian poet, Nizar Qabbani, entitled *On Poetry, Sex and Revolution* (Beirut, 1972).

In this book Qabbani argues that sex is the 'fundamental problem' of Arab society and that once this problem is solved all other problems will likewise.

'Sex [he writes] is our eternal headache, the incubus which devours us day and night. If you ask me about the size of the sexual problem, I will tell you that it has exactly the same size as our cranium, so that there is not a single convolution in the Arab brain which is not tumescent with sex.'

Qabbani believes in revolution which is 'a total change in the geography of Arab man', and in this change sexual and political emancipation go hand in hand.

177

In the quarter of a century since the end of the second world war, they at last took their destiny in their own hands, and tasted to the full the disappointments and the disasters of the life of politics. Autonomous political action coincided with—and led to—the disaster in Palestine, a disaster the like of which had never befallen the Arab world when it was governed by the Ottomans. To this defeat at the hand of a hitherto-despised group has been added the bitter spectacle of soldiers laying rough hands on the body politic, plotting with and occasionally murdering one another, ranting about liberation, revolution and the other slogans which in an evil hour Europe had let loose over the east, and all the while steadily extending their dead hand over a society which may have been in the past ruled by aliens, but which for all its poverty and 'backwardness' still had some precious graces, still allowed the individual some elbow-room, and mercifully permitted a retreat into privacy.

The life of politics has thus brought to Arabs humiliation abroad and impotence at home; and the disappointment is proportionate to the great rewards which, deceived by the European mirage, they had come to expect from political autonomy. The western 'Arabophiles' who proliferate in universities, public life and the 'communications industry'—the kind of friends from whom one must pray to be protected—have managed to give currency to a picture of the Arab as a humourless, solemn, sententious, tediously strident creature. To penetrate beyond this caricature is to discover that the Arabs are 'men like us all,' who weigh in the same balance as ourselves justice and oppression, tyranny and freedom, loyalty and faithfulness, honour and dishonour.

There is no better way of realizing this than to read some of the political memoirs which have been coming out in large numbers in the last decade or so. They provide a valuable clue to the character of recent Arab politics, and paint a melancholy picture of the disappointments and disasters which its practitioners have had to suffer. Apart from some fiction from the pen of one or two gifted authors, like the Egyptian Najib Mahfuz, these memoirs constitute perhaps the most lively and the most interesting portion of Arabic literary production today.

By far the largest part of this literature, it is significant to observe, is published in Beirut where it is still possible for writers to escape censorship and suppression. It is mostly written by refugees, or émigrés, or by those who have lost out in whatever ghastly game they have chosen to play. That they apologize, or palliate or embellish or suppress, in no way diminishes the value of what they write. For unwittingly or not, this literature testifies alike to the endemic distemper which afflicts most middle-eastern polities, and to the fact that so much disorder and misfortune has not yet entirely deadened the critical faculty, or banished all liveliness and independence of mind.

It is appropriate to begin this account of some of the most noteworthy of these political memoirs with a short and modest work by an Iraqi professional soldier who, as a member of the royal guard, witnessed the murder of the King of Iraq and his family in 1958.

In *The Secrets of the Assassination of the Royal Family in Iraq, 14 July 1958* (Beirut, 1971) Lieutenant Falih Hanzal in a modest and unassuming way, with the precision and economy of a military despatch, sets the scene of the crime, shows how the *coup d'état* started and quickly snowballed, and in what manner the royal household were, suddenly, in a terrible exhibition of blood-lust, indiscriminately mowed down with machine-guns by a handful of junior officers. But it is not only the physical scene which Hanzal sets. During the two years that he served in the royal guard, he had many opportunities to observe the royal family at close quarters, and particularly the young king, Faysal, and his uncle and heir-apparent, Abd al-Ilah. Faysal himself, as Hanzal reports, was a cypher, content to leave all important matters in the hands of his uncle who, in effect, exercised ultimate power and authority in the state. To him the politicians, the secret police and military intelligence reported, and from him they took their instructions. According to Hanzal, in the two years that he knew Abd al-Ilah, the latter was oppressed with a heavy sense of fatality, and seemed utterly weary of the burden of power which he had borne since 1939 when his brother-in-law, Ghazi, died in an accident, and he was made regent for the infant king. He was kept accurately informed of the plots against his régime which were constantly being hatched in the army. But this information seemed only to induce in Abd al-Ilah a feeling of resignation. He seemed resigned to the fact that, aliens as they were, with no roots in the country, it was vain for him and his family to struggle against the dislike and the hatred of the Iraqis. In the last few months of his life he was repeatedly given details of army plots, and his reaction was that the officers who were implicated were patriotic and devoted to the country, which they might serve better than he; if they did not want him, then he was ready to leave the country together with his nephew. Hanzal describes an interview toward the end of April 1958 in which he reported information that had come to his knowledge:

> ... he did not comment in any way on the news, or ask for further details. He nodded and thanked me, his face showing his desire to be left alone, and that I should not add to the oppression of his spirits. For he was no longer in need of news, or information, or even friends. I may almost say here that he was no longer in need of Iraq either.

It is this failure of nerve, this intimate conviction that the régime he headed was alien and illegitimate which proved fatal to Abd al-Ilah and his family. Hanzal describes how a handful of soldiers arrived opposite the main gate of the modest villa which served as the royal residence in the early morning of 14 July 1958 and started firing desultorily at the building. In and around the villa Abd al-Ilah had at his orders a large body of disciplined and loyal troops who could have easily overcome the attackers. But Abd al-Ilah ordered them to refrain from firing at the assailants. Within half-an-hour the original attackers were joined by mutinous cadets from an infantry school in an army camp nearby. They were armed with bazookas and anti-tank guns and quickly set fire to the house, compelling the royal family to take refuge in the basement. The house was not yet entirely surrounded, and it would still have been possible to escape through the back garden. His entourage implored Abd al-Ilah to do so; but he refused adamantly either to do this, or to order a counter-attack. He would negotiate with the rebels, Faysal would sign his abdication and they would all leave Iraq. Hanzal was convinced that the regent was seized with a fatalism which made him utterly sceptical of any attempt to resist the mutineers. This fatalism was 'a deadly mistake'; it was inspired by the example of his father Ali, who had preferred to surrender together with four thousand soldiers to a handful of Saudi soldiers, thus giving up the throne of the Hejaz in 1924 in order to escape with his life. An emissary was sent outside with a white flag and he brought back with him rebel officers for negotiation. At the point of the gun they ordered the royal family to leave the basement by a side-door for the garden. When they had all filed out, another officer (Abd al-Sattar Sabi' al-'Ubusi) who was then standing on the steps leading to the main door, observing the cortège coming out, suddenly and impulsively fired a burst from his machine-gun at the backs of the prisoners. Hanzal declares that he had an opportunity afterwards to discuss the killings with 'Ubusi, who told him that when he fired he was in 'a state of madness,' as though a black cloud had obscured his vision, that he fired his machine-gun without knowing what he was doing or taking in what was going on in front of him. A year after the *coup d'état*, Hanzal adds, 'Ubusi retired from public life. In 1969 he committed suicide for reasons still unknown.

'Ubusi's burst of machine-gun fire plunged the other officers in the garden into a murderous frenzy. They also began firing their weapons at the inmates of the royal villa, and in a few minutes slaughtered the king, his uncle, and the latter's mother and sister, together with the servants who had been compelled to join the procession of their masters.

The sight of blood, together with the sound of shooting [Hanzal writes] maddened the officer in the armoured car and he opened fire with his heavy machine-gun on the bodies which were lying on the ground, riddling them with bullets. The orphan boy Ja'far who was being brought up by the princess Abdiyya [the regent's sister] tried to take refuge in some corner of the palace, but the soldiers soon pursued him with their rifle fire and finished him.

Only the regent's wife escaped alive from this massacre; she had been left for dead, but an officer later realized that she was still alive and managed to get her into a hospital.

Shortly after the massacre, the bodies were piled in a van to be taken to the morgue. By that time a dense crowd had assembled near the villa and was impeding the passage of the van. It appears that the pressure of the crowd threw the officers who were in the van into a panic; and they decided to abandon Abd al-Ilah's body to the mob. They tipped it out of the van and made their escape. Ropes were quickly brought, and the regent's body was attached by the neck and the armpits to the back of a lorry which proceeded to drag it through the streets, the increasingly numerous mob escorting it with shouts of *Allahu akbar*. During all this, men armed with knives and choppers began to get to work on it. The regent's sex was first cut off, and then his arms and legs; they were thrown to groups of young men who ran off waving these members with joyful shouts. By the time the procession reached the ministry of defence on the other side of the river, the body was no more than a bruised and mutilated trunk. Opposite the ministry men with ropes appeared on a first-floor balcony. By means of these ropes the body was hoisted from the street and secured to the balcony:

a young man with a knife in his hand climbed a lamp-post nearby, and stabbed the corpse repeatedly in the back. He then began cutting off the flesh, working from the buttocks upwards. From the street a long white stick was brought which was inserted into the corpse and forcibly pushed inside.

What was left of the regent's body that evening was soaked with petrol and set on fire, the burnt remains being thrown into the Tigris.

Hanzal concludes his precise and unassuming account by recording the symmetrical fate which befell the body of Abd al-Karim Qasim who had overthrown the monarchy. He, in turn, was overthrown by another *coup d'état* on 9 February 1963, carried out by some of his original fellow-conspirators, and immediately executed. He was secretly buried in a shallow grave outside Baghdad. Some dogs came upon the corpse and started to eat it, to the horror of some *fellahs* nearby. These provided a coffin and gave the body a decent burial.

When the secret police came to hear of this, they disinterred the body and threw it into the Tigris.

Hanzal's account is that of a close, well-informed observer who narrates with quiet fatalism what his eyes saw and his ears heard. The same matter-of-fact quality may be found in the memoirs of another officer. But since, unlike Hanzal, the latter adopts this tone to describe what he did and not what he saw, the impression of horror carried away by the reader is scarcely less powerful than that emanating from Hanzal's book, even though there is nothing here like the demoniacal orgy of 14 July 1958 which Hanzal describes with such powerful restraint.

Fadlallah abu Mansur is a Druze from Salkhad in Syria who in 1928 joined the *troupes spéciales* raised by the French in the Levant states which they administered under a League of Nations mandate. By 1945 he had been promoted to lieutenant, and when Syria became independent he naturally joined the new Syrian army. He took part in the Palestine war in 1948, and between 1949 and 1954 was involved in the successive *coups d'état* which took place in Syria during this period. It is to these events that his memoirs, *Damascus Hurricanes*, published about 1959, are mostly devoted.

The first of these *coups d'état* took place in March 1949 when a senior officer, Husni al-Za'im, taking as his pretext the maladministration and corruption which he claimed had led to defeat in Palestine, toppled the civilian régime, and himself exercised all the powers of the state. Very soon other officers, who had started by supporting Za'im's *coup d'état*, began conspiring against him, and abu Mansur took a prominent part in the conspiracy. One night in August 1949, Fadlallah abu Mansur drove with a small troop to Za'im's residence in Damascus, surrounded it, overpowered the sentries and, hammering on the door of Za'im's palace, called on him to surrender. When Za'im did not immediately give himself up, abu Mansur machine-gunned the door, broke it open, and strode into the palace. Za'im then came down, buttoning a pair of trousers over his pyjamas. He was taken into an armoured car and driven to the outskirts of Damascus. The whole operation took no more than fifteen minutes. Abu Mansur then waited with his prisoner for instructions. Za'im was in a state of shock and did not at first recognize his captor, for, says abu Mansur, 'I was in field dress, and had let my black thick beard grow, so that I looked hirsute and frightful. . . .' Za'im first tried to bribe his captor into letting him escape, and offered a large sum of money:

> I answered 'How did you acquire such a fortune? Did you not say that you would leave power as poor as when you came to it? How has your poverty become wealth?' He began to mutter: 'By God, I am innocent,

I am innocent. This is a plot by the British to destroy the independence of the country.' I said to him: 'Do not be afraid for independence. We are jealous for it and will know how to preserve it.'

Some two hours or so later, a detachment of troops came with another prisoner, the civilian Muhsin al-Barazi who was Za'im's prime minister. He was brought to abu Mansur, still in his pyjamas, trembling with fear and shouting: 'Take pity on me. I have nothing to do with what happened. Take pity on me. Take pity on my children. I throw myself on your mercy.' With the new prisoner came instructions from the leaders of the *coup d'état* that Za'im and Barazi had been condemned to death and were to be immediately executed. Abu Mansur therefore took hold of Barazi with his left hand, and of Za'im with his right and led them to a depression by the road where a squad of soldiers duly executed them. While awaiting his fate Za'im, who had not had time to dress properly, felt cold and begged for abu Mansur's overcoat. The latter gave it to him, and Za'im died wearing it. But abu Mansur resumed possession of it, and he reproduces in his memoirs a certificate from the leader of the new *coup d'état*, attesting the fact and declaring that the holes and the traces of blood appearing on the overcoat were caused by the execution, 'to certify which he was given this document'.

Hinnawi thus succeeded Za'im. But shortly after he took power, some of his fellow-conspirators began to be discontented, and to conspire in turn against him. The leader of the new conspiracy was Shishakli with whom abu Mansur was on close terms of friendship rendered even closer by the fact that they both sympathized with the ideology of the movement known as the *Parti populaire syrien*, which in the early 1950s was the great rival of Ba'thist ideology among young army officers. Hinnawi suspected something, and tried to discover where abu Mansur's sympathies lay. In order to detach him from Shishakli, he dangled before abu Mansur the prospect of rapid promotion. In reply, abu Mansur held to the same elevated language as he had when Za'im had tried to bribe him:

> I swear to you, General [he said] that I do not seek anything of what you have promised me. The only honour I seek is to serve my country faithfully and loyally, and to be a man of principles and action. I therefore solemnly promise to do all that in my power lies to serve the interests of my country. Please therefore have no anxiety in this respect.

A politician encouraging him to save the country from Hinnawi heard exactly the same exalted sentiments:

> Be at ease, Akram bey, we act only at the behest of our conscience and our patriotism. We take no action except to serve our country and preserve its sovereignty and independence. We offer our blood to this

end, and no power in the world can turn us away from our duty. We here are ready to protect Syria, whatever the price.

Duty called one morning in December 1949. At dawn that day, abu Mansur moved into Damascus with a small force. In half-an-hour he had arrested Hinnawi and his key men, and occupied the police headquarters and the police station. Shishakli came to power.

> Our purpose in the third *coup d'état* [writes abu Mansur] was to save the country from disorder and anarchy, and entrust government to loyal and faithful men known for their patriotic devotion, and their truthful and upright character. This would enable the army to withdraw from politics and things to return to their normal course. These aspirations were disappointed, and Shishakli concentrated all power in his hands.

Abu Mansur was horrified by such cavalier treatment of responsibilities and prerogatives . . . by this open attack on the pillars of the state and its fundamentals. But even though Shishakli was abusing his power in this way, and though he persecuted abu Mansur and in the end retired him from the army, yet the latter refused to conspire against him. Two officers approached him with an offer of two hundred thousand liras if he would go to Damascus and form a gang to murder Shishakli. He turned down the offer because his party—the *Parti populaire syrien*—was opposed to murder, and 'I personally disapprove of murder and consider it a species of villainy.' However, though he was retired, he took some part in the army movement which toppled Shishakli in February 1954.

In spite of his services, he was not reinstated. Ba'thist officers were now in charge of army appointments, and they were wary of his politics. Further, as one of them said: 'abu Mansur would make a *coup d'état* even in his grave.' When one of these Ba'thist officers was murdered by a member of the *Parti populaire syrien*, abu Mansur had to flee from Syria and take refuge in the Lebanon. The book ends with a dithyramb addressed to Mount Hermon which the author had to cross on his flight:

> O Hermon! Brother of time! Pole of history! Twin of the gods! . . . O summit in my country, proclaim that my nation is a summit among nations! O Hermon! I testify that your meaning and significance is in our breasts, in our faith, in our blood; that we hold it aloft as a torch to illumine and guide until right shall awake and falsehood die!

The rhetoric of sensibility, patriotism and the public interest sits ill with conspiracies against the lawful government and executions at dawn. It is this contrast which gives abu Mansur's memoirs so repulsive a quality, and produces in the reader so vivid a sense of the degradation of politics in large parts of the Arabic-speaking world today. But the gap between what is said and what is actually done is not always so hopelessly wide. The *Memoirs* of Haza' al-Majali (Amman, 1960) show us a public man whose discourse patently attempts confrontation with a political situation which, however dangerous and disturbed, yet does not inspire the same terror as the blood-intoxicated Baghdadi mob, or the treacherous and relentless conspirators of Syria.

It is not that Haza' al-Majali remained immune from terror. On the contrary, born about 1918 into a notable family at Kerak in Trans-Jordan, he was to die in August 1960, a few months after the publication of these memoirs, victim of a bomb placed in his office in Amman. This was said to be the work of agents of the United Arab Republic, whose president considered Majali and King Husayn an obstacle to his vaulting ambition.

Majali went to school in Kerak and Salt, and he gives an engaging and illuminating account of the relentless politicization to which schoolboys were subjected, even in that out-of-the-way part of the Arab world, as early as the 1920s and '30s:

> I remember that I was in the fifth form of the primary school when Sulayman al-Nabulsi [one of his teachers and later a Jordanian prime minister] came into the class-room on the morning of 2 November. As soon as he came in, he asked us in English what day it was. Some said it was Sunday, others that it was the second of November. But he shouted at us with excessive emotion: 'Today is the anniversary of the Balfour Declaration'. He went on shouting in English, ' *Down with the Balfour Declaration!*' We had never heard of Balfour or the Balfour Declaration. He began to explain to us the Declaration, its circumstances, its meaning, and the necessity of protesting and demonstrating against it. We went out of the class-room and got all the other schoolboys out, and marched in a noisy demonstration, which may have been the first one to take place in Kerak. Those who understood the aims and watchwords of this demonstration were very few, for the large crowd were shouting slogans. Some were shouting, ' *Down with Krikor!*', Krikor being an Armenian shoemaker who had joined the demonstration and was shouting at the top of his voice, ' *Balfour! O group of Balfour!*' Some were shouting ' *Down with the balcony!*', others ' *Down with one who is upstairs!*'

Of his years at the secondary school in Salt, Majali says that there he and his fellow-pupils perfected the art of demonstrating with or without a pretext.

At the end of the second world war Majali was a law student in Damascus. In May 1945, the Syrian government clashed with the French mandatory, and there were noisy anti-French student demonstrations. The students asked to share in the struggle for

liberation and the Syrian government allowed them to volunteer
for the Syrian army:

> We went to the barracks and, after a formal medical examination, put
> on uniforms. What drew my attention was that most of those who had
> made speeches that day asking to be allowed to bear arms obtained
> medical certificates prescribing a rest at home in order to recover from
> the exertions of the *jihad!*

By the third day the number of volunteers, which had begun by
approaching the thousand mark, dwindled to a hundred or less.
Majali was to observe similar happenings in Amman at the beginning
of the Palestine war three years later. 'Volunteering', he observes,

> was in most cases mere showing off, a means of boasting and self-
> glorification or even, regrettably, of making a living. I myself have seen
> with my own eyes this phenomenon in Amman and elsewhere. The
> volunteers paraded the streets amidst the applause of the crowd and
> their shouts, and the traditional trilling of the women. They would fire
> off their guns with such frequency that when they reached their battle
> station in Palestine their ammunition was all but exhausted. It is not
> out of place to mention here, with much regret, that many of these
> volunteers were a heavy burden on the Arab villagers and town-
> dwellers, and that volunteering was sometimes a means to robbery and
> plunder!

The Palestine war, which was to have a profound and nefarious
influence on Majali's life and career, can be said to have been finally
made inevitable by the ambitions and policies of the ruler of Trans-
Jordan, King Abdullah.* His régime was, however, somewhat
different from those of Iraq and Syria, of which Hanzal's book and
abu Mansur's memoirs are such a lurid reflection. Majali, on his
return from Syria, was soon much in demand as a lawyer and was
eventually tempted to play a part in politics. He joined a small
group who opposed the king's reliance on a number of elderly
ministers of non-Jordanian origin. But Abdullah took up and
befriended the able young lawyer who soon became a prominent
member of his entourage. Majali's memoirs provide an affectionate
and well-observed picture of Abdullah's personality, and his very
idiosyncratic way of conducting public business:

> He had a special way of greeting known to the Jordanians, which
> enabled one to gauge the extent of royal favour. It was his custom to
> allow his hand to be kissed. Sometimes it would be extended wide open
> which would be a sign of approval, and sometimes it would be clenched

---

* See Kedourie, *The Chatham House Version*, pp. 230–1, where the evidence in
support of such a judgement, including a significant episode described in Majali's
memoirs, is examined.

to indicate displeasure. Occasionally he would put his hand on some-one's chin as a particular sign of approval. Sometimes he would extend his hand to be kissed on both sides, and would then allow his cheeks to be kissed, as a sign of complete approval. These various manifestations were often the subject of comment and the basis of various rumours about ministerial changes or appointments to high office or to important positions.

Abdullah's favour opened to Majali the career of a high official, of a minister, and eventually of prime minister. Jordanian politics were—and still are—very much dominated by the king, who rules the country through a small number of notables and courtiers whom he tries to balance against one another. On to this essentially simple arrangement, elections and a parliament have been grafted. In what sense, if any, members of this parliament represented those who elected them was very obscure, and what went on in parliament had usually little relation to the realities of power. It was rather an elaborate game of shadow-boxing which, however, sometimes proved lucrative to the participants. Majali describes how, when he was an opposition leader, he put down a motion of No Confidence in the government, which compelled it to mobilize its supporters. For their services in the voting lobby these exacted financial and other rewards—

> and how often [adds Majali] some of these members described to me the way in which the government responded to their demands and served their interests. They went so far as to wish me to put down continuously motions of No Confidence so that gifts and grants might be repeated.

Majali became prime minister at a crucial moment in Jordanian history. The British and their middle-eastern allies were pressing Jordan to join the Baghdad pact, while Egypt and Saudi Arabia opposed this strongly. In order to prevent such an outcome, they organized demonstrations, particularly among the discontented and volatile Palestinians whom Abdullah had, to his own undoing, incorporated into his kingdom. It fell then to Majali to deal with the serious agitation and rioting which the opponents of the pact were fomenting. Majali was invested with office on 15 December 1955. But he clearly did not have the stomach to invoke that *ultima ratio* which, as King Husayn showed in the summer of 1970, the rulers of a state like Jordan must not hesitate to invoke, or else face ruin and destruction. Four days later, on 19 December, he resigned.

> I remember [Majali writes] the morning of the day on which I presented my resignation. ... The demonstrations in Amman had become more tumultuous, and when they [a delegation of West Bank politicians] were with me, I heard the sound of shots. I communicated with police head-quarters, asking the reason for these shots, and strongly reiterating the

instructions not to open fire on anybody. Shortly afterwards, General Radi Innab, the assistant chief of staff, spoke to me and asked me to allow army and police sharp-shooters to pick out and shoot the leaders of the demonstration and nobody else. I vehemently refused, and said to him that I preferred to resign rather than have anybody fired on or harmed. . . .

I could have imposed the [Baghdad] pact by force . . . but I preferred to resign and stay at home, rather than adopt a policy of violence, I who had always disapproved of and combated it.

There is incongruity here between the reality and what is said and done in order to cope with it. Parliament, constitution, party, etc.— such a vocabulary has little meaning in a polity such as Jordan and, Majali's use of it, which seems not entirely rhetorical, increases the pathos with which his violent death has invested these memoirs.

During and before the outbreak of the Palestine war in May 1948, Majali was in King Abdullah's entourage and thus was able to observe events across the Jordan from a privileged vantage-point. He states that the course of the struggle between Jews and Arabs in the period before the British evacuation led them to feel anxious and fearful over the eventual outcome. The catastrophe, he observes, would have been easier to bear and narrower in its scope if the Arabs of Palestine had realized the true position. As it was, they erroneously believed themselves able to confront the Jews, and 'their confidence in the Arab states and their armies was one of the most potent causes of the extensive catastrophe.' When Palestinian villagers were worsted in some fight with the Jews they would take refuge in a more distant village, or even cross the Jordan, leaving all their possessions *in situ*,

hoping to come back a few weeks later and find everything in order. Were not the Arab armies on the point of invading the country to gain a quick victory over the Jewish 'gangs' and purify the Holy Land from their filth? Why should they carry away even what it was possible to carry away?

The attitude of the Palestinians towards the Zionists of which Majali gives here an example, the over-confident belligerence and the refusal to compromise or even negotiate with an adversary traditionally held in contempt, has been a standing feature of the Palestine dispute ever since the Balfour declaration. It figures prominently in the memoirs of one of their leaders, Ahmad al-Shuqayri. These memoirs, *Forty Years of Arab and International Life* (Beirut, 1969), the first in a series of six volumes, are worth noticing not only because they give a valuable glimpse into Arab politics in and relating to, Palestine over many decades, but also because Shuqayri is exceptional among Palestinian Arab leaders in having published political memoirs.* Shuqayri began to be active in Palestinian Arab politics in the early 1930s, though it was only after 1948, when he was Syrian and then Saudi Arabian delegate at the United Nations, and subsequently head of the Palestine Liberation Organization, that he came to be widely known. His memoirs clearly reveal that, early or late, his fundamental and unvarying attitude (and in this, of course, he is representative of his people and of their leaders) is an utter refusal of any accommodation with Zionism. Typical of his views is the statement he made as a spokesman for the Arab Office in Jerusalem calling for armed struggle, the setting-up of emergency committees throughout the country, 'making the whole fatherland a military barracks, and sending women and children into the neighbouring Arab countries, so that we might set a conflict aflame not to be extinguished until victory and independence. . . .' His attitude remained the same thereafter, as is strikingly shown by a conversation with Count Bernadotte during the conversations at Rhodes in the summer of 1948 which eventually led to an armistice in Palestine. Count Bernadotte had proposed that the Arabs and the Jews should hold informal discussions without prejudice to their respective positions. As spokesman for the Arab delegation, Shuqayri declared that talking, let alone negotiating, with the Jews was out of the question. Bernadotte then pointed out that Arab leaders had in the past frequently met Jewish leaders. This, conceded Shuqayri, had been the case, but that was before the rise of the Jewish state; only if this state disappeared, would they be ready to talk or negotiate.

As must again be emphasized, in expressing such sentiments and judgements—whether or not they were politically wise—Shuqayri was expressing the attitudes and feelings of his countrymen. Another passage provides a glimpse into their state of mind during the early part of the second world war. He describes the great excitement with which they used to listen to German and Italian broadcasts, how he would follow during the night the military communiqués, marking on a map the places being occupied by the victorious Germans, and meet his friends the following morning to discuss triumphs exceeding those of the previous day:

> Our sympathies were with the Axis powers being led by Hitler from victory to victory and with our sympathies went our prayers for the victory of Germany and her allies, and defeat for Britain and her confederates. . . . When the British government announced the formation of a Palestine force to help the war effort, our young men received the directive: do not join the Palestine force, and the response was quasi-

* The Mufti of Jerusalem, Hajj Amin al-Husayni, published some years ago a short, scrappy and disappointing book which cannot bear comparison to any of the works discussed here.

unanimous. . . . The activity of the Italian and German air force extended to Palestine, and in September 1940 their airplanes bombed certain targets in Tel-Aviv and Haifa. The joy and excitement produced in our circles was indescribable. An Italian bomb happened to fall in the Acre quarter where I lived, making a large crater but causing no damage. The assistant governor of Acre . . . visited me to report that the British governor . . . had told him jokingly that the bomb was destined for Ahmad Shuqayri. I said: This is fine; upon me and upon my enemies, O Lord!

As this passage suggests, Shuqayri is a man of eloquence and repartee. It is this gift which made for him a world-wide reputation. His position as United Nations delegate for Syria, and later on Saudi Arabia, gave him a large audience and wonderful scope for oratorical jousting. As his memoirs show, he is very proud of his verbal campaigns against Zionists in New York, giving long summaries of his interventions and rejoinders, and recording the fact that eight volumes of his United Nations speeches have been published.

I put him [Abba Eban] to flight and with him Golda Meir, the Prime Minister of Israel, and with them all the Israeli delegates in all the committees of the United Nations. I rubbed their faces in the dust and their noses in the mud, on the battlefield of justice and logic.

The fight was wide-ranging, and the most unlikely subject became the occasion of a skirmish, or even a regular battle. For example, Mrs. Meir referred in a speech to the slave trade in Africa and alluded to the role of the Arabs in this traffic. Shuqayri, in reply, makes a speech, quoting from various encyclopaedias, to show how the Jews had been the prominent slave traders in various epochs.

I was reading these extracts to [the delegates of] the African states. They were listening to me while their eyes were on the Israeli minister, who was either smoothing down her hair with her fingers, or leaning towards her assistant. I said, addressing Mrs. Golda Meir: 'If the minister returns to the subject of the slave trade, I will speak on the role of Israel in white slavery. You understand what I mean.' The minister kept silent, because in fact she knew what I meant and knew the role of Jewesses beginning with the story of Esther, down to our own day.

Shuqayri's account of his United Nations days has an epic quality about it, but the battle is a mere battle of words, and the epic is therefore a mock-epic. Grandiloquence has replaced the deeds of valour which epic celebrated. These memoirs, therefore, in their fashion also mark the failure of political action, the terrible hazards lying in the exercise of political power—the hazard of emasculation, impotence, or even (as in the Palestinian case) ruin pure and simple. Owing to his antecedents Shuqayri himself is aware that to take one's political fate into one's hands does not necessarily lead to success.

Shuqayri comes from a family of Acre notables, and his father As'ad Shuqayr was a pillar of the Young Turk régime in the Levant, the Mufti of the Ottoman fourth army and the confidant of its commander Jamal Pasha. After the first world war he used to witness many debates in his father's *divan* between those (like his father) who believed that the Ottoman connexion would have been best for the Arabs, and those (like his father-in-law) who sympathized with Arab nationalism. He tells us that these discussions came back to him some forty years later after the Six-Day war of 1967

> ... and the old question recurred: Was it better to stick with the Otto-man state or to follow the Allies? I went back, in my mind, to this old question, and reviewing the progress of Zionism during a period of fifty years, I decided that our generation had been grievously at fault, and that Ottoman rule with all its dangers—with which I was familiar—was preferable to these Arab 'autonomies', these defeated statelets, put to flight by Zionism in three wars.

Shuqayri not only evokes gratefully Sultan Abd al-Hamid who—as he told the Turkish foreign minister—knew how to resist Theodor Herzl's blandishments, he is also at times very bitter at the record of the Palestine Arab leaders between the wars. Of these leaders undoubtedly the most prominent was the Mufti of Jerusalem, Hajj Amin al-Husayni. Suqayri is in no doubt that what he sought was personal power:

> The glory of 'His Eminence' came before the glory of the homeland. The homeland fell and with it the glory. During the festival of Nabi Musa there was a glorious and splendid slogan: The sword of religion is Hajj Amin (*sayf al-din al-Hajj Amin*). The festival is gone and with it the slogan.

He compares the mufti with his relative Musa Kazim who preceded him in the leadership of the Palestine Arabs. The latter led the move-ment for a decade or so with his limited mentality and narrow views, but this is how he was and he could not help it. Hajj Amin was the leader for another decade or so 'during which the great catastrophe happened. There were many differences between them ... among which', Shuqayri says in an eloquent play on words, 'was that Musa Kazim was much mourned [on his death] while Hajj Amin has caused many people to mourn (*Musa Kazim bakahu al-nas kathiran wa'l-Hajj Amin abka kathiran min al-nas*).'

The sanguinary character of Palestine Arab politics in the late 1930s touched Shuqayri very closely and may explain the bitterness of this remark. His brother was a doctor and used to treat the wounded among the Arab guerrillas in the north of Palestine. He was called out one day to take care of a wounded man, and was murdered by fellow-Arabs while on his way to answer the call. Shuqayri was then in Beirut, and the mufti—who was a refugee there—came to offer his condolences. An Arab diplomat was also present and Shuqayri quotes this 'immortal' remark which the latter addressed to Hajj Amin:

> The Arabs, the Jews, and the British differ over everything, but agree on one thing: the British kill the Arab, the Jews kill the Arab, and the Arab kills the Arab.

The mufti's flight from Jerusalem in 1937 may be seen in retrospect to mark a decisive change in the fortunes of Arab Palestine.

Up to then it was the Palestine Arabs who had the initiative in deciding through their own leaders—however such leaders came to assume their position—what to do in order to fight the Zionist menace. Thereafter the neighbouring Arab states took up the defence and protection of their interests. Shuqayri's memoirs are equally copious on the lamentable results this intervention has produced, as on the mistakes and failures of the native Palestinian leadership. Another recent book of memoirs, *Roving Ambassador* by Nasir al-Din al-Nashashibi (Beirut, 1970), is particularly devoted to the way in which the cause of Palestine has been defended by the Arab states.

Nashashibi comes from a well-known Jerusalem family, and as we learn from Shuqayri's memoirs he—along with Ruhi al-Khatib (who was to become Mayor of Jerusalem), Raja'i al-Husayni, Burhan al-Dajani (both members of prominent Palestinian families), Albert Hourani and Wasfi al-Tall (who later became prime minister of Jordan and was murdered by terrorists in Cairo)—worked with Shuqayri at the Arab Office in Jerusalem, set up by the Arab League to disseminate information about and propagate the Arab case in Palestine. After 1948, Nashashibi made a reputation for himself in Cairo as a journalist of talent. In 1965, at the suggestion of President Nasser, he was appointed Arab League ambassador to Europe charged with presenting and defending the case of the Palestinians in western Europe. *Roving Ambassador* is the account of his European experiences and of the ways of Arab diplomacy.

From this book, too, there emanates a powerful impression of futility, powerlessness and despair. To believe Nashashibi, the countries of western Europe are, as he puts it, so many 'Zionist fortresses' which it is vain to hope to reduce or capture. Thus, he found the West Germans to be mere slaves at the feet of Israel; the Israeli ambassador to Bonn behaves 'as though he had a thousand heads, a thousand eyes and ears, and a thousand mouths.' The chapter in which he gives an account of his visit to Holland is entitled: 'Out of fear of the Jews, the Arabs here are Jews'; that on France: 'In the whole of France, we have only de Gaulle, while our enemies have the whole of France.' This demoralization in the face of Zionist activity is not peculiar to himself, but seems rather to be widely prevalent among Arab diplomats serving in Europe. He reports, for instance, a dialogue with a counsellor at the Egyptian embassy who comes to meet him at the railway station in The Hague:

> He quickly pulled me by the hand and bundled me into his car, saying: 'May God preserve!'
> Surprised, I said: 'What?'
> He said: 'The Jews. . . .'
> I said: 'What about them?'
> He said: 'God be praised they did not know who you were, or else you would have been involved in a catastrophe.'
> I said: 'Why?'
> He said: 'A week ago the secretary-general of the Arab League, Mr. Hassuna, was here and we had to meet him at the back door of the station, for fear of a Jewish attack.'
> I said: 'And who told you that the Jews were going to attack the secretary of the Arab League?'
> He said: 'No one. But it was by way of taking precautions!'
> I started laughing like a madman.
> But the embassy counsellor was driving at a prodigious speed while saying to me: 'Holland is no more than a Jewish colony! The Dutch are more Zionist than the Jews of Tel-Aviv! The atmosphere is poisoned, the air is poisoned, the work is poisoned. We find ourselves here in a worse state than prisoners of war. It is no use!'

Nashashibi, as may be seen, uses this dead-pan style of reporting for an ironical purpose. But his most mordant satire is reserved for Arab statesmen, and particularly for the officials of the Arab League. The League, which the Lebanese ambassador at London described in a conversation with him as 'an old people's home', Nashashibi holds responsible for the disaster which befell his people. He in fact dedicates his book to Jerusalem, 'one of the victims of the League of Arab States.' A victim, one gathers, of the selfishness and frivolity of a bureaucratic organisation which regards its own self-preservation as the highest public interest.

The suggestion for Nashashibi's appointment, as has been seen, came from President Nasser. But the secretary-general of the League was ill-disposed to Nashashibi, and sent him a message to say that he was being appointed to New Delhi. Nashashibi answered that the President of the Republic had not asked the secretary-general to send him into exile. Hassuna ceased his obstruction and Nashashibi received his appointment. He then paid the secretary-general a visit in order to seek instructions, and the comic dialogue which ensued crisply and savagely proves and illustrates his point. The secretary-general advises Nashashibi to avoid, while on his mission, any controversial subject:

I said: 'But supposing I was invited to a press conference, say in Bonn, and a foreign journalist asks me about the attitude of the Arab League to Socialist propaganda, how do I answer?'

Hassuna said: 'Do not answer him!'

I said: 'If another journalist asks me about the attitude of the League to the Islamic Alliance, were I to attack the alliance I fear Saudi Arabia would be vexed with me, while if I were to support it Cairo would disapprove; and both are members of the League. What shall I do?'

Hassuna said: 'Confine your remarks to Islam, and ignore the Islamic Alliance!'

I said: 'And Arab unity, what shall I say about it? A state such as the Lebanon is a member of the League and does not support Arab unity; while some of the other states do support it. What are your directives on this subject?'

He said: 'Tell them that the Arabs are one nation!'

I said: 'But this is not the view of the Lebanon.'

He said: 'Make use of your diplomatic tact and do not go into details.'

I said: 'And the Arab Common Market, should I speak in support of it?'

He said: 'Indeed.'

I said: 'But seven Arab states have refused to join the Market, thus showing that they do not believe in it or in its advantages.'

He said: 'We hope that a long time will not elapse before these states will come to believe in the utility of the Market.'

I said: 'When?'

He said: 'Within the next ten years.'

I said: 'But I am leaving for Europe tomorrow.'

He said: 'Use your discretion, Sir, use your discretion!'

I said: 'There is also an Arab state which calls, by the voice of its President, for peace with Israel. Is this the policy of the Arab League, or do I have the right to attack the President of this state?'

Hassuna said: 'Beware of attacking anybody!'

I said: 'Should I defend the idea of a peace with Israel?'

He said: 'Certainly not.'

I said: 'How do I answer a journalist who asks about the view of the League on this subject?'

Hassuna said: 'I am tired, O my brother, why do you want to increase my weariness?'

I understood, and passed on to another subject. I said to the secretary of the League: 'Where do you wish me, I mean in which European country shall I begin my work?'

He said, as though he were a great army commander making dispositions for a battle: 'Do you know those round counters with which children play? Take a number of red counters and spread before you the map of Europe. Put a red counter on Germany, and a similar one on London. Put a green counter on Geneva, another on France, and a third on Italy.'

I said: 'What shall I put on Holland, Belgium and the Scandinavian countries?'

He said: 'On Holland put a counter which is neither red nor green, a yellow one for instance. As for Brussels, it is the headquarters of the Common Market so it would be a good idea to put a red counter on it. As for the Scandinavian countries, they are not very important for us, so put no counter on them. When you have done all this, write to me and I will reply.'

Another conversation which Nashashibi reports is also worth quoting at length. It took place in Paris in the autumn of 1965 between him and Dr. Mahmud Fawzi, when the Egyptian foreign minister was accompanying Marshal Amer, vice-president of the Republic, on an official visit. If the comic writer is one who uses laughter and ridicule to make his audience aware of the human predicament, then in this passage Nashashibi shows himself a very skilled writer of comedy. The author visits Dr. Fawzi at breakfast in the Crillon hotel to find out news of Amer's discussions with the French government, and the following dialogue ensues:

Myself: 'What news, Doctor?'
Fawzi: 'The machine is working as usual . . . working.'
Myself: 'I mean the news of the Marshal and his Paris visit.'
Fawzi: 'The important thing is not the preface but the book!'
Myself: 'Do you mean the preface to the visit?'
Fawzi: 'I mean that the essence should be as clean as the appearance, or else everything is lost.'
Myself: 'Do you mean the essence of the visit and its appearance?'
Fawzi: 'I mean that we must not lose ourselves in formalities, and let go of the basic things.'
Myself: 'I hope that the Marshal has achieved something through the visit?'
Fawzi: 'The important thing is to achieve the achievement of success.'
Myself: 'Do I understand that the Marshal has not succeeded?'
Fawzi: 'Success may come in either way: through the strength of your own arm or through the weakness of others.'
Myself: 'In which way has the Marshal succeeded?'
Fawzi: 'I admire Montesquieu's saying that one of the requirements of success is that you should appear like a stupid man donning the dress of a wise man.'
Myself: 'And has the Marshal donned the wise man's dress?'
Fawzi: 'The most important thing is conviction.'
Myself: 'And have the French become aware of the solidarity of the Marshal's conviction?'

Fawzi: 'We work with an ebullient spirit.'

Myself: 'And has this spirit made an impression on the government in Paris?'

Fawzi: 'I did say to you, O my brother, that the important thing is not the preface but the book.'

Dr. Fawzi handed me a piece of buttered bread saying: 'Paris butter is like Paris . . .'

I said: 'Tasty?'

He said: 'Transparent.'

I said: 'Light?'

He said: 'Rich.'

I said: 'Wholesome?'

He said: 'Necessary.' . . .

Dr Fawzi accompanied me to the door of the apartment, saying: 'Please treat what you have heard as a secret between the two of us.'

Biting satire and a parade of the pompous and shifty incompetents in authority are Nashashibi's means for comprehending the Arab political predicament. It is the spirit of comedy which presides over his enterprise. But in the memoirs of Munif al-Razzaz, *The Bitter Experience* (Beirut, 1967), we discover the workings of a sombre and tormented spirit.

Razzaz is a prominent Ba'th ideologist who comes from Jordan. In April 1965, following internecine and ferocious disputes within the Ba'th leadership, he was appointed national secretary-general of the Party, in succession to the well-known Michel Aflaq—one of the original founders of the Ba'th—to whom some of the most powerful Syrian Ba'thist officers were by then implacably opposed. In the event, Razzaz retained his office for less than a year. He was rudely ejected by the *coup d'état* of 23 February 1966, notorious for the manner in which the partisans of General Jdid mowed down the followers of General Hafiz and then hosed their blood off the streets. The victors announced Razzaz's arrest and forthcoming trial, but he succeeded in escaping and found refuge in Beirut where he wrote and published these memoirs.

In them, Razzaz makes a great effort to account for a disaster for which the ideology he embraced and expounded had not prepared him. The ideology of the Ba'th was democratic, populist and socialist. It looked forward to the spiritual and political liberation of Arab Man, and the union of all Arabs in one state which ensured for everyone dignity and prosperity. That the state should become the sport of conspiratorial and murderous officers was envisaged in the writings neither of Aflaq, Bitar, Arsuzi—the founding fathers—nor of Razzaz himself. What, then, had gone wrong? To provide an explanation Razzaz goes into long ideological disquisitions, and manages to get entangled in his own explanations. These explanations, the reader suspects, serve not so much to explain as to provide comfort and justification to one who has seen his political world tumbling about his ears. The one possibility which it does not occur to Razzaz to consider is that the very ideological style which is the hallmark of the Ba'th itself can lead to the degraded and sanguinary politics which so horrify him. In effect, his explanation itself begs the question. The misadventures of the Ba'th Razzaz somehow attributes to the fact that the party was in reality two parties,

> one party on the side of the people, of liberty, of unity and of socialism; and another party against the people, against liberty, against unity and against socialism, and that the *coup d'état* slaughtered the aims of the people and its expectations.

The people, he also believes, was with the party against the members of the party.

However implausible this explanation is, the situation for which it purports to account is not in dispute. It is one which, as Razzaz puts it,

> Governments have taken the place of the masses, and become identical with politics and politicians. In each country a very insignificant number of politicians rule, nay in many of them only one citizen has the right of political action, and even the prime minister becomes an executive official.

One of the most valuable features of Razzaz's memoirs is that they describe graphically how this came to pass. Razzaz tells us that at the *coup d'état* of 8 March 1963 when the Ba'th—following its vicissitudes in the United Arab Republic and after—once more came to power in Syria, there was only an 'insignificant' number of Ba'thist officers in the army. What the successful conspirators therefore began by doing—without, it would seem, any objection from Aflaq, Bitar, Razzaz or the other civilian ideologues who later raised a hue and a cry against the militarization of the party—was to pack the army with Ba'thist officers. This done, and Nasser's followers bloodily eliminated, the various Ba'thist factions began a long, tortuous and bloody struggle which ended eight years later with the triumph—for the time being—of the present ruler of Syria, Hafiz al-Asad, and one of the many casualties of which was Razzaz. To Razzaz this internecine struggle was

> a military struggle between two groups occasionally invoking the support of civilian and political elements on which they leaned, and by which they covered their nakedness, a mere struggle for power, paltry,

ridiculous, humiliating and depressing. As for the people, it had to be content with looking on and grieving. It understood the reality of the struggle better than the contestants themselves, knew itself to be helpless and quite unable, even if it had wanted to, to shift the balance in this or in that direction.

It was not only the people which was powerless to influence the struggle; the Party organization, its leadership and its congresses were likewise powerless. The national Command [i.e. Aflaq, Razzaz *et al.*] had speech for its weapon, in a fight where no weapon except the tank, the cannon, and the machine-gun was any use.

Razzaz has many arresting descriptions of this fight. The two rivals at the time were the Sunnite Amin al-Hafiz and the Alawite Salah Jdid. We see them confronting one another like birds of prey with hooded, watchful, expressionless eyes, waiting for the enemy to make a false step, to stumble or relax his attention, in order instantly to pounce down with a shriek and tear him apart with beak and claws. A casual footnote conjures up a picture of these chieftains always moving about under the protection of a gang of armed officers. Hafiz, says Razzaz, used to come to Party meetings with forty of his own bodyguard, while Asad—then Jdid's ally—would come with twenty retainers; and these mobsters would occupy the corridors, and the staircases, the offices and the reception rooms of the Party headquarters. We follow the manœuvrings, the patient and devious tactics, the secret and complicated intrigues by which the lieutenant-general (Hafiz) and the major-general (Jdid) for something like a year undermined and sought to destroy one another. Razzaz gives, for instance, the details of a pretty stratagem by which Jdid contrived to detach from Hafiz some of his most important supporters. He nominated as minister of war and as chief-of-staff two of Hafiz's followers. The latter, taken by surprise, hesitated to endorse his enemy's nomination. This convinced his partisans that Hafiz wanted to monopolize all positions for himself, and they turned against him. In the end the Sunnite bit the dust, and the Alawite succeeded him. His victory may have been due to the clannishness and secretiveness inculcated in the Alawites by their esoteric sect. But, if so, then Jdid met his superior in his fellow-Alawite and fellow-villager, Asad, who toppled and imprisoned him in 1971. The fortunes of those who seek to govern a polity like Syria irresistibly remind one of the priest of Nemi who, as Frazer recounts, has to slay his predecessor in order to become the guardian of the golden bough, but who is himself, in turn, fated to be slain by his successor.

The bloody rites of Syrian politics in the 1960s inspired not only Razzaz's bitter and disillusioned chronicle, but also what is perhaps the most remarkable and revealing book of political memoirs to appear in the Arab world in recent decades. This is *The Ba'th* (Beirut, 1969) by Sami al-Jundi. Jundi—a Syrian Isma'ili from the Syrian Isma'ili centre, Salamiyya, by profession a dentist and a Ba'thist of long standing—played an active role in Ba'thist conspiracies and political activities in the first half of the 1960s. But his known Nasserite sympathies led to his removal from the centre of the stage and his appointment as ambassador to Paris. After the Six-Day war he was accused—in what he claims to have been a frame-up by his own foreign minister—of conducting clandestine negotiations with the Israelis. He was recalled to Damascus and imprisoned for a time in the notorious Mezze prison. Upon his release, he was allowed to leave, and is now—as appears from his latest book—again practising dentistry, in Tunis.

For Razzaz, the mishaps of Syria and the Ba'th are the consequences of, and to be explained by, ideological deviation. Jundi's vision may, by contrast, be called tragic, if by tragedy we mean the exhibition of a *peripeteia* which inspires in the spectator surprise, pity and terror. In this sense *The Ba'th* is a tragedy. Its tragic effect is enhanced by Jundi's style, which surely makes him one of the masters of modern Arabic prose. It is a style which breaks the neck of that empty magniloquence which has been the hallmark and the bane of literary Arabic in the period of its decadence. It is subtle, sinuous and allusive, blending in a successful amalgam foreign words with colloquial and literary expressions; it glows with a sombre fire, smouldering with a desolate, anguished lyricism which, uncontrolled, might have spilled over into hysterical lamentation. The style is evoked by and adapted to the subject and to the profound despair which the situation of the Arabs inspires in him. He speaks of this despair in the preface of his latest collection of short stories, a despair the expression of which, whether in the memoirs or in the fiction of which he is an accomplished writer, he presents as an offering to his bruised and maltreated country.

Jundi begins his account with the early history of the party which came to be known as the Ba'th or Resurrection. Its origins lie in the activities of two schoolmasters, Zaki al-Arsuzi (an Alawite from Alexandretta) and Michel Aflaq (a Greek Orthodox from Damascus). Arsuzi was a leader of Arab resistance to the Turks in Alexandretta. When this mixed region was closed to Turkey by the French mandatory in 1939, Arsuzi settled in Damascus where Jundi, then a young student, came to know him as the leader of a small group, the Arab Nationalist Party, the principles of which, established by Arsuzi, were the embryo of later Ba'thist doctrines. Arsuzi 'was good-looking, elegant, and of a gentle appearance, but when he spoke he became a fierce rebel, his big green eyes flashing with a

ferocious, destructive gleam, as though he was revolution personified
. . .' Jundi records the occasion, on 29 November 1940, when he
and four other young men met in the room of one of them and listened
to a four-hour lecture by Arsuzi on Democracy, Communism and
Nazism, beginning with Descartes and ending with H. S. Chamberlain. At the end of this discourse which 'plumbed the depths' and
was 'warm and emotional', Arsuzi suggested the formation of an
Arab Resurrection Party. Jundi became the treasurer of the small
group, and with the subscriptions bought a high chair for the master
and low stools made of straw for the disciples. On a wall in the room
where they held their meetings one of them wrote in pencil: 'We live
here under the banner of Arab unity,'

> We lived [writes Jundi of this period] through this hope, strangers in
> our society which gradually increased our isolation: rebels against all
> the old values, enemies to all the conventions of humanity, rejecting all
> ceremonies, relationships and religions. We sought the fight everywhere;
> we were an unrelenting pickaxe. Society persecuted us, and so we defied
> it and began to destroy all institutions with much intelligence and much
> stupidity, like children growing up who with time became more
> childish. . . .
> We were accused of atheism, and this was correct in spite of what the
> Ba'thists later pretended by way of exculpation. We believed in religious
> feeling, in the mysticism of all religions, and in their wholly human
> tendency. As for the religion of the others, we were wholly opposed to it.
> We were racialists, admiring Nazism, reading its books and the
> source of its thought, particularly Nietzsche's *Thus Spake Zarathustra*,
> Fichte's *Addresses to the German Nation*, and H. S. Chamberlain's
> *Foundations of the Nineteenth Century* which revolves on race. We were
> the first to think of translating *Mein Kampf*.
> Whoever has lived during this period in Damascus will appreciate
> the inclination of the Arab people to Nazism, for Nazism was the power
> which could serve as its champion, and he who is defeated will by
> nature love the victor. But our belief was rather different. . . .
> We were idealists, basing social relationships on love. The Master
> used to speak about Christ, and I think he was influenced by Nietzsche's
> book, *The Origin of Tragedy*. He took the pre-Islamic period for his
> ideal, calling it the golden age of the Arabs. Like Nietzsche, he believed
> that Socrates was the beginning of that logic and dialectic which
> destroyed the spontaneity of Greece; and he saw in *kalam* [philosophical
> theology] the decadence of the Arabs. He went even further and took
> up only what was pre-Islamic in Islam. He was a man who rejected, and
> with him we also rejected.
> In discussion with him in 1946 I invoked the Koran. He took excep-
> tion to my religious tendency, saying: 'You are a monk in the guise of a
> revolutionary.' I objected, saying: 'Belief in ideas takes on a religious
> character.' He answered: 'Revolution itself is a mystic belief.' I found

in conversation that he had not, up to then, read the Koran seriously. When he did so later on, many of his views changed. Few may know that he began to study Arabic in 1940, having preferred until then to speak in French.

We used to read, write, and translate. The foundation of the group library preceded that of the Party. We did not have the means to buy many books, so we brought together in the Master's house all those which we possessed and they filled the sill of the small window over-looking the street.

This small group of young disciples—never more than twelve university students and a scarcely greater number of pupils from the main secondary school in Damascus—worked upon by this fervent schoolmaster who unveiled, in French, all the glittering marvels of the European ideologies, excited by this daring rejection of the traditions of their society, and seized by the dream of its total renovation, constituted, then, a nucleus of the Ba'th Party. What they were like we may gather from Jundi's description as quoted above, and from another passage of his describing the change which came over them as a result of Arsuzi's indoctrination: '. . . . the Party became a collection of anarchists who were one in their thinking and logic, explaining events in almost the same way, trusting in nobody, loving the people and hating individuals, venerating the whole and hating the parts.'

Arsuzi's group dispersed when he left Damascus in 1944. Almost all of them were, however, also members of another group also calling itself the Ba'th and led by the two schoolmasters, Salah al-Din al-Bitar and Michel Aflaq. It was this latter Ba'th which was to flourish in post-war Syrian politics, and of which Aflaq became the acknowledged and venerated ideologue. Aflaq began first to be known not as a political thinker, but as a writer of short stories. And it is as an artist that Jundi sees him, who by going into politics betrayed his real vocation. Aflaq, thinks Jundi, looked upon the Ba'th as his artistic creation. 'He wished the Party to be a painter's canvas, but the colours turned out to be violent, and he sometimes hated it as much as he loved it.' 'I always used to say about him,' continued Jundi, 'that the Arab Ba'th Socialist Party was Michel Aflaq's suicide.'

All these young Syrian intellectuals, then, whether inspired by Arsuzi or Aflaq—who themselves took their ideas from Nietzsche or H. S. Chamberlain or Alfred Rosenberg (Jundi says that in 1940 he was looking for a copy of the *Myth of the Twentieth Century* in Damascus, and finally found a French abridgement of it belonging to Aflaq which he borrowed from one of his students)— were radically disaffected towards the political institutions and the social arrangements of post-war Syria. Their fervour was incandescent, their intentions of the highest, and they were determined by their exertions and example to save Syria and the Arabs. Looking back now on a quarter-of-a-century of Syrian politics, Jundi contrasts the high hopes of the past with the present degradation.

> Who would have believed during the school year 1940–1 [he begins his memoirs by asking] that the Ba'th would end in all this mockery?*
> Who among us would have thought that the word, Ba'thist, would become an accusation which some of us would rebut with bitter scorn?
> Who among us would have supposed that a day would come when we would be ashamed of our past; would flee from it as from a sin we have deliberately committed and for which we are treated with ignominy; would almost deny having been part of it; and would hide our identity? Was it, then, delusive to have been proud of it and to have cherished it?
> Our sacrifices, our youth wasted on the roads among the people, our dreams and our faith, were they then all a mockery?
> Almost nobody credits the fact that we believed in a cause. They insist that we are informers, writers of delations, torturers, killers. They accuse us of treason. They pretend that all that we had said was opportunism and trickery, that we so perfected the actor's art that the people were deceived by us.

The evil, for Jundi, began with a fatal illusion:

> We thought that the epochs of decadence had come to an end with our predecessors among the politicians, and that we were the glorious beginning of a new civilisation, when in fact we were the last exemplars of backwardness, and a desolating expression of it.
> We wanted to be a resurrection [ba'th] of signal deeds and of heroism, but what was resurrected through us—when we came to power—was no more than the period of the Mamlukes.

The Ba'th, then, has proved to be, Jundi laments, the pall-bearer of the Syrian people. This sad and unexpected outcome is a consequence of the Party's involvement with the officers. The soldiers whom the Ba'th had hoped to make the servants of its ideology have in fact taken it over and become its masters. When two civilian nominees were elected to head the party's politburo at the instigation of the three military leaders Hafiz, Jdid and Asad (who were then allies), a joke—which Jundi recounts—became current in Damascus. It was to the effect that three soldiers governed Syria by means of two shoes [shoes being lowly unclean objects].

A second aspect of Ba'thist misgovernment can be seen in its economic policy. The nationalization of industrial enterprises was

---

* Untranslatable play on words: ba'th, resurrection and 'abath, mockery.

ill thought out and, finally, ruinous. Jundi gives as an example the fact that in a Japanese textile factory a worker looks after 260 shuttles, while in a Syrian nationalized establishment the figure is only 7 shuttles per worker. As for land reform, its real basis, declares Jundi, was not the welfare of the peasant class but the mere dispersal of private property to satisfy local animosities.

A third aspect of Ba'thist rule was its terrible capriciousness. The ministry of information of which he was for a while in charge gives a true picture of the régime: 'In it I was everything and nothing. I could dismiss and punish whom I wished and as I wished, but I had no power to appoint even a temporary announcer. Official appointments followed a curious routine on the pretext of doing away with routine. . . . The appointment of an announcer had, and still has, to be approved by the council of ministers.' It was the same in other ministries, and chaos reigned supreme: 'The lists of dismissals were the index of a minister's success. The members of the Party, their relatives and fellow-tribesmen were claiming the rewards of the struggle and the rights of kinship. . . . Dismissal was therefore necessary in order for new appointments to be made.' What Jundi is describing here is clearly only a modern version of the most ancient and the most durable form of government, namely Oriental despotism. A further characteristic of Oriental depotism is what may be called its Thousand-and-One-Nights quality: overnight the beggar becomes a king, and almost immediately reverts to a beggar again. This quality is also present in Ba'thist rule, as appears from another remark of Jundi's:

> In the whirlpool of March [1963] you thought yourself to be exercising responsibility, planning and making history, but you became suddenly nothing. A little while later you saw yourself again as very important, and then, again, nothing.

But what recurs like a sombre litany through Jundi's book is the illegal and atrocious violence which the official classes inflict and suffer in turn. This violence came in with military rule, and owing to Ba'thist involvement with the military, it hangs like a millstone round the neck of the Ba'th Party. Torture as a method of government came in with Za'im at the first *coup d'état*, and all his successors have had recourse to it, 'as though', exclaims Jundi, 'the whip has become the warp of modern Syrian history. Governments and régimes succeed one another so that the whip may be transmitted from hand to hand. If one becomes tired of holding it, one entrusts another with it, and the latter becomes skilful and expert in branding the victims' bodies with its fire.'

Za'im was the victim of what he had initiated, and his execution was plain murder. His successor Shishakli was clearly possessed by blood lust. Jundi sees himself as both the victim and the accomplice of violence. He was imprisoned twice, the second time by the Ba'thists in 1968, but the first time was in 1962, after an abortive Ba'thist *coup d'état* in which he was implicated:

> I found that the only reality in modern Syrian history was Mezze military prison and the whip, everything else being an illusion. . . . During August torture reached an inconceivable height. . . . They used to wrap the prisoners from head to foot in woollen blankets leaving only one small orifice to enable them to breathe. They left them for days like this in temperatures which burned and scalded, forbidding all movement and speech, with the guard standing ready to whip whoever dared so much as to whisper.

Exactly a year after his prison experiences, Jundi was minister of information following the *coup d'état* of 8 March 1963. In this *coup* Ba'thists and Nasserites worked together, but they later fell out with one another over reunion with Egypt. On 18 July of the same year the Nasserites attempted to topple their erstwhile partners, but the Ba'thists foiled them, killing that day alone 170 Nasserites. A bloody repression followed. Military courts handed down death verdicts on the nod, and they were executed on the spot. One evening Jundi was at the ministry of information, and an official told him of a television film which was going to be shown and about which he was doubtful:

> I went to the projection studio and saw something unbelievable. The members of the court had decided that the people should share in their sport, and not miss the joys of victory. They arranged therefore for the scenes of the executions to be recorded: the prisoner led from the cell to the place of execution, the blindfolding, the order to fire, the blood pouring out from the mouth, the knees folding under the victim, his body leaning forward as the cords were loosened, his mouth open in order to kiss the earth his mother. I said nothing, I went out and an officer asked me gaily: 'How did you like it, Doctor?' I said: 'Is this the Ba'th?' He said: 'I do not understand.' I said: 'You will never understand!'

Some months later those Nasserites who were not executed in July began coming out of Mezze prison, and he saw the tortures which they had suffered. When he recalls the oath that he and other Ba'thists had taken to transform Mezze into a tourist hotel, he laughs with bitterness, for was he not one of those who held the whip, a torturer among torturers? That it should all have come to this, that the schoolboy's fervour and the student's aspiration should put him in the end alternately among the hunters and the hunted, this is the tragic irony which gives Jundi's accents their poignancy.

The bleak light of despair illumines the writer's vision, and this vision is his gift to his countrymen. As the dedication to a haunting allegorical work of his, *My Friend Ilyas* (Beirut, 1969), declares:

Damascus, O fountain of my tenderness,
O blonde among cities, O branch of jasmine,
I offer up to your sorrows this strangled corpse.

12. Anti-Marxism in Egypt

Political thought in modern Egypt is, in its categories and arguments, derivative from European thought. It has been entirely produced by the small westernized minority which, ever since Muhammad Ali's time, has increasingly dominated the intellectual and official classes. Both before and after world war I, the trend of thought of these classes has revolved around two issues, namely: how to rid Egypt of the British occupation; and what ought to be the character and limits of government. Both issues were formulated in European terms and debated according to European assumptions and categories. They were thus of little import or significance for the mass of the Egyptians whose universe of discourse was quite different from that of their westernized rulers.

It is true that the Wafd party, both under Zaghlul and Nahhas, attempted now and again to mobilize the masses, by appealing to them in the traditional Islamic terms,[1] but such attempts were intermittent, adventitious, opportunistic, non-systematic and never buttressed with a theoretical foundation or justification. In fact, before 1952, only three groups in Egypt possessed a theory by which they justified an appeal to, and a mobilization of, the masses. The first was the Communist party which, under the monarchy, was a small, clandestine group inspired and led to a very large extent by non-Muslim foreigners. What was even more incapacitating was that their notion of Egyptian politics, based as it was on a Marxist-Leninist analysis of class divisions and revolutionary action, was as irrelevant to Egyptian conditions as the political thought of the westernized politicians who called themselves Wafdist or Sa'dist or Liberal Constitutionalists.

The second group was Ahmad Husayn's Young Egypt party.[2] Its doctrine did recommend and require mobilization of the masses, in the European totalitarian style, and its ideology of Egyptianism, Islam, and xenophobia was more intelligible and acceptable to the masses. But the Young Egypt party did not prove very successful. This was perhaps owing to the fact that it became involved in political intrigues with Fu'ad and Faruq very soon after its foundation in 1933, before having seriously recruited and organized a mass following. The powerful political opponents which it thus attracted were able therefore largely to limit and even at times to suppress its activities. The outbreak of war in 1939 added to its difficulties, since it was suspected of having Nazi connexions, and was thus in bad

206

odour with the British. But, what is perhaps equally important, the ideology of Young Egypt could not rival that of the third group which seriously and systematically attempted to mobilize and indoctrinate the masses.

This group was that of the Muslim Brothers which Hasan al-Banna founded at Isma'iliyya in 1928. While the ideology of Young Egypt was an artificial hodge-podge made up of Islamic and European elements, that of the Muslim Brothers was purely Islamic, deliberately evoking and recalling beliefs, ways of thought and behaviour, and exemplary deeds which the ordinary Egyptian Muslim held in familiar affection. Thus, where Young Egypt adopted for its slogan 'God, Fatherland, and King,' the Muslim Brothers proclaimed that Islam was their banner and the Qur'an their constitution. There can be no doubt that the latter was incomparably more powerful and attractive than the former. To say that the Muslim Brothers appealed to purely Islamic sentiments is, of course, by no means to deny that they were themselves profoundly touched by European ways of thought. For their very reaction to, and attack upon, what they considered as deeply harmful western-Christian influences forced them to deal with and in European concepts and categories. In this respect, the thought of the Muslim Brothers is quite similar to modern Islamic apologetics, whether emanating from al-Azhar or from writers who have no official connexions. All these writings, those of the Muslim Brothers included, consciously and militantly defending Islam against the west, are traditionalist rather than traditional in character. They are impregnated by European thought.[3] But the fact remains that, whatever its underlying tendency, the thought of the Muslim Brothers is expressed in traditional Islamic terms, and thus appeals to those Egyptians who have not been much touched by Europe, as well as to those who have become acquainted with, and been discomforted by it. Another reason for the superior appeal of the Muslim Brothers lay in the fact that, unlike the Young Egypt party, Hasan al-Banna and his lieutenants were at the outset, and for many years afterwards, not directly concerned with politics. Originally they looked upon their mission as one of social reconstruction. Their mission was directed toward the urban workers who were in acute danger of disorientation and alienation. The Muslim Brothers worked to recuperate these lost souls for the Islamic community, to make a place within the body politic for 'the inhabitants of the caves who were outside the laws and the constitution,' and give them a pride in their heritage.[4] It was really only after 1945 that the energies of Hasan al-Banna and the other leaders began to be mainly directed to political intrigues and terrorism.

Of the success of the Brothers in creating a very large and tena-
ciously loyal following there can be no doubt. They were throughout
a private organization. Unlike the Wafd and the other political
machines under the monarchy or the military régime, the Brothers
had no access to official patronage and could by no means reward
their adherents or punish their opponents in the way these machines
could. But in spite of this fact, they managed to attract a very large
following indeed. Professor Mitchell has estimated that in 1946–8
the society had some half-million members and another half-million
sympathizers, and that in 1953, a year or so before its dissolution
by the military régime, there were between 200,000 and 300,000
Brothers.[5] Such figures in a country like Egypt are remarkable on
any reckoning, and it is difficult to believe that the loyalties and
commitments which these figures represent should have disappeared
so quickly. Such scant evidence as we have leads us rather to suspect
that even now, persecution, repression and proscription have
succeeded in driving them underground rather than in absolutely
destroying them. The vicissitudes of the Brothers may be laid at the
door of their leaders who twice misjudged the political situation and
their own power, and thus wrecked the organization which had been
built up with such arduous labour and devotion. In 1948–9 they
resorted to terrorism in order to gain power, and proved unequal to
the contest with the authorities. The *coup d'état* of July 1952 gave
them new hope of playing a large role on the political scene. But the
scene was extraordinarily confused. Nasser and his fellow-officers
were, it is true, very unpopular in the period 1952–4, and the leaders
of the Brothers may have thought that in trying conclusions with
these officers they could not possibly lose. But again they were
proved wrong, and discovered to their cost that in an oriental
despotism to him who controls the tanks obedience is due. So they
suffered their second repression in the autumn of 1954. They were
allowed to re-emerge briefly in 1965, but even in their enfeebled
condition they must have represented a threat to the régime which
subjected them to a new repression and condemned their most
prominent surviving leaders to death. They have now been bludgeoned
into passivity; but to judge by the nervousness of the authorities in
1965–6, their criticism of the military régime must enjoy a wide
audience among a population still staunchly Islamic, more alienated
from its westernized rulers, and more sceptical of their purposes than
ever.

Under the monarchy, the Brothers criticized the west and westernization in Egypt for encouraging sexual immorality, unrestrained,
cupidity, the merciless exploitation by man of his fellow men,
corruption and atheism. That society in Egypt was a chaos and a

shambles, that an increasingly large number of Egyptians were living in conditions of increasing misery was attributed to 'the abandonment of Islam by the rulers of this Muslim society, and to their infatuation with the west. The Muslim Brothers were not at that time particularly interested in Marxism or Communism, which seemed to them mere variants of European materialism and godlessness. After the *coup d'état* of July 1952 and the subsequent abolition of the monarchy, a great change came over the terms in which political debate was conducted in Egypt. The officers now in power—many of them greatly influenced by the outlook and doctrines of the Muslim Brothers—declared that, as the Brothers had argued, the miseries of Egypt stemmed from the corrupt political institutions of the monarchy, whose parties pursued their own narrow and selfish interests at the expense of the people. All this was now to be changed: the welfare of the masses would become the object of government, the magnates would be divested of their extensive landholdings, and the administration would become clean, and be put at the service of the citizens. There was a moment when all this must have seemed very promising to the Brothers, to be indeed the vindication of their teaching and their struggle. But, as has been seen, these hopes were soon dashed and if Ibrahim 'Abd al-Hadi in 1949 had chastised the Brothers with whips, Nasser in 1954 began chastising them with scorpions. Furthermore, from the arms deal of 1955 onwards, the military régime was becoming increasingly tied to the Soviet Union, increasingly inclined to adopt 'socialist' policies—which to the Brothers were tainted with a European origin—and increasingly tolerant of literary and publicistic activity by Egyptian Marxists and Communists. The defeat of June 1967 seemed to the Brothers—and no doubt also to a large number of Egyptians—proof conclusive that the foreign policy which the régime had pursued for 12 years, with its dependence on the Soviets, and the internal economic and social policies which were believed to be the concomitant of this dependence, were an unmitigated catastrophe. If political debate had been free in Egypt, the Egyptians would surely have manifested their dislike of the military régime, in the same way in which they spontaneously manifested it in February 1954 before Nasser had been able fully to establish his hegemony.[6] As it was, this feeling of discontent had perforce to remain inchoate, expressed more in the gallows humour of which the Egyptians are such masters, than in reasoned criticism or in putting forward alternative policies.

To this there is an exception. A trenchant criticism of the régime, its tendencies, and the ideology it favours, of what is alleged to be its betrayal of Islam (and hence of Egypt) has been expressed by the Muslim Brothers and by those who seem sympathetic to their tenets.

It is true that the Brothers were subject to great persecution in 1954–5 and 1965–6, but this does not seem to have led them to abandon their views, and we may suspect that these views find a large audience of passive sympathizers. Before the repression of 1965–6, in which he was executed, Sayyid Qutb published, in 1964, a remarkable work *Ma'alim fi'l-tariq* (Signposts on the Road) which was thought by the authorities inportant enough to warrant a refutation which the Arab Socialist Union published in 1966 under the title *Ma'alim fi tariq al-kihyana wa'l-raj'iyya* (Signposts on the Road of Treason and Reaction). Significantly, the title of this pamphlet echoed that of Qutb's book, and the layout and design of its cover were an exact copy of the work it was attempting to refute. One of the grave charges which this pamphlet levels against Qutb is that he is a 'reactionary inimical to socialism,' and the charge is proved from his statement that the west is bankrupt because it has begun to adopt socialism from the eastern camp. The writer of the pamphlet comments: 'There are some who disagree with him, and who consider that the necessity for the capitalist system to adopt socialism is a confirmation of the triumph of socialism, which realizes the sublime principles which Islam has proclaimed.'[7] The pamphlet's author is at any rate right in asserting that Qutb is strongly opposed to socialism. For him it is one species of that *jahiliyya* which now has the world in its grip. Communism, he declares, is class-rule 'based on the union of the proletariat (*al-sa'alik*), and the sentiment which is dominant in it is a black hatred for all other classes! Such a petty and hateful union could not but bring out what is worst in the human being. For it is *ab initio* based on emphasizing the animal characteristics alone, on allowing them to strike root and to grow, in the belief that the basic needs of man are food, shelter and sex—and these are the basic needs of the animal—and in the belief that the history of man is the history of the quest for food.'[8] Communist society, Qutb also says, is, like all the other societies existing in the world today, a *mujtama' jahili*, an idolatrous society which denies the sovereignty of God. Communist society is such because it denies the existence of God, making matter or nature the active principle in the universe, and economics and the means of production the active principle in human history. Communist society is also idolatrous because it establishes a régime in which complete submission is given not to God but to the party.[9] Qutb's criticism, however, reaches beyond communism and the Soviet régime. His readers are left in no doubt that he rejects equally some of the most basic notions by which the military régime justifies itself, and the very foundations of its ideology. A régime, he asserts, cannot claim inspiration from God or Islam unless it proclaims that it is God, not the people or the party, or any other human being, who is the source of authority. It is not only Communism and Capitalism which are idolatrous, we Muslims are also living in a *jahiliyya:* 'All that is around us is *jahiliyya.* Peoples' imaginings, their beliefs, customs and traditions, the sources of their culture, their art and literature, their laws and statutes, much even of what we take to be Islamic culture, Islamic authorities, Islamic philosophy, Islamic thought: all this too is of the making of this *jahiliyya.*' It follows, that the fatherland of the Muslim, his *watan,* is where Islam is supreme; as for the solidarity based on clan, tribe, nation (*qawm*), race (*jins*), colour and land, all these are petty and retarded types of solidarity which humanity adopts only when it is in a state of spiritual degradation. This kind of solidarity the Prophet had described as 'rotten,' an expression denoting repugnance and disgust.[10]

The repression of the Brothers in 1965–6 made it difficult if not impossible for such views to be publicly expressed. But the very fact of the repression showed perhaps that the authorities feared the popularity of views such as Qutb's. After the defeat of 1967, and the shock which it administered to the military régime, the passive sympathizers with the Brothers and their ideas must have increased. Criticism of the régime, of its Soviet connexions, of its emphasis on 'socialism' and its tolerance of Marxist writings most likely gained an increasing audience. But such criticism, though certainly voiced in private conversation, could not possibly find public expression in Egypt. To gain an idea of their tenor we may refer to two pamphlets; published in Beirut by the Egyptian publicist and journalist, Muhammad Jalal Kishk. Though the pamphlets were published outside Egypt, the author himself was apparently still living in Egypt at the time of their publication, and what he has to say in these pamphlets may therefore be taken as an exposition by a close and interested observer of the vicissitudes affecting Egypt, and of their causes and remedies. As will be seen, what he has to say makes it unlikely that his is an isolated and unrepresentative voice. His criticisms and proposals seem rather the continuation and the echo of what the Muslim Brothers, and all those Egyptians who have desired to transform Egypt into a true Islamic polity, have been saying for many decades now. The pamphlets therefore may be considered a sign of the obstinate continuity of certain currents of thought which, in spite of repression and persecution by different governments, have had the power to attract and hold for many decades now a large proportion of the Egyptian intellectual classes.

The first pamphlet, *What the Egyptian Students Want* (*Madha yurid al-talaba al-misriyyun*), was published in November 1968, and dealt with the student demonstrations of the previous February. The second, *What the Egyptian People Want* (*Madha yurid al-sha'b al-misri*), taking the form of an open letter to President Sadat, was published in October 1970, and thus at the very moment when the latter was chosen to succeed Nasser.

Of the two pamphlets the second is the more cutting and outspoken but many themes are common to the two publications, though since they are *oeuvres de circonstance* the emphasis changes from the one to the other. Writing in 1968 Kishk has no doubt that the Egyptian people is the absolute enemy of Communism: 'The Egyptian people is a people which has faith, which clings to Islam. It has never known fanaticism in all its history, but it likewise will not allow itself to be uprooted.' The Egyptian opposition to Communism has been on the increase since 1964 after Khrushchev's provocative visit, when he behaved as though he was a Cromer or an American vice-president visiting South Vietnam. This enmity became clear when the Soviet Union adopted a defeatist attitude in May–June 1967, the crowd going so far as to throw stones and spit at the car of the Soviet ambassador on 9 June 1967. Kishk goes on to affirm that this dislike extends to the Egyptian Communists who have followed one of two policies: beginning by attacking the régime as fascist, they then changed their policy and gave it absolute support. They thus formed 'the greatest reactionary force opposed to any criticism or change' and became the enemies of democracy and the supremacy of law. But who, anyway, are these Egyptian Communists? They are either Copts or Jews or Baha'is whose main interest is the struggle against Islam. Consider for instance their support of Emperor Haile Selasie in spite of his inimical position toward the Arabs, or how they have taken Makarios' side in the Cyprus dispute and prevented any publicity being given to the Turkish case. Many of them are opportunists who have taken up Marxism in order to teach in Government institutes, so that they may earn high salaries and 'smoke American cigarettes imported in an illegal fashion.'[11]

But it is clear that Kishk's attack is directed against a wider target than that of the Egyptian Communists. His quarrel is really with the military régime itself. This régime, he argues, is in effect composed of a congeries of organizations (*tashkilat*) whose members form a new ruling class. In order to perpetuate its rule, this new class has to repress the people, since if the people were in control of politics, these organizations would lose their *raison d'être*: they are 'a natural phenomenon of class rule transforming the government into a secret group, and politics into a conspiracy'. In order to describe the character of these organizations, Kishk has recourse to an analogy drawn from an earlier period of Egyptian history: it is mamlukes, he says, who run *al-Ahram,* and this newspaper is in effect their fief (*sanjaqiyya*). The Egyptian Communists are but part of these organizations where they have succeeded in lodging themselves.[12]

What Kishk has been describing is in fact Nasserism, the bankruptcy of which appeared in 1967. Why, asks Kishk in his 1968 pamphlet, did the masses maintain Nasser in power on 9 June 1967? Because the disastrous alternative was Nasserism without Nasser, and what they wanted was Nasser without Nasserism. It is this again which the Egyptian students wanted in their demonstrations of February 1968. The passage is eloquent enough to warrant extensive quotation:

> When the régime sustained a military defeat, the justification for its existence disappeared, having previously lost any justification in internal affairs. If the President had not announced his retirement and the retirement of all the leadership of the régime, the masses would have marched on Cairo after the cease-fire, and it is impossible to foresee what would have happened.
>
> But President Nasser was able, on the evening of 9 June, to prevent this march, rather to deflect it to another direction, when he faced the masses with the only possibility contingent on his resignation, namely the continuation of the Nasserite régime without Nasser; he was careful to emphasize this by appointing a successor.
>
> Since this was the worst possible solution, the masses put forward immediately the contrary solution: Nasser without the Nasserite régime.
>
> It seemed to the people that from June [1967] to February [1968] this was the direction events were taking. The trials began to take place, the press was allowed to publish the scandals of the régime, and proclaim the slogan of change.
>
> When it began to be apparent after the formation of the ministry, the return of the youth organizations to their activity, the reconstitution of the branches of the Arab Socialist Union, the interference in the elections to the journalists' [union], the refusal to allow the formation of a students' union, the coming forward of the old faces on the pretext of continuity, the coming into prominence of new forces, and the swelling of the old forces which escaped the liquidation, then the students came out in February, reminding with a greater emphasis and sharpness [the authorities] of the demand of the people on 9 and 10 June, which was: Down with Nasserism and long live Nasser.[13]

Kishk's open letter to Sadat is even more daring in its ideas and expressions. Nasser, he tells his successor, was a President (*ra'is*), but he was also a Leader (*za'im*). No successor to the Presidency can, however, hope to succeed to Nasser's leadership which the people had acknowledged and accepted. But if his successors should attempt to exercise tutelage (*wisaya*) over the Egyptian people, this will end in a dictatorship such as that which ravages Iraq or that of

Papa Duvalier in Haiti. There must be an end to minutely organized demonstrations, with rigidly prescribed slogans; an end to elections without a plurality of candidates. He congratulates Sadat on welcoming the fact that three-quarters of a million voters had rejected his candidature; Sadat, however, had declared that in saying no to him, these voters did not oppose the revolution of 1952 or its continuation. Kishk for his part would like to ensure that even if they did oppose the revolution and all its works, they would still be free to express their opinions, and to organize themselves politically in order to do so.[14]

Kishk, then, proposes an alternative régime for Egypt. Organizations such as the Arab Socialist Union have to go. Under the leader, they were a harmless mockery; without him, they become dangerous instruments in the struggle for power, opening the door to endless civil war. An end has likewise to be made of these parliaments which 'have been elected by nomination, or nominated by election' (*untukhibat bi'l-ta'yin aw 'uyyinat bi'l-intikhab*), and to which Egyptians have never conceded the quality of representativeness. If there has to be a Pharaoh, he must be accessible to the people:

> The ugliest régime is that in which Pharaoh has the sole prerogative in deciding on peace and war, and in confiscating the peasants' donkeys, and where the people are prevented from approaching him, the right of speaking to him being reserved to the priests and the guardians of the temple of Dandara.[15]

In his 1968 pamphlet, Kishk points out that the students were shouting Islamic slogans in their demonstrations, and that their leaders insisted, in their speeches, on religious education and religious values. This, he points out, is in great contrast to the tepid attitude of the official representatives of Islam to their religion: shaykh Baquri, the rector of the University of al-Azhar, omits the invocation to God (the *basmala*) at the beginning of his speeches, while the student leaders invoked not only God but his Prophets as well. In this they were more representative of the Egyptians than Baquri, for it is not to be denied that interest in Islam, and the desire for a return to Islam are very strong in Egypt. How else can one explain the great opposition which arose when it was proposed—before June 1967—to omit the provision that Islam is the official religion of the state when an official committee was considering a draft constitution? How otherwise to account for the steadily increasing popularity of religious books among the Egyptians? In short, Islam in Egypt is not the result of a plot by the Muslim Brothers; the Egyptians are loyal Muslims, and nothing can shake their loyalty. Therefore to belittle or repress Islam in Egypt is to go against the desires of the Egyptian people. It is also to harm Egypt's international position by isolating it from the Arab world and the world of Islam where its true strength lies, and where it has a fundamental role to play.[16] In his open letter to Sadat, Kishk reiterates that Egypt's safety and salvation lie in cultivating relations with the Muslim and the Arab world. Under his predecessor, these relations worsened considerably. Egypt became known as a centre of subversion where every conspirator or fugitive or intriguer found a ready welcome at the Voice of the Arabs. The result was a remarkable diminution of Egyptian influence and almost total Egyptian isolation. Egyptians were expelled from every country. Arab capital ceased flowing into Egypt. Egyptian industrial, commercial and cultural presence has almost disappeared from every Arab country. Compare the Lebanese Middle East Airlines and Misr Airlines: which is the larger, and which earns more revenue from the Arab countries? And this 'in spite of the fact that the Egyptian air force has roamed freely (*sala wa jala*) in almost all Arab skies "hitting the bases of the enemy," extirpating the supports of imperialism and reaction, defending "Arab unity" and its "vanguard," while it is impossible to record a single instance of the Lebanese air force going beyond its frontiers.' Again, what kind of Egyptians are now chiefly to be seen in Arab countries? They are domestics. Socialist Egypt and revolutionary socialist Syria are the two main suppliers of domestics to the capitalist Arab countries.[17]

Egypt, then, is isolated in the Arab and Muslim worlds. Such is the outcome of Nasserite policies which have thus made even more disastrous the Soviet connexion, which is again the outcome of the same policies. Egypt has become a Soviet satellite: Kosygin's intervention in the affair of Nasser's succession, the way in which they had earlier imposed Ali Sabri on him are the outward signs of this state of affairs. The Soviet position in Egypt is now reminiscent of the earlier British domination, when British advice had the force of an order. How did this come to pass? It is true that the Soviets do not use their soldiers in Egypt as an army of occupation like the British—they make use of another army of occupation to effect their purpose, namely the Israeli army. The first deal in 1955 was represented both as necessary in the circumstances, and as delivering Egypt from a western monopoly in arms. This may have been the case then, but, in fact 'the purchase of Soviet arms has delivered us into the power of an absolute monopoly. The western arms market, with its competition and contradictions, with its smugglers even, allows room for manœuvre and bargaining, in contrast to Russian arms where the grip of the state is absolute and undisputed.' Taking Soviet arms has in effect disarmed Egypt, and delivered her into the hands of the great powers. The proper answer to the Israeli threat would have been to develop an Egyptian arms industry as China had shown it possible to do. Since this was not done, Egypt has become a pawn in a great-power game. It is an illusion to think that Egypt can play off the U.S.S.R. against the U.S.A. The latter power would prefer to see Egypt a Soviet protectorate and settle matters directly with the U.S.S.R.[18]

In sum, then, Egypt's security lies in cultivating and strengthening ties with the Arab and the Muslim world. It is only Arab and Islamic solidarity which can save Egypt from enslavement to the great powers, from the stultification of its foreign policy (the overriding aim of which is the removal of the Israeli threat), from its Islamic traits disappearing and from a repressive and divisive police régime at home. Egypt must 'practise a dynamic Islamic policy.' This is Kishk's prescription, and he ends his 1970 pamphlet on an uncompromising and defiant note. He implores God 'to make use of those who straighten the crookedness of the rulers by means of their swords' (*min al-ladhin yuqawwimun i'wijaj al-hakimin bi-suyufihim*).[19]

It is, of course, impossible to say what 'a dynamic Islamic policy' really means. Nor are Kishk's pamphlets best seen as a blueprint for a practical policy. Rather, they constitute a criticism, at once reasoned and biting, of the 18 years of Nasserism. The pamphlets, as has been said, were published outside Egypt, and it is doubtful whether their importation would have been allowed. But their author is an Egyptian, and apparently still living in Egypt. The incisiveness and originality with which he formulates the grievances and discontents of his fellow-Egyptians must not lead us to think that he is an isolated eccentric. On the contrary, we may suspect that Kishk is giving body and shape to widespread fears and dislikes, and that what he has to say would find a wide audience in a country where so many had so recently sympathized with the doctrine of the Muslim Brothers. And this for two reasons: first, he speaks a familiar and acceptable Islamic idiom; and second, his frank and common-sensical discussion of burning political issues has a concreteness and a solidity which would make it immediately intelligible to his fellow-citizens, in contrast to the alembicated disquisitions of Cairo progressive intellectuals. These would fall on deaf ears, or be rejected with suspicion as officially inspired. The fate of the European-inspired idioms of politics which the ruling classes adopted under the monarchy, and which have now disappeared without trace shows how little attractive such importations are.

But popular as Kishk's themes might be, this does not mean that they would have the slightest effect on a régime which does not have to reckon very much with public opinion, or at all with representative assemblies. Certain circumstances might make it advantageous for the present régime, or a succeeding one, to make its own some or all of Kishk's themes, just as other circumstances might make more advantageous the continued suppression of such views. But these would have little or nothing to do with the wishes of the public. The reason why this is so is not likely to give pleasure to Kishk: for it is precisely because Egypt is Islamic, and because the most persistent political tradition of Islam is oriental despotism, that his plea for a 'dynamic Islamic policy' is likely to go unheeded.

NOTES

1. For an example, see Kedourie, *The Chatham House Version*, p. 140.
2. On which see James P. Jankowski, 'The Young Egypt Party and Egyptian Nationalism 1933–1945,' unpublished Ph.D. dissertation, University of Michigan 1967.
3. The distinction between tradition and traditionalism has been worked out in exemplary fashion for modern China by the late J. R. Levenson in his *Confucian China and its Modern Fate*. What he has to say of China is, *mutatis mutandis*, equally true of Islam. For the impregnation of modern Islamic thought by European modes and categories see Wilfred Cantwell Smith, *Islam in Modern History* (Princeton 1957), particularly pp. 115–56; Hamid Enayat, 'Islam and Socialism in Egypt,' *Middle Eastern Studies*, vol. IV, no. 2 (January 1968); G. E. von Grunebaum, 'Approaching Islam: a Digression,' *Middle Eastern Studies*, vol. VI, no. 2 (May 1970); and Idem 'Some Recent Constructions and Reconstructions of Islam,' in Carl Leiden (ed.), *The Conflict of Traditionalism and Modernism in the Muslim Middle East* (Austin 1969).
4. Richard P. Mitchell, *The Society of the Muslim Brothers* (London 1969), p. 80.
5. Mitchell, *op cit.*, p. 328.
6. Mitchell, *op. cit.*, p. 129.
7. *Ma'alim fi tariq al-khiyana*, pp. 63, 37–8.
8. *Ma'alim fi'l-tariq* [1964], n.p., n.d., p. 66.
9. *Ibid.*, p. 110.
10. *Ibid.*, pp. 117–18, 21, 177.
11. *Mahda yurid al-talaba . . .*, pp. 28, 36, 55–9.
12. *Ibid.*, pp. 52, 77ff.
13. *Ibid.*, pp. 70–1.
14. *Madha yurid al-sha'b . . .*, pp. 7, 9, 26–8, 32, 91.
15. *Ibid.*, pp. 33, 29, 6.
16. *Madha yurid al-talaba . . .*, pp. 25–9.
17. *Madha yurid al-sha'b . . .*, pp. 45–59.
18. *Ibid.*, pp. 65–9.
19. *Ibid.*, pp. 83–4, 93.

13. The Arab-Israeli Conflict

At its beginnings just over half a century ago, what is now known as the Arab–Israeli conflict was relatively simple and limited, but since then—and this is perhaps its most important and ominous characteristic—it has become progressively more complicated and envenomed.

The Zionists in whose favour the Balfour declaration was issued in November 1917 had been neither numerically important nor politically significant before the world war in the territory which shortly afterwards came to be officially called Palestine. They were known to the original inhabitants as immigrant foreigners upon whom the Ottoman authorities—whether at the time of Abd al-Hamid or later—did not look with much favour and whose ingress they tried to restrict as much as possible; and known also for their agricultural settlements which were occasionally involved in friction and dispute with their rural and nomadic neighbours.

The Balfour declaration, therefore, could not but come as a shock to a population which, being overwhelmingly Muslim, was already disoriented by the collapse of a Muslim authority which had lasted for four centuries, and its replacement by Christian European conquerors. And these conquerors were proposing to bestow privileges, the extent of which was uncertain, on this handful of foreigners, privileges which in the end might even lead Jews to exercise power over the Muslims who had hitherto believed in their divinely ordained right to rule over Christians and Jews. This feeling of Muslim superiority which a century of reverses at the hands of Europe had shaken but also exacerbated, goes far to make intelligible the uncompromising opposition which from the very beginning the Palestinians offered to Zionism. Also the very vagueness of the Balfour declaration, while arousing the worst fears of the Palestinians, encouraged them to hope that unyielding and strenuous opposition might lead to the declaration being interpreted restrictively, or even actually disowned.

But, when all is said and done, the conflict between the Zionists and their opponents all through the 1920s and the first half of the '30s, remained confined to Palestine. Opposition to Zionism erupted in riots and violence in 1920, 1921 and 1929. The first two incidents may be seen as unsuccessful attempts by the Palestinians to overawe and intimidate a new government and compel it to bow to their wishes. Whilst the third—and most serious—outbreak, that of 1929, coming as it did after a period of actual Jewish emigration from Palestine, may be interpreted as a bid by the mufti of Jerusalem at once to demonstrate his supremacy in Palestinian Arab politics, and to hurry the Jews on their way out. But such incidents, serious as they were, involved only the Mandatory, the Zionists and the Arabs of Palestine, and hardly involved other governments or groups. Indeed, it may be argued that the mufti may have been right in 1929 when he reckoned that Zionism was a declining force.

The advent of Hitler in 1933 introduced an entirely new and unforeseen element in the Palestinian problem. It increased, beyond any previous expectation, the demand for immigration into Palestine; imbued the Zionist leaders with a new sense of urgency and imposed new pressures on them; and by upsetting the European balance, indirectly weakened the British position in the Mediterranean and encouraged those who wanted to challenge it. Nazism, in short, seriously complicated the Palestine problem, made it perhaps wellnigh intractable. The British, we may note in passing, have been repeatedly blamed for encouraging Zionist settlement in a country occupied by a large group of people naturally unwilling to be swamped and dominated by another, aggressive and enterprising, group. This, however, is to condemn *ex post facto*, for no one in 1917 could have reasonably foretold the rise and triumph of Nazism which, by confronting European Jewry with sudden ruin and destruction, overturned the assumptions and expectations on which the Balfour declaration policy implicitly rested.

The next complication which befell Palestine dates from 1938–9. in 1936 strikes organized by the Arab higher committee, degenerated into serious disorders. This compelled the British government to look anew at the problem. A Royal Commission was appointed which recommended in 1937 partition of the country into Arab and Jewish areas as the measure most likely to issue in appeasement and to produce a settlement. The government first accepted this line of policy, but soon afterwards it began to have second thoughts. It appointed in 1938 a technical commission ostensibly to examine further the detailed scheme of partition proposed by the Royal Commission, the chairman of this commission, however, being given secretly to understand that partition was no longer the policy which the government favoured. A new departure was clearly being envisaged.

The new policy was unveiled at the end of 1938, when the government announced the convening of a conference on Palestine, to which were to be invited not only the Jewish Agency and representatives of the Palestinian Arabs, but also, on the one hand, representatives of Arab states—even of a state as far away as Yemen—and on the other, of world Jewry, the latter being, in point of political importance or sovereign attributes, by no means the equal or the equivalent of the Arab states. This was a fateful and perhaps fatal move, the consequences of which even now are far from being exhausted. For this move recognized and sanctioned the intervention of a number of sovereign states in the affairs of a territory under British control. For the administration of Palestine, Great Britain was indeed responsible to the League of Nations, but it had certainly hitherto not acknowledged responsibility to a collection of states who shared more or less vaguely the vague epithet 'Arab'. Indeed, up to the middle of 1937, we find the British government firmly resisting Egyptian and Iraqi attempts to intervene officially in Palestinian affairs.

Whatever the various reasons and justifications for this new policy, it was one which appreciably limited British freedom of action, since the right to intervene, once conceded to outsiders, would be difficult if not impossible again to withdraw. This was to burden future British policy, as well as Palestine and the Palestinians with— to use a legal metaphor—a heavy servitude. There is no evidence that the British government was disquietened by this prospect. When an annex to the Charter of the Arab League in 1945 officially stated that the signatories had a collective right of intervention, the British government never protested at a claim now all the more enhanced for being enshrined in a formal instrument.

This development exacerbated the conflict in Palestine by introducing a large number of sovereign states, each with their particular, and conflicting, interests into what had been a relatively limited dispute between two groups in a mandated territory. The consequence of such a step appeared clearly in the Palestine war of 1948–9. After the U.N. vote, in November 1947, to partition Palestine—the very solution proposed by the Royal Commission ten years before—and the British decision to lay down the mandate which followed, King Abdullah decided that here at last was an opportunity to enhance a position which he had ever regarded as beneath his abilities and deserts. First he hoped that, supported by Iraq, he would compel the Zionists to accept his overlordship without a fight. When this failed, he embarked on war. Up to the end of April 1948, Egypt was not contemplating military intervention, but she could not allow the Hashemites to aggrandize themselves by annexing Palestine. At the last minute, therefore, an Egyptian army, by all accounts unprepared for battle, was ordered to march into Palestine. Syria, fearful of Abdullah's ambitions, likewise intervened. The conflict between Palestinians and Zionists thus became embroiled with the discordant ambitions of Egypt and Syria, Jordan and Iraq, all the more intransigent for being proclaimed in the ideological vocabularly of pan-Arabism, rather than expressed in the more modest language of interests.

The next complication in the Palestine problem first appeared in 1955–6, and became manifest in all its danger during the Six-Day war and since. The conflict, which initially was local to Palestine, and then was transformed into a regional conflict, now became inextricably involved in the rivalries of the great powers. This happened because the Soviet Union began to exert the power and influence which Tsarist Russia used traditionally to have in the region and which, so to speak, unnaturally disappeared between 1917 and 1955 In the Suez affair, the Israeli government deliberately took advantage of the British and French quarrel with Egypt in order to defeat and neutralize the most important of its enemies. An American–Soviet 'collusion'—an appropriate term to use in this context—prevented it from gaining its object. This American–Soviet collusion ruined British and French power and influence in the Mediterranean and the middle east, thus destroying the possibility of the rivalry between the two super-powers being effectively mediated or moderated by the action of other powers as used to happen in the classical eastern question before 1914. As became clear during and after the Six-Day war, the U.S.A. and the Soviet Union now stand face to face in the middle east, and their conflict is linked precisely with the Arab–Israeli conflict. This is an inherently unstable and dangerous position, made even more dangerous by the fact that neither super-power is fully in control of the actions of its clients, and is thus liable to get drawn into quarrels neither sought nor foreseen.

These then are the parties involved in this conflict: the Zionists, who have succeeded in creating and maintaining the State of Israel; the native Palestinians; the Arab States; and the U.S.A. and the U.S.S.R. Each of these parties will influence, more or less as the case may be, the further course of the conflict and any possible settlement. There is a great deal of variety in the aims and purposes of these parties, as well as in the price which they are prepared to pay for attaining them. But for all of them the conflict may be said to be primarily political (and therefore, at times, military). Political in the sense that two groups (the Israelis and the Palestinians) dispute sovereign control over a territory; political also in the sense that this original dispute has become for other local states a means for attaining regional primacy or increasing their territory; political lastly in the sense that each of the super-powers sees in this dispute a way of increasing its power and influence in the Mediterranean and middle east, and of diminishing that of its rival.

But the political conflict between Israel and its neighbours is further complicated by what might be called a cultural conflict, or perhaps misunderstanding. A clue to its nature may be gathered from the frequency with which the dispute between Israel and her neighbours is described as a conflict between 'Jews' and 'Arabs'. Are these two groups actually in conflict? Jews as a group certainly have an identity supplied by a religion which has kept them together. So far as 'culture' goes—if by culture we mean broadly a way of life— the Jews have experienced huge variations of culture throughout their history. Some of them, in particular, have shared, or still share, the culture of those called 'Arabs'. To the extent that there is cultural conflict, it must be between the 'Arabs' and those Jews who have not shared in their outlook, values and way of life.

But who are the 'Arabs'? Some sixty years ago, the term 'Arab' generally meant Bedouin. Since then this term has undergone a great change. It has ceased primarily to designate a group of nomads; it has rather become an ideological term indicating an aspiration to create a new political order, in which all 'Arabs' would be members of an autonomous, sovereign entity. In this new usage, who the 'Arabs' are has changed from time to time, and even now the notion in not yet quite stable. But one thing at least can be affirmed, namely, that they are, in an overwhelming majority, Muslim, that they are, and have been part of the Muslim world and of an Islamic culture. Islam has generally looked upon Jews as a subject community docile and unwarlike, to be treated with contemptuous tolerance, and whom it is quite unthinkable to consider as political equals. This surely accounts for a great deal of intransigence with which the Palestinians and the Arab states have refused sometimes in clear disregard of their interests to negotiate directly or to sit at the same table with Zionists or Israelis. But the Jews with whom they had to deal in Palestine were, in fact, the antithesis of the Jews to whom the Muslims were accustomed. They were politically activist, aggressive and by no means deferential towards Muslims.

On the contrary, the Jews who invented Zionism and worked for the establishment of the State of Israel, coming from eastern Europe, and imbued with European notions and prejudices, were wholly pre-occupied with European issues and European problems. They knew little about the indigenous inhabitants of Palestine, and looked down upon them as backward, primitive and incompetent. The history of the Palestine problem from the Balfour declaration to the Six-Day war must have served to confirm them in this view. The political conflict over Palestine has thus been further complicated by mutual incomprehension, to which have contributed, on the one hand, the European prejudices of the Zionists, and, on the other, the Muslim prejudices of the Arabs. Misunderstanding, it has been said, makes the world go round. Mutual contempt is another story.

To review this conflict and its progressive exacerbation is thus to admit the unlikelihood of a speedy settlement. What must increase pessimism is that a state of war between Israel and its neighbours has now lasted for almost a quarter of a century and that, as we may suspect, it has become for various governments a cosy habit and a convenient state of affairs. It is said, no doubt with a great deal of truth, that a state of war enables the Israeli government to transform a heterogeneous collection of immigrants into a homogeneous nation-state, and to mobilize the sympathies and resources of world Jewry. It is probably just as true that military régimes, such as those of Egypt, of Syria and of Iraq, apprehend in a state of peace a serious threat to their stability, or even to their very existence.

But let us review in turn the various parties to the conflict, their ability to make peace, and the inducements and pressures which may incline them thereto. On the Arab side, it seems to be the case that ability to influence the course of the quarrel is almost in inverse proportion to a party's vital interest in it. This is, and has been, most true of the Palestinians. For some twenty years, from the British occupation until the end of 1938, the Palestinian leaders attempted by continuous pressure and protest, as well as by occasional violence, to resist the establishment and extension of the National Home to which the mandatory was committed. This campaign almost from the beginning went hand in hand with the campaign of Hajj Amin al-Husayni, whom Sir Herbert Samuel had tacitly allowed to become mufti of Jerusalem in 1921, to establish his dominance over the Palestinians. In declaring his uncompromising hostility to Zionism the mufti indeed faithfully expressed the sentiments of those whom he claimed to lead; but it remains true that he was leader not because he was elected or appointed by the Palestinians, but only owing to the initial support of the mandatory, to his subsequent use of the *Waqf* resources which the government allowed him to control without any supervision, and in the later stages to a campaign of murder and terrorism. He was thus practically free to pursue whatever policy he liked, and in the end was tempted by armed rebellion, intrigues with Italy and Germany, and with elements in Syria and Iraq who wanted to use the Palestine issue as a weapon in their own struggle for power. His policies failed, and he may fairly be said to have served his people ill.

The period 1937–9 may be considered a watershed in the sombre, disaster-strewn history of the Palestinians. It was then that the mufti fled to the Lebanon, an action which, in retrospect, marks the failure of his policies. Self-appointed and self-seeking as he was, yet his policies, however unwise or undesirable, in their fashion were primarily concerned with the interests of the Palestinians. When the

Arab states were invited at the end of 1938 to intervene in the Palestine problem, Palestinian interests necessarily became a pawn or a weapon in the hands of these states in their pursuit of power and primacy. Between 1939 and the Six-Day war the Palestinians had no say or no control over their affairs. Such leadership as Hajj Amin and his lieutenants had provided was dispersed and destroyed, and the Arab states and the Arab League undertook to defend the Palestinians' interests. During this period, successive catastrophes befell the Palestinians which they have been utterly powerless to avert.

Since the Six-Day war the Palestinians have once again come to the fore. Once again leaders claim to speak in their name and to defend their particular interests. The character and the tactics of these leaders bear a disturbing resemblance to those of the 1930s. In so far as they are not promoted or supported for its purposes by one or other of the Arab states, they too are self-appointed. Undoubtedly in their utter hostility to Israel, they speak for all the Palestinians, but these have no say whatever over policies or tactics, which are decided by small groups in secret. Again like Hajj Amin, the new leaders have a partiality for guerrilla warfare. This partiality has indeed been reinforced by the great popularity which the doctrine of Mao, Guevara and the Vietcong have found in Asia and Africa. Quite recently, Yassir Arafat, the leader of the Palestine Liberation Organization, declared in an interview (*Le Monde*, 12 November 1970): 'I will tell you why the Americans, in spite of their undoubted power, do not have, and will never have the upper hand over the Vietcong: a guerrilla movement which has popular support is invincible. No electronic machine is able to measure the will of our people to conquer their right to life and freedom. Their ability to resist is practically infinite'.

The words were uttered after three years of fruitless guerrilla action against Israel—fruitless itself, and fruitless in that guerrilla warfare has not been changed (as the theory requires) into a 'people's war'. These words also followed the clash with King Husayn's army which has decisively shown that, in middle eastern conditions at any rate, a resolute government disposing of planes, tanks and artillery, is more than a match for guerrillas who wish to take it over. Even if Husayn were killed or deposed, it is by no means clear that the guerrillas would be able to take over Jordan. If this is so, then the future for Palestinian resistance is not bright. At best, the guerrillas may become a kind of IMRO (Internal Macedonian Revolutionary Organization), able to use spasmodic terror, but quite unable to effect a substantial change. There is another reason for pessimism: if as has been here argued, it was a misfortune for the Palestinian cause to be, so to speak, pan-Arabized, then the guerrilla organizations in relying, as they must, on this or that Arab state, are doing nothing to save the Palestinians from the ruinous attentions of their protectors.

The guerrillas then are unlikely to achieve military victory over Israel, or to force it to give in to their demands. The clash with the Jordanians indicates that they are also unlikely to be able to force an Arab state to wage war on their behalf. It follows that they are not in a position, should they want it, on their own to negotiate or conclude a compromise peace with Israel. A peace of this kind which did not suit Jordan or Syria or Egypt can easily be upset by them. Jordan which, after the Palestinians, is the party most vitally interested in the conflict, is in scarcely a better position.

To Abdullah's ambitions, as has been seen, must be attributed in large part the outbreak of war in 1948. But bold and ambitious as he was, yet he was not a man to persist in a manifestly unprofitable enterprise. Having emerged from the war of 1948 as the only beneficiary on the Arab side, he was quite willing to attempt a settlement with his fellow-beneficiary Israel. But Jordan was no longer the pastoral emirate over which he had ruled for a quarter of a century. It now included a large and turbulent population of Palestinians, many of them refugees: it was he who had made this bed and he must now lie on it. He had to reckon with these Palestinians in his attempts at a settlement, and with the trouble which a defeated and embittered Egypt would make for him among the Palestinians. His room for manœuvre became very exiguous, and the final reckoning came when they assassinated him in that Jerusalem which he had wanted so much to possess. His grandson was at no time in a better position to negotiate. Much as he wanted a settlement, particularly after the Six-Day war, he too has never been in a position to conclude it on his own. A satisfactory peace for him must include the return of the west bank, if not of east Jerusalem. A Jordan permanently confined within the frontiers of the old emirate would destroy his prestige and put his throne at risk. But even if he could make a satisfactory deal with the Israelis, he would not be in a position to go through with it in the face of opposition from other members of the Arab League, and particularly Egypt.

Let us consider the character of this opposition, leaving aside Egypt for the moment. The opposition is likely to come from countries like Syria, Iraq, Libya or Algeria—none of them as intimately touched by the conflict as Jordan, the two latter being indeed very far from the scene. This opposition would be expressed in activist and doctrinaire terms, in the style customary to a party like the Ba'th in Syria or Iraq, or the FLN in Algeria. A passage in a recent article by the Algerian minister of information and culture, Ahmed Taleb-Ibrahimi, provides an excellent specimen of this style and outlook. He wrote (*Le Monde*, 12 September 1970):

> No smoke-screen and no inspired article will make us forget the decisive importance of the potential power of the Arab masses who are already impressing on those who were meditating a treacherous blow, that the Palestinian cause cannot be betrayed with impunity.
>
> Today's struggle [referring to Husayn's recent attack on the guerrillas] must not be taken for a classic battle, as was the case in the Spanish civil war, where some parties try out their weapons. It is not a matter of tanks or rockets. The resistance must be organized and must spread to all the Arab countries. For those who think to justify their defeatism (which, of course they call realism) by declaring that the struggle in the East takes place under peculiar conditions, is different from the struggle of the Vietminh or of the FLN, examples are not lacking which prove that resistance can develop in mountains as well as in cities, in the steppes as well as in deserts of sand or ice. The problem is not one of terrain, but of will: what in the end is victorious is not war material, however perfected, but rather the man who operates the weapon, and the faith which moves the man.
>
> To take another point, how can Algeria advise the Palestinian resistance to accept that which it had refused to accept for itself twelve years ago? A cease-fire in present-day conditions reminds us too much of that '*paix des braves*' by means of which it was hoped to undermine the morale of the Algerians.

Rhetoric of this style invites, and sometimes compels, political activity of a similar style. But even if it did not, even if those who use it have no intention of themselves being carried away by it, they may yet consider that their interest requires the encouragement of intransigence. Algeria is a rival of Egypt in north Africa, and one way by which to assert her claim is to adopt an uncompromising stand over Palestine. Again, Syria and Iraq, both governed by Ba'thist officers consumed with mutual dislike, confronting each other in a gladiatorial posture, and in any case looking on King Husayn as fair game for revolutionaries, would also have good reason to encourage, singly or in unison, an uncompromising stand.

But by themselves, neither Iraq nor Syria nor Algeria are decisive, just as the Palestinian guerrillas and Jordan can effect nothing on their own. For all these parties are dwarfed and overshadowed by Egypt which, it is no exaggeration to say, holds, among Israel's enemies, the key to a settlement. Egypt's involvement in the Palestine conflict was a deliberate step by Faruq to secure primacy in the middle east. The adventure, in a sense, cost him his throne. But his ambition was taken over by those who overthrew him, and from beginning to end Nasser sought, by means of a victory over Israel, to crush his opponents in the Arab world and establish Egypt as *the* middle-eastern great power. Egypt's resources and military capacity did not prove equal to such an aim, the pursuit of which has brought so far nothing but loss and catastrophe. But Nasser's régime and his prestige had become intimately bound up with this policy. As is known, so long as he was unwilling to consider a settlement which might advertise and consecrate the failure of this policy, no other Arab state or group would have dared even enter into negotiations. This was because Nasser's prestige and Egypt's power were too great to be challenged by the other Arab states. Whether Nasser himself would have been prepared to abandon the policy he took over from Faruq, and to work for a purely Egyptian–Israeli settlement will never now be known.

His successors do not enjoy his prestige either inside or outside Egypt, and this may in fact be one potent reason why they dare not abandon a policy associated with one who, because of his death in office, has so to speak become the tutelary deity of the régime. What is clear at any rate is that they persist in using the rhetoric of pan-Arabism and in proclaiming themselves the champions of all the Arabs against Israel. Thus, in a declaration in the National Assembly, Anwar al-Sadat said that the struggle was for them 'the priority of all priorities'. By struggle he meant 'the total liberation of all occupied Arab territories, with no exception whatever. To give up anything whatever means giving up everything'. Again: 'To give up the total liberation of these territories is tantamount to submitting to the Israeli imperialist aggressor and those who give him support. No one in the Arab world will agree to the liberation of one portion of the territory, and the abandonment of another. Let the world understand that we are against all half-solutions, all bargaining and all auctions.' The U.A.R. he stated, 'is unshakeably convinced that the Arab nation is one, that its progress is one and that its aspirations are the same for all the Arabs.' (*Le Monde*, 21 November 1970). This is the language of Nasserism. But Sadat has also introduced a new, Islamic, accent which must greatly appeal to, and move, his audience. In an eloquent address delivered in April 1972 on the anniversary of the Prophet's birthday he compared the struggle on which his people were engaged to the trials which faced Muhammad at the beginning of his apostolate. We are fated, he said, to fight the battle to liberate our land and, with our land, Jerusalem, the first *qibla* and third *haram*. 'We will, with God's help' he affirmed, 'take it back from those of whom our Book says that lowliness and submissiveness is their lot.' Sadat also declared that he refused to negotiate directly with people whom the Prophet had found, in his dealings with them, to be vile, treacherous and faithless. (Text of Sadat's address reproduced in an appendix in Fu'ad Matar, *Russya al-nasiriyya wa Misr al-misriyya* (Nasserite Russia and Egyptian Egypt), Beirut, 1972, pp. 202–5). Whether these words represent an extension of Nasserism, or are used to cover a retreat from it, time will tell.

Egypt has never been powerful enough to win, or even to maintain its position—witness the occupation of Sinai and the closure of the canal, but has been powerful enough to prevent a settlement. Israel, contrariwise, has been powerful enough to win many campaigns and improve its position, but not powerful enough to impose a settlement. Hence the deadlock, and the mutual and cumulative mistrust. But as between Israel and its neighbours the position is asymmetrical in one respect which is crucial. The Israelis are convinced that the conflict is for them a life-and-death issue, that a defeat or a retreat for them will end not merely in a humiliating peace but in the destruction of their state. Hence another element of intransigence. But what kind of a settlement, one may ask, does Israel envisage? The answer is by no means clear, and this very lack of clarity is in itself yet one more obstacle to a settlement. Israel's objective has always been twofold: recognition and secure frontiers. The Six-Day war put it at least in the short term in a better bargaining position, but did not bring the attainment of these aims nearer. It may have even perhaps made this more difficult, since the conquest of so much territory in 1967 has tempted some Israeli politicians to believe that they could attain both recognition and a larger Israeli territory, or else that Israel, secure behind the shield of its new conquests, need not sacrifice anything for recognition by its neighbours. Since Israel's is a parliamentary régime in which government has been carried on from the start by means of coalitions, it has always been easier to register disagreement over policies, than to resolve on a particular policy. Moreover, disagreement about policy is accompanied by confusion about the character of the conflict in which Israel is engaged.

The conflict at the outset was one with the indigenous population of Palestine. During the 1920s and '30s the belief widely prevailed among Zionist leaders that this local conflict could somehow be dissolved if the Palestinians could be submerged in a wider Arab entity. The Zionists, in other words, were themselves pan-Arabs. Events have shown this line of reasoning to be quite fallacious, but many Israeli leaders still hanker after it. They now do so in the belief that to admit the existence of Palestinians as Palestinians is somehow to throw doubt on the legitimacy of Israel and its right to the territory is occupies. Hence the curious immobility of Israeli policy after 1967. Internal deadlock—political and intellectual—in Israel reinforces the external deadlock.

But Israel and its enemies, checkmated by one another, find themselves further constrained by their dependence on the super-powers who, of course, are primarily concerned with the safeguard and advancement of their own interests, and for whom the middle east is merely one element in a world-wide rivalry and the Arab–Israeli conflict by no means the most important issue in the middle east. It was to outflank and neutralize the American and, generally, the western positions in the middle east that the U.S.S.R. began an active policy in Egypt in 1955. In the decade which followed the Soviet stake in the middle east and in the Mediterranean increased enormously. Its naval contingent in the Mediterranean, its liberal supply of arms to Egypt, Syria, Iraq and other Arab states, its financing of the high dam: all these meant that Soviet prestige became bound up with the survival and success of those Arab states which had become its clients. It is the logic of this situation, rather than deliberate choice, which has made the U.S.A. the patron and protector of Israel. For it has been a constant theme of Soviet propaganda that just as the Soviets were committed to the protection of the Arab states, so the United States was committed to the protection of Israel. The Six-Day war and the events which followed somehow seemed to give body and reality to this propaganda. By espousing so unconditionally the cause of the defeated Arab states, the U.S.S.R. forced the U.S.A. to link its prestige to the survival of Israel and to its protection against defeat. Such a position is necessarily irksome to the U.S.A. which, by reason of its interests elsewhere in the middle east, cannot afford to seem unconditionally to support Israel. Hence the continuous ambiguity and tension in the relations between these two states. One reason, presumably, for American initiatives to break the deadlock between Israel and its neighbours is eagerness to escape from the position into which the Soviets has cornered them.

The American position, seemingly weak, is not, however, without its strength. Its protégé, Israel, has a stranglehold over the Suez Canal, to open which is a more pressing Soviet than American interest. Israel, again, is militarily superior to its neighbours and does not need the kind of direct support which the U.S.S.R. has had to give Egypt. Lastly, so long as the protégés of the Soviets are involved with Israel, they cannot busy themselves very much with subverting states such as Saudi Arabia or the Lebanon to protect which is an American interest. Whether the U.S.A. considers these as strong cards, and whether it would consider them nonetheless worth sacrificing for the sake of a local settlement with the Soviets, we do not yet know. If the former is the case then the deadlock is likely to last for some time, if the latter then a new situation will emerge about which it is fruitless to speculate. For in such a situation what will be important will be not the exact territorial character of an Arab–Israeli settlement, but rather the stance in which the super-powers and their protégés will find themselves for prosecuting their ambitions in an area which seems doomed to turbulence and disorder for a long time to come.

14. Sir Hugh Foot's Memoirs

The author of this book,* now Lord Caradon, comes from a well-known Liberal and non-conformist west country family. He joined the British colonial service in 1929 as a young man just down from Cambridge. His first post was that of a junior assistant secretary in Palestine; he remained a member of the Palestine administration until 1938 and after a short interval at the colonial office went back to the middle east as assistant British resident in Amman, where he stayed until 1942. After a short period in the military administration of Cyrenaica, he was appointed in 1943 colonial secretary of Cyprus; as is well-known, he afterwards became governor of this territory during the fateful years 1957–60, when it was ravaged by a civil war for which he helped to effect a settlement which transformed the colony into an independent state presided over by Archbishop Makarios. The author also served in Nigeria and Jamaica, and on his retirement from the governorship of Cyprus was appointed by Mr. Harold Macmillan as a member of the British delegation to the United Nations, to advise on problems affecting the 'emergent and newly emerged countries' and to represent the United Kingdom in the Trusteeship Council and the Fourth Committee of the General Assembly. From this post he resigned in October 1962, because he disagreed with official policy in respect of central Africa and southern Rhodesia.

These memoirs provide a glimpse into the outlook, beliefs and attitudes of one who had much to do with colonial administration and policy during the last days of the British empire. In his introduction the author indicates (p. 15) that he intends his account to serve as a record not only of his own particular experience but of the colonial service in general, for he writes: 'I began to think that I should try to put down something of what I had seen and learnt, and give some account of how we worked to give colonial peoples a good start in independence'. And he adds: 'When I say "we" I mean those of us who worked overseas in the Colonial Administrative Service.' The book, we must therefore remember, claims to be more than merely autobiographical, claims rather to give some account of the attitudes and methods of the British colonial service.

One of the illustrations contained in the book (opposite p. 177) shows the author on horseback attired in the official dress of a colonial governor reviewing a body of British(?) troops; the caption

* *A Start in Freedom* by Sir Hugh Foot.

(a phrase attributed to Mr. Macmillan) reads: 'A Colonial Governor who ran out of Colonies.' This picture of bygone and somewhat absurd imperial trappings, together with its piquantly contrasting caption is presumably intended to indicate in a humorous fashion the author's satisfaction at so happy a conclusion to a long official career. But it is not this picture alone which provides evidence of the author's sentiments. When he relinquished the governorship of Cyprus he thought of taking employment with the United Nations, and he gives (p. 188) the text of a telegram which he sent to the secretary-general: 'Have just finished', he told Hammarskjöld, 'my assignment as Governor of Cyprus having completed thirty years' work in Middle-East Africa and West Indies Stop All the countries in which I have worked are now self-governing or about to be Stop.' His discussion, again, of the final steps leading to the handing-over of Cyprus begins (p. 181): 'Nineteen fifty-nine was a year of sheer happiness. It was the year of agreement, of reconciliation, the year in which we had to create a Republic from nothing', and his account of this genesis is prefaced by a burst of that Burkean rhetoric which so often in recent decades has done duty in justifying abdication of imperial rule—whether forced or voluntary—as noble and beneficent. 'From that moment', says Burke, as quoted by Sir Hugh Foot, 'as by a charm, the tumults subsided, obedience was restored, peace, order and civilization followed in the train of liberty'. The moment here in question is when Archbishop Makarios made sure of power—*his* start, as it were, in freedom. We who know what followed in this and like cases and who compare it with the vision which Burke is pressed into conjuring up, are much tempted to exclaim with Halifax—the Trimmer not the foreign secretary—that rhetoric is indeed the harlot of the arts. In this book there is altogether too much of this hopeful rhetoric which has become the customary idiom of British politics, and too little—indeed an absence of—awareness, that the disappearance of imperial rule, whether inevitable or not, is an occasion to inspire sheer happiness, may be—but surely also some fear and foreboding?

Still, what will most interest readers of this book is perhaps not so much the author's attitude to alien rule and self-government, as his account of his middle-eastern years to which five of his eleven chapters are devoted. This account of his early career in Palestine and Transjordan is particularly valuable for it gives us a picture not only of the author's apprenticeship in colonial administration but of the *ambience* created by his colleagues and superiors. Most of the first fifteen years of his overseas service had been, as he says (p. 100), spent with Arabs: 'No one', he goes on, 'lives with Arabs without becoming devoted to them and, although my years in Arab countries had been years of disorder and violence and war, I had understood something of the Arabs' language and religion and increasingly admired them'. The quality of his understanding and his admiration, as they are seen in the book, indicate fairly clearly that we have here a mild case of romantic Arabophilia, all the more interesting for being so mild and modish, and therefore so much more useful as a typical specimen than better-known but extreme cases where romantic Arabophilia has been a *grande passion*. Sir Hugh Foot, in describing his establishment at Amman, affords us a nice glimpse of this Arabophiliac atmosphere which pervaded British official circles during his time in the middle east and afterwards. Owing to the war, his family had been evacuated to South Africa and his house in Amman 'had been turned into a mess. Gawain Bell, of the Arab Legion—later to be governor of northern Nigeria—shared the house with me and one or two other Arab Legion officers. From time to time other officers came to stay with us. . . .

'We became Arab enthusiasts. We didn't drink or smoke. We carried the string of Arab beads which we would run through our fingers as we talked of an evening. I gave more and more of my time to Arabic. I have no ear for languages but I went at it the hard way, often working for four or five hours at night at the grammar. With much preparation and anxiety I gave a lecture to the Arab Club in Amman. I became obsessed with the regularity and richness of the language' (pp. 76–7).

'We became Arab enthusiasts': the expression is apt for, as the dictionary tells us, enthusiasm is a rapturous intensity of feeling on behalf of a person or a cause, but also, originally and more literally, an ill-regulated religious emotion or speculation.

The author's understanding of Arab and Islamic history conforms to a well-known modern European version which has little connexion with the facts. 'The Arabs', he tells us (p. 86), 'are children of the desert', 'the purest Arab characteristics are the result of the influences of the remotest desert', but these qualities 'have been blurred and half-forgotten in the towns', while 'the springs of Islam remain pure in the desert'. This account, both romantic and *romancé*, is followed by a passage the sincerity of which there is no reason to doubt: 'I have never ceased to rejoice', declares Sir Hugh Foot (p. 87), 'that I had the privilege of spending my early years in overseas service with the Arabs. I was never in any doubt that, however politely they received me and whatever trouble they took to put me at my ease, they regarded me as an inferior, an infidel'. The author goes on to speak of his shame, embarrassment, and discomfort at what he considered to be a display of superiority or aristocratic condescension by British officials towards their subjects in Africa. This passage is a most arresting description of the feelings of an imperial ruler towards his charges, and becomes even more remarkable when we remember that the author was serving among a people long accustomed to venerate the ruler and render passive obedience to him, and that it is very unlikely that they would have considered a representative of imperial power and authority as an inferior unless, of course, he himself were openly to doubt his own right to rule. We may therefore consider the passage to be a description not so much of attitudes which the author encountered as of his own feelings and emotions. He speaks of embarrassment, shame, of rejoicing at being considered an inferior: when we examine the last stages of British colonial rule and the failure of nerve it exhibits, we must not forget to make due allowance for these vague but powerful and pervasive feelings of guilt. Other imperial powers like the French and the Russians seem to be quite immune to them, and we may suspect that they have their origin not in what the British did in colonial territories—for their record is in general far better than that of other rulers, whether native or foreign—but in complex and obscure emotions which, for the last half-century or so, have taken hold of the British official and intellectual classes.

The author's career in Palestine began at the time of the Wailing Wall incident and had to be terminated in the middle of another, more serious challenge to the lawful government when it was feared that as assistant district governor of Samaria he might be on the terrorists' assassination list. It was during this period that he must have become convinced that the Arabs considered him an inferior. It is a curious belief for a ruler to harbour in such circumstances. Some explanation may perhaps be afforded by the author's view of the Palestine problem. He adopts the arid moralism to which so many English writers seem fatally prone when they discuss Anglo-Arab relations: 'the main responsibility was ours', the British have been guilty of 'prevarication', 'procrastination', 'fundamental dishonesty' and 'double-dealing' (p. 36). It is this immorality, the author seems convinced, which 'made disaster certain'. Sir Hugh Foot goes on as though the world were designed to illustrate a pedagogue's manual, as though he had never heard of good intentions and honesty and straight dealing also leading to disasters, as though it were not the oldest worldly wisdom that the wicked can flourish like the green bay tree. But what exactly does this strong language denounce? We gather that the dishonesty and double-dealing somehow reside in the fact that in 1915 'we supported King Faisal's desert rising' and in 1917 'we signed the Balfour Declaration'. Is not this breast-beating superfluous, supererogatory, or at least misplaced? For it is as well established as these things can be, that in 1917 the British government was neither dishonest towards, nor engaged in double-dealing with, its Zionist and its Arab nationalist clients, that in fact it is the French who have reason to complain of double-dealing. But then the French have never been ones to inspire much guilt in an English breast.

A story told in this book shows Clio once more as the supreme ironist. As is well-known, the British troops who fought to capture Damascus in 1918 were deliberately prevented from entering the city, so that Faysal's Arabs could formally claim its capture and forestall French claims to a privileged position in Syria. Sir Hugh Foot reveals here (p. 72) that in order to support the Free French privileged position in Syria, the British troops who fought to capture Damascus in 1941 were deliberately prevented from entering the city, so that the Free French might formally claim its capture.

15. Sir Mark Sykes and Palestine 1915–16

The role of Sir Mark Sykes in the formation of British middle-eastern policy in the first world war has always been thought to be prominent. But it is only now, when most of the relevant archives have been made available, that his role is coming to be exactly known, and the degree of its prominence to be appreciated.

It is with the so-called Sykes–Picot Agreement that his name has been mostly associated. In a book published in 1956 I remarked that 'Very few people believed in the Sykes–Picot Agreement, and among those on the English side who did, it is a moot point whether Sir Mark Sykes can be included.'[1] This tentative judgement has now found confirmation in the foreign office files which show that on more than one occasion after its signature Sykes disclaimed responsibility for its provisions, and expressed disagreement with them. This need not occasion surprise, for in carrying out the negotiation with Picot, Sykes was acting not as a principal but as an agent, bound by the views and decisions of ministers.

Indeed, on one crucial issue in particular, he held and continued to hold views quite at variance with the arrangements envisaged in the agreement. This was the issue of Palestine. What his views on Palestine were at the start of the war appears quite clearly from the alternative plans for dealing with the Ottoman empire which he put before the Bunsen committee. At the committee's meeting of 17 April 1915, Sykes proposed either that the non-Turkish portions of the Ottoman empire should be annexed by the various allies, or that the empire should be maintained intact and divided into zones of commercial and political interest. In the first case Sykes proposed that Britain should acquire the territory from Haifa in the north to Egypt in the south; if the second alternative were to be adopted Britain ought to have the predominant position in the same area.[2]

In a most interesting letter which Sykes wrote after Kitchener's death to his biographer, he explained how he came to be a member of the Bunsen committee. On the outbreak of war he was introduced by Lancelot Oliphant of the foreign office to Kitchener's personal military secretary, Colonel O. A. G. Fitzgerald, to whom he began giving his views on eastern affairs, for Kitchener's benefit. 'When the Dardanelles expedition was decided upon,' Sykes went on, 'I was sent for to the War Office and worked under General Callwell, preparing books, memoranda, etc. for the forces. I was told I was going with the expedition, but at the last moment was ordered to remain in London, and then returned to my battalion for a short time, but was sent for again, and appointed at the personal request of Lord Kitchener as a member of the committee formed to ascertain British desiderata in Asiatic Turkey. . . .

'Through Fitzgerald Lord Kitchener told me that he wished to keep him in touch with the situation, . . . I used to report to Fitzgerald each night at York House on the various problems that had come up for discussion, and received instructions as to the points Lord Kitchener desired should be considered; this I did as best as I could by explaining the views which he approved of or suggested.' Sykes, then, may be considered Kitchener's representative on the Bunsen committee. It is therefore all the more interesting to note that on one particular issue he differed from Kitchener, and that in the end he succeeded in converting the latter to his own view. 'When Lord Kitchener's views differed from my own', his letter to Sir George Arthur went on, 'I used to argue the case out with Fitzgerald, and prepare memoranda, etc. until we could agree. There was only one real point of difference and that was on Alexandretta. Lord Kitchener wanted Alexandretta to be a British port with a through connection to the Euphrates', Sykes wrote, 'but was ultimately reconciled to Haifa.'[3]

It must have been from Sykes, then, rather than from Kitchener, that the proposals which the former put before the Bunsen committee at its meeting of April 17, 1915 originally came. Such a view gains confirmation from what Kitchener said at a meeting of the war council on 10 March 1915, a month or so, that is, before Sykes broached his plan for Palestine to the Bunsen committee. The council, considering Russia's demand for Constantinople, was led to discuss whether British interests required the acquisition of any Ottoman territory. In the course of this discussion, Kitchener declared in his usual categorical manner that 'Palestine would be of no value to us whatsoever', and that Alexandretta was far more important; he even went so far as to say that Britain could not count on holding Egypt if Alexandretta were in other hands.[4]

In the letter to Arthur mentioned above, Sykes went on to describe how, after the Bunsen committee made its report, Kitchener 'decided that I ought to go right round the Middle East and report on the various situations', and how after his return 'Lord Kitchener told me personally to get hold of the Franco-British negotiations which were at a deadlock, and I worked through Picot the Franco-British agreement on Lord Kitchener's lines, every detail of which I discussed with Fitzgerald nightly.' It was during this period that Sykes appeared before the war committee in order to give evidence on the Arab question. Here too he made clear his desire that Britain should annex

Palestine. To Balfour's question as to the sort of arrangement he would like to have with the French, Sykes answered: 'I should like to retain for ourselves such country south of Haifa as was not in the Jerusalem enclave, which I gather the French themselves admit. I think it is most important that we should have a belt of English-controlled country between the Sharif of Mecca and the French.'[5] In the event, this did not prove possible, and as is well known, under the Sykes–Picot scheme only an enclave round Haifa was to become British, the rest of Palestine being internationally administered territory. This scheme received the approval of a meeting of ministers and officials on February 4, 1916, at which Kitchener was present.[6]

'When the agreement was completed,' we learn from Sykes' letter to Arthur, 'I reported to Lord Kitchener in person, and of my own initiative suggested that I should go to Russia and finish it up there; this was the only suggestion I made myself. This was agreed to, and oddly enough was the only occasion on which he gave me a direct order as regards policy; he said, "In doing this job you will make it clear to the Russians, that it is to settle up the Entente as regards Turkey and not because we particularly desire to get anything for ourselves."' But while he was in Petrograd, a new development occurred which made Sykes hope for a moment that a way might yet be found of increasing the British stake in Palestine, even though Kitchener, from whom he took his instructions, seems to have resigned himself to the Sykes–Picot scheme. On 11 March 1916, the foreign office sent a telegram to the embassy at St. Petersburg, stating that a proposal had been received for a declaration to be made holding out to the Jews the prospect of a Jewish settlement in Palestine. Such a declaration was thought to appeal 'to a large and powerful section of the Jewish community throughout the world', and if this was so then 'the Zionist idea has the most far-reaching political possibilities', enabling the Entente Powers to bring to their side 'the Jewish forces in America, the East and elsewhere which are now largely if not preponderantly hostile to us.' The foreign office added that 'some influential Jewish opinion would be opposed to an international protectorate, but we do not desire to state a preference in favour of any particular solution of the problem'.[7] It may be interesting to note in passing that this telegram was drafted by Hugh O'Beirne, who was present at the meeting of the war committee on 16 December 1915 when Sykes had insisted on the necessity of Palestine coming under British control.[8]

A few days later, Sykes reported that he had discussed this proposal with Picot, and made a suggestion that one of the sons of the Sharif of Mecca should be made Sultan of Palestine, that a privileged chartered Zionist land company be formed, and that the

British government should arbitrate in any dispute between this land company and the projected Palestine sultanate. But, Sykes said, Picot was violently against such proposals.[9] This telegram seems to have aroused the disquiet of Grey and of Nicolson, the permanent under-secretary at the foreign office, since both considered the maintenance of good relations with France vastly more important than territorial gains in the middle east. A telegram which Grey himself drafted was sent to Sykes on 16 March to the effect that 'Sir E. Grey considers that matter should not have been discussed with M. Picot', and that if it were to arise on a subsequent occasion then Sykes should make clear that there was no question of a British protectorate in Palestine. Two days later Sykes replied with a telegram, declaring that: 'I have never mentioned Palestine to Picot without making it clear that His Majesty's Government have no idea to protect Palestine.'[10]

On the same day Sykes wrote a letter in amplification of this telegram. The letter, preserved among the Nicolson Papers,[11] is a document of great interest, and its text is printed below. In his study on 'The Balfour Declaration and its Makers' mentioned above, Professor Vereté has remarked that the 'entire stage (end 1915–autumn 1916) in the evolution of matters leading to the Declaration calls for further research and elaboration'.[12] Sykes' letter of 18 March 1916, has its contribution to make in clarifying this somewhat obscure period. In the letter, Sykes apologizes for 'having caused you some uneasiness in regard to Picot and Palestine'. But no harm, he declares, has been done in relations with the French or the Russians, and he goes on to give his estimate of Zionism. We see that at this period already, Sir Mark Sykes was utterly convinced of the worldwide importance of Jews and Zionists. 'To my mind', he writes, 'the Zionists are now the key of the situation—the problem is how are they to be satisfied?—with "great Jewry" against us there is no possible chance of getting the thing thro'—it means optimism in Berlin—dumps in London—un-ease in Paris—resistance to last ditch in C'ople—dis-sension in Cairo—Arabs all squabbling among them-selves—as Shakespeare says "Untune that string and mark what discord follows"—Assume Zionists satisfied the contrary is the case, of that I am positive—'. Such sentiments may now seem extravagant, but belief in the power, or rather in the omnipotence, of the Jews was then very widely held. In his authoritative work on *The Balfour Declaration*, Mr. Stein quotes a letter from Sykes to Samuel written on 26 February 1916, on the eve of his departure for Petrograd, which clearly shows his interest in a Zionist scheme,[13] but this letter does not lead the reader to suspect how impressed Sykes was with the power of Jewry and Zionism.

Remembering his steady and undeviating belief, from the beginning of the war, that possession of Palestine was necessary for the British empire, and putting it side by side with this belief in the universal power of the Jews, so clearly and vehemently expressed in his letter to Nicolson, we may not doubt that for Sykes a British Palestine and a Zionist Palestine became complementary schemes, the realization of which would put a tremendous weapon in the allies' hands and, precisely in so doing, satisfy a legitimate British ambition.

By the end of 1916 Kitchener was no more, and Lloyd George had taken Asquith's place. With him as prime minister, the prospects of a Zionist scheme for Palestine, which would be used as a lever to bring about British control of the country, became much brighter. Lloyd George, as Mr. Stein has established, was 'predisposed to be receptive' to Zionism.[14] He also seems to have wanted a British Palestine from the start. Kitchener's categorical words that 'Palestine would be of no value to us whatsoever', which he uttered at the War Council of 10 March 1915, were in fact addressed to Lloyd George who had just expressed 'considerable misgivings about the expediency of occupying Alexandretta' and actually suggested Palestine as an alternative 'owing to the prestige it would give us'. Again, in April 1917, a few months after his becoming prime minister, he bluntly told the British ambassador at Paris that the French would have to accept a British protectorate in Palestine: 'we shall be there by conquest and shall remain.' Lord Bertie accurately summed up his attitude then and later as being: '*J'y suis, j'y reste.*'[15] His being at the helm meant that patronage of Zionism would be used to establish and maintain the British control of Palestine which Allenby's victory had made possible. And in the execution of this policy Sykes was certainly a key figure.

APPENDIX

18 March 1916

Dear Sir Arthur,

I am afraid from your telegram that I have caused you some uneasiness in regard to Picot & Palestine.

But I can assure you no harm has been done, P[icot] is in the highest spirits over his new Castle in Armenia, and S[azonow] is apparently delighted to get out of having to take over any more Armenians than he can help. To my mind the Zionists are now the key of the situation—the problem is how are they to be satisfied?—with 'Great Jewry' against us there is no possible chance of getting the thing thro'—it means optimism in Berlin—dumps in London,—un-ease in Paris—resistance to last ditch in C'ople—dis-sension in Cairo—Arabs all squabbling among themselves—as Shakespeare says 'Untune that string and mark what discord follows'—Assume Zionists satisfied the contrary is the case, of that I am positive. The question is what is their minimum—International solution they dislike—I put it to Picot this way 'H.M.G. hate Palestine and don't want it—Zionists want us for obvious reasons' there was no harm in saying this as P. knew it all along—so he and I set to work to draft a scheme which I forwarded. As regards that scheme if it will satisfy Zionists, I think it can be worked, but always on terms, if the Zionists think [the] proposal good enough they will want us to win—If they [want] us to win they will do their best which means they will (A) calm their activities in Russia, (B) Pessimise in Germany (C) stimulate in France England & Italy (D) Enthuse in U.S.A. This will be subconscious, unwritten, and wholly atmospheric. P. now sees this and understands it and will put it to those who count in France, and will appeal to the ancient French sentiment not of St. Louis but Henri IV 'Paris etc' only now 'Alsace, Paris, Verdun, are well worth a land company in Palestine'—But the rub lies in one point is a land company enough? can its charter be made sufficient to meet Zionist *real* aspirations?—because further neither Islam nor Christendom can go—if the Caliphate of Berlin can go further then we are up a tree—but I don't believe it can—I don't see how it can—to go further compromises the Mosque of Omar and that is impossible.

What has to be done, requires very careful handling and London is the place to do it, under Sir Edwards eye and within reach of Paris—That is why I suggest the Arabs being sent to London—so that when we have got the Zionists fixed up, we can settle the Franco-Arab difficulty and so have our situation ready and martialled in order.

I am afraid this sounds rather odd & fantastic but when we bump into a thing like Zionism, which is atmospheric, international, cosmopolitan, subconscious, and unwritten nay often unspoken, it is not possible to work and think on ordinary lines—This letter is only for yourself—I apologise a 1000 times for troubling you with what reads like a rigmarole.

Yours very sincerely,

Mark Sykes

NOTES

1. *England and the Middle East*, p. 66.
2. Cab. 27/1, 'British Desiderata in Turkey in Asia', minutes of meeting of 17 April.
3. Sir Mark Sykes to Sir George Arthur, 12 Sept. 1916, in Kitchener Papers, PRO 30/57/91. For Kitchener's preference for Alexandretta, see Jukka Nevakivi, 'Lord Kitchener and the Partition of the Ottoman Empire, 1915–16', in K. Bourne and D. C. Watt, eds., *Studies in International History*, 1967, pp. 315–29.
4. Cab. 42/2/5.

5. Cab. 42/6/10.
6. Cab. 37/142/10, F.O. note on 'Arab Question'.
7. F.O. 371/2817, file 42608/43776. See Leonard Stein, *The Balfour Declaration*, 1961, ch. 14, 'Sir Edward Grey's proposal, March 1916'. Also D. Z. Gillon, 'The Antecedents of the Balfour Declaration', *Middle Eastern Studies*, vol. 5, no. 2.
8. Cab. 42/6/9. O'Beirne had shortly before written a memorandum in which he stated that 'an arrangement completely satisfactory to Jewish aspirations in regard to Palestine' would have 'tremendous political consequences', see Mayir Vereté, 'The Balfour Declaration and its Makers' in *Middle Eastern Studies*, vol. 6, no. 1, pp. 56 and 70–1. The article gives the inner history of the telegram of 11 March.
9. F.O. 371/2767, file 49669, Buchanan's telegram, St. Petersburg, 14 March 1916. Gillon, *loc. cit.*, quotes at length from this telegram and the exchanges which followed.
10. F.O. 371/2767, *loc. cit.*
11. F.O. 800/381.
12. *Loc. cit.*, p. 72.
13. *Op. cit.*, p. 233.
14. *Op. cit.*, ch. 8; the expression cited above is at p. 142.
15. *The Diary of Lord Bertie of Thame*, ed. by Lady Algernon Gordon Lennox, 1924, vol. II, pp. 123, 312.

16. Young Turks, Freemasons and Jews

It is related that when Kamil Pasha was Ottoman grand vizier at the beginning of 1913, he complained of lack of support from the British ambassador, Sir Gerard Lowther, and exclaimed in despair: 'Alas, where is White, where is Currie?'[1] Kamil Pasha's bitterness over Lowther's attitude was certainly justified, but it is most doubtful whether his nostalgia for White and Currie has any historical warrant. In fact, whether we look at British policy towards the Ottoman empire from the morrow of the congress of Berlin to the eve of the first world war, or whether we examine the attitude of successive British ambassadors in Constantinople during the same period, our dominant impression is likely to be quite negative. On the very morrow of the Cyprus convention of 1878, by which Britain engaged to join the Sultan in defending Ottoman possessions in Asia 'by force of arms', mutual disenchantment was already apparent. The British government on the one hand found itself unable or unwilling to give financial or other support to Abd al-Hamid, and on the other suspected that the sultan was not in earnest about those 'necessary reforms' which he had bound himself by the Cyprus convention to introduce. By the end of 1879, British influence was at a low ebb in Constantinople, and the pro-Ottoman Layard had, as Salisbury put it, 'lost his temper with the Sultan, and like a Portuguese sailor in a storm is disposed to beat the idol he worshipped'.[2] Anglo–Ottoman relations thereafter remained tepid. The British occupation of Egypt, on the one hand increased Abd al-Hamid's suspicion of his ostensible ally, and on the other considerably decreased British interest in an Ottoman alliance.[3] British attitudes toward Abd al-Hamid became one of increasing dislike and mistrust: he was believed to be cynical about reforms and to propagate a mischievous and possibly dangerous Pan-Islamism. The Armenian troubles of the 1890s served to give him, in addition, a sinister reputation as an unscrupulous and bloodthirsty despot. It was now thought practically useless and morally wrong to have any truck with 'Abdul the Damned', and the 'unspeakable Turk' was undoubtedly the wrong horse to have backed in the Crimean war and in 1876–8. 'I believe,' Salisbury wrote in 1898, 'that under the guidance of Palmerston and Lord Stratford de Redcliffe we made a grave blunder in deserting the alliances of 1805. We sacrificed the alliance of a Power that was growing, for a Power that was evidently decaying.'[2] Fear of Germany finally brought about an *entente* with Russia some nine years after the date of Salisbury's letter. This *entente* was bound to, and did make, Anglo-Ottoman relations more difficult and ambiguous than ever.

The outbreak, a year later, of the Young Turk revolution seemed, however, at first sight to herald a warmer relationship between Britain and the Ottoman empire. The newly appointed ambassador, Sir Gerard Lowther (1858–1916), was given an enthusiastic popular welcome on his arrival at Constantinople, and Sir Edward Grey described the revolution as 'marvellous', declaring that: 'We were against the Turkish government when it was bad, but between us and the people there was not, and never had been, any barrier.'[5] But it soon became clear that the Young Turk revolution had not effected any fundamental change in Anglo-Ottoman relations. British policy, after all, was still governed by the need to maintain the *entente* with Russia, no matter what the character of the Ottoman régime. If this was the case, then to afford the Ottomans solid and whole-hearted support—whether political or financial—would have been considered as at best unproductive, and at worst downright harmful. In this attitude Lowther seems to have been at one with the foreign office. One may even go further and say that his reports on the political situation at Constantinople, and on the character and activities of the Young Turks instilled within the foreign office the belief that the Young Turks were much worse than Abd al-Hamid. Lowther thus reinforced the long-standing anti-Ottoman prejudice in the foreign office, and encouraged its tendency to believe that the Ottoman government was made up of men who were at once sinister and incompetent, corrupt and infantile.

In conveying such an impression to his colleagues and superiors in London, the ambassador seems to have been wholly guided by his chief dragoman, G. H. Fitzmaurice (1865–1939). No biography either of Lowther or Fitzmaurice exists, and it is difficult for us to know how passive and receptive the former was by character, or how forceful and persuasive the latter. But this at least we do know, that Lowther was a newcomer at Constantinople while Fitzmaurice was an old hand there, and that the ambassador admired his subordinate's abilities and relied on him. 'As to Fitzmaurice, who is indefatigable,' he wrote to the permanent under-secretary at the foreign office in July 1909, 'I am quite satisfied that he is in touch with all the various elements of the local political world, and that no embassy, except perhaps the Russians, who have a Jew dragoman in close touch with the Jew Committee of Union and Progress, is better informed than we are'.[6] When, some two years later, the Young Turk newspaper *Tanin* attacked Fitzmaurice for allegedly intriguing in favour of an Arab caliphate, and for attributing pro-Zionist policies to the Ottoman government, Lowther strongly defended his chief dragoman, and endorsed Fitzmaurice's explanation of the attack by *Tanin*. This attack Fitzmaurice attributed to his investigation of the influence of freemasonry over the Young Turks. He believed that it was his duty to carry out such an investigation because masonry had become 'the instrument of political intrigue in matters affecting British interests'. Fitzmaurice also believed that his inquiries into masonry 'were not free from danger'.[7]

It is clear from this language that the chief dragoman believed that in Constantinople things were not what they seemed, that political incidents had hidden implications and esoteric explanations. His outlook may be exemplified by a remarkable letter which he wrote to William Tyrrell, Grey's principal private secretary in November 1912, when the Balkan allies appeared on the point of capturing Constantinople. Fitzmaurice's letter was dated from Tzarigrad as he now called the Ottoman capital, and began: 'Swan-like, let me write you a last letter from Pekin before the Court and Porte flee bagless and baggeless (Gladstonese) to the shores of Asia.' He believed that the 'drama of 1453' was being 'undone' and that the 'Turkish Army rotted by C.U.P. doctrines and politics could not fight in the name of Djavid Bey, instead of the Padishah and collapsed before the avenging Balgar and the armies of the new Great Power—the "United States of the Balcans" which are undoubtedly the right horse besides the favourites of the Gladstonian tradition. Art. 23 of the Treaty of Berlin has been set right by reverting to San Stephano and if bad massacres, etc., occur here within the next 36 hours, the lurid wave may sweep over Anatolia and force the 10,000 Russians at Urmia to step in and redress Art. 61 of Berlin.' His imagination was just as lurid as the scene he envisaged, for he went on to say: 'If a general massacre, etc., etc., like Turner's picture in the National Gallery "Wind, Rain and Speed" sweeps over Anatolia and Syria in an expiring spasm of Panislamism now for four years harnessed to the chariot of Panjudaism, the prairie fire may even reach Egypt.'[8]

There is no doubt that Lowther shared Fitzmaurice's outlook. As has been seen, in a letter of 1909, he speaks of the 'Jew Committee of Union and Progress'. Other letters make his views on Ottoman politics fully explicit. 'Have you read the Nineteenth Century?', he asks Hardinge, in a letter of April 1910. 'Freemasonry in France, *mutatis mutandis*—this will explain a lot of what is going on here. The Jews, Socialists and Freemasons are all supreme latter making great strides. That will probably produce another Counter revolution unless it gets too strong.' A week later, he speaks of the 'combination of self-seeking spurious freemasons and Jews that represent the

Committee of Union and Progress' and he affirms that 'this Albanian business has been created by a few Salonica Jews'.[9] Three years later his opinions are quite unchanged: 'Great Britain and her agents,' he wrote in March 1913 to Sir Arthur Nicolson, Hardinge's successor at the Foreign Office, 'do not appeal to the reckless and the violent who pull the strings here, so we are not popular. I do not think Mahmoud Shefket [the Grand Vizier] dreads or need dread the Ententists [i.e. the Hurriyet ve Itilaf Firkasi] Moderates or peace men or whatever you like to call them but rather the violent section of his own party who care not what happens to the country, but who, encouraged by the Jews, merely seek their own ends.'[10]

The mysteries of the Judeo-masonic and Young Turk conspiracy uncovered by the ambassador and his dragoman fortunately do not have to be pieced together from mere *obiter dicta*. They are actually set out in a long and detailed letter, 'private and confidential', dated 29 May 1910, from Lowther to Hardinge. It is reproduced in an appendix. The story which Lowther here unfolds in all its labyrinthine complexity involves many actors in various parts of the Mediterranean—and even perhaps beyond—all bound together by the occult ties of freemasonry: 'Nathan, the Jewish Lord Mayor of Rome, is high up in Masonry, and the Jewish Premiers Luzzati and Sonnino, and other Jewish senators and deputies, are also, it appears, Masons'; 'The Italian Government appointed a Jew and Mason called Primo Levi, who was not in the consular career, as consul-general at Salonica, and Oscar Strauss [*sic*], who together with Jacob Schiff, had influenced the American Jews in favour of Jewish immigration into Mesoptamia as opposed to other Territorialist plans and as an extended form of Sionism, was appointed American Ambassador here.' If to Nathan, Levi and the others, we add another name, we will have revealed a crucial link in this invisible chain: 'Some years ago Emanuele Carasso, a Jewish Mason of Salonica, and now deputy for that town in the Ottoman Chamber, founded there a lodge called "Macedonia Risorta" in connexion with Italian Freemasonry. He appears to have induced the Young Turks, officers and civilians, to adopt Freemasonry with a view to exerting impalpable Jewish influence over the new dispensation in Turkey.' These were the conspirators. But Nathan and Levi, Sonnino and Luzzati, Schiff and Strauss and Carasso, what was their purpose? 'The immediate purpose for which they are working is the practically exclusive economic capture of Turkey and new enterprises in that country.' Behind this immediate aim lay an ultimate purpose '[the Jew] seems to have entangled the pre-economic-minded Turk in his toils and as Turkey happens to contain the places sacred to Israel, it is but natural that the Jew should strive to maintain a position of exclusive influence and utilize it for the furtherance of his ideals, viz. the ultimate creation of an autonomous Jewish state in Palestine or Babylonia as explained by Israel Zangwill in his article in the "Fortnightly Review" of April.' It was through Carasso that the Young Turks were harnessed to these aims, and they in return have made the Ottoman Empire a mere instrument of the Jew: 'Talaat Bey, the Minister of the Interior, who is of Gipsy descent . . . , and Javid, the Minister of Finance, who is a Crypto-Jew, are the official manifestations of the occult power of the Committee [of Union and Progress]. They are the only members of the Cabinet who really count, and are also the apex of Freemasonry in Turkey. . . . Since he became Minister of the Interior about a year ago, Talaat Bey has been spreading the net of the Freemason Committee over the Empire by appointing to provincial posts as governors, sub-governors, etc., men who are Masons or reliable Committee adherents, and, in most cases, both. . . . The invisible government of Turkey is thus the Grand Orient with Talaat Bey as Grand Master.' These were the main lines of Sir Gerard's story, but it also had some baroque and highly significant embellishments. The Jew hates Russia, England is friendly to Russia, therefore the Jew is anti-British, 'a consideration to which the Germans are, I think, alive'. The Jew and the Young Turk, again, have combined to push out and estrange Armenians, Greeks and Arabs, and many of the latter 'secretly turn their eyes towards the Khedivate as the one "Arab Government" which, they cherish the hope, may one day, under British auspices, exercise a centripetal influence on all Ottoman Arabs.'

The fustian fantasies recorded in this document are worth noticing for their own sake, for they exhibit the extremes of credulity to which succumbed the two men[11] to whom the foreign secretary looked for the provision of reliable information about an important and sensitive area. The document shows how tenuous was their hold on reality. Rule by doctrinaire officers such as the Young Turks was, of course, an ominous development in the Ottoman empire; but to represent it as the outcome of a Juedo-masonic conspiracy was entirely to miss its significance. It was to be gulled by fuddled fabulosities.

If Lowther and Fitzmaurice were so easily led astray on so fundamental an issue, then their judgement regarding other aspects of Ottoman politics becomes suspect. How this judgment influenced policy is, however, a different and a more complex issue. But that it had an influence may not be doubted. Acknowledging Lowther's report of 29 May, Hardinge declared that it was 'most interesting reading' and that copies were being sent privately to the India office, to Cairo and Teheran.[12] This is a indication of how seriously it was taken. As has been argued above, anti-Ottoman prejudice more or less pronounced is a standing feature of British policy from the 1880s onwards. Lowther's letter, encouraging the belief that the new Ottoman rulers were a band of sinister conspirators, must have confirmed this prejudice and given it a new strength. Such a prejudice, incalculable as its effects are, must be reckoned with in considering British policy towards the Ottoman empire in the years immediately preceding the outbreak of the first world war. In a recent paper, Professor Allan Cunningham has remarked that by 1914 'a British government was no longer inclined by temperament to make any sort of major sacrifice to win over Turkey'.[13] It is reasonable to assume that Lowther's reports had their part to play in the making of this temperament.

Two echoes of Lowther's and Fitzmaurice's views are perhaps worth mentioning, both for their intrinsic interest, and as an indication of the wide prevalence of these views. The *Arab Bulletin* of 26 September 1916, carried an anonymous article entitled 'Notes on Freemasonry in Turkey under the New Régime (1908–1914)', which seems to reproduce, with embellishments, the account given in Lowther's letter of 29 May 1910. Carasso, 'a low-class, and dishonest lawyer, an obsequious, venal and secretive scoundrel, with a mysterious manner' was responsible for inducting Talaat, Javid, Dr. Nazim and Behaeddin Monastirli into freemasonry; he was a 'useful jackal to the lions and tigers of the C.U.P.'. The Committee of Union and Progress, freemasonry and Judaism were inextricably connected: 'Certain Turks of Constantinople who knew Salonika remarked a curious similarity between the emblems of the Committee and those of the Macedonia Risorta Lodge, and of the Jewish Beni Brith Society'; the inauguration of the Grand Orient of Turkey in June 1909 was 'graced by the presence of numerous Jewish gentlemen from Haskeui (the Whitechapel of Constantinople), Salonika, Smyrna and various cities in Hungary, and the Central Empires'. The *Bulletin* listed the members of the 'Supreme Council of the Grand Orient of Turkey', three or probably four of whom were Jews,[14] three Dönmés and four only Muslims. Certain foreign observers, the *Bulletin* remarked, had begun to wonder whether 'the Young Turk might not prove to be an old Jew with German affinities'. After going through various complicated reasonings, the article concluded that 'as far as is known Turkish Freemasonry is now dormant, and will probably remain so, till the present governing group in Turkey is driven from power, and resumes its underground methods against the next Turkish régime or a foreign conqueror'.[15]

The other echo worth noticing occurs in a letter from G. F. Clayton, director of Intelligence at Cairo, to Wingate, the governor-general of the Sudan. The letter is written from London where Clayton was on an official mission, and is dated 3 August 1916. Clayton describes to his correspondent his impression 'which confirmed what I have always thought' of the widespread influence of the Jews; the letter went on: 'There are English Jews, French Jews, American Jews, German Jews, Austrian Jews and *Salonica* Jews— but all are JEWS, and moreover practically all are anti-Russian. You hear peace talk and generally somewhere behind is the Jew. You hear pro-Turk talk and desires for a separate peace with Turkey— again the Jew (the mainspring of the C.U.P.)'.[16] The letter sheds a peculiar light on the judgement of one who, during and after the first world war, was a main architect of British policy in the middle east. But, of course, Clayton was not the only one to be impressed by the ubiquity and omnipotence of the Jews. If he was suspicious, others were impressed by so much power and it may well be that such fictions helped to persuade the British government to fall for and to take up Zionism: Clio is indeed an ironic muse.

APPENDIX

Secret

Sir G. Lowther to Sir C. Hardinge*

(Private and Confidential.)

Dear Charles   Constantinople, May 29, 1910.

Gorst's telegram of the 23rd April and your telegram of the 25th April about the rumoured appointment of Mohammed Farid as delegate in Egypt of the Constantinople Freemasons, 'said to be intimately connected with the Committee of Union and Progress', prompts me to write to you at some length on the strain of continental Freemasonry running through the Young Turk movement. I do so privately and confidentially, as this new Freemasonry in Turkey, unlike that of England and America, is in great part secret and political, and information on the subject is only obtainable in strict confidence, while those who betray its political secrets seem to stand in fear of the hand of the Mafia. Some days ago a local Mason who divulged the signs of the craft was actually threatened with being sent before the court-martial, sitting in virtue of our state of siege.

As you are aware, the Young Turkey movement in Paris was quite separate from and in great part in ignorance of the inner workings of that in Salonica. The latter town has a population of about 140,000, of whom 80,000 are Spanish Jews, and 20,000 of the sect of Sabetai Levi [*sic*] or Crypto-Jews, who externally profess Islamism. Many of the former have

* F.O. 800/193A (Lowther Papers).

in the past acquired Italian nationality and are Freemasons affiliated to Italian lodges. Nathan, the Jewish Lord Mayor of Rome, is high up in Masonry, and the Jewish Premiers Luzzati and Sonnino, and other Jewish senators and deputies, are also, it appears, Masons. They claim to have been founded from and to follow the ritual of the 'Ancient Scottish'.

Some years ago Emannuele Carasso, a Jewish Mason of Salonica, and now deputy for that town in the Ottoman Chamber, founded there a lodge called 'Macedonia Risorta' in connection with Italian Freemasonry. He appears to have induced the Young Turks, officers and civilians, to adopt Freemasonry with a view to exerting an impalpable Jewish influence over the new dispensation in Turkey, though ostensibly only with a view to outwitting the Hamidian spies, and gave them the shelter of his lodge, which, meeting in a foreign house, enjoyed extra-territorial immunities from inquisitorial methods. Abdul Hamid's spies got cognisance of the movement, and a certain Ismail Mahir Pasha, who was mysteriously murdered shortly after the revolution in July 1908—an accident after dark—appears to have learnt some of their secrets and reported on them to Yildiz Palace. Spies were posted outside the lodge to take down the names of officers and others who frequented it, a move which the Free-masons countermined by enrolling of the secret police as 'brethren'. The inspiration of the movement in Salonica would seem to have been mainly Jewish, while the words 'Liberté', 'Egalité' and 'Fraternité', the motto of the Young Turks, are also the device of Italian Freemasons. The colours of both, red and white, are again the same. Shortly after the revolution in July 1908, when the Committee established itself in Constantinople, it soon became known that many of its leading members were Freemasons. Carasso began to play a big rôle, including his successful capture of the Balkan Committee, and it was noticed that Jews of all colours, native and foreign, were enthusiastic supporters of the new dispensation, till, as a Turk expressed it, every Hebrew seemed to become a potential spy of the occult Committee, and people began to remark that the movement was rather a Jewish than a Turkish revolution. The Italian Government appointed a Jew and Mason called Primo Levi, who was not in the consular career, as consul-general at Salonica, and Oscar Strauss, who, together with Jacob Schiff, had influenced the American Jews in favour of Jewish immigration into Mesopotamia as opposed to other Territorialist plans and as an extended form of Sionism, was appointed American Ambassador here. As you probably know, the orthodox Moslem has a very strong prejudice against Masonry, which he looks upon as worse than irreligious, and in the movement against the Committee which culminated in the mutiny of the 13th April, 1909, this feature figured rather prominently. Those events have not so far been satisfactorily explained, but it did not escape notice at the time that the four battalions which had been specially dispatched from Salonica to the capital, and which Kiamil Pasha wished to have sent back to the IIIrd Army Corps, started the mutiny or 'so-called reactionary movement', and were commanded by a Crypto-Jew and Freemason from Salonica, a Colonel Remzi Bey, who, instead of being court-martialled on account of the behaviour of the troops confided to his charge, was appointed Chief Aide-de-camp to Sultan Mehmed V. Carasso was one of the bearers of the message of deposition to Abdul Hamid, who was conveyed to Salonica and confined in the house of the Italian Jewish bankers of the Committee, while a brother of Remzi Bey was set over him as keeper. After the deposition the Jewish papers of Salonica sent up a loud cry of deliverance from 'the oppressor of Israel' who had twice turned a deaf ear to the appeals of Herzl, the Sionist leader, and who, by the imposition of the red passport, like our own Aliens Act, against Polish Jewish immigrants, and otherwise, had thwarted the realisation of the ideals of Sionism in Palestine. The ninth Sionist Congress in December 1909 at Hamburg announced that the divisions in the Jewish world between Territorialists and Sionists, 'as a miracle of the Turkish revolution', had been healed. At the same time Javid Bey, Deputy for Salonica, an exceedingly clever and gifted Crypto-Jew and Freemason, was made Minister of Finance, while Talaat Bey, also a Freemason, became Minister of the Interior. Hilmi Pasha, the Grand Vizier, had applied to become a Mason, but did not 'proceed'. Martial law was proclaimed for two years, and most of the officers on the courts-martial were Freemasons. Parliament was 'ordered' to pass a very stringent Press Law, and a Salonica Crypto-Jew and Freemason was made 'Directeur du Bureau de la Presse', a post of enormous power, as its holder can suppress a paper for severe 'criticism of the new régime' (dubbed 'reaction'), or have the proprietor or editor court-martialled. A semi-inspired Ottoman telegraph agency, which gives the Committee view of events external and internal concerning things Ottoman, was started under the direction of a Baghdad Jew, and an all but successful attempt was made to appoint a Salonica Jewish lawyer and Mason as adviser to the Ministry of Justice. The Constantinople head branch of the Committee of Union and Progress is also run by a Salonica Crypto-Jew and Mason. Another Salonica Crypto-Jew and Freemason made determined attempts to be appointed 'Préfet', i.e. Lord Mayor, of the capital, but has not yet succeeded in his aim, though Prince Said Ha[lim] an Egyptian Freemason, has become Deputy Mayor. The 'Préfet' of Constantinople, like those in France, wields enormous power in all matters concerning the lives and movements of the citizens, and especially in matters connected with municipal elections and those for the Constantinople deputies in the Chamber. At the same time, the old Ministry of Police was replaced by the 'Sûreté Publique' controlling the police and gendarmerie, and put in charge of a Salonica Freemason. 'Parliament' was further ordered to pass the 'Loi sur les Associations', which enabled the Committee of Union and Progress to suppress all similar or rival associations among the Bulgars, Greeks, etc., after which muzzling process it went through the sham of transforming itself from a secret revolutionary society into a 'political party and social society' with published statutes.

It was, however, noticed at the same time that Freemasonry lodges began to spring up like mushrooms in all the principal and small towns of Macedonia and also in the capital, where some twelve lodges have been started within the last year, and it did not require much investigation to learn that the secrecy of the craft was being partly used to conceal the inner workings of the Committee, which had professedly ceased to be a 'secret society'. A subterranean propaganda seemed to be carried on, and officials and others holding important posts seemed to be given to understand that their position, advancement, and consequently their livelihood depended on their becoming 'brethren'. Some were told that, by becoming Masons, Egypt, Crete, and other questions affecting the national greatness of the country would be settled in favour of Turkey, that the innermost arcana of the political world would be revealed to them, that they would become the brothers of the late King of England, and could shake hands and exchange signs with him when he visited Constantinople, etc. Many of these new recruits began to visit, and some actually succeeded in joining, the old-established British lodge, 'La Turquie', and every endeavour was made to induce them to believe that in becoming Masons they were joining an English institution. The new lodges, like similar ones in Egypt, claimed to follow the 'Ancient Scottish' rite, and falsely gave out that they indirectly held a charter from the Grand Lodge of Scotland, of which the King of England was Protector, their idea being to inspire the confidence which attaches to the English name among all Ottoman classes. To maintain the Committee's hold on the army, crowds of officers, especially the juniors were made Masons, and received into a lodge called 'Resna' after the birthplace in Macedonia of Niazi Bey, and with Major Osman Fehmi Bey, the brother of Niazi Bey, as Master. Most of the Committee deputies and senators also became Masons, belonging to the lodge 'La Constitution' of which Talaat Bey, the Minister of the Interior and Javid Bey, Minister of Finance, were the principal officers. Some opposition deputies, especially Arabs, seeing that they were being left out in the cold and out of the current of local political secrets and intrigues, started or joined lodges, e.g. the 'Ukhuvet Osmanié' (i.e. 'Ottoman Fraternity') and the 'Muhiban-i-Hurriet' (i.e. 'Friends of Freedom'.) Further the close on 1,000,000 adherents of the unorthodox Islamic sect of Bektashis, to be found mostly in South Albania and Macedonia, and possessing secret tenets and an organisation akin to those of Freemasonry, manifested a desire to join the Freemasons. These, however, were animated rather by the true spirit of Freemasonry as opposed to the political and atheistic form to be met with in some continental countries.

In addition to the above-mentioned lodges, the following were founded in Constantinople during 1909–10: The 'Vefa Oriental' (or 'Oriental Fidelity'), 'Les vrais Amis de l'Union et Progrès', 'Byzantio Risorto', 'La Véritas', 'La Patrie', 'La Renaissance', and a branch of 'Macedonia Risorta' and the 'Shefak' (or 'Dawn', i.e. 'L'Aurore'), a name not unknown to the students of Egyptian underground politics. All these lodges, like the network of Freemasonry in Salonica and Macedonia, seem to be mainly directed or inspired by Jews, the Greek, Armenian, and other native Christian elements being almost entirely non-represented, if not excluded. Mention has been made above of Prince Said Halim of Egypt. He, his brother Abbas Halim, Prince Aziz Hassan, and other

Egyptians animated with a violent dislike of His Highness the Khedive have worked in with and financially helped the Committee of Union and Progress. The process by which the Freemasonry of Young Turkey, introduced into the capital through Salonica, became linked up with Egyptian Masonry was subject to the cross-currents that usually characterise politics on the shores of the Bosphorus, and is a bit obscure. Masons themselves giving conflicting accounts of what occurred.

Idris Bey Raghib, the Master of the Grand Lodge of Egypt, which is said to be recognised by the Grand Lodge of Scotland, was the founder of, and held supremacy over, a number of lodges in Egypt, Syria, Palestine, and the Lebanon, in which latter district the curious phenomenon of large numbers of Roman Catholic Masons is to be met with.

Mahomed Orfi Pasha was also the founder of some lodges in Egypt, Jerusalem and Southern Syria, and aspired to bring the Constantinople lodges into his 'system', and arrived here for that purpose in the Spring of 1909. He met with certain difficulties, and when the mutiny of the 13th April occurred, he got scared and fled precipitately to Egypt. Some time before those events Idris Raghib had delegated Prince Aziz Hassan who had attained the 17th degree in the Italian lodge at Alexandria, to bring the Constantinople lodges under the Grand Lodge of Egypt, and some time after the entry into the capital of the Macedonian forces who were led and inspired by Masons, and the dethronement of Abdul Hamid, who was bitterly opposed to Masonry, held by him to be a dangerous secret political society, the negotiations began. The necessary authority was obtained from the Italian Grand Orient, and Prince Aziz Hassan, in virtue of special powers emanating through Yusuf Bey Sakakini, from the Belgian Supreme Council of Freemasonry, was raised to the 33rd degree, and empowered to constitute the Grand Orient de la Turquie. This took place in July or August 1909, and Mehmed Talaat Bey, Minister of the Interior, was made Grand Master. It would thus appear that the victory of the Macedonian forces in April 1909 over Abdul Hamid and the conquest of Constantinople also meant the victory of Italian inspired Freemasonry over the British recognized Grand Lodge of Egypt. All the lodges in Constantinople were gradually affiliated to it, as also those in Macedonia, and it was decided to bring all the Ottoman lodges in Syria, Egypt, etc., under the Ottoman Grand Orient. Prince Aziz Hassan, accompanied by Sakakini, returned to Egypt for that purpose, but Idris Bey Raghib and others were opposed to the idea, and maintained that Egypt and the Lebanon, being privileged provinces, ought to be independent even in (political) Freemasonry. Prince Aziz Hassan then fell out with Idris Raghib, who had originally dispatched him to Constantinople, and, in virtue of instructions from Talaat Bey, Grand Master of the Ottoman Grand Orient, appointed Mahomed Farid, the Egyptian Nationalist leader, as delegate in Egypt of the Constantinople Grand Orient, the investiture being carried out at a lodge at Tantah. Halil Hamade Pasha, Shahin Makarius of the 'Mukattam', and other prominent Egyptian Masons who do not sympathise with the Nationalists, raised strong opposition to the appointment, while His Highness the Khedive also deprecated a step which linked up by the bond of political Freemasonry the Egyptian Nationalists and the Committee of Union and Progress, but the appointment once made could not be undone. Halil Hamada Pasha suggested as a remedy the founding of a separate Egyptian 'Grand Orient Ottoman', with the express stipulation that Mahomed Farid should not become its Grand Master or Grand Venerable. By the establishment of an Ottoman Grand Orient in Egypt, and the investiture of its Grand Master, Mahomed Farid's appointment as delegate of the Constantinople Grand Orient will *ipso facto* lapse. Halil Hamada Pasha is now in Constantinople and is endeavouring to get Carasso, the Jewish deputy and Venerable of the Italian Lodge of Salonica, to use his good offices with Talaat Bey to bring about the above consummation. Prince Aziz Hassan and Mahomed Farid are also on their way to Constantinople. When Talaat Bey declared it was untrue that Mahomed Farid had been appointed delegate in Egypt and that he and his Committee friends would not commit such a *gaffe* it would appear that he deliberately lied, presumably under pressure of the engagements of the Committee not to betray their secrets.

In the meantime Sakakini has also arrived in Constantinople, after passing from Egypt to Syria, and spending some time in the latter country linking up its lodges with the Ottoman Grand Orient.

Should the Committee of Union and Progress Grand Orient of Turkey get control of the Egyptian lodges and fill the latter with Nationalists, there is no doubt that the tendency will be to work secretly and subterraneously, with a view to one day bringing about an unexpected explosion like that which in July 1908 took the world by surprise at Salonica. In this connection I may mention a somewhat curious incident. Some time ago the new Grand Rabbi of Turkey, a clever, energetic and accomplished man, who was the schoolfellow of some prominent Young Turks, and who under the old régime made several attempts to be employed in Abdul Hamid's palace as librarian, solicited the good offices of the Embassy in the case of a Jewish Mason, named Ventura, of Italian nationality, who many years ago posed as an Ottoman subject, started business in the Soudan, and was expelled thence by the Sirdar on the ground that he (Ventura) was connected with the smuggling of tobacco through two Jews in Suakim for a certain Corporal White. The latter was also expelled and degraded. Ventura brought his case before the Mixed Tribunal at Cairo and obtained a semi-favourable sentence against the Ministry of War, but the Court of Appeal quashed the sentence. The Grand Rabbi presented a long memorandum of nearly 200 pages exposing the details of the alleged injustice of which Ventura was stated to be the victim, and begged that I should give Ventura a letter of introduction to Sir E. Gorst, with a view to the latter exercising his influence in favour of Ventura's case, which was again to come before the Egyptian courts. I pointed out that any such action of mine was impossible as it would constitute an attempt to influence justice, and that the man was, moreover, professedly an Italian subject. Some time after a Jewish Mason here, called Dr Farhi, got an introduction, through the Master of the local British lodge, to a member of my staff, and again, in a quiet, determined, and semi-minatory tone, begged for the letter of introduction to Gorst on behalf of Ventura. On its being explained to him that such a course was impossible, even in the case of a British subject, he adopted a defiant tone, and declared that this case of crying injustice must be remedied; that the highest influences in the world, including that of Jewish members of the House of Lords, would be brought to bear; and that, if necessary, measures would be taken to bring about the downfall of the Egyptian Government, and the British position in Egypt would be compromised. The man was not a lunatic, and spoke in very measured tones.

Talaat Bey, the Minister of the Interior, who is of Gipsy descent, and comes from Kirjali, in the Adrianople district, and Javid Bey, the Minister of Finance, who is a Crypto-Jew, are the official manifestations of the occult power of the Committee. They are the only members of the Cabinet who really count, and are also the apex of Freemasonry in Turkey. That they would use an agent of Sakakini's antecedents is more than suspicious. Since he became Minister of the Interior about a year ago, Talaat Bey has been spreading the net of the Freemason Committee over the Empire by appointing to provincial posts as governors, sub-governors, etc., men who are Masons or reliable Committee adherents, and, in most cases, both. The intention is that, should a majority of the present Chamber, by accident or despite the terrors of the state of siege, carry opposition to the point of endangering the Ministry of Talaat and Javid, the latter should instantly reply by a *coup d'état*, dissolve the Chamber, and have fresh elections, which would be manipulated by the Committee clubs and Freemasonry lodges in the provinces and return more malleable deputies. The invisible government of Turkey is thus the Grand Orient with Talaat Bey as Grand Master. Eugène Tavernier, in his article in the April number of the 'Nineteenth Century', describes the French Republic as the 'daughter of the Grand Orient'. The same epithet might perhaps be appropriately applied to the Ottoman Committee of Union and Progress, for as Masons seem to be adherents of the Committee, most non-Masons, i.e. the vast majority of the population, are secretly opposed to its rule. Like French Republicans and Freemasons, the words most frequently on its lips are 'reaction' and 'clerical'. Its first tendency was not to modify and modernise the Mahommedan sacred law, but to undermine and smash it. Most of its leaders, while frankly rationalist, also paradoxically endeavour to use the Islamic fervour of the masses as a political weapon and to divert it into chauvinistic channels on the lines of national, i.e. Asiatic, Pan-Islamism. It is intolerant of opposition, and one of its principal methods of destroying its adversaries is to drive them into overt opposition and then crush them as 'reactionaries'. Several of the Ulema have been induced to become Masons, and their example is being used to overcome the scruples and prejudices of the people. A Turk described it as a process of 'drugging the latter with Jewish hashish'.

From the foregoing or any close inspection of the Young Turkey movement in its present stage, it will appear to be principally Jewish and 'Turkish' as opposed to other Ottoman elements, e.g. Arabs, Greeks, Bulgarians, Armenians, etc. The Turk is mainly a soldier, and under constitutional forms he strives to preserve his race predominance, which he can only do through the army. On the latter he spends half his revenue and uses it to reduce the other elements to a state of terror and mute subjection. A constitution in a way implies economic progress, but the economic organism of the Turk is of the feeblest kind, and, unsupported, could not stand alone a week. It was hoped in the beginning that the Armenians, Bulgarians, Greeks and the Ottoman Jew would serve as economic props, but the Young Turk seems to have allied himself solely with the Jew, Ottoman and foreign, and to have estranged the other races. The same result has been witnessed in Hungary, where the Hungarian, who is of Turkish stock and is similarly devoid of real business instincts, has come under the almost exclusive economic and financial domination of the Jew. The latter seems to have entangled the pre-economic-minded Turk in his toils, and as Turkey happens to contain the places sacred to Israel, it is but natural that the Jew should strive to maintain a position of exclusive influence and utilize it for the furtherance of his ideals, viz. the ultimate creation of an autonomous Jewish state in Palestine or Babylonia, as explained by Israel Zangwill in his article in the 'Fortnightly Review' of April. He would kill two birds with one stone if he could obtain from the Turk unrestricted immigration of Jews into Turkey, an aim that he has been pursuing for years back, and transfer to Mesopotamia some millions of his co-religionists in bondage in Russia and Roumania. In return for 'unrestricted immigration' of foreign Jews, he has offered the Young Turk to sacrifice his mother-tongue and replace it by Turkish, and even to take over the whole of the Turkish National Debt. Dr. Nazim, one of the most influential members of the Salonica Committee and said to be of Jewish extraction, has, in company, with his *fidus Achates*, a certain Faik Bey Toledo, a Crypto-Jew of Salonica, visited the Paris branch of the I.C.A. (Judaeo-Colonisation Association) and has since openly advocated importing 200,000 Roumanian Jews into Macedonia and some millions of Russian Jews into Mesopotamia. Israel Zangwill, in the article in the 'Fortnightly Review' of April alluded to above, expresses the hope that Hakki Pasha, the present Grand Vizier, 'may be trusted to advise the Porte soundly on the subject', i.e. in favour of a Jewish autonomous state in Mesopotamia. Hakki Pasha has been given a Jewish private secretary, and frequents a certain Jewish house more than any other, but the Jewish projects have not yet materialised. Doubtless, when Young Turkey with its heavy military expenditure is in need of borrowing, further pressure will be applied by the Jewish lenders. Abdul Hamid, when in dire financial straits, refused similar offers from Herzl, the Sionist leader, and the same idea seems to be in Zangwill's mind when he remarks: 'For, unless the Young Turks have even less common sense than money, the enormous advantages to their Empire of permitting the peaceful penetration of an industrial and non-militant white population must be borne home to them.' Zangwill says the four Jewish deputies in the Ottoman Parliament are 'violently anti-Sionist'. They may pretend to be so in the Palestine sense of the word: they are certainly not in the Mesopotamian sense.

This feature of Young Turkey politics cannot be overlooked by those who would be connected with projected enterprises in Mesopotamia, Syria and even Egypt. For the 'Aurore' ('Shefak'), a Sionist organ started a year ago in Constantinople, is never tired of reminding its readers that the domination of Egypt, the land of the Pharaohs, who forced the Jews to build the Pyramids, is part of the future heritage of Israel. This theory certainly sounds far-fetched, but it is apparently held and preached by some idealists. Mesopotamia and Palestine are, however, only the ultimate goal of the Jews. The immediate end for which they are working is the practically exclusive economic capture of Turkey and new enterprises in that country. It has been shown above that already they hold or control all the pivotal points in the machinery of the Young Turkey Government, though the Ministry of Public Works, which can influence the granting of concessions, is still held by an Armenian, Halajian Effendi. When his predecessor, another Armenian, was got rid of, a determined attempt was made to appoint a Jew or a Jewish nominee. But, especially after the massacres of Armenians at Adana, it was felt that the Armenians should continue to hold one portfolio in the Ministry. Two months ago Halajian seemed on the point of falling, but obtained a new lease of life on becoming a Mason in the same lodge as Talaat Bey and Javid Bey. His position is now still shaky, and the most bitter and constant attacks on him come from a Jewish-financed paper, 'Le Jeune Turc', while there are rumours that his successor will be a Jew, or a Turk with a Jew at his elbow.

It is obvious that the Jew, who is so vitally interested in maintaining his sole predominance in the councils of the Young Turkey, is equally interested in keeping alive the flames of discord between the Turk and his (the Jew's) possible rivals, i.e. the Armenians, Greeks, etc., while it is to be inferred that he would not be averse to the new régime increasing the national indebtedness to the Hebrew financiers. This aspect of the Turkish Revolution has been dwelt on at some length, as, apart from its historical interest, it is not without its direct and indirect bearing on side problems of the Near East. The Jew hates Russia and its Government, and the fact that England is now friendly to Russia has the effect of making the Jew to a certain extent anti-British in Turkey and Persia—a consideration to which the Germans are, I think, alive. The Jew can help the Young Turk with brains, business enterprise, his enormous influence in the press of Europe, and money in return for economic advantages and the eventual realisation of the ideals of Israel, while the Young Turk wants to regain and assert his national independence and get rid of the tutelage of Europe, as part of a general Asiatic revival, on lines and at a pace which must appear chauvinistic to the average Western. The Jew has supplied funds to the Young Turks and has thus acquired a hold on them; but in order to retain this hold he has to appear at least to approve and aid the Young Turk towards the accomplishment of 'national' dreams. Secrecy and elusive methods are essential to both. The Oriental Jew is an adept at manipulating occult forces, and political Freemasonry of the continental type has been chosen as the most effective bond and cloak to conceal the inner workings of the movement. It has been mentioned above that, at the outset, this new form of Masonry in Turkey 'fraternised' with the members of the British, i.e. Scottish, lodge founded in Constantinople fifty years ago, but the latter soon began to discover that the ways of the native lodges, which were mostly run by Jews, were but a travesty on and a prostitution of true Freemasonry, and eventually the Grand Lodge of Scotland pronounced them 'spurious', with the result that the English lodge closed its doors to all the new Masons, including the all-powerful Ministers Talaat Bey and Javid Bey. The latter, who control the armies of Turkey, its finances, martial law, Parliament, and, in short, the destinies of the Empire generally, naturally took umbrage at this 'rebuff from the English', as it was styled in the version which rapidly spread through the whispering galleries, and may have become a trifle less pro-British in consequence. They were described as 'furious at this insult', but there is no reason to suppose that it led them to essentially alter the friendly policy of their Cabinet towards us. We may, perhaps, also give them the benefit of the doubt, and suppose that they have little or no positive knowledge of the extreme views and policy of some members of local lodges that are in touch and sympathy with Egyptian Freemasons and working in the same subterranean way in Cairo, Alexandria, etc. For some of the ultra-chauvinistic Masons here are working in with the anti-Khedive and anti-English parties in Egypt, and an Arab deputy and Mason stated recently that he had good reason to suppose that one of their back-thoughts was, by propaganda, occasional display of the Ottoman fleet at Alexandria, to foster unrest and eventually lead up to disorders, in the course of which His Highness the Khedive would be made to disappear by the 'black hand', and a member of the Halim branch be appointed regent of the Khedive's son on the lines of the recent dynastic change in Persia. The Committee of Union and Progress undoubtedly encouraged and co-operated with the Persians in this latter event, and there is now question of starting a Persian Grand Orient, Ferrajullah Khan, the new Persian *chargé d'affaires*, having recently become a Mason. The type of chauvinistic Young Turk who holds such views is an 'Asiatic Nationalist', and, no matter how grateful he may feel to a European Government for services rendered, would consider it his 'patriotic' duty to help other Orientals 'rightly struggling to be free' in Egypt or in India, to attain their freedom from European 'bondage'. The Committee's policy is not guided by sentimental considerations, and any Power that expects gratitude for services rendered to Young Turkey would be making an egregious miscalculation.

Ismail Hakki Bey, Babanzadé, Deputy for Baghdad, and one of the Committee's experts on foreign affairs, is said to have a brother Hikmet Bey employed under Reouf Pasha in the Ottoman Agency in Cairo. Hikmet Bey appears to have doubtful dealings, mostly through some Syrians, with Mahomed Farid and other such Nationalists, despite the correct behaviour of his chief. The 'Jeune Turc', which, like some other organs in the Ottoman capital, is subventioned by the Jews, has from time to time violent anti-English articles on Egyptian affairs. One of the writers is a young Cretan, Jelal Noury by name, who is a member of the

Committee, and son of a Committee senator called Noury Bey. Another writer in the same is a renegade Pole, called Seiffeddin T. Gastowtt, who once had financial relations with Oppenheim, the German Jew well known in Cairo at the time of the Akaba incident and since. Seifiddin T. Gastowtt, with an Egyptian called Hussein Hassib, has recently started in Constantinople a Pan-Islamic organ in French and Turkish called 'La Tribune des Peuples' (in Turkish 'Kursi-i-Millel'), the avowed object of which is to awaken and arouse to a sense of their solidarity with Young Turkey Moslems the millions of 'oppressed' brethren in India, Egypt, Russia, Tunis, Algiers, etc. It declares that Europe's policy is anti-Islamic and anti-Asiatic and that Turks should put no faith in European hypocritical professions of friendship. As for England, it quotes Ahmed Riza Bey's statement: 'L'écrasement de l'Empire ottoman augmentera et consolidera sa force en Egypte et en Arabie.' Hussein Hassib Bey is a sort of delegate here of the Egyptian Nationalists, and has interested himself in getting some young Nationalists taken into Turkish schools. He has a brother working with Mahomed Farid.

What are then the likely tendencies of Young Turkey? Its representative civilians are Talaat Bey, who was a telegraph clerk in receipt of £T.3 per month, Javid Bey, Minister of Finance, who was a schoolmaster earning some £T.10 a month, and Hussein Jahid Bey, deputy and editor of the 'Tanin', who at one time translated into Turkish novels at the rate of fourpence a page for Abdul Hamid. Their natural instinct has been and is to reduce others to their own level. The Turkish element numbers some 6,000,000 in an Empire of some 30,000,000. Under a real constitutional régime, allowing a certain fair play and free play to the other elements, it would be swamped, more especially as it is inferior to the majority (Arabs, Greeks, Bulgarians, etc.), in intelligence, instruction and business qualities. It can only maintain its position as the dominant race by its fighting qualities, i.e. by the army. The capital and Parliament it dominates through martial law. The Armenians were cowed by the Adana massacres, the Greeks have been terrorised into a sullen silence, the political life of the Bulgarians was crushed by the forcible closing of their clubs and societies. So much for the potentially 'obstreperous' Christian elements. The Turkish army is now levelling the non-submissive Moslem Albanians, and the Kurds and Arabs will probably in turn undergo the same process. As the Turkish element cannot shine by intellectual or commercial achievements, its instincts lead it to display its superiority by military 'activity'. If it succeeds in reducing the Empire to mute subjection internally, its impulse will probably be to adopt an active chauvinistic policy as regards Persia, Egypt, Greece and perhaps Bulgaria. For the moment it is withheld by prudential considerations connected with the Cretan question, where it still requires the good-will of Europe to secure a favourable solution. The attainment of the latter may only whet its appetite for similar successes in Egypt, etc. But all this is dependent on European, i.e. mainly Jewish, financiers supplying it with the sums required to keep up an army which is disproportionate to its actual state of economic development. At present the Turkish constitutional régime is a sham;

but, looking into the future, how the Turkish element can maintain its supremacy by force alone under a genuine constitutional régime is almost an insoluble problem. As it is, Young Turkey regards itself as the vanguard of an awakened Asia. It fancies itself bound to protect the nascent liberties of Persia 'now endangered by the selfish and over-bearing policy of Russia and England'. Hence its policy of adventure in Western Azerbaijan and its subterranean links with Young Persian anjumans, with German efforts at intervention in Persia, as in Morocco in 1906, and with Caucasian revolutionaries. It also has affiliations with Jewish and extreme Armenian (Tashnak) revolutionaries in Russia, which it hopes to weaken and render innocuous by fostering unrest and currents of internal upheaval. It is also coquetting, assisted by the Jews, with its Hungarian brethren of Turanian origin, and tries to create a sympathetic current in Afghanistan and among Indian Moslems.

The Young Turks, partly at the inspiration of Jewish Masonry, and partly owing to the fact that French is the one European language extensively spread in the Levant, have been imitating the French Revolution and its godless and levelling methods. The developments of the French Revolution led to antagonism between England and France, and should the Turkish revolution develop on the same lines, it may find itself similarly in antagonism with British ideals and interests.

The Young Turkish policy so far has almost completely estranged Ottoman, and especially Syrian, Arabs, who, like Greeks, Bulgarians, etc., have lost all hope of the establishment of a really constitutional régime in Turkey, fear the heavy hand of the Turk, and are looking around for some rallying centre in defence of Arab interests. They hate and despise the Turk, to whom they feel themselves intellectually and culturally superior, will not submit to be turcised, and dread Sionism and Jewish invasion in Syria and Mesopotamia, but they are separated by deserts, differences of dialect, and a racial inability of cohesion, and many of them, deputies and others, secretly turn their eyes towards the Khedivate as the one 'Arab Government' which, they cherish the hope, may one day, under British auspices, exercise a centripetal effect on all Ottoman Arabs. With many this idea has taken definite shape, with others it is inchoate or semi-inchoate; but all these have no sympathy with Egyptian extreme Nationalists or their methods. Some of them suggest that the Grand Lodge of Egypt, which is recognised by British Freemasonry, should try to bring under its wing the 'spurious' Egyptian lodges of political Masons. The notion, of course, is ridiculous, and only testifies to their fallacious conception of the true principles of British Masonry, which is, of course, non-political, and presumably British recognised Masons in Egypt will have to follow the injunctions of the Grand Lodges of England and Scotland to eschew all relations with the 'spurious brethren' who merely use Masonry as a cloak for their political scheming. All the above facts and appreciations concerning our local Masonry have been obtained from Masons under the seal of confidence, but, like all secret political organisations of the kind, it is very elusive and tends to bury itself deeper if it suspects that its secrets are being discovered, and I would therefore beg that this document be treated as strictly secret. Most of it interests Cairo, and I suppose you will forward it confidentially to Gorst. It might also be expedient to similarly communicate it to Tehran and, perhaps, the Government of India. For if the prominent Indian Moslems were discreetly given to understand that the Young Turkey movement is seriously influenced by Jewish and atheistic political Freemasonry, the effect would be to counteract any potentially anti-British national Pan-Islamic propaganda carried on by extreme chauvinist Young Turks.

I have reason to believe that my German colleague is aware of the extent to which Jewish and Latin Masonry inspires the Committee, and that he has confidentially kept his Government informed as to this feature of Young Turkey politics.

Yours very sincerely,

GERARD LOWTHER.

P.S.–It has been said above that the Grand Lodge of Scotland refused to recognise the new 'Grand Orient Ottoman', whose Masonry it pronounced 'spurious'; but I learn that efforts are being made to indirectly get round this difficulty by inducing the Grand Lodge of England to recognise the new Turkish creation. In view of the curious developments in Egyptian Masonry, it would seem desirable that the Grand Lodge of England should follow the example of its Scotch sister and refuse its imprimatur to an institution so coloured by politics.

NOTES

1. Quoted from the memoirs of Ali Fuad Turkgeldi by B. Lewis, in *Bulletin of the School of Oriental and African Studies*, vol. XXIII, 1960, p. 147.
2. Gwendolen Cecil, *Life of Robert Marquis of Salisbury*, vol. II, 1921, p. 320.
3. See, for instance, Cromer's report of a conversation in 1896 with Baron Calice, the Austrian Internuncio at Constantinople. Discussing British policy towards the Ottoman Empire, Cromer declared that there had been a change in public opinion of late years. 'More especially,' he added, 'since we had been in occupation of Egypt, many influential newspapers had urged that excluding the Russians from Constantinople was a matter of less importance to England than to Austria.' Cromer to Salisbury, Cairo, 2 December 1896, Public Record Office F.O. 633/6 (Cromer Papers), no. 267.
4. Salisbury, to the Duke of Rutland, quoted in E. Kedourie, *England and the Middle East*, 1956, p. 21.
5. Kedourie, *op cit.*, p. 33.
6. F.O. 800/193B (Lowther Papers). Lowther to Nicolson, 5 May 1911, enclosing a memorandum by Fitzmaurice; see also in F.O. 800/193B a letter of 26 April previous, same to same, also in defence of Fitzmaurice.
7. F.O. 800/193B (Losther Papers), Lowther to Hardinge, 6 July 1909.
8. F.O. 800/80 (Grey Papers), Fitzmaurice to Tyrrell, 5 November 1912.
9. Hardinge Papers, vol. 20, pp. 230 and 235, Cambridge University Library, Lowther to Hardinge, 19 April and 27 April 1910. *The Nineteenth Century* had just published an article on French freemasonry; see Appendix.

10. F.O. 800/193B (Lowther Papers), Lowther to Nicolson, 13 March 1913.
11. There is little doubt that the details in Lowther's letter were supplied by Fitzmaurice. There is great resemblance between it and Fitzmaurice's memorandum of 1911 mentioned above, in F.O. 800/193B.
12. Hardinge to Lowther, 'Private and Confidential', 26 June 1910. F.O. 800/193A. With this letter was included a printed copy of Lowther's letter of 29 May. It is this copy which is reproduced in the Appendix. Lowther's original does not figure in the Hardinge Papers. Lowther copied his letters to Hardinge and Nicolson in a series of notebooks (F.O. 800/193B), but a copy of this letter does not figure in these notebooks. This may confirm the suspicion that it was not so much a genuine private letter from Lowther to Hardinge, as a report written by Fitzmaurice and couched in the form of a private letter from the ambassador to the permanent under-secretary. In his memoirs, Hardinge wrote: 'Turkey, under a Parliamentary Government, required a strong and judicious hand to control its policy, but it was the Army under the direction of a corrupt Committee of Jews and aliens that dominated the situation'. *Old Diplomacy*, 1947, p. 175.
13. Allan Cunningham, 'The Wrong Horse?—A Study of Anglo-Turkish Relations before the First World War' in *St Antony's Papers*, no. 17, 1965, p. 75.
14. The fourth, doubtful, name was that of Yusuf Sakakini, also mentioned in Lowther's letter. It is curious that an intelligence bulletin written in Cairo should be so ignorant as not to know that Sakakini in fact belonged to a Syrian Christian family long settled in Egypt. The *Bulletin* describes him as 'a French protected subject of most uncertain origin, but probably a Syrian Jew, resident at Alexandria, who had lived by exploiting Freemasonry, in various parts of the Levant, and, by rendering a variety of mysterious services to the then Khedive for whom he spied, to Aziz Pasha Hassan, an Egyptian Prince of Prusso-Turkish morals . . . and other notables'.
15. F.O. 882/25, Arab Bulletin, no. 23; the passages cited above are at pp. 294–6 and 298.
16. Wingate Papers, Sudan Archives, School of Oriental Studies, Durham University, 139/1. It is also perhaps worth noticing that the Judeo-masonic character of the Young Turks is touched on in one of the handbooks prepared in the Historical Section of the Foreign Office for the use of the British Delegates to the Peace Conference and subsequently published. The handbook on *Mohammedan History* (1920), declares, p. 57; 'That the Committee of Union and Progress could be in earnest in its Pan-Islamic policy has been denied on various grounds. In the first place it has been pointed out that the leaders of that Committee are, without exception, Freemasons; and such religious fanaticism conflicts with the principles of the Masonic Society . . .'; and again on p. 80: 'The Salonika Jews are inseparable from the Committee of Union and Progress.' The author of the first assertion was Sir Thomas Arnold and of the second Arnold J. Toynbee; see list established by Professor G. W. Prothero, the editor of the handbooks, F.O. 370/245 L455 and L959/14/405. A recent author, Professor Z. N. Zeine, seems to accept the truth of these and similar assertions. He also compounds his error by also affirming, on his own account, that 'The Arab Muslim leaders doubted the sincerity of the Committee of Union and Progress' because of these alleged Jewish and masonic connections. There is no evidence for such an affirmation; see *The Emergence of Arab Nationalism* (Beirut, 1966), p. 89.

17. The Jews of Baghdad in 1910

The world evoked by Sir Gerard Lowther's letter on the Young
Turks, the Freemasons and the Jews, and by Sir Mark Sykes' letter
on Zionism is a world of fantasy, incompatible, surely, with the
practical concerns of diplomacy and foreign policy. But bizarre as
these ideas may seem to us, yet they were taken very seriously by
those who propounded, and those who listened to, them. One
wonders if they thought of comparing these imaginings about the
occult power of Jewry with the activities and the way of life of actual
Jews. Did Lowther and Fitzmaurice, for instance, read the solid
'Account of the Jewish Community at Baghdad', which the consul-
general in Baghdad sent them in February 1910? And did they ask
themselves if the picture it drew of this large and active community
was in any way to be reconciled with the lurid fictions which they
were then compiling?

The 'Account', which J. G. Lorimer annotated and enclosed with
his despatch of 27 February 1910,[1] was signed H.D.S. The initials
seem to refer to Haron Da'ud Shohet, then employed as a dragoman
at the British consulate-general. The report has a claim to our
attention because it comes to us under the auspices of the learned
Lorimer (author of the *Persian Gulf Gazetteer*), because it brings
together details which are not easily, if at all, available in any
other source, and because it constitutes an inside view, intelligent and
well-informed of this community at that point in its history. In
short, the report provides an instructive and striking contrast
between the sober sense of reality of the humble native dragoman,
and the wild flights of the august ambassador's fancies. It is reproduced in an appendix below.

A few salient points are worth noticing. Shohet shows how
marginal a position the religious leadership of the community had
come to occupy: the Chief Rabbi, he says, is 'simply a mouth-
piece', a 'mere puppet'. The rabbinate, whom he calls 'the clergy',
'enjoy no influence over their co-religionists'. The writer is aware
that this constitutes a change from what used to be the case, and
that the change is an outcome of the educational activities of the
Alliance israélite universelle. These had begun in the eighteen-sixties
and, steadily expanding for half a century or so, had gradually—
though not without encountering some resistance[2]—propagated a
secular outlook within large and influential sections of the community.

It is also to those educational activities that Shohet attributes the
growing prosperity of the community. The education provided by
the *Alliance* made the Jews of Baghdad open to the outside world,
and enabled them, earlier than the Muslims or the Christians, to
take advantage of Mesopotamia increasingly becoming drawn into
the world economy. The methods of education introduced by the
Alliance were inspired by French pedagogical doctrine and practice,
and seem to have been from the outset extraordinarily efficient.
Within a decade or so after its establishment, the *Alliance* school was
attracting favourable comment. Grattan Geary, editor of *The Times
of India* who visited Baghdad in 1878, wrote that instruction in this
school was 'of the best modern kind. Arabic is the mother tongue
of the Baghdad Jews, and the pupils are taught how to write and
speak that language grammatically. They are also taught Hebrew,
Turkish and French; within the last few months English has been
added to the curriculum. . . . I went to the school to be present at
the final examination of the boys in English. . . . Many of them
spoke and read English with wonderful fluency, and some of them
wrote to dictation without an error of spelling or punctuation. Most
of them had been learning French before they began the study of
English, and they all declared that their knowledge of French greatly
helped them in acquiring our more difficult tongue. . . . They speak
French with singular purity of accent and expression.'[3]

Important as the role of the *Alliance* was, yet it would seem that
the Jews of Baghdad had other channels by which to become
acquainted with the outside world. Gobineau remarks, in *Les
religions et les philosophies dans l'Asie centrale* which was published
in 1865, that Hebrew books were what European presses had most
exported to Asia in the preceding hundred years. Once made, the
remark is at once seen to be true and indeed obvious. During this
period there was very little acquaintance in the middle east with
European languages, and publications in Arabic, Persian and
Turkish on other than religious subjects were very scant. During the
same period, what has been called the Jewish Enlightenment was in
full flood in Europe, and some of the large number of Hebrew
publications produced by this Enlightenment must have made their
way into the Ottoman empire and Persia along with the prayer books
and the traditional religious works which constituted, no doubt, the
bulk of what was imported. Gobineau himself records how astonished
he was to find a Jew in the depths of Persia speaking of Spinoza
with admiration and asking for details regarding Kant's doctrine.
Gobineau adds: 'Ces noms, ces idées, des lueurs d'autres idées
qu'on devrait leur supposer inconnues arrivent jusqu'à eux dans les
ouvrages qu'ils font venir surtout d'Allemagne et dont l'entrepôt est

Baghdad.'[4] It so happens that as regards Baghdad itself, Gobineau's observation finds support from another source. The Austrian Jew, Jacob Obermeyer, who lived in Baghdad from 1869 to 1880, has reported that the periodicals *ha-Lebanon*, published at Mainz, and *ha-Magid*, published at Koenigsberg, were both known in the city, and that the latter, a weekly, actually had some twenty subscribers and was read by hundreds of Baghdadi Jews. Both periodicals were solid, serious publications which aimed at promoting among their readers an informed opinion about the main issues of the age, whether religious or secular.[5]

It is no doubt this wide, and gradually widening, experience of the outside world, together with their connexions in India, the far east, Manchester and Vienna, established over half a century or so, which made the Jews of Baghdad into the active and dynamic community which Shohet portrays. In the covering despatch transmitting his dragoman's report, Lorimer declared that: 'There can be little doubt that, given political freedom (if not political equality) and economic development, the intelligent and energetic Jews of this province will play an important part in the future of the Turkish Empire.' Events were soon to falsify this prophecy, and some forty years after these words were written, the Jews of Baghdad, caught in a crossfire of political messianisms (both simultaneously promoted by the consul-general's government), were destroyed as a community. Shohet's report indicates how far such messianisms were from their political outlook and experience, how little interested indeed they were in politics. The community, he says in his last paragraph, 'is anxious to co-operate with the Government for the improvement of the country, if only the Government gain their confidence. It may be said that some of the Jews are sceptical about the future and do not believe much in the so-called "convalescence" of the "Sick Man".' This business-like and sceptical attitude to government and politics characterized their leaders and spokesmen to the very last. Two notable instances of this attitude are worth giving. The first occurs in a letter of September 1922 to the Zionist Organization written by Menahem Salih Daniel, a very large landowner, and one of the notables mentioned in Shohet's report. The letter discusses Zionist activities in Baghdad and describes the ferment which they had created in the poorer classes: 'We have had, since Dr. Bension's arrival to this country [as a Zionist emissary], a sad experience of the regrettable effects which an influx of Zionist ideas here may have. There was for some time a wild outburst of popular feelings towards Zionism, which expressed itself by noisy manifestations of sympathy crowded gatherings and a general and vague impression among the lower class that Zionism was going to end the worries of life, and that no restraint was any longer necessary in the way of expressing opinions or showing scorn to the Arabs. This feeling it is needless to say', the writer goes on to say, 'was altogether unenlightened. It was more Messianic than Zionistic. To an observer it was merely the reaction of a subdued race, which for a moment thought that by magic the tables were turned and that it [was] to become an overlord. ... In this state of raving the Jews could not fail to occasion a friction with the Moslem, specially as the latter were then high up in nationalist effervescence, and a feeling of surprise and dissatisfaction ensued. . . .' 'The Jews', Menahem Daniel went on to warn, 'are already acting with culpable indifference about public and political affairs, and if they espouse so publicly and tactlessly as they have done lately, a cause which is regarded by the Arabs not only as foreign but as actually hostile, I have no doubt that they will succeed in making of themselves a totally alien element in this country and as such they will have great difficulty in defending a position, which ... is on other grounds already too enviable.'[6] With perspicacious wisdom this letter foresees the danger to its author's community posed by the style of politics which Zionism and Arabism shared in equal measure, a danger rendered all the more deadly by the indifference about public and political affairs which, as he correctly observes, was a characteristic of the Baghdad Jews.

Widespread though this was, yet as his letter shows, Menahem Daniel himself did not share it. Another notable exception was a prominent Baghdadi lawyer, Yusuf Elkabir. It is, again, of interest to quote from a letter of his published in *The Iraq Times* in November 1938. The letter comments on a report that a number of U.S. senators, representatives and governors had signed a petition in favour of the Jewish National Home in Palestine. Elkabir declares that the problem which the Balfour declaration purported to solve, 'is, and remains, a European problem both by origin and present incidence'. The declaration was 'a very risky piece of political acrobatics', a scheme 'founded on a manifestly unworkable partnership'. And in the course of discussing the difficulties which Zionism was bound to encounter in Palestine, Elkabir puts his finger on the absurdities of nationalist argument. He comments on the idea that Jews are entitled to Palestine now because two thousand years ago the country was theirs: 'Reconstructions of historical geography, if accepted as a practical theory,' he writes, 'would for instance bring the case for Ulster to the ground, and provide a recognized legal basis for German claims on Eastern Europe. In a certain influential section of the German press the theory is now being held out that Eastern Europe, up to the Volga, was in some remote time wholly occupied by Germans. If the legal basis for a reoccupation is conceded, there will remain nothing but to work out history in detail for a suitable epoch, and everyone knows that modern science can do anything. Moreover, if one goes reconstituting history two thousand years back, there is no reason why one should not go still farther back, say four or five thousand years, and presently have the world ruled by militant archaeology.'[7] Though in its shrewd grasp of the implications of an unfamiliar political rhetoric it is certainly uncharacteristic, yet the letter is representative of that sobriety and common sense which Shohet's report mirrors, and which were to prove of no avail against the political fantasies and fanaticisms into addiction to which modern Europe has seduced the rest of the world.

APPENDIX

ACCOUNT OF THE JEWISH COMMUNITY AT BAGHDAD

The Jewish community at Baghdad is, after that of Salonica, the most numerous, important, and prosperous in Turkey. According to a revised census made by the authorities about two years ago, the Jews here number about 35,000; but in well-informed circles the belief is held that they are as many as 50,000. In their last reports the *Alliance Israelite Universelle*, in Paris, and the Anglo-Jewish Association have attributed to this community a total of 45,000 souls.*

The Jews may roughly be divded into four classes viz.:

(1) A rich and well-off class, consisting almost entirely of merchants and bankers, 5 per cent;

(2) A middle class, consisting of petty traders, retail dealers, employees, etc., 30 per cent;

(3) A poor class, 60 per cent; and

(4) Beggars, 5 per cent.

Most of the professional beggars come from Kirkuk, Musal, and their environs in a very miserable condition.

The community is headed by a Chief Rabbi who is, as a rule, provided with a Farman from the sultan. He can be removed by the Jewish community at Baghdad through the Chief Rabbinate at Constantinople, as he draws his salary from the Treasury of the Baghdad community. He is not under the orders of the Chief Rabbi at Constantinople; but, in special cases, he applies to him for help. He attests documents and keeps an eye on Hebrew education. He is the medium of correspondence between the Turkish authorities and the community.

* In a despatch, no. 5 of 24 January 1904, the French Vice-Consul at Baghdad estimated that the Jews of Baghdad numbered 40,000, out of 60,000 in the whole vilayet; they constitute, he wrote, 'la communauté de beaucoup la plus nombreuse, la plus riche et la plus laborieuse'. Correspondance politique, Turquie, N[ouvelle] S[érie], vol. 137—E.K.

This is merely a matter of form: the Chief Rabbi is simply a mouth-piece. He exercises no real influence over either the Turkish authorities or the members of his own community.

There is an Ecclesiastical or Religious council, composed of three Rabbis, to settle purely religious disputes. Some other Rabbis teach Hebrew literature and are paid by the community. The council and the educational Rabbis are not connected with the Chief Rabbinate; but, in special cases where authoritative help is required, they apply to it for assistance.

In contradistinction to past days, the clergy enjoy no influence over their co-religionists, and this may confidently be ascribed to the effect of education diffused among the classes of the community.

The chief and really influential personages in the community are the following who belong to the richest class: Mir Elias, a stock-holder: M. Daniel,* a land-holder; Joseph Shemtob, banker; Shaool Hakham Ezkell, merchant; Hiskel Yehooda, merchant; Yehuda Zeloof, merchant; Shaoul Shaashoua, banker, merchant and land owner; and Sion Aboodi, money-lender. It is these persons who discuss measures together in cases of emergency, and who form deputations in important questions, to the Wali and other high officials. The Chief Rabbi is under the influence of these persons, and is, so to speak, a mere puppet in their hands. Two of them, viz.: Mir Elias and M. Daniel, are liberal in money matters; and all are intelligent, tactful, and energetic.

The Jews are particularly interested in trade. They have literally monopolized the local trade, and neither Muhammadans nor Christians can compete with them. Even the few leading Muhammadan merchants owe their prosperity to the capable and industrious Jews whom they have for years employed as clerks. The Jewish clerks are practically the managers of their firms.

The chief item of Jewish trade is Manchester piece-goods and the local merchants have amassed riches by importing these goods from Manchester and exporting them to Persia.

In Manchester and London there are over 20 Jewish firms belonging to Baghdad, and there are a similar number at Kirmanshah and Hamadan in Persia.

The Jews† also trade in groceries, drugs, iron, coffee, tin, loaf sugar, soft sugar, copper, and the like. A trade by the Jews in haberdashery, with Germany and Austria, is gradually increasing.

There is a large export by them of wool, skins, gum, carpets, etc. Owing to the aggressive nature of the Arab tribes, to lack of protection on the part of the Government, and to various other reasons, the Jews as a body have never speculated in land. The only real land holders are Mr. M. Daniel and other members of his family. Their holdings are said to be worth about £T. 400,000.

* This is Mr. Manahim Salih Daniel, mentioned in my monthly summary for December/January 1909–10, and my tour report No. 1 of 1909.—J.G.L.

† The principal dealers in precious stones and jewellery and the leading gold and silversmiths are Jews.—J.G.L.

Shaool Shaashoua, Ezra Daood, Asher Salem, Joseph Shemtob and Eliahoo Danoos own real estate* at Baghdad, Basrah, and Karbala. The three first named own certain lands also in the suburbs of Baghdad. Ezra Waddan at Hillah, is said to hold large rural property in that district.

It is a well-known fact that the emancipation of the Jews in Baghdad, their prosperity, and the development of their trade are mainly due to the very generous work done in this city by the *Alliance Israélite Universelle* during the last 45 years. The *Alliance* has three flourishing† schools for boys and a fourth for girls. Mr. Kadoori in Shanghai, who is himself a native of Baghdad, and is deeply interested in the education of the Jewish girls here, has purchased a site on which he is building, at his own expense, a school which will accommodate 1,000 pupils and will be fitted up with every modern improvement. The total cost to this gentleman will, it is estimated, not fall short of £T 10,000.

The schools have always been managed by capable and energetic representatives. They are admitted to be the best schools in Baghdad. The community owns and supports a large Hebrew school (or Midrash) containing about 2,000 pupils, all poor.

Since the declaration of the constitution, the Jews have not failed to give signal proofs of their tendency towards education and progress. Mr. M. S. Daniel some time ago moved the *Alliance* to open an Infant School, offering at the same time to provide a building and contribute the fixed sum of one hundred Lires per annum. This School has been open for the last five months and is in excellent condition.

Mir Elias, the most generous member that the Jewish community has ever had, is making a fine hospital at the north gate for poor Jews, to which Christians and Muhammadans will also be admitted. The cost will not be less than £T 5,000.

Seven Jews of the rising generation have lately formed a committee and started a school for Turkish instruction. The subjects are the same as in the government Military school. The idea is (1) to diffuse Turkish among the young, and (2) to qualify them for superior military service, thus enabling them to obtain positions as officers and not merely to serve as rank and file. This "Mutual Help School" (تعون مكتبي) is partly supported by the community and partly by voluntary contributions, and it is managed by the said Committee. It has been open for a month and promises very well.

Six or seven small houses at the east gate have lately been purchased by some of the rich Jews, which are to be reconstructed as a large Hebrew school for the poor. Mir Elias, already mentioned, is going to build this school at his own expense. The total cost will be £T 3,000 at least.

The community has a Council known as the 'Majlis-al-Jismani',

* The general impression that the price of property near Baghdad will rise rapidly is leading many Jews to invest in land suitable for building in the vicinity. —J.G.L.

† The only native schools at Baghdad in which English is seriously taught are those managed by the Jews.—J.G.L.

composed of ten unpaid members with a paid secretary, the members being elected for a period of three years.

The Communal Council levies taxes and directs the expenditure of the proceeds of the same.

A large tax on meat has *ab antiquo* been enforced. The tax was a few years ago recognized by the Turkish Authorities at Constantinople and is known as the Gabelle. The origin of this tax is that sheep, after being slaughtered, must be examined by trained persons (Shohets) who are provided with certificate from the Ecclesiastical Authorities. The Shohets are paid by the community.

The following is an approximate statement of the proceeds of internal taxation in the Jewish community and of how the money collected is expended.

Receipts

	£T
Gabelle	2,650
Tax on Intestines	800
Fees for verification of signatures etc. . . .	100
Marriage fees	180
Total:	3,730

Expenditure

	£T
Yearly contribution towards the new hospital mentioned above	500
Yearly contribution towards the *Alliance* School .	366
Yearly contribution towards the new Turkish School	200
Chief and other Rabbis salaries ⎫	
Slaughterers and other employees ⎬ . . .	1,900
The Hebrew School ⎭	
Dispensary for poor Jews	380
Help to other communities	185
Miscellaneous	200
Total:	3,730

The Jews are very ambitious, hard-working, capable, and economical. They are also very cunning, timid, and tactful. They are becoming richer day by day; and, as a result of education, a great many of them now understand that happiness in life does not only consist in massing money, but also in living well in the meantime. They have taken a fancy to the Christian quarter of the city because it is comparatively clean and airy. They are enormously increasing the rents in that quarter and are literally turning out old Christian tenants, who cannot cope with them from a financial standpoint.

In the Christian quarter a pretty good house cannot be had now for less than 40 liras a year. This exorbitance of rents is due solely to the

Jews, and it is a source of annoyance to the Christians. The Jews have distanced and out-done the Christians in education, standard of living, etc. The community is full of initiative, especially the younger generation. The Jews on the whole are practical people; their ideal is to work hard and make money. They are awaiting with breathless impatience, the result of Sir William Willcocks' inspection, because they hope that Baghdad will soon acquire increased importance from the irrigation works and the projected railway line across the Syrian desert. They think that Baghdad will soon be a very important centre of commerce and residence, and that they will then be able to throw themselves into a stream of speculations.

The Jews of Baghdad are no longer persecuted and despised. They are now placed on the same footing as the Muhammadans and the Christians.

The Turkish Government fully realize that the Jews are one of the chief elements in the progress of the country. The Turks have all along regarded the Jews as very faithful subjects of the Sultan and have placed confidence in them. On the other hand the Jews of Baghdad have borne feeling of gratitude towards the Turkish government ever since the immigration* of their co-religionists from Spain into Asia Minor some hundreds of years ago. The community is anxious to co-operate with the government for the improvement of the country, if only the government gain their confidence. It may be said that some of the Jews are sceptical about the future and do not believe much in the so-called 'convalescence' of the 'Sick Man'.

Baghdad   H. D. S.
17 February 1910

NOTES

1. F.O. 195/2338, file 79. The report also figures in the foreign office confidential print, F.O. 424/223, no. 4.
2. See 'The Alliance Israélite Universelle 1860–1960' above.
3. Grattan Geary, *Through Asiatic Turkey*, 1878, pp. 132–5. Geary also mentions the opposition which the *Alliance* initially encountered. When the school was first founded in 1864, he reports, 'great difficulties were encountered amongst the conservative Jews of the place, who imagined that the faith of Abraham might suffer if new-fangled notions were introduced from Frangistan. Few pupils could be got together, and the whole affair was so disheartening that the principals of the school were constantly giving up the task in disgust.'
4. *Op. cit.*, p. 65.
5. Jacob Obermeyer, *Modernes Judentum im Morgen und Abendland*, Vienna and Leipzig, 1907, pp. 43–4. I am much obliged to Mr. Emile Marmorstein for drawing my attention to this source.

* I am informed that the greater number of the Jews of Baghdad are supposed to be descended from those of the Captivity; but there has also been considerable immigration of Jews from Persia, and the Arabic spoken by the Jews here contains a number of Persian words. Baghdad was Persian in the seventeenth century. There has also been some immigrations of Jews from Syria.—J.G.L.

6. The letter is printed as an appendix in Hayyim Cohen, *ha-Pe'iluth ha-sionith be-'Iraq* (Zionist Activity in Iraq), Jerusalem 1969, pp. 237–40.
7. Letter in *The Iraq Times*, 5 November 1938, enclosed in U.S. minister's despatch no. 1180, Baghdad, 25 November, National Archives, Washington, Department of State records 867 N. 01/1346.

18. Wavell and Iraq, April–May 1941

It is a matter of great regret that Mr. Connell's untimely death means that we shall not see a sequel from his hand to this first volume of Wavell's biography.* An earlier military biography, *Auchinleck*, published in 1959, showed Mr. Connell's great talent for this genre and the present volume confirms and enhances his reputation. Its qualities are great lucidity in narration, a mastery of the political and military issues involved, and a generous but apposite and discriminating quotation from the Wavell Papers which form the basis of this work.

Field Marshal Lord Wavell (1883–1950) was, as this biography well establishes, a great military leader, brilliant in his grasp of strategy and fecund in stratagems; Rommel hardly exaggerated when he said that he 'showed a touch of genius.' Wavell's reputation as a commander was made in the middle east, and this book is therefore necessarily much concerned with the campaigns in the western desert, Greece and Crete and with their political aspects. But Wavell's connexion with the middle east dates not from the second but from the first world war. In the summer of 1917, while a brevet lieutenant-colonel, he was appointed to act as liaison officer between the C.I.G.S. in London and Allenby, who had just assumed command of the Egyptian Expeditionary Force. He was later to write a notable biography of Allenby and a classic analysis of his campaign in Palestine. Before taking up this appointment he had been for a few months British military representative on the staff of the Grand Duke Nicholas, governor and commander-in-chief in the Caucasus. A minor incident which took place during Wavell's time in Tiflis and which throws some light on Allied strategy and politics is recounted by Mr. Connell (p. 117). At the beginning of 1917 General Maude was mounting an assault on Ottoman positions in Mesopotamia and was expected shortly to capture Baghdad. Wavell was asked to request the Russians to advance simultaneously on Mosul. Now by the terms of the Sykes–Picot agreement Mosul had been assigned to France, who would thus constitute a buffer between the British and the Russian empires. Unwittingly or not, therefore, this request—to which the Russians could not in the end respond—meant abandonment by the British government of a particularly important consideration which had governed its proposals for the partition of Ottoman territories. The French liaison officer in

* *Wavell Scholar and Soldier: To June 1941*, by John Connell.

273

Tiflis received similar instructions; he, however, sought to ensure that the French flag would fly over Mosul on its capture, but 'Wavell knew that the very idea would be fatal to any hopes of inducing the Russians to advance. Pretending complete ignorance of the Sykes–Picot agreement, he refused to back Chardigny on this point.'

Wavell was next involved in middle-eastern affairs when for a short period, from September 1937 to March 1938, he commanded British troops in Palestine. His predecessor in this command was Sir John Dill and Mr. Connell prints (p. 188) a most interesting letter which he sent to Wavell in October 1936, when the Arab rebellion was not yet far advanced. In this letter Dill expresses his great disagreement with the policies of Wauchope, the high commissioner, who opposed the declaration of martial law and who believed that the mufti of Jerusalem meant to give up armed resistance when he responded for a time to the appeal of the Arab kings: the peace, wrote Dill, was only an armed truce and furthermore it was 'a fatal error' to bring in the Arab kings: 'From henceforth they will consider themselves entitled to a say in Palestinian affairs. Moreover they prevented the declaration of Martial Law, because we obviously could not act while the conversations, which we had encouraged, were going on. And so the [Palestinian] Arab leaders slipped out with honour and renown instead of being scattered to the four winds.' Dill's verdict on Wauchope's handling of the rebellion was severe: 'As I see it,' the letter ended, 'Arthur Wauchope loves greatly, administers with knowledge and imagination, but he does not rule.' The attitude of the Palestine administration to the mufti a year later, when Wavell was in command, was much the same. Wavell, it seems, wished to arrest the mufti, who had taken refuge in the temple area; he also had plans for kidnapping him, which were not allowed for fear of provoking a disturbance in the mosque. The administration seemed here to be taking the right of sanctuary in a mosque more seriously than Sunni divines or rulers have usually been disposed to, seemed indeed to be equating it to the established right of *bast* which obtains in Shi'ism. But, whatever his disagreement with the administration on this issue, Wavell's attitude to the disturbances was not the same as Dill's. Whether this was because the situation in 1937–8 when he held command was different from that of 1936 or for some other reason, Wavell refused, in spite of urging both by the Government in London and by the Palestine Administration, to proclaim martial law. His biographer states (p. 193) that he considered the troops at his disposal insufficient for the maintenance of effective control and the administration of martial law. Instead he set up a system of military courts and increased the penalties for offences connected with the rebellion. It does not seem that this policy met with much success.

Wavell was opposed to Zionism and disliked British support for it. 'He believed, too,' Mr. Connell writes (pp. 189–90), 'that the fulfilment of Zionist aspirations would lead to trouble in the Middle East and—since it was the one subject on which all Arabs were united—would focus antagonism against Britain throughout the region.' When he became commander-in-chief, middle east, he remained firm in the conviction 'that every response to Zionist aims and aspirations, every acceptance of Jewish offers to help in the war effort, would jab and inflame Arab resentment.' (p. 255). This anti-Zionism is, of course, in itself nothing remarkable or eccentric, since it is perfectly reasonable to believe that the Balfour declaration policy was for Great Britain unwise and harmful. The anti-Zionism is rather worthy of notice because it led Wavell and the multitude of British officials who shared these opinions to take up other positions which anti-Zionism by no means logically or necessarily entailed. There has grown a whole literature in English about British policy in the middle east since the first world war, which is irredeemably mediocre, the mediocrity of which resides mostly in the fact that it attributes to the conflict between the Zionists and the Palestinians an exorbitant importance in explaining the tangled and tortuous rela- tions between Arab States in this period, as well as every reverse to the British position in the middle east and its ultimate and total ruin. The literature may be dismissed as of little lasting consequence or value, as so much *littérature*, the production of foolish academics and excitable journalists. What is of much more consequence is that these views were, in their time, widely current among officials and politicians. What these views are may be illustrated from a minute by Churchill written in 1941. We learn from Mr. Connell (p. 264) that in August 1940 Churchill broached to Wavell the idea of arming the Jews of Palestine for their defence and that Wavell's answer was 'courteously and firmly negative.' Churchill's minute which he publishes in his memoirs (*The Second World War*, III, p. 658) was addressed to the Colonial Secretary and dated 1 March 1941. It seems to deal with a telegram from Wavell objecting to the project of a Jewish army, containing arguments which Churchill dismissed as 'all this stuff'. What they were may be surmised from the first paragraph of the minute: 'General Wavell,' wrote Churchill, 'like most British military officers, is strongly pro-Arab. At the time of the licences to the shipwrecked illegal immigrants being permitted he sent a telegram no less strong than this, predicting widespread disaster in the Arab world, together with the loss of the Basra-Baghdad-Haifa route.' We may then say that Wavell allowed his anti-Zionism to have a by no means necessary corollary, namely pro-Arabism, and that this pro-Arabism led him to harbour the fallacy that there was a monolithic 'Arab world' which moved in unison and which, if crossed, was likely to rise in fearful and irresistible wrath. As will be seen, this fallacy governed in large measure his appreciation of the Iraqi situation in April and May 1941. He was of course not alone in holding such views, but it is curious that an intellect so powerful and commanding in military affairs should betray such poor judgement in politics; in this, however, he was exactly like Allenby, whom he so much admired.

Wavell was appointed commander-in-chief, middle east, in the summer of 1939 and reached Cairo on 2 August. He was to remain Commander for two eventful years, until at the end of June 1941 Churchill, having lost confidence in him, replaced him by Auchinleck. One of the most important reasons for this loss of confidence was the manner in which Wavell tried to tackle the Iraqi affair. In the present work and in *Auchinleck*, Mr. Connell has printed a wealth of documents which, taken together with the material found in Churchill's memoirs, enable us to form a reasonably full picture of the evolution of British policy towards Rashid Ali's régime.

In considering Wavell's reaction to the Iraqi events, we have to bear in mind that one of his great qualities as a military commander was a wary caution, a refusal to be distracted from his main objective, a dislike for committing his forces unless he could be sure of dealing the enemy a decisive blow. These qualities appear in his attitude to the French authorities in Syria in the summer of 1940 immediately after the French collapse. The foreign office had urged him to encourage Frenchmen to cross over from Syria to British-controlled territories, but he resisted this pressure: 'My view,' he wrote, 'was that I wanted a stable and neutral Syria on my northern flank, in view of my general weakness; and that to disrupt it by removing large numbers of the best French officers would be bad policy' (p. 241). We must also remember that in the spring of 1941, what with the reverses in Greece and the western desert, his position was quite perilous. It is therefore easy to understand that he should have been strenuously opposed, on purely military grounds, to a new commitment in Iraq. But, as we see from the documents, the military objections were buttressed and themselves made to seem more imposing than in the event they proved to be, by other weighty-sounding and awesome political objections. In *Auchinleck* Mr. Connell had argued that these political objections were being canvassed by the proliferating Arab experts in Cairo who were saying that it was highly dangerous to take any step, political or military, which would hurt Arab interests or offend, however briefly, what they described as Arab public opinion, and thus result in a 'general Arab uprising'; that Wavell shared neither the fears nor the pre-judices of these experts, but merely allowed himself to use their arguments to support his purely military objections. In *Wavell* the matter is somewhat differently put: aware of his military weakness, Mr. Connell here says, Wavell strove to discover a political solution to the Iraqi issue, a solution desired and 'energetically canvassed' by middle-east experts in both London and Cairo. But nothing much turns in practice on this particular point. Whether he used the experts' opinions as a matter of convenience in order to impress Churchill, or whether he himself actually shared their views—as was more likely—Wavell and no one else was responsible for the appreciations and recommendations he was sending to London.

What, in any case, were the military reasons which made him dislike intervention in Iraq? The most obvious one was that he was overstretched, but there was also something else, as appears from a telegram he sent to the C.I.G.S. on 25 May. 'My task, defence of Egypt and Palestine,' he wrote, 'would be made more difficult but would not be greatly jeopardised by hostile control of Iraq, whereas hostile control of Syria would affect me more closely and danger-ously... India on the other hand regards Iraq as absolutely vital outpost of their defence...' (p. 444). Coming from a commander of Wavell's stature, this is a most curious document. It seems incredible that he should have believed that axis control of Iraq would not have made axis control of Syria—administered as it was by Vichy—highly likely, and even more remarkable that he should make so clear-cut a distinction between what might affect his Command and what might affect India—he who was among the first to under-stand and practise the war of movement. It would seem then in this Iraqi question Wavell's military judgement faltered, and if as Churchill said, war is a contest of wills, we may detect here a weakening in Wavell's will to confront and attack the enemy wherever he manifested himself. This weakening was corrected by the prime minister's aggressive and urgent prodding, and in words quoted by his biographer (p. 446) Wavell recognized that Churchill had been right.

But specious arguments are heard from time to time to the effect that Churchill need not have pressed Wavell to occupy Iraq since Hitler in the spring of 1941 was busy with the coming invasion of Russia, and the German danger in Iraq was therefore illusory. To this the short answer is that Churchill's policy eliminated once and for all any possibility of German intervention then or later, and as Churchill said to Boothby: 'If you back a winner it doesn't really matter much what your reasons were at the time.' But further observations are in order. As Wavell later stated, it was not known in the early months of 1941 that Hitler would attack Russia. Wavell himself believed that the Germans would most likely concentrate on the middle east (p. 330). To argue that Churchill need have done nothing about Iraq in April and May because Russia was going to be invaded in June is to argue from hindsight, and a rather imperfect hindsight at that. For the invasion of Russia need not have prevented the Germans from exploiting any favourable openings in the middle east. Hitler's directive no. 30, dated 23 May 1941, when his decision to invade Russia was already irrevocable, states: 'I have decided to push the development of operations in the Middle East through the medium of going to the support of Iraq.' Again, it is well-known that Hitler had been very cautious and rather reluctant to be involved in north Africa, and that it was Rommel's military genius which in a twinkling transformed a limited operation in support of Italy into a deadly threat to the British position in the whole middle east. How can the possibility of another Rommel be ruled out in the case of Iraq?

Ever since the fall of France, the British authorities had watched Iraqi politics with anxiety. We learn from this work (pp. 250–1) that in July 1940 an Indian Division was going to be sent to Basra, but that Wavell and Cassels, the commander-in-chief in India, thought this might provoke Russia and create a graver situation for dealing with which they would have no reinforcements to send: 'They were all aware of the risk of having a repetition of the First War's Mesopotamian campaign.' The war cabinet accepted their advice. But the Iraqi situation showed no sign of improving, rather, in spite of the inaction which Wavell favoured, steadily deteriorated. On the eve of Rashid Ali's *coup d'état* which took place at the beginning of April 1941 we find Dill, the C.I.G.S., writing on 13 March from Cairo, where he was on a short visit, to Auchinleck, the new Commander-in-Chief in India: 'Conditions in Iraq are, as you know, bad and show little sign of improving. We have had that nasty little red fox, Tewfiq Suwaidi, the Foreign Minister, over here. He has been all honeyed words but is obviously quite unreliable' (*Auchinleck*, p. 197). Immediately after the *coup d'état*, Churchill took action. Amery, the secretary of state for India, had some time before offered an Indian division for the middle east. In a minute of 8 April (*The Second World War*, vol. III, p. 225), the prime minister suggested that this division should be sent to Basra. Auchinleck promptly agreed and on 12 April the troops sailed from Karachi. But on 10 April Rashid Ali had stated that his *coup d'état* was a purely internal affair and that he would honour his obligations under the Anglo-Iraqi treaty. This led Cornwallis, the British ambassador, to send on 11 April a 'most immediate' telegram requesting that the despatch of troops to Basra should be held up. But both Auchinleck and Linlithgow the viceroy protested strenuously against this advice. In a letter of 12 April to the viceroy's private secretary, Auchinleck wrote: 'I view with the gravest misgiving the proposal of H.M.G. to temporize and compromise'; and the viceroy himself telegraphed on 13 April that he felt no doubt himself 'that the definite line is the wise one. I express no view,' he went on, 'as to whether we have not been much too tender over the prewar period with Iraq, from which we have had no cooperation that has mattered, and which essentially owes her existence to us.' Linlithgow saw the main point which seemed to elude both Cornwallis and Wavell, for his telegram continued: 'But we are moving into a position that affects our general standing in the Middle East, that has most important potential repercussions on India and Iran, that affects our oil supplies (so vital to the Admiralty) in Iran and in Bahrein (and to a lesser extent Kuwait); and I have no doubt that we must be prepared to take a strong line now.' (*Auchinleck*, pp. 202–5).

India's advice was heeded, and troops disembarked without opposition at Basra on 18 April. Cornwallis, in a telegram of 21 April which throws grave doubt about his judgement at this particular juncture, urged that no more troops should be sent. Churchill however had decided the previous day, rightly, that more troops should be sent to Basra 'as fast as possible' (*The Second World War*, vol. III, pp. 225–6).

When the second contingent of Indian troops reached Basra at the end of April, hostilities broke out. Wavell had always advised negotiation with Rashid, and he now pressed his advice on the chiefs of staff, but they rejected it, as well as his proposal to accept an offer of Turkish mediation. Wavell replied brusquely on 5 May that the chiefs of staff took little account of realities: 'You must face facts,' he told them, and went on in ominous and portentous language: 'I feel it my duty to warn you in gravest possible terms that I consider prolongation of fighting in Iraq will seriously endanger defence of Palestine and Egypt. Apart from the weakening o strength by detachments such as above, political repercussions will be incalculable and may result in what I have spent nearly two years trying to avoid, serious internal trouble in our bases.' (*Wavell*, p. 437). But these highly alarmist views were not all. In a telegram of 8 May Wavell gave the impression that he considered Rashid Ali and his army to be on a par with that of a great power: 'Forces from India can secure Basra, but cannot, in my opinion, advance north-wards unless the cooperation of the local population and tribes is fully secured.' Again: 'Force from Palestine can relieve Habbaniya and hold approaches from Baghdad to prevent further advance on Habbaniya, but it is not capable of entering Baghdad against opposition or maintaining itself there.' To this solemn and heavy ponderousness, Churchill from London opposed a deft touch, an eye for essentials, a gay and gallant willingness to take a risk. Thus in a telegram on 7 May: 'audacious action now against the Iraqis may crush the revolt before the Germans arrive. . . We must forestall the moral effect of their arrival by a stunning blow'; and again on 9 May: 'You should exploit the situation to the utmost, not hesitating to try to break into Baghdad even with quite small forces, and running the same kind of risks as the Germans are accustomed to run and profit by' (*The Second World War*, vol. III, pp. 229–31). As has been said, Wavell's reaction to the Iraqi affair may be explained by the great strain under which he then laboured. Was the strain on the prime minister in the spring of 1941, we may now ask, any less?

Ordered to take military action against Rashid Ali, Wavell now raised another matter. In a telegram of 10 May, he stated that the proper objective in Iraq should be to secure oil and communications, but above all the 'avoidance of major conflict with Arabs'. He asserted that India did not appreciate the effect on his position of 'a large-scale Arab uprising in Iraq' which 'would have repercussions in Palestine, Aden, Yemen, Egypt and Syria which might absorb very large proportion of my force in maintaining internal order.' The way to avoid this catastrophe, Wavell thought, was 'to get back to normal relations with well-disposed Iraqi Government' and to scotch any suggestions that the British wanted to occupy the country. 'Already,' Wavell added, 'loyalty of Transjordan Frontier Force is in grave doubt.' That Wavell should bring up such a point shows that his argument was founded on doctrine—whether his own or that of his advisers—rather than on realities. It is perfectly true that the Transjordan Frontier Force was unreliable: in the Iraq operation one squadron refused to take part in operations and many officers and men actually refused to cross the frontier into Iraq; what this showed, however, was that the Force—and other Arabs—were unfriendly to the British, not because they suspected their designs on Iraq or 'the Arab world', but simply because at that point they expected Germany to win the war, and they were backing the winner. The way to guard against subversive action on their part was not to make polite noises about Iraqi independence, but to show by deeds that the Germans could be checkmated and defeated.

Wavell raised this point about the future treatment of Iraq because Auchinleck was insisting that the British should establish themselves quickly with sufficient force at Baghdad and other key points. His attitude emerges from a letter to the viceroy in which he makes a cogent and illuminating criticism of Wavell's strategic outlook: 'As I see it,' Auchinleck wrote on 11 May, 'Mideast are looking at the Asiatic strategic situation from a parochial angle and visualize North Africa and the Levant as one fortress, India as another and Malaya-Burma-Hong Kong as a third.' Auchinleck himself preferred to look on the situation 'as being one continuous and united front divided into three sectors, each interlocking and interdependent on the other.' (*Auchinleck*, p. 224.) Wavell, however, was suspicious of Delhi's motives. What India wanted, he told the chiefs of staff, was 'obviously military occupation.' and added that 'without exception all in Middle East with experience [of] Arab affairs' were against such a policy and in favour of endeavouring to instal a friendly government in Iraq. This belief that a 'friendly government' in Iraq would make a British occupation unnecessary was a curious fallacy. Rashid Ali's *coup d'état* was enthusiastically supported by the army, and the great majority of the intellectual and official classes. If it meant anything, it meant the rejection by all these of the dynasty and the politicians who were imposed on the country by British action in 1921. If a 'friendly government' was wanted in Iraq, British occupation was a necessity. One of these politicians, Midfa'i, a refugee from Rashid Ali in British-occupied Basra, made the point to Wavell and Auchinleck when they met at Basra on 24 May that a 'friendly government' and a British occupation, far from being antithetical, rather went hand in hand: 'He was forthcoming,' reported Auchinleck to Dill, 'and was firm on the point that if a friendly government under the auspices of the Regent were to survive, it would require the physical support of our forces to hold the important towns and areas' (*Auchinleck*, p. 229). This was straight indeed from the horse's mouth.

Installing a 'friendly government' and leaving it to its own devices was, as the sequel showed, quite out of the question. In a letter full of sound common-sense Linlithgow saw that the undoing of Rashid Ali entailed the occupation of the country. 'What is ... essential,' he wrote in a letter to Amery of 13 May, 'is that we should have our lines of communication, and that of course involves, in the conditions of that somewhat lightly organized state, effective arrangements to ensure that those lines of communications are properly held and not cut.' 'I am quite sure,' he went on, 'that if we are to avoid infiltration on a scale that may be very dangerous indeed to us, given the vital importance of this area and of the head of the Persian Gulf, we must be pretty strongly represented on the spot. Even if we can get rid of Rashid Ali and get the Regent back with a Cabinet sufficiently responsive to our control, we shall have to buttress them against German intrigue, and to do that effectively we must be on the spot in sufficient strength.'

Events after Rashid Ali's defeat demonstrated that Linlithgow was stating the obvious and the inevitable, but while operations were going on in Iraq, Wavell's view received the support of the Arab experts, of the foreign office, and eventually of Cornwallis in Baghdad. So that when at the end of May the Iraqis asked for an armistice, the terms granted by the British negotiators were, in the words of the official historian 'lenient and brief, because the British thought it best to limit their demands to what the Iraqi military authorities could be persuaded to accept[!]. The great thing was to get a friendly government established in Baghdad quickly.' 'The terms,' recited the preamble to the armistice agreement, echoing so much fanciful doctrine then and long afterwards current in official circles, 'have been drawn up in harmony with the declared policy of His Britannic Majesty's Government, which is to abstain from any infringement of Iraq Independence as formally laid down by Treaty, and to afford His Highness the Regent every assistance in re-establishing legal government and assisting the Iraq nation to resume its normal and prosperous existence. His Britannic Majesty's Government have been led to adhere to these two bases of policy by the fact that they realise that the recent regrettable incidents in Iraq were not the outcome of any feeling of hostility between the British and Iraqi nations or any divergence of interests between the two friendly peoples, but that these incidents were engineered solely by a small political party for their own private ends.' The official historian records that the chiefs of staff in London expressed their concern at these terms (I. S. O. Playfair *et al., History of the Second World War: The Mediterranean and Middle East*, vol. II, pp. 192–3 and 332). But the concern was needless, since the point of view of Wavell and his advisers—as unreal as the words of the armistice preamble—prevailed only formally, and in practice until the end of the war Iraq was—and had to be—under British occupation. Prevailed only formally except in one respect. In his telegram of 10 May cited above, Wavell had said: 'As regards Baghdad do not consider occupation desirable except temporarily to secure favourable Government or at request Iraqi Government.' In the event, British troops remained passive onlookers at the gates of Baghdad while the city was given over to murder and rapine. This was meant to show a generous and forgiving forbearance, but was in fact taken for a foolish and mean pusillanimity. It did not enhance British prestige in the eyes of the country's official classes whose friendship was thus being courted, but only succeeded in leaving a stain upon the British name.

19. The Sack of Basra and the *Farhud* in Baghdad

Somerset de Chair's book, *The Golden Carpet*, which describes its author's adventures as intelligence officer of 'Habforce' which marched from Palestine on Habbaniyya and Baghdad in May 1941, appeared in a general, trade, edition in 1944. But it had been published the previous year in a limited, private press, edition. This earlier edition has a passage in the preface which the trade edition omits. In this passage, de Chair recounts a story which he had heard from a British officer serving in the Indian army, Colonel W. G. Elphinston, concerning Colonel T. E. Lawrence and the capture of Damascus. Elphinston, wrote de Chair,

> threw a new light on [Lawrence's] abrupt departure which appears to have been wrung from a reluctant Allenby at the close of the *Seven Pillars of Wisdom.*
>
> Lawrence had begged Allenby's permission for the Bedouin to occupy Damascus, but they massacred the occupants of the Turkish hospital and hurled the bodies through the windows. Allenby arrived, saw the sickening pile of corpses, said 'enough' and Lawrence was given a single ticket home.[1]

As we now known, there is a large element of truth in Elphinston's story,[2] but when de Chair disclosed it in his book, it gave rise to much indignation on the part of Lawrence's admirers. Sir Percy Sykes, reviewing the work in the *Royal Central Asian Society Journal*, declared that such a statement could not go unchallenged, and to refute it quoted a letter from Colonel Peake Pasha to the effect that the Ottoman army hospitals had been deserted by their staff fully two days before the occupation of Damascus. The review elicited a letter from de Chair in which he declared that discussion with Lord Winterton and Peake Pasha had convinced him that there was no substance whatever in the suggestion that Allenby had given Lawrence 'a single ticket home' and that he was omitting the whole passage from the forthcoming trade edition. Elphinston, who was the head of the combined intelligence centre, Iraq, himself wrote a letter following Sykes' review which throws a significant light on the circumstances in which his conversation with de Chair had occurred:

> The only fact [wrote Elphinston in a letter dated 25 November 1943] connected with the story which he relates of which I can speak with first-hand knowledge is that, when riding through Damascus the day

after the city was taken, we passed the hospital and saw a considerable number of naked corpses piled in the courtyard in heaps, five or six feet high, apparently—from their condition—comparatively recently dead and thrown from the windows of the upper storey.

It was not surprising that such a sight gave rise to considerable comment and it was said that General Allenby was exceedingly angry about it. When it was known that Lawrence had left for England there were those who connected his departure with this incident, on what authority I do not know.

When [Elphinston went on], after our recapture of Baghdad on May 31, 1941, British forces remained on the right bank of the Tigris and attacks were made on Jewish life and property in the city on the other bank, I was reminded of Damascus in 1918 and may have mentioned it to de Chair, to emphasize the importance of adequately policing a newly captured Arab city until its normal administration has been restored. That such gossip should be repeated in print, is in my opinion, quite unjustifiable, and I hope Captain de Chair will expunge from his book all reference to this statement, for which, so far as I know, there is no justification whatever.[3]

That the events of June 1941 in Baghdad reminded Colonel Elphinston of what had taken place in Damascus in October 1918 is interesting in more than one respect. Not only were rioters, looters and murderers suffered in both cases to go unchecked for two days; but also, in both cases the conqueror's inaction was deliberate, the outcome of decisions the consequences of which had not been foreseen. And, again, since these consequences cast little credit on those responsible, what exactly took place became, in both cases, somewhat difficult to piece together. Curiously enough, the foreign office files contain no reports whatever about the Damascus events, the only relevant documents to be found in them being two telegrams from Brigadier G. F. Clayton, the first of 6 October 1918, an example of *suppressio veri* and *suggestio falsi*, in which Clayton declares that the Arabs 'have established in Damascus an Arab administration which was in being when our troops entered the city' and that 'a certain amount of looting by Druses took place when Arab troops first entered which was suppressed by Arab authorities who employed Sherifian troops to restore order'; the second, of 8 October, containing a propaganda piece (written by Lawrence) destined for publication in *The Times*.[4] For Elphinston in 1943, as has been seen, these events were still in the realm of gossip. The Baghdad events of June 1941 are, it is true, less difficult to establish. But British official reports on the subject are somewhat curt and uninformative, by no means reflecting the shock which the disorders are known to have produced in British official circles, and of which Elphinston's conversation with de Chair is only one expression.

The outbreak of 1–2 June 1941 in Baghdad followed a lightning campaign in which a small force, 'Habforce', assembled at short notice in Palestine demoralized and put to flight the Iraqi army. At the end of May, 'Habforce' had reached the western outskirts of Baghdad, and Iraqi army representatives were forced to ask for an armistice which was signed on 31 May. The expedition, conducted with great panache, was under the ultimate authority of Wavell, the commander-in-chief in the middle east. But if matters had rested with him alone, the expedition would probably never have started. For Wavell kept on urging his government to reach a settlement with Rashid Ali, lest the whole Arab world should go up in flames. It would seem that Wavell's views were shared at the foreign office. Squadron-Leader A. D. Macdonald, of the intelligence directorate at the air ministry, spoke in a minute of 6 May of

> the vague and ambiguous manner in which we are at present operating in Iraq. At the moment [he went on] I am not at all clear what it is that we are trying to do....
>
> I understand from my conversation at the F.O. this afternoon that we would accept the withdrawal of the Iraqi forces at Habbaniyya as a basis of negotiations with the present Government, and that we still have hopes that negotiation on such a basis is possible.

Macdonald, who knew Iraq very well and was the author of one of the best books on Iraq under the monarchy, *Euphrates Exile* (1936), declared himself to be pessimistic about the possibilities of negotiating with Rashid Ali and urged that plans based on such an appreciation should be seriously and speedily considered.[5] In the event it was pressure by the government of India and by Amery, the secretary of state for India, and above all Churchill's urgent prodding which moved the reluctant commander-in-chief to mount 'Habforce'. His views are accurately summarized by a letter from Amery to Churchill

> Wavell's telegrams [wrote Amery on 8 May 1941] have been very unsatisfactory. There was, first of all, the agonised appeal for us to negotiate with Rashid Ali at all costs, then the refusal (which the Chiefs of Staff have sat on) to allow our Air Force to attack the Iraqis except in the immediate neighbourhood of our posts, then the telegram fishing for an excuse to open negotiations with Rashid Ali.[6]

But as has been said, Wavell was compelled by Churchill to organize an attack on Rashid Ali, and he was given responsibility not only for 'Habforce' but also for the Indian troops which had landed in Basra in April. This involved him in exchanges with Auchinleck, the commander-in-chief of the Indian army. In a telegram to the war office on 8 May Wavell expressed misgivings about a proposal by the government of India to send to Iraq 'large numbers of political and administrative officers'. He believed that the first essential in dealing with Iraq

> must be to avoid any action to suggest that we have any intention of infringing Iraqi independence or introducing British administration or control. This would unite the whole population behind Rashid Ali and against us and would not only involve us in most serious commitments in Iraq itself but would have repercussions in Palestine Syria and Arab world generally.

Auchinleck and the government of India disagreed with Wavell's view. In a telegram of 9 May, the defence department of the government of India argued that it was necessary for the British to ensure that the Iraqi administration did function, and it therefore followed that there had to be British officials with knowledge of the Iraqi administration to establish an effective liaison with the British military authorities. 'We must also be prepared', they sensibly added, 'temporarily to administer any local function of Government that may break down for one reason or another e.g. Port, railways, post and telegrams, local currency.' Even if there were a friendly government in Iraq, Auchinleck also argued in a telegram of 12 May, this would not be enough: 'Any such Government must be backed by our armed occupation of key points or ability to do so at short notice.' As for the general uprisings predicted by Wavell, India had no information to indicate that such were impending. If these were to happen, they would be a consequence not of strong action, but rather of passivity on the part of the British:

> we consider [Auchinleck declared] that failure to take strong action in Iraq immediately with forces available is more likely than anything else to bring about an Arab uprising and further Axis activity in Iran and Afghanistan. Any appearance of weakness at a time when circumstances are in our favour [he concluded] will in our opinion be fatal.[7]

The sequel showed that Auchinleck's appreciation was sounder than Wavell's. As the British quickly found out, the only way to make sure that Iraq was a secure base was in fact to occupy it, to control its key points and to cover its territory with an intricate network of intelligence officers and political 'advisers'. There was no other way of ensuring that a friendly Iraqi government would stay friendly, and would not be toppled by Nazi sympathizers. Wavell's attitude may have been influenced by his over-riding preoccupation with Cyrenaica and by the exiguity of his resources. But there may have been something else as well. In his letter of 8 May cited above, Amery gave an indication of what this might be:

> I am inclined to suspect [he told Churchill] that the cause is not so much any loss of nerve or undue strain upon Wavell himself, but an

undue reliance on his part on Brigadier Clayton, his Intelligence Officer, for all Arab questions. Clayton certainly knows his Arab world well but is so pro-Arab that this may have warped his judgement. Also I am struck by the fact that our Political Officer for the Persian Gulf telegraphing from Bushire to India with reference to a suggestion, I think of negotiations, asked if this was due to Clayton, whom he then proceeds to describe as 'a defeatist of the first water'. This may possibly be quite unfair, but I think I ought to pass it on to you as a possible explanation of Wavell's otherwise inexplicable attitude.

Whether Amery was right or not, the fact remains that Auchinleck failed to convince Wavell who remained adamant that a forceful British action in Iraq would be disastrous. This attitude was reflected in the directives which he issued to 'Habforce' and to the Indian troops in Basra who had also been placed under his command. In a telegram of 8 May he gave their orders to the force headquarters in Basra. Their task was to secure the port of Basra and the adjoining British airbase at Shaiba. Wavell went on to lay down that it was essential

> at once to convince local authorities and Iraq people that we have no intention whatever to occupy country setting up British administration or infringing Iraq independence. You will therefore encourage local Iraq administration to function so far as is consistent with your own force and will do everything possible to avoid conflict.[8]

Three days later, Wavell reiterated his instructions and added:

> As long as Iraqi administration meets our Military requirements it is not, repeat not, to be interfered with or superseded because it is inefficient in other directions.[9]

Wavell's instructions were misconceived and fanciful. In the eyes of the population Rashid Ali, backed by the triumphant Nazis, was challenging the British, hitherto the paramount Power in Iraq. For the British to protest that they were not infringing Iraqi independence while in fact mounting an expedition against a régime which was challenging them was to engage in meaningless rhetoric. For them actually to leave unmolested the Iraqi administration which was known to support Rashid Ali overwhelmingly, would have seemed at best a sign of weakness and at worst an involved and sinister plot. The events of Basra during May illustrate the operation and the consequences of such a policy.

Indian troops had landed at Basra on 19 April, and a second convoy arrived ten days later. It was the arrival of this second convoy which precipitated open hostilities between Rashid Ali and the British. The British commander at Basra decided on 1 May to occupy the port area, and to demand that Iraqi troops evacuate military barracks in the vicinity and retire fifteen miles up the river. The Iraqis adopted delaying tactics, and General Fraser issued an ultimatum. A short skirmish followed, and the Iraqi troops withdrew according to his demand. The port of Basra was now occupied by the British, but the Iraqi administration resorted to arrests and intimidation in order to hamper the working of the port, and there was no doubt, the British consul later wrote, 'that they were encouraging the non co-operative attitude of certain sections of the population and even instigating it'.

The state of affairs eventually led General Fraser to occupy 'Ashshar where the government offices, the consulates and the principal business houses were situated. The occupation was to be 'limitated and temporary' with the object of preventing the Iraqi administration from hampering him. The occupation of 'Ashshar took place on 7 May. The area where most British firms had their offices and houses was quickly occupied, but the attempt to advance into the bazaar quarter encountered 'considerable rifle and machine-gun fire from both police and populace'.

It will be recalled that Wavell's orders not to interfere with the Iraqi administration were issued only on 8 May, the day following the occupation of 'Ashshar. From the language of the consul's later report it would seem that General Fraser's decision not to occupy the 'Ashshar bazaar at that point was motivated by immediate military exigencies, namely the resistance of the Iraqi police, and not by Wavell's orders. The consul wrote in his despatch of 16 July:

> The military authorities were not prepared forthwith to undertake the difficult and costly operation of cleaning up the bazaars having already lost two men killed and twenty six wounded and they contented themselves for the whole of that day and the next with holding the area already occupied.

When the troops had occupied the main part of 'Ashshar the British consul then accompanied General Fraser to the government headquarters where they saw the acting *mutasarrif*:

> He immediately got up and offered his own desk to the General who, however, explained that he had no intention of taking over the administration or of usurping any of the functions of the Mutasarrif.

General Fraser induced the acting *mutasarrif* to persuade the police, who had attacked his force, to withdraw from 'Ashshar under a white flag and with their arms. It so happened that when the police were evacuating 'Ashshar, a Ghurka soldier was mortally wounded by a sniper, his comrade opened fire on a police column marching under the white flag, and three policemen fell. The others fled, many handing their arms to the crowd. According to a well-informed local notable, following this incident, the acting *mutasarrif* told the police in an eloquent sentence 'which Plato could not have equalled': 'I am free and you are free.' Rioting and looting in 'Ashshar followed on 7 and 8 May.[10]

The British consul gives one or two interesting details of the disorders:

> Lawless elements [he wrote] seized the opportunity thus provided to loot the 'Ashshar bazaars. In at least one case the members of a rich and respected family did not, at any rate, restrain their retainers from taking part in the disorders and there are strong grounds for thinking that, faced with the alternative of loot or be looted they chose the former.
>
> In actual fact [the consul was careful to point out] the looting was not by any means as thorough as it might have been, and any shopkeeper who showed courage and determination seems to have escaped. One Indian trader who had only just imported £5,000 worth of goods saved his entire stock for a re-insurance of twenty dinars by the simple expedient of standing at the door and offering anyone who threatened to break in the sum of one dinar to go and loot someone else.

According to the Iraqi chronicler, Abd al-Razzaq al-Hasani a delegation of Basra notables went to see the British authorities at 'Ashshar on 8 May and asked them to occupy Basra city. They said that the mob had looted the bazaars, and they were afraid that it was now the turn of private houses and women to be attacked. By then Wavell's orders had been received. The delegation were told: 'We see no need to occupy Basra, and the British government is not required to preserve order either in Basra or 'Ashshar. The British army entered 'Ashshar only to ensure its own supplies.'[11] The British consul wrote:

> For the next seventeen days 'Ashshar was deprived of all administrative and municipal services except electric current and water...[12]

It would seem however that the British military authorities were not so solicitous of Iraqi independence as to abandon the unfortunate inhabitants of 'Ashshar to the full rigours of a state of nature. Hasani reproduces the text of proclamations by the British commander ordering a curfew and threatening those caught looting with execution. We also read in the war diary of the 10th Indian Division that on 17 May, prisoners were escaping from the jail, and that a company was sent in order to prevent this.[13]

Such flagrant interference in the affairs of the Iraqi administration did not however extend to Basra city proper, where the acting *mutasarrif* had retired, and where he maintained law and order, carrying out the orders of Rashid Ali's government to which he remained loyal. On 14 May Wavell reported to the war office that the Iraqi authorities in Basra would not dissociate themselves from Rashid Ali and that local notables, for fear of reprisals, were unwilling themselves to set up a friendly local administration. Wavell was sure that the British themselves could do nothing to modify this situation:

> For British [he affirmed] to turn out hostile Iraqi officials and make new appointments even if latter would co-operate would provide further propaganda for Rashid. Only way to get over this is for Regent [who was now a refugee in Jerusalem] to set up alternative government which HMG could then recognise. This would also remove lurking suspicions of Regent's entourage that we intend to take over administration of country.[14]

It is, again, striking how fanciful and unbusinesslike Wavell's preoccupations were. Rashid Ali and his supporters were doing their best to vilify and blacken the British name, using a wide range of arguments and pretexts to further their campaign: what the British did or did not do in Basra was unlikely to have much bearing on their strident and unrestrained propaganda. As for the Regent and his entourage, they were refugees, clients and suppliants waiting for their fortunes to be restored by British arms. Their suspicions—and Wavell adduced no evidence that they did in fact harbour the suspicions he attributed to them—were strictly of no consequence.

On 16 May, on orders from Baghdad the acting *mutasarrif* left Basra and took with him his officials. Basra was left without a government. On 19 May, the British consul telegraphed that all parts of the town were virtually deprived of administrative services, that no police were functioning in the city and that the situation was obviously chaotic. Minorities, and especially Jews, were fearful and anxious to leave for India. 'I am', declared the consul, 'in consultation with G.O.C. discouraging this by every means.'[15] In his later report, the consul amplified the picture which his telegram had sketched out:

> the telephone [he wrote in his despatch of 16 July] rang without ceasing and notables, professional men and merchants begged that the British should take steps to prevent the looting, rape and murder which was universally expected. I could only reply that the policy of His Majesty's Government was not to interfere in any way with the local administration or to occupy any quarter which was not essential to the safety of the troops and that therefore the military could not intervene.
> The notables then took steps to recruit night watchmen and many gave asylum in their own homes to Jews and other members of minorities who were in fear of their lives.

What the notables had told the consul would happen did come to pass:

> That night and the following day [the despatch continued] the city was looted with considerable thoroughness but [the consul was careful to point out] I have not heard of any cases of murder, rape, or even wounding. Undoubtedly the temper of the crowd never approached that degree of ferocity shown by the Baghdadis in the first days of June.

The sack of Basra was an outcome of Wavell's orders. These orders falsely assumed that Rashid Ali would be reconciled to the British connexion if he were shown that the British did not want to do away with Iraqi independence; or that the population of Iraq could be brought to the side of the British by the same argument. These were all illusions. The reality was that Rashid Ali and his supporters had irrevocably committed themselves to the Nazis who were then at the crest of the wave; and that so long as the Nazis were victorious, and himself successful in defying the British, Rashid Ali would be able to elicit—for what it was worth—the vociferous enthusiasm of the Muslim population, and to count on the loyalty of the official and intellectual classes. In this respect, the behaviour of the acting *mutasarrif* of Basra and of his officials was entirely typical. To establish themselves in Iraq therefore the British had to incapacitate or destroy the Iraqi army and the Iraqi administration. To do this and then refuse to do anything about the breakdown of public security which followed was dishonourable. The dishonour is not made less by the fact that it was infatuation with a false doctrine, rather than cowardice, which allowed British troops to neglect an elementary duty, and to look passively on while the life and property of defenceless civilians was at the mercy of the mob.

Wavell's orders applied not only to Basra but to 'Habforce' as well. The instructions of 11 May sent to Basra were also sent to Palestine and the air base at Habbaniyya.

> Any action suggesting that we have any intention of infringing Iraq independence or introducing British administration or control is to be avoided. Every encouragement is to be given to local Iraq administration to function so far as is consistent with safety of our forces. Political officers are to be regarded as liaison officers between Iraq administration and British forces and not as administrators except where Iraq administration is inoperative.

The instructions went on to lay down, in words already quoted, that

> As long as Iraq administration meets our military requirements it is not (repeat not) to be interfered with or superseded because it is inefficient in other directions.[16]

The mission of Major-General J. G. W. Clark, the commander of 'Habforce' was to reach and raise the siege of Habbaniyya; thereafter, if possible, to send a portion of his forces to Baghdad to regain contact with the British ambassador, Sir Kinahan Cornwallis, who was being held by the Iraqis incommunicado in his embassy. The objective of the expedition was

> to bring about the collapse of the Rashid Ali régime and to enable Emissaries from the Regent at Amman to restore legitimate government in Iraq.

As soon as contact with Cornwallis was re-established, he was to be responsible for all policy connected with Iraq 'and directives will then be issued to the missions with his approval'.[17]

Cornwallis, newly appointed to the Baghdad embassy, arrived in Baghdad at the beginning of April. He had been one of the pillars of the Sharifian régime, having arrived with Faysal in 1921 and served for fourteen years as adviser to the ministry of the interior in Baghdad. His first reaction to Rashid Ali's *coup d'état* was that it had to be opposed and the regent, Abd al-Ilah, reinstated. But he soon came to change his views. On 9 April he told the foreign office that Rashid Ali's propaganda was now so strong that if force was to be used against him 'we shall have to take careful precautions to ensure that our action is not resented by the people'.[18] Two days later, he concluded that the opportunity for taking swift action against Rashid Ali had passed. The reason was a speech in which Rashid Ali had explained that his movement was purely internal and that he intended to honour his obligations under the Anglo–Iraqi treaty. If forceful action were taken against him he could represent this as an attack against the independence of the country 'and it is quite likely that he could rouse such a fanatical and unreasoning people against us'. Cornwallis therefore asked that the regent should be removed from Basra where his presence on a British warship Rashid Ali would consider a provocation. The foreign office acquiesced and Abd al-Ilah was removed to Jerusalem. The regent's removal from Basra may have actually emboldened Rashid Ali and his supporters, for this may have been taken as a sign of British weakness. Such a view is supported by a situation report compiled on 9 April by air intelligence in London on the basis of local information. The report declared that 'a dangerous lie' was current in Mosul that the British had abandoned the regent 'owing to his having tried to seize the throne'.[19] Such a rumour was damaging precisely because it would persuade people that it was dangerous to support the British, because they were weak enough and treacherous enough to abandon their friends.

Cornwallis also wanted the departure of the Indian troops for Basra, which Churchill and Amery had concerted, to be postponed so that he could prepare Rashid Ali and thus avoid some 'unfortunate incident'. This request was considered by the defence committee meeting under Churchill's chairmanship with Eden and Amery present, and on 13 April its conclusions were sent to the ambassador. These were that the expedition to Basra was to proceed, and that no faith could be reposed in Rashid Ali. He was not to be apprised in advance of the movements of the troops, but was to be presented with a *fait accompli*, and to be informed at the last possible moment that the British government has noted his declaration that the treaty would be observed and were disembarking troops at Basra who were in transit to Palestine.[20]

Churchill's hand is clear in this swift and decisive response. Before he was informed of the defence committee decision Cornwallis sent two more telegrams, on 12 April, which show signs of cold feet. In the first he said that Rashid Ali now strengthened 'in the eyes of public opinion' by his speech, would expect a quid pro quo for allowing the transit of British troops through Iraq:

> In the circumstances [he argued], I feel that in the last resort we should be prepared to accede to some form of recognition which would depend on [Rashid Ali] honouring treaty obligations towards us simply in order to enable us to get a foothold in the country without incident. I realise loss of prestige involved, though I hope it might be largely offset by the peaceful landing of British troops and concession would have to be regarded as our contribution in return for Rashid Ali's first concrete step in implementing Anglo-Iraqi Alliance. Once we are established in the country, we should be in a far stronger position to control Rashid Ali and rally our own supporters. Failure to recognize now [Cornwallis warned] might play into the Axis' hands.

Cornwallis' second telegram of 12 April also tried to persuade the foreign office to allow him to negotiate with Rashid Ali:

> If you wish me to approach Rashid Ali [he wrote] I should of course endeavour to strike best possible bargain.

And when the instructions of the defence committee reached him on 14 April Cornwallis urged that the announcement of the landings (in which he saw 'grave dangers' involved) should be accompanied by the offer of *de facto* recognition to Rashid Ali: this, he declared, would be a small price to pay for the peaceful landing of the force. But London was not to be persuaded. Cornwallis was prudently refused permission to offer recognition outright, but allowed to dangle the bait of future recognition 'as soon as [the régime's] position has been finally regularized'.[21]

Rashid Ali was caught unprepared by the troop landings and had to agree to them without the *quid pro quo* which Cornwallis had believed essential. But he persisted in thinking that the way to deal with Rashid Ali and his military supporters was to establish 'a more normal atmosphere'. In a telegram of 21 April he said he 'must have a quiet period in which I can get in social touch with old friends and during which inevitable opposition to Rashid Ali will have chance to grow'. He therefore attached 'particular importance to immediate entry into formal relations with the Government'.[22] He was not allowed this quiet period. Churchill directed that another contingent of troops from India should land at Basra. They arrived towards the end of April and Rashid Ali was thus compelled to declare his hand, and engage in hostilities before the Nazis could come to his help. By the end of May his régime had collapsed and he was in flight. Churchill had been proved right, and Wavell and Cornwallis wrong. But even if Churchill's policy had failed, they would still have been demonstrably wrong. Cornwallis was wrong in the same way as Wavell was wrong. He misconceived the character of the Iraqi polity, attributing an autonomous character to its public opinion, and attaching enormous importance to one speech by Rashid Ali, and to its formal—and specious—arguments. In spite of his long years in the country he could not see that Rashid Ali's régime did not depend on speeches, arguments or legitimation by a cowed parliament, but on brute military power which was beyond anyone's control. The régime was no doubt popular with the mass, but this was because it was thought to be on Hitler's side, the winning side. The only way for its popularity to be destroyed was to establish that it was not on the winning side, or that Hitler's protection could avail it nothing. To hope for 'a quiet period', 'a more normal atmosphere', and 'inevitable opposition' which would act on its own, was to be deluded with mere words.

The sudden total collapse of Rashid Ali's régime which he had thought very difficult if not impossible to dislodge does not seem to have led to any change in Cornwallis' views. Just before he fled from Baghdad, anticipating an emergency in the capital, Rashid Ali set up, on 28 May, a 'committee of internal security' composed of the mayor, the director-general of police and an army representative. On 30 May this committee asked for an armistice. On the following day the armistice was signed on behalf of the British by the commander of 'Habforce', General Clark, and the commander at Habbaniyya, Air Vice-Marshal J. H. d'Albiac. As Clark's instructions required, before granting the armistice he consulted Cornwallis (who had now been released from his embassy by the 'committee of internal security') and its terms, Cornwallis subsequently wrote, 'were drawn up in consultation with me and with my approval'.[23] The terms of the armistice were extremely lenient, the only important provision being that laid down in clause 6, to the effect that 'All facilities will be accorded immediately to the British military authorities for unimpeded through communication by rail, road and river'. Clause 2, it is also important to remember declared that 'the Iraq Army will be permitted to retain all its arms, equipment and munitions, but all units of the Army must proceed forthwith to their normal peace-time station.'[24] These terms were predicated upon, and in furtherance of, the fiction that British operations in Iraq had not been undertaken against the Iraqi army and in order to assert British rights, but, as the preamble to the armistice had it, 'to afford His Highness the Regent every assistance in re-establishing legal government and assisting the Iraq nation to resume its normal and prosperous existence'. This fiction was sedulously maintained, and carried to absurd lengths. In a telegram of 3 June, Cornwallis asked that public statements should avoid the word 'occupation':

> If it were used [he feared] Iraqi suspicions would be strengthened and the Germans would seize on it at once to make out that our purpose was a military occupation of the country.[25]

On 6 June he was asking that the terms of the armistice, which had not been published in Iraq, should not be published elsewhere as 'some of the terms might expose new Government to embarrassing criticism'.[20]

The attempt to maintain the fiction that British troops had not clashed with the Iraqi army—a fiction which could deceive nobody[27] —was not confined to the avoidance of indelicate words and embarrassing publicity. Cornwallis also made sure that no British troops would be in Baghdad or even in its vicinity. A provision for the stationing of British troops in Baghdad was conspicuous by its absence from the armistice terms. On 1 June the ambassador telegraphed to the commander of the Basra troops that the Iraqi authorities were expressing concern over the continued advance towards Baghdad by British forces in Basra and were suggesting that movements of British troops should be suspended until the new government was formed. Cornwallis suggested that the commander or a senior staff officer should go to Baghdad to discuss the matter. The movement of troops from Basra was accordingly stopped and a colonel was sent to Baghdad on 2 June for talks with the ambassador.[28]

Similarly, 'Habforce' avoided entering, or even coming near Baghdad. On the contrary, the left column of the detachment commanded by Brigadier Kingstone which was known as 'Kingcol' and which had advanced to Kazimayn on the north-western outskirts of Baghdad actually withdrew to Habbaniyya, on 1 June.[29] The following day an official at the foreign office, P. M. Crosthwaite, noticed a report of this withdrawal in the situation report which had been telegraphed from Habbaniyya, and also that the terms of the armistice did not stipulate the stationing of British troops in Baghdad. He minuted:

> It looks . . . as though the military authorities do not propose to station troops in Baghdad West. That seems to me an extraordinary line to take, and one would have expected Sir K. Cornwallis to press for troops there.

Crosthwaite gave details of previous telegrams from the government of India and from Cornwallis himself in which the necessity of stationing troops in Baghdad was affirmed and added:

> The arguments in favour have surely increased, and the opportunity, if it has not already been lost, the best possible.
> Could we not at least ask H.E. what is proposed?

Crosthwaite submitted a draft telegram. Cadogan, the permanent under-secretary approved it, and it was sent on 2 June. Cornwallis replied the following day, simply stating that the column returning to Habbaniyya was 'probably ours' and vouchsafing no further explanation. He added that he was 'trying' to arrange for 'Kingcol' to have a few days' rest in a camp in Baghdad West, but that the newly formed Iraqi cabinet was 'doubtful'! This was not the whole story for, according to the operations record book of the air head-quarters at Habbaniyya, it had been decided on 31 May that 'a portion of [Kingcol's] main column would enter Baghdad on 2nd June'.[30] When the disorders broke out, these orders must have been countermanded. By Cornwallis? In the event, it was not until 5 June that a detachment of British troops did move into a camp in Baghdad.[31]

There is little doubt that the retreat of the British column from Kazimayn back to Habbaniyya was at Cornwallis' initiative. As has been seen, Wavell's instructions to 'Habforce' had stipulated that once contact had been made with Cornwallis, the ambassador's approval had to be obtained for any directives issued by the commander of 'Habforce'. This may serve to explain why Wavell's own instructions came to be superseded. Wavell had informed Clark that

> it is not intended that your force should cross R. Tigris as it is important that a small force should not get involved in street fighting in disadvantageous conditions.

Considering how small 'Habforce' was such an instruction was only prudent. But Wavell had added:

> It is considered that your operations should be designed to effect the following:
>
> (a) Reach the British Embassy
> (b) Control the bridges over R. Tigris at Baghdad.[32]

With the collapse of Iraqi resistance on 30 May the embassy was no longer under siege. But control of the bridge of boats from Kazimayn to Baghdad and particularly of the two bridges from Baghdad West to Baghdad East could have been secured by the detachment which was sent back to Habbaniyya. This would have been of vital importance, as will be seen, during the disorders of 2 June. It was most probably at Cornwallis' behest that Wavell's directives on this subject were not put into effect.

As the preamble to the armistice terms made clear, Cornwallis' policy was to pretend that the whole regrettable episode was at an end, now that trouble-makers were no longer coming between the regent and his loyal subjects, and a legitimate government was once more in being. The regent, in fact, reached Baghdad on 1 June in the morning. On the afternoon and evening of this day Jews were attacked and murdered in both Baghdad West and Baghdad East. Attacks, now accompanied by extensive looting, resumed early the following morning and went on unchecked until the late afternoon.[33] During these events, known locally as the *farhud*, notwithstanding the official fiction promoted by the preamble to the armistice, there was no government in Baghdad, and no one had the courage to exercise authority, to assume responsibility for law and order, or to take any steps to protect the life and property of helpless civilians.

After Rashid Ali's flight, the 'committee of internal security' as has been seen assumed authority in Baghdad. The committee, it seems, was fearful of disorders and it agreed on a plan for dealing with them.[34] The plan depended on prompt action by police and army detachments who were each made responsible for a particular neighbourhood. But once the disorders started the plan totally broke down, for the simple reason that the soldiers and the police, debauched by Nazi propaganda, and bereft of leadership, ran amuck and themselves began the attacks on the Jews. As the report of the Iraqi investigation committee later showed, neither the director-general of police, nor the army representative, nor the *mutasarrif* nor the mayor of Baghdad were willing to assume the responsibility for ordering that the rioters should be fired on. Each and every one of them shuffled off the responsibility on to some unspecified higher authority. Cowardice was universal. On the evening of 1 June, when rioting had been going on for some hours, some officers suggested to the director of operations, a colonel, that it would be advisable to proclaim a curfew. He agreed, but refused to sign the order. So did his superior, a general, until he had obtained by telephone the regent's permission.[35] In any event, the curfew was not enforced. As for the police, the report of the investigating committee pertinently pointed out that they had no need to seek orders from their superiors for firing on looters and murderers caught in *flagrante delicto*. The director-general of police and his assistants and the *mutasarrif* forgot or feigned to forget, the report declared, that every member of the police had the right to fire in such circumstances. The report also found that the commander of the first division stationed in Baghdad acted negligently in not confining his soldiers to barracks following the incidents of 1 June in which they took a prominent part.[36]

In any case, the superior authority to which all these high officials looked for orders, namely the regent, was present in Baghdad. But it was not until the late morning of 2 June that the regent gave a written order in which he stated that, having 'assumed full powers', he was authorizing the army to use such force as was necessary in order to suppress the disorders.[37] It was then, and only then, that the army commanders dared to move their troops against the rioters. They found no difficulty in putting them to flight and clearing the streets in a very short time. The official investigating committee reported officially that the numbers of those killed 'including Jews and Muslims' was one-hundred and thirty, but one of its members later told the chronicler Hasani (who had the story confirmed by the then Baghdad chief of police) that the true figure was nearer six hundred, but that the government was anxious for the lower figure only to appear in the official report.[38] The report did not attempt to evaluate the damages sustained by householders and commercial establishments, but the Jewish communal authorities advanced a figure of £650,000 which seems realistic and was in any case never disputed.

Why was the regent so tardy in issuing his orders? The answer probably lies in the fear of responsibility which almost all of those concerned—British or Iraqi—showed in this incident, and in the elaborate constitutional fictions invented and persevered in by Wavell, the foreign office and Cornwallis. The pretence, as has been seen, was that the Iraqi army had not been defeated by the British army, but that the regent was merely resuming his lawful authority which had been momentarily interrupted by a handful of conspirators now in flight. To conform to this fiction, the foreign office impressed on the regent as early as 19 May that he should set up a government. The regent found this difficult. As G. de Gaury, the chargé d'affaires who had just been appointed British representative with the regent explained in a telegram of 22 May, the regent had three ex-prime ministers with him, 'and so whichever is selected to form a Government, the other two will be disgruntled, and probably cease to co-operate'. Instead of a government, therefore, the regent formed a 'Council of State', consisting of these mutually suspicious and jealous politicians—Jamil al Midfa'i, Nuri al-Sa'id, Ali Jawdat and Da'ud al-Haydari. De Gaury agreed with this step. But these 'Eminent Persons' (as the regent desired them to be described) had no constitutional or political attributes of responsibility.[39] So it was that when the regent arrived in Baghdad on 1 June he had not yet formed a government. In a book published in 1961, de Gaury declares that this fact led to 'the good name of the Regent and those with him being blackened' in the course of representations subsequently made in London on the subject of the disturbances of 1–2 June. The papers show no trace of such representations or indeed of the 'blackening' of anyone's reputation. De Gaury may, of course, be alluding to conversations of which no record was kept, similar to that between Elphinston and de Chair which, but for an accident, would have remained unknown. De Gaury went on:

> It was said incorrectly that, had there been formed a government-in-exile to take over in Baghdad on entry, no one would have suffered, but Ministers could have done no more or acted no faster than did the city authorities, who took immediate measures to quell the trouble.[40]

The evidence does not quite support de Gaury's assertions. There is obviously no knowing what action ministers, endowed with powers and duties under the law, would have taken in this emergency, but it is not the case that the city authorities took 'immediate steps to quell the trouble'. For two days they took no steps whatever, shuffling off the responsibility onto one another, and asking for orders from a higher authority. It is possible, perhaps likely, that ministers appointed by the regent would have shown the same fecklessness, but this is not exactly what de Gaury intends to convey. Cornwallis who was, at this stage, in a better position to observe events, directly controverts de Gaury's judgement, declaring that if a government had been formed earlier 'it is improbable that such a serious situation would have arisen'.[41]

The regent, then arrived in Baghdad towards midday on 1 June without a government. Cornwallis had gone out some distance to meet him and delivered the advice—which in the circumstances was more than mere advice—which the foreign office had instructed him to deliver the previous day. For in a telegram of 31 May the foreign office had expressed the view that the new government should be formed 'on broadest possible basis'. In particular, 'every effort' had to be made to avoid a situation arising in which the government was formed by 'an alleged "pro-British" clique'. Nuri al-Sa'id was therefore not a suitable prime minister in the circumstances, and Jamil al-Midfa'i was preferred.[42] The regent, according to Cornwallis, did not like Midfa'i and 'sought anxiously for alternatives'. But, the ambassador reported, 'my enquiries failed to reveal anyone else who had the courage and influence to step into the breach'. However, Midfa'i was not exactly a lion himself. Telegraphing at 4.15 in the afternoon on 2 June Cornwallis reported:

> I told the Regent both yesterday and this morning that the immediate formation of a Government was imperative. Jamil Madfai refused to accept responsibility last night but this morning sent two emissaries to me and on my promising that I would give him my full support providing he carried out the Treaty in the letter and spirit, he consented. I saw him later. He seems to have grown slow and rather senile so may prove a broken reed but he was the only available candidate with public support.

Considering the circumstances, Cornwallis' reference to 'public support' partakes of black comedy. Midfa'i assumed office 'when the rioting was at its height. As every minute almost was of importance, the Regent gave him a free hand.'[43]

But the regent's tardy haste availed him nothing, for he did not succeed in saddling Midfa'i with the responsibility for giving the necessary order to deal with the rioters. He himself had to issue the order which, as has been seen, he did in the late morning of 2 June. Dr. Hayyim Cohen has rightly pointed out that to issue this order, the regent did not have to wait for a ministry to be formed. He was, after all, head of the state and commander-in-chief. Dr. Cohen ventures the explanation that the regent had to wait for the arrival of Kurdish soldiers from the northern division (stationed in Kirkuk) who were uncontaminated by Nazi propaganda before taking action to suppress the riots.[44] But it does not seem to be the case that the riots were suppressed only by soldiers from Kirkuk. Action against the rioters was also taken by a cavalry brigade which formed part of the general reserve on the Baghdad front, and which was therefore in the neighbourhood of the city at all times.[45] The conclusion seems inescapable that like others, British and Iraqi, the regent was unwilling to face up to his responsibilities, and tried to shuffle them off on to someone else. But if he was so anxious for a minister to assume responsibility, he should not have delayed making an appointment for reasons which, in an emergency, were simply footling and frivolous.

The riots of 2 June were more extensive than those of the previous day by reason of the fact that hordes of beduins and others, attracted by the possibility of loot, began streaming across the bridges from Baghdad West at a very early hour. If Wavell's original orders had been followed these bridges would have been controlled by British troops and the looters would have been unable to use them. But Cornwallis' policy required the troops to stay at a distance from the city, and the bridges remained open and unguarded. In any case British troops abstained scrupulously from interfering with the rioters. Various explanations have been given for this inactivity. Dame Freya Stark has written that 'the British troops, encamped some miles down Baghdad were anxious not to enter the town unless invited, and the Iraqi forces of law were equally anxious to win their own fight unaided'.[46] The picture of gallant Iraqi policemen 'anxious to win their fight unaided' is perhaps only an instance of the 'sympathetic tact' and the 'light touch' for which Cornwallis praised her when proposing to employ her for propaganda work at the Baghdad embassy,[47] for in a book published over twenty years later Dame Freya Stark quotes an entry from her diary for 2 June 1941 in which the information is recorded that 'there is looting all down Rashid Street, chiefly by army and police taking a rake-off'.[48] De Gaury also repeats the allegation that it was the army which decided that it could not force its way into Baghdad: 'their commander [Clark or Kingstone presumably] had refused to do so on the grounds of danger to his troops in the narrow streets, quoting, as an example well-known to military men, Amritsar'.[49] But there is no evidence that this in fact was the attitude taken by the British commanders. The war diaries are silent on this matter, but there is a signal sent from Habbaniyya on 1 June which indicates that the fears of which de Gaury speaks could not have been very prevalent:

> Baghdad populace extremely friendly and appear relieved [the signal reported] to see British officers and civilians moving about the city again. Villagers on road Fallujah to Baghdad most friendly. Only discordant note were people on Khadimain and north of that town who show signs of fierce hatred possibly inspired by propaganda but in keeping with past record. . . . Iraqi troops returning in lorries this afternoon from Khadimain area were well turned out and showed no loss of morale. Surrender appears due to disinclination to continue fighting after leaders had bolted plus fear of intensive bombing . . . Baghdad airport was being used today by R.A.F.[50]

Again, de Chair's testimony to which, by reason of its author's functions, a great deal of weight must be given, totally contradicts de Gaury's and Dame Freya Stark's assertions. De Chair wrote:

Having fought our way, step by step, to the threshold of the city we must now cool our heels outside. It would, apparently, be lowering to the dignity of our ally, the Regent, if he were seen to be supported on arrival by British bayonets. It was apparently believed in Whitehall to be beyond the imagination of the wily Baghdadis to see that his return was brought about by the victory of British arms. 'Were there not Iraqi troops enough in the city, now loyal of course to the new Government, to keep order?'

De Chair went on to refer in a crucial passage to the disorders during the evening of 1 June:

So we waited and, as darkness settled like a mantle over the domes and minarets across the river, the shooting began. We did not hear it, but to the Brigadier's [i.e. Kingstone's] ears sleeping in the white colonial house of the British Embassy, came the growing crescendo of rifle and machine-gun fire. Baghdad was given up to the looters. All who cared to defend their own belongings were killed, while eight miles to the west [de Chair affirmed] waited the eager British force which could have prevented all this. Ah, yes, but the prestige of our Regent would have suffered.

De Chair's account also indicates that if the disorders had gone on longer, Cornwallis would have been compelled to call in the British troops. On 2 June de Chair saw Kingstone at the embassy, who gave him 'a slip of paper on which he had written three codes, should the Ambassador want me to send for help: "Brigadier come" (which would bring Joe [Kingstone] alone); "Cassano come" (which meant the armoured cars); or "All come" (which meant the whole shooting match)'. This account is confirmed by Colonel Skinner who on 2 June arrived in Baghdad from Basra in order to discuss the movement of British troops from the south which Cornwallis had asked to be halted. He telegraphed:

Situation which is being handled by Iraqi Government, detachment of Habforce standing by to enter if necessary, appears to be in hand.[51]

It was only subsequently that inaction during the riots was excused by the fear of possible Iraqi recalcitrance if the British were to enter Baghdad, and this not by the commanders of 'Habforce'—who had conducted their campaign with panache and gallantry—but by the embassy. De Chair writes:

It was argued afterwards in the Chancery of Baghdad that the Iraqis would have gone on fighting rather than agree to an armistice on the basis of our immediate entry. Again, it was argued that our arrival would have precipitated street fighting with the brigade which we had pushed back into the town. Yet why, I asked, if they crumpled up on the outskirts, should they have stiffened in the middle?

Diplomacy is the continuation of war by other means, but it should not begin too soon.

Genius is a grasp of the essential; and, after victory, the essential is to keep control of the situation.[52]

It is no doubt the echo of these apologies which we hear in Dame Freya Stark's and in de Gaury's books. But if these questions were agitated among British diplomats and officers, it is interesting to note that no trace of their discussions is to be found in the official correspondence. The disorders elicited a brief mention in a telegram on the afternoon of 2 June:

> Sporadic shooting with murderous assaults on Jews seems [Cornwallis reported] to have gone on throughout the night and from early this morning armed mob looted principal shopping streets of the town. Eventually orders were given to the Police and the army to open fire and this afternoon the position is much quieter. Disturbances are at present limited to the left bank of the Tigris [i.e. not the bank where the embassy is situated]. Casualties not yet known.[53]

Crosthwaite at the foreign office was moved to minute:

> What the Baghdad populace need is a little rough handling. They do not get bombed, and their only reaction is to get cocky. It looks more than ever as if British troops were needed in Baghdad itself, and a roomy concentration camp opened for the reception of the most obstinate mischief-makers.[53]

This telegram of 2 June is the only one in which Cornwallis thought it necessary to mention the disorders. More than a month later, on 11 July, he sent a despatch in which part of a paragraph was devoted to these events. A few sentences of clipped, brisk business-like prose concluding with a creditable sentiment about brutal outrages 'which all right minded persons will for long remember with shame and horror', tidily disposed of the incident. A curious and suspicious reader might perhaps wonder whether—even from a narrowly political point of view—an incident in which, as the despatch said, 'several hundred Jews were brutally murdered' should not have been more fully examined. For, after all, even in the bloodstained history of Iraq a few hundred murders in the capital city still constituted in those days a noteworthy happening. But readers of despatches, particularly in wartime, no doubt are busy men.

Cornwallis' despatch was received in the foreign office on 29 July. A few days earlier a letter from L. B. Namier, of the Jewish Agency, dated 21 July, had been received in which he stated that according to information from Jerusalem there had been anti-Jewish riots in Baghdad which had gone on for two days before being stopped by the intervention of British troops. Namier enquired about the truth of these reports, and about other reports that incriminated police had not been dismissed from the service, and that no investigation of the outbreak was being carried out or punishment administered. The foreign office had then no information about these events apart from what was contained in Cornwallis' telegram of 2 June and in two paragraphs of an air force situation report of 2 June which spoke of a 'slight' disturbance in Baghdad organized by agents of Rashid Ali which had resulted in 'a few' Jews and Christian Arabs being killed.[54] They therefore telegraphed to Cornwallis on 24 July for information. His reply, on 29 July, confirmed that the Jewish Agency report was 'substantially true', though he declared it 'too highly coloured'. He firmly rejected the accusation that British troops had stopped the rioting and pillaging. This, he forthrightly affirmed, was 'wholly inaccurate'. As for the punishment of the guilty,

> it must be remembered [the ambassador explained] that large numbers of rioters were shot down [in the] streets (Iraqi troops probably killed as many rioters as rioters killed Jews) and the military court which was set up in Baghdad to try those arrested has already committed many guilty men to severe terms of imprisonment, and three (including one policeman) have been publicly executed. There has been difficulty [Cornwallis pointed out] in persuading Jews to give evidence.[55]

The impression which this telegram conveys of things being firmly under control, of condign punishment being as speedily meted out as the reluctance of the Jews to give evidence allowed, is quite false. Baghdad had been abandoned to looters and murderers for two days in order that it should not be said that the government which was now in power had been imposed by the British army. This administration was headed by Midfa'i who was pressed on the regent by the foreign office in order that it should not be said that the British had put in power a pro-British politician. It was no wonder that these subtle and alembicated moves should have produced a government by no means eager to seek out and punish the rioters, or to banish Nazi sympathizers from public life, or even to be moderately friendly to those who had put it in power. The evidence, then belies the impression which Cornwallis' telegram of 29 July sought to give. Thus, in a letter of 16 June 1941 included among the fragmentary archives of the Baghdad embassy, the British adviser to the ministry of the interior, C. J. Edmonds (who had succeeded Cornwallis in this office in 1935) wrote that the director general of police and the minister of the interior had expressed some concern over British troops going through the main street on their way to a railway station, and had said that it would have been better for these troops to follow another route or go by night. Edmonds 'took the opportunity of saying to each that it was out of date and a mistake to be ashamed of their friends or their friendship'. On 2 July Edmonds again reported that he had spoken several times during the preceding fortnight to his minister about punishing the rioters and those who had conspired against the regent: 'On Ist July I said straight out that people were saying that Ministers were trying, by their leniency, to "secure their line of retreat".' On 12 July, Edmonds reported a conversation with the Egyptian *chargé d'affaires* who had expressed concern at the supine inaction of the government and declared that there was a limit to what could be achieved by the policy of co-operating with Midfa'i whom he described as 'absurdly weak'. Edmonds himself did not on the whole dissent from these views. He believed that

> both the army and the educational system and perhaps even the adminis-
> trative system require drastic overhaul; that the old gang of Baghdad
> politicians ([Midfa'i] himself, Rashid Ali, Nuri, Taha [al-Hashimi] and
> the rest, are lumped together in the same condemnation) have lost all
> prestige in provincial eyes (notably in Kurdistan and on the Shia
> Euphrates) as costly failures who have added the crime of treachery
> to their native misfortune of incompetence.[56]

Dame Freya Stark wrote in her diary that when an Iraqi delegation came to see Cornwallis on 30 May to ask for an armistice 'and beg that the constitution of Iraq may not be taken away from them', Cornwallis 'made a wonderful speech in Arabic telling them that as he and King Feisal *made* the constitution, it is safe in his hands'.[57] Edmonds' letter constitutes a telling commentary on the leadership of the Iraqi state which Cornwallis had done, and was doing so much, to foster and protect.

But the most acute appraisal of the consequences of Cornwallis' policy still extant may be found in a letter to the ambassador written from Kirkuk on 1 September 1941 by Colonel Lyon, the political adviser in the northern area, who knew the country well. The letter is reproduced in an appendix, but one particularly pointed passage is worth citing here:

> Let us look at the problem from the point of view of our Iraqi friends.
> They thought that having broken the rebellion British influence would be
> paramount in every department, that exemplary punishments would be
> meted out at least to certain important leaders who fell into our hands.
> That the British would control political appointments, kick out the rotten
> officials, appoint our friends, remedy the many injustices that have
> occurred, disarm or at least re-organise the Iraq Army, and stop con-
> scription. They expected a puppet government and after all what else
> could they expect since without British support they could only have
> Nazi Government. After three months what do they think? They see

the high places in government as well as many of the lower ones still occupied by traitors, they see that practically no disciplinary action has been taken, that the Iraq Army is filled with sullen and Pro Nazi Officers whose influence can thwart the police and successfully cow and estrange such other officers as would like to support us.

The intelligence summaries for July and August produced by the combined intelligence centre confirm and amplify Lyon's estimate of the situation.[58] When Midfa'i in the end had to go, a much closer British control over Iraq was instituted. Reviewing the record of the Midfa'i administration a few months after its demise, Cornwallis passed some strictures on its policies which are more justly applicable to him who had, after all, put Midfa'i in power.

Rapid and drastic action against known partisans of Rashid Ali and pro-Axis sympathisers [wrote Cornwallis, wise after the event] could have been carried out without risk of opposition and such action would have gone far towards convincing the large body of time-servers that it was prudent to identify themselves with the democratic cause.[59]

One outcome of the sack of Basra and of the *farhud* of Baghdad was to confirm Iraqis in their belief that the British were unreliable and devious.[60] The belief that the British willed and organized these two events, unfounded as it was, became quite widespread. This is what Hasani and other partisans of Rashid Ali assert,[61] explaining that the British fomented these disorders in order to confuse the population and weaken their resistance to the occupation. We find even a pro-British politician, Da'ud al-Haydari, one of the 'Eminent Persons' who formed the regent's council of state, seriously maintaining that 'All this has come from the British, and no one will admit that it has come from the British'.[62] The underlying assumption in all these suspicions was that since the Jews were the friends of the British, for the victors to allow an attack on them made sense only as a sinister machiavellian plot. To Iraqi minds with their robust and uncomplicated approach to power, the idea that practical and experienced men like Wavell or Cornwallis allowed riots and looting in Basra and Baghdad because to stop them was to interfere with Iraqi sovereignty would have been simply incredible. They would have agreed with Dame Freya Stark who, in her diary for 2 June 1941 wrote that 'the pretence that this is an Iraqi spontaneous Restoration is just nonsense.'[63]

In his telegram of 29 July answering the enquiry occasioned by Namier's letter Cornwallis reported that anti-Jewish talk continued 'as part of pro-German move worked up by Rashid's administration' and that the Jews would have a bad time if Rashid and 'his pro-Nazi friends' were to return to power. Cornwallis was undoubtedly correct in attributing anti-Jewish sentiment in Iraq to Nazi propaganda. This is one of the conclusions of the report of the committee which investigated the *farhud*. This propaganda had been spreading since the middle thirties and had greatly intensified since about 1938 when the Nazi government had decided to pursue an activist policy in the middle east. A main theme of this propaganda was that the British were the allies of the Jews. By a natural chain of reasoning, it came to be accepted in Iraq both among the educated classes and the masses, that since the Nazis were the enemies of the Jews, the Jews must therefore be the friends and the allies of the British. It was therefore not so much because of Zionism—a theme then much less in evidence than it subsequently became—as because of their alleged pro-British sympathies that the Iraqi Jews were intimidated and occasionally persecuted by Rashid Ali's régime. This is widely known, and it is confirmed by the witness of a diary which a Baghdad Jew, Abraham Twena, kept at the time. On 6 May he wrote:

> A number of British aircraft flew over Baghdad. The hostile population started accusing Jews of signalling to the airplanes. The Jews suffered greatly that day. A large number of Jews were arrested.

Again, on 7 May:

> the patients of the Jewish hospital, Meir Elias, were accused of giving signals to airplanes. A large angry crowd broke into the hospital with cudgels and knives; the officials ran for their lives. The police intervened and restored order, and from that day the hospital was closed and its patients were sent to their homes.[64]

And again on 8 May:

> [the radio] repeated the following information many times: 'We wish to inform the public that in their joy over the victory they are spending their ammunition in vain. We wish peace to prevail in every place, and after the victory over the British, revenge shall be taken on the internal enemy, and we shall hand him over to your hands for destruction'.
> It was not difficult to guess who this internal enemy was, nor why this instruction was given.[65]

It was also alleged that in Basra they had welcomed the British troops with open arms. Again, it is significant that, according to the report of the investigating committee, the incident which sparked off the *farhud* on 1 June took place on the outskirts of Baghdad when some soldiers and civilians attacked and wounded some Jews who had joined the crowd welcoming the regent on his return to Baghdad.[66] It was thus as supporters of the British that the Jews of

Baghdad were murdered and looted. This was common knowledge and it is indeed what Cornwallis' language implies both in his telegram of 29 July, and in his despatch of 11 July where he links the anti-Jewish outbreak to the popular resentment aroused by the regent's return.[67] The tone of a letter of his written towards the end of September 1941 comes therefore as a surprise. In this letter, written to Sir Horace Seymour at the foreign office, Cornwallis advances a new explanation for the outbreak. Responsibility for it, we discover, did not lie with those who actually looted or murdered or with those who neglected their duty to protect peaceable and law-abiding civilians. It lay rather with the Balfour declaration and with the Zionists of Palestine:

> I am anxious [Cornwallis assured Seymour] to do what I can to help the Baghdad Jewish community. As you know, this community has for long justly prided itself on its culture, its enterprise and its admiration for British ideas and institutions. The names of Sassoon and Kadoori are only the best known of many Iraqi Jews who have done well by their community and Great Britain.
> Recently, Baghdad Jewry has fallen on evil days. This is largely due to the unfortunate reactions of Zionism. Despite the proviso of the Balfour Declaration safeguarding the rights of Jews in other countries, those of the Baghdad community never seem to have been taken into consideration. Inevitably, though quite falsely, they have been regarded as Zionists, and have paid the price not only in 'benevolences' running into thousands of pounds, but also with their blood. They are naturally bitter at the attitude of the Zionists towards them. While I was in Palestine, the 'Palestine Post' reported that three Iraqi Jewesses had been fined for demonstrating outside the premises of the Jewish Agency, when the Agency had refused them immigration certificates, and I learn that even so moderate a man as Rutenberg when the murder of the Baghdad Jews was mentioned, replied: 'That is their contribution'.

The purpose of this seemingly irrelevant and wilfully misleading disquisition becomes clear as Cornwallis comes to the point of his letter:

> I have mentioned this background [he continued], because not only is Zionism in great measure responsible for the present difficulties of the Jewish community, but it also makes it vitally necessary for us to be most careful how we assist the community, if both helper and helped are not to be involved in a common charge of being Zionist agents.

Cornwallis went on to discuss ways of helping the Jews. The British Council could perhaps extend some educational help, but:

> I appreciate that the council may possibly feel that in a Moslem country they should not be too forward in helping a Jewish community ... the greatest discretion [he insisted] must be used in offering any help.

Again, the Anglo-Jewish Association might be approached. There were, so far as Cornwallis knew, no 'ardent Zionists' on its council. But one could not be too careful: the council did probably include some Zionists and

> if the matter came before them officially there is a danger that they might try to make a 'case' out of the plight of Baghdad Jewry.

It was therefore better to sound some discreet member of the council first. Cornwallis certainly wanted to help but, he solemnly warned,

> we shall have to go very carefully.[68]

It is a mean-spirited letter.

Burke wrote: 'To a people who have once been proud and great, and great because they were proud, a change in the national spirit is the most terrible of all revolutions'. Sir Kinahan Cornwallis may perhaps claim a modest share in this revolution.

APPENDIX

LETTER FROM THE POLITICAL ADVISER, NORTHERN AREA TO SIR K. CORNWALLIS, KIRKUK, 1 SEPTEMBER 1941 (F.O. 624/60, PART II).

Sufficient time has now elapsed to permit of a review of the administration since it came into power and from the point of view of the political advisory staff it is not very heartening. It was thought that the present cabinet some members of which had to flee the country to escape arrest would have taken a much firmer line than they have done with those persons who are since proved to have taken a prominent part in throwing out the properly constituted Government with such disastrous results to the country's prestige and economy.

There are numerous instances one could quote from various reports which have been circulated but for the purpose of this report examples are quoted in appendix attached of *Nazi Sympathizers past and present, active and passive, going unpunished and retained in lucrative government appointments.** This being so it is almost farcical to try and get action taken against the unquenched Nazi propaganda that is still extant in a variety of forms. Further I feel that decent officials will become soured and even wish that they had taken no initiative from the commencement if the result is to be intrigue, stalemate, and equally good or better appointments for those who behaved so despicably in April and May last and who have not even yet shown any signs of repentance. Moreover the deplorable effect on the populace at large must now be considered. Minorities are already complaining that those who have been reported because of their

* The appendix to this letter is not reproduced here—E.K.

fanatical threats under the guise of Nazi propaganda in one form or another are still at large. But what can be done to help when we know that so many much more glaring instances have met with no punishment. In fact treatment has been such that the man in the street can only come to the conclusion that the Government is lukewarm about the matter. Well disposed people both officials and others are frankly puzzled and not a little disquieted at the course events are taking.

Another point of great importance is that the Iraq Army is still as a whole sullen, behaves churlishly in public and disregards the civil administration in the execution of its function. Those living in towns turn their radios on to Germany and encourage others to listen in defiance of instructions to the contrary. The army is completely useless as a force to defend or even assist in the defence of the country and although I quite realise that a well paid force like this cannot be thrown onto the streets without creating an even greater evil, yet I find it hard to understand why the worst have not been court marshalled and many lesser lights removed from the Army into a concentration camp. Why should these people escape penalty and exist as an obstacle to the mending of the situation they have been principally instrumental in bringing about? To make matters worse men continue to be called up under the Military Service Act a policy under present conditions which is quite unfathomable.

Let us look at the problem from the point of view of our Iraqi friends. They thought that having broken the rebellion British influence would be paramount in every department, that exemplary punishments would be meted out at least to certain important leaders who fell into our hands. That the British would control political appointments, kick out the rotten officials, appoint our friends, remedy the many injustices that have occurred, disarm or at least re-organize the Iraq Army, and stop conscription. They expected a puppet government and after all what else could they expect since without British support they could only have Nazi Government. After three months what do they think? They see the high places in government as well as many of the lower ones still occupied by traitors, they see that practically no disciplinary action has been taken, that the Iraq Army is filled with sullen and Pro Nazi Officers whose influence can thwart the police and successfully cow and estrange such other officers as would like to support us.

The Adviser to the Ministry of Interior the most important in the administration experiencing difficulty in influencing the Minister has suggested that we who have no official standing within the Iraq Government should attack problems with the local administrative authorities, rather than call for action from the Top. Experience proves as I have already outlined that in spite of local successes scored this does not produce the hoped for results with an uncooperative minister. The other British officials of the Iraq Government are few in number and politically impotent. In fact the Iraq Government is behaving just the same as it did at the zenith of its national frenzy which followed its newly bestowed independence in the piping times of peace. The tribesmen who are our friends can still be subjected to the oppression of officials petty and medium of the Nazi colour who should ere now have been summarily dismissed and many of the directors and directors general of departments are people who are unreliable, uncooperative or disloyal. The few Mutasarrifs who have been loyally endeavouring to punish offenders have had their decisions quashed by the Minister, or courts and cannot be expected to continue loyally under such adverse conditions. Court Martials have for the most part been a farce. They think that the Cabinet is weak because they see it does not rule as it should, did its members really have faith in the ultimate success of British Arms. Our Iraqi friends both rulers and ruled want an atmosphere of political confidence to enable them to come into the open under the auspices of a strong and loyal government. They want to see proper action taken against those who have undoubtedly plotted against the State. They want to see more signs of an active British influence, without interference with domestic affairs. The minorities are frankly frightened of what they have been promised after the disappearance of British troops.

At the head of the State we have a Regent, admittedly weak in personality but not unfriendly. His weaknesses can be fortified by H.B.M's Government through the firm support and advice of the British Ambassador. The Prime Minister and Minister of Foreign Affairs are men who could not survive a British defeat and their loyalty is [not] beyond question. There are others outside the Cabinet in the same category. The Prime Minister is naturally blamed for the weaknesses of his Cabinet but it must be said in his favour that he gives full authority to his Ministers in the exercise of their functions and I have yet to hear of any case in which he has used his influence to shield guilty men. The problem therefore resolves itself into the activities of Ministers and I maintain that this is where the weakness lies. Given the right Ministers the various departmental officials, Mutasarrifs, Qaimaqams and Mudirs will obey the crack of the whip as they did during the Régime of Rashid Ali. It is up to us to get such Ministers by hook or crook. I feel sure they can be found. If the present occupants cannot be persuaded, bought or bullied into action then let the Prime Minister resign and choose (with the Ambassador's guidance) others who can. If men of the highest integrity cannot be found let us augment by search among less scrupulous personalities. Provided they will carry out a policy which will safeguard our interest it should be possible to ensure their individual welfare come what may. The present Mutasarrif of Basrah though having by no means an unsullied past has never-the-less shown ability and firmness in dealing with disloyal elements. The strange end of Keokha Mejid-I-Shahnashin suggest a second personality, and there are others.

In the event of future German pressure the Iraq Army can only be regarded as a menace in its present state. The country is ruled by officials a large proportion of whom are disloyal and not afraid to show it. The Iranian Army and probably its government has followed suit with Iraq, ducked the swing and saved its arms for future fifth column activities. How much Danegeld will bring about the desired change? Certainly very much less than the cost of extra troops over a long and vulnerable Line of Communication and in any case it may be regarded as a loan to be subsequently met from oil royalties. In the event of Danegeld proving ineffective then it is surely more economical to use force for our ends while the common enemy is far away than to have to use it when he is at our gates. The Iraqis are all at heart great admirers of strength, let us use it while there is yet time.

I trust that you will not form the impression that I am despondent, or that I shall cease to exert every effort. I am merely trying to draw you a picture of the political situation as I see it.

NOTES

1. Somerset de Chair, *The Golden Carpet*, limited edition, 1943, pp. 8–9.
2. See Kedourie, 'The Capture of Damascus, 1 October 1918' in *The Chatham House Version*. To the evidence there quoted may be added a graphic (and horrifying) account of the conditions in the military hospital in Damascus by the U.S. special agent William Yale, written in 1938. Copy in St. Antony's College Middle East Centre Library.
3. *Royal Central Asian Society Journal*, vol. XXX, 1943, pp. 330–2, for Sykes' review, and vol. XXXI, 1944 pp. 107–8, for de Chair's and Elphinston's letter. Peake and Winterton, it will be observed, do not deny the allegation that Lawrence begged Allenby to let the Arabs go into Damascus first, and that the Ottoman soldiers in the hospital were in consequence massacred.
4. F.O. 371/3883, 169058 and 169562/747/44.
5. Air 40/1425.
6. Premier 4, 32/6, folio 200. On Wavell's policy see generally 'Wavell and Iraq, April–May 1941', above.
7. F.O. 371/27069,2171 and 2176/1/93, and F.O. 371/27070, 2314/1/93.
8. W.O. 169/1085, war diary of 'G' Branch, Force H.Q. 7 May to 31 May 1941, appendix M/8/14.
9. W.O. 169/1085, *loc. cit.*, appendix M/15/C.
10. Hassun Kazim al-Basri, *Dhikra . . . al-Shaykh Salih Basha'yan al-Abbasi* (In Memory of . . . shaykh Salih Basha'yan al-Abbasi), Beirut 1949, pp. 37–8. Basha'yan put himself later at the head of the committee of notables who tried to secure law and order in Basra when the acting *mutasarrif* left and the British refused to protect the inhabitants.
11. Abd al-Razzaq al-Hasani, *al-Asrar al-khafiyya fi hawadith al-sana 1941 al-taharurriyya* (Hidden Secrets of the Events of the Liberatory Year 1941), Sidon 1958, p. 162.
12. F.O. 371/27079, 4820/1/93, despatch no. 17 from Wolstan Weld-Forster, Basra, 16 July 1941.
13. Hasani, pp. 164–5. W.O. 169/3326. The British consul reported on 19 May (F.O. 371/27071, 2418/1/93) that only 'Ashshar was being patrolled by British troops which may serve to confirm Hasani's account.
14. F.O. 371/27070, 2372/1/93.
15. F.O. 371/27071, 2418/1/93.
16. F.O. 371/27069, 2180/1/93, copy of Wavell's telegram, 11 May 1941.
17. W.O. 169/1039, war diary of 'Habforce' May 1941, appendix 4A, Instructions to Major General J. G. W. Clark, 11 May, and appendix JA, Operations Instructions no. 48 'Task of Habforce', 12 May 1941.
18. F.O. 371/27063, 1386/1/93.

19. Air 40/1425. To judge by their weekly intelligence summaries for the month of April, the air headquarters at Habbaniyya were better informed, and their judgement sounder than the ambassador. The reports are in Air 24/830. They make an instructive contrast with Cornwallis' telegrams.
20. F.O. 371/27064, a series of telegrams from Cornwallis all dated 11 April, 1408, 1409, 1410 and 1414/1/93, and telegram from foreign office 13 April (in 1414). The government of India expressed their disagreement with Cornwallis' recommendations in telegrams of 12 and 13 April, *ibid.*, 1456/1/93; see also 'Wavell and Iraq April–May 1941' above.
21. F.O. 371/27064, 1439 and 1467/1/93.
22. F.O. 371/27066, 1618/1/93.
23. F.O. 371/27077, 3426/1/93, Cornwallis' despatch no. 148, Baghdad 6 June, 1941.
24. Text in I.S.O. Playfair *et al.*, *History of the Second World War: The Mediterranean and Middle East*, vol. II, p. 332.
25. F.O. 371/27074, 2803/1/93.
26. F.O. 371/27074, 2918/1/93. Cornwallis was wrong in saying that the terms had not been published in Iraq. They appeared in an official notice from the ministry of defence on 6 June, see Mahmud al-Durra, *al-Harb al-iraqiyya-al-britaniyya* (The Anglo-Iraqi War), Beirut 1969, pp. 408–9.
27. The intelligence summary for the week ending 7 June 1941 produced by the combined intelligence centre (Air 24/831) declared (para. 43): 'Although it has been announced that the British Government have not been fighting the Iraqi nation, but only Rashid Ali and his small group of Generals, it would be unwise to take this statement too seriously. In fact the leaders who started the rebellion against the Regent Abdul Ilah, had a very large following in the country.'
28. W.O. 169/1085, war diary of H.Q. 'G' Branch, June 1941, appendix J/2/A.
29. W.O. 169/1259, war diary of H.Q. 4th Cavalry Brigade, 1 June 1941.
30. Air 24/820, operations record book for May 1941, p. 26.
31. F.O. 371/27073, 2724/1/93; W.O. 169/1259, war diary of H.Q., 4th Cavalry Brigade, 5 June 1941.
32. W.O. 169/1039, *loc. cit.*
33. The events are well set out in Hayyim J. Cohen, 'The Anti-Jewish *Farhud* in Baghdad, 1941' in *Middle Eastern Studies*, vol. 3, no. 1 (October 1966).
34. Text of plan in Hasani, Hidden Secrets, pp. 207–8.
35. Durra, *op. cit.*, pp. 409–10.
36. Hasani, Hidden Secrets, prints the report, pp. 226–36. The point about the police and the army is made on p. 231.
37. Text in Hasani, Hidden Secrets, p. 224.
38. Abd al-Razzaq al-Hasani, *Tarikh al-wizarat al-iraqiyya* (History of the ministries of Iraq), vol. 5, new ed., Sidon 1967, p. 268, footnote 1. Hasani's informants were Abdullah al-Qassab, a member of the investigation committee and Ali Khalid al-Hijazi, Baghdad chief of police.
39. F.O. 371/27071, 2427, 2451 and 2482/1/93.
40. G. de Gaury, *Three Kings in Baghdad*, 1961, pp. 128–9.
41. F.O. 371/27078, 4231/1/93, Cornwallis' despatch no. 185, Baghdad 11 July, 1941.
42. F.O. 371/27073, 2694/1/93.
43. F.O. 371/27078, 4231/1/98, despatch of 11 July cited above. The telegram of 2 June no. 491 is in F.O. 371/27074, 2763/1/93.
44. Cohen, *loc. cit*, p. 14.

45. Durra, *op. cit.*, pp. 389 and 410–11. The intelligence summary for the week ending 7 June (Air 24/831) records (para. 8) that on '2 June, just before noon, 2 battalions railed from Kirkuk were marched into the city and, firing to kill, they quickly cleared the streets of all rioters'.
46. F. Stark, *East is West*, 1945, p. 160.
47. F.O. 371/27101, 3066/1015/93, Cornwallis' telegram no. 502, Baghdad 4 June 1941.
48. Freya Stark, *Dust in the Lion's Paw*, 1966, pp. 114–15.
49. De Gaury, *op. cit.*, *loc cit.*
50. Air 20/6026 where the signal is cited in an account of the defence of Habbaniyya by Squadron-Leader A. G. Dudgeon written on 14–21 July 1941.
51. W.O. 169/1085, war diary of H.Q. 'G' Branch, June 1941, appendix J/2/C.
52. Somerset de Chair, *The Golden Carpet*, 1944, pp. 118–19.
53. F.O. 371/27074, 2763/1/93, Cornwallis telegram no. 491, 2 June, 4.15 p.m. cited above.
54. Air 24/831, appendix 2/6/41/1, situation report no. 90.
55. F.O. 371/27078, 4060/1/93.
56. 624/60.
57. *Dust in the Lion's Paw*, p. 111. The episode is proudly recounted in the article on Cornwallis (who died in 1959) in the Dictionary of National Biography.
58. Air 24/832.
59. F.O. 371/31371, 2595/204/93, Cornwallis' despatch no. 55, Baghdad 8 March 1942.
60. On the origins of this reputation see Kedourie, 'The Kingdom of Iraq: A Retrospect', in *The Chatham House Version*, and particularly p. 278.
61. See for instance Hasani, Hidden Secrets, pp. 157 and 223.
62. Quoted in 'The Diary of Abraham Twena' in *The Scribe* vol. 2, no. 11 (May–June 1973), p. 7.
63. *Dust in the Lion's Paw*, p. 114.
64. The crowd destroyed the X-ray machine suspecting that it was a wireless transmitter. Private information.
65. Abraham Twena's diary translated in *The Scribe*, vol. 2 no. 11 (May–June 1973), p. 4.
66. Hasani, Hidden Secrets, p. 226.
67. F.O. 371/27078, 4231/1/93 cited above.
68. F.O. 371/27116, 6613/5126/93, Cornwallis to Seymour, Baghdad 25 September 1941.

Works Cited

Place of publication London, unless otherwise indicated

'Abbas al-'Azzawi, *Tarikh al-Iraq bayn ihtilalayn* (History of Iraq between Two Occupations), vol. VIII, Baghdad, 1956.

'Abd al-Latif Hamza, *Adab al-maqala al-suhufiyya fi Misr* (The Art of the Newspaper Article in Egypt), vol. II, Cairo, 1950.

'Abd al-Rahman al-Rafi'i, *Mustafa Kamil*, Cairo, 1939.

'Abd al-Razzaq al-Hasani, *al-Asrar al-khafiyya fi hawadith al-sana 1941 al-taharuriyya* (Hidden Secrets of the Events of the Liberatory Year 1941), Sidon, 1958.

'Abd al-Razzaq al-Hasani, *Tarikh al-wizarat al-'iraqiyya* (History of the Ministries of Iraq) vol. 5, new ed., Sidon, 1967.

Adib Ishaq, *al-Durar* (The Gems), 1st edition, ed. by Jirjis Mikha'il Nahhas, Alexandria, 1886.

Adib Ishaq, *al-Durar* (The Gems), 4th edition, ed. by Awni Ishaq, Beirut, 1909.

Iraj Afshar and Asghar Mahdavi, eds., *Documents inédits concernant Seyyed Jamal al-Din Afghani*, Tehran, 1963.

Ahmad Lutfi al-Sayyid, *Qissat hayati* (The Story of My Life), Cairo, 1962.

Ahmad al-Shuquayri, *Arba'un 'amm fi'l-hayat al-'arabiyya wa'l-duwaliyya* (Forty Years in Arab and International Life), Beirut, 1969.

J. Alexander, *The Truth About Egypt*, 1911.

'Ali al-Balhawan, *Tunis al-tha'ira* (Tunisia in Revolt), Cairo, 1954.

Alphonse d'Alonzo, *les Allemands en Orient*, Brussels, 1904.

Alphonse d'Alonzo, *Cardinal et ministre général*, Jerusalem, 1902.

Alphonse d'Alonzo, *la Russie en Palestine*, Paris, 1901.

American University of Beirut, *Annual Reports, Board of Managers, Syrian Protestant College, 1866–7/1901–2*, Beirut, n.d.

Amin al-Rayhani, *al-Muhalafa al-thulathiyya fi'l-mamlaka al-hayawaniyya* (The Triple Alliance in the Animal Kingdom) [New York 1903], 2nd ed., Beirut, 1972.

Amin Sa'id, *al-Thawra al-'arabiyya al-kubra* (The Great Arab Revolt), Cairo, 1934.

Rufus Anderson, *Memorial Volume of the First Fifty Years of the American Board of Commissioners for Foreign Missions*, Boston, 1861.

George Antonius, *The Arab Awakening*, 1938.

Negib Azouri, *le réveil de la nation arabe*, Paris, 1905.

Negib Azouri and Eugène Jung, eds., *l'Indépendance arabe*, Paris, 1907–8.

James L. Barton, *Daybreak in Turkey*, New York, 1908.

James L. Barton, *Human Progress through Missions*, New York, 1912.

John Batatu, '*Some Preliminary Observations on the Beginnings of Communism in the Arab East*', in J. Pennar, ed., *Islam and Communism*, Munich, 1960.

315

Gertrude Bell, *Amurath to Amurath*, 1911.

Gertrude Bell, *The Desert and The Sown*, 1907.

Frederick Bliss, *The Religions of Modern Syria and Palestine*, New York, 1912.

Frederick Bliss, *The Reminiscences of Daniel Bliss*, New York, 1920.

Howard Bliss, 'The Modern Missionary', in *The Atlantic Monthly*, Boston, (May 1920).

Joel Carmichael, *The Shaping of the Arabs: A Study in Ethnic Identity*, New York, 1967.

Gwendolen Cecil, *Life of Robert Marquis of Salisbury*, vol. II, 1921.

Somerset de Chair, *The Golden Carpet*, limited ed., 1943; trade ed., 1944.

André Chouraqui, *Cent ans d'histoire: L'Alliance israélite universelle et la renaissance juive contemporaine (1860–1960)*, Paris, 1965.

Winston Churchill, *The Second World War* vol. iii, 1950.

Hayyim J. Cohen, 'The Anti-Jewish *Farhud* in Baghdad 1941' in *Middle Eastern Studies*, vol. 3 no. 1 (October 1966).

Hayyim J. Cohen, *ha-Pe'iluth ha-sionith be-'Iraq* (Zionist Activity in Iraq), Jerusalem, 1969.

M. Confino and S. Shamir, eds., *The U.S.S.R. and the Middle East*, 1973.

John Connell, pseud., *Auchinleck*, 1959.

John Connell, pseud., *Wavell Scholar and Soldier: To June 1941*, 1964.

Miles Copeland, *The Game of Nations*, 1969.

Allan Cunningham, 'The Wrong Horse?—A Study of Anglo-Turkish Relations before the First World War', in *St. Anthony's Papers*, no. 17, 1956.

Bayard Dodge, *The American University of Beirut*, Beirut, 1958.

Hamid Enayat, 'Islam and Socialism in Egypt', in *Middle Eastern Studies*, vol. 4 no. 2 (January 1968).

Fadlallah abu Mansur, *A'asir Dimashq* (Damascus Hurricanes), n.p., n.d., [c. 1959].

Falih Hanzal, *Asrar maqtal al-'a'ila al-malika fi'l-Iraq 14 tammuz 1958* (Secrets of the Assassination of the Royal Family in Iraq, 14 July 1958), Beirut, 1971.

Nadia Farag, 'The Lewis Affair and the Fortunes of al-Muqtataf', *Middle Eastern Studies* vol. 8 no. 1 (January 1972).

Farah Antun, '*Hizb al-nasyunalist fi Misr*' ('The Nationalist Party in Egypt'), *al-Djami'a*, vol. v, New York, 1906.

David Farhi, 'The *Seriat* as Political Slogan—or the "Incident of the 31st Mart"' in *Middle Eastern Studies* vol. 7 no. 3 (October 1971).

Sir Hugh Foot, *A Start in Freedom*, 1964.

G. de Gaury, *Three Kings in Baghdad*, 1961.

Grattan Geary, *Through Asiatic Turkey*, 1878.

H. A. R. Gibb, ed., *Whither Islam*, 1932.

D. Z. Gillon, 'The Antecedents of the Balfour Declaration', in *Middle Eastern Studies*, vol. 5 no. 2 (May 1969).

Pierre Grandchamp, *Etudes d'histoire tunisienne*, Paris, 1966.

P. Graves, 'The Story of the Egyptian Crisis', *The Nineteenth Century and After* (March 1938).

G. E. von Grunebaum, 'Approaching Islam: a Digression', in *Middle Eastern Studies*, vol. 6 no. 2 (May 1970).

G. E. von Grunebaum, 'Some Recent Constructions and Reconstructions of Islam', in Carl Leiden, ed., *The Conflict of Traditionalism and Modernism in the Muslim Middle East*, Austin, 1969.

Sylvia G. Haim, *Arab Nationalism*, Berkeley, 1962.

Sylvia G. Haim, 'The Ideas of a Precursor', unpublished Ph.D. dissertation, Edinburgh University, 1953.

Charles Hardinge, *Old Diplomacy*, 1947.

Hassun Kazim al-Basri, *Dhikra . . . al-Shaykh Salih Basha'yan al-'Abbasi* (In Memory of . . . Shaykh Salih Basha'yan al-'Abbasi), Beirut, 1949.

Haza' al-Majali, *Mudhakkirat* (Memoirs), Amman, 1960.

Albert Hourani, *Arabic Thought in the Liberal Age 1798–1939*, 1962.

H. N. Howard, *The King-Crane Commission*, Beirut, 1963.

A. M. Hyamson, 'The Damascus Affair 1840', in *Transactions of the Jewish Historical Society of England*, vol. xvi (1952).

al-Ittihad al-'arabi al-ishtiraki (The Arab Socialist Union), *Ma'alim fi tariq al-khiyana wa'l-raj'iyya* (Signposts on the Road of Treason and Reaction), Cairo, 1966.

Jabran Khalil Jabran, *al-Arwah al-mutamarrida* (Rebellious Spirits), New York, 1908.

Jamal al-Din al-Alusi, *Muhammad Kurd Ali*, Baghdad, 1966.

James P. Janowski, 'The Young Egypt Party and Egyptian Nationalism 1933–1945', unpublished Ph.D. dissertation, University of Michigan, 1967.

Henry Harris Jessup, *Fifty-Three Years in Syria*, New York, 1910.

Henry Harris Jessup, *Mohammedan Missionary Problem*, Philadelphia, 1879.

Eugène Jung, *La Révolte arabe*, 2 vols., Paris, 1924.

Elie Kedourie, *Afghani and 'Abduh: an Essay on Religious Unbelief and Political Activism in Modern Islam*, 1966.

Elie Kedourie, *The Chatham House Version and Other Middle-Eastern Studies*, 1970.

Elie Kedourie, *England and the Middle East: the Destruction of the Ottaman Empire 1914–1921*, 1956.

Malcolm Kerr, *The Arab Cold War, 1958–1967: A Study of Ideology in Politics*, 2nd ed., 1967.

Malkam Khan, 'Persian Civilisation', in *The Contemporary Review* (1891).

Khayri al-'Umari, *Hikayat siyasiyya min tarikh al-'Iraq al-hadith* (Political Episodes from the Modern History of Iraq), Cairo, 1969.

Rom Landau, *Search for To-Morrow*, 1938.

W. Z. Laqueur, *Communism and Nationalism in the Middle East*, 1956.

K. S. Latourette, *A History of the Expansion of Christianity*, vol. vi, 1945.

Lady Algernon Gordon Lennox, ed., *The Diaries of Lord Bertie of Thame*, 2 vols., 1924.

R. le Tourneau, *Evolution politique de l'Afrique du Nord musulmane 1920–1961*, Paris, 1962.

Narcisse Leven, *Cinquante ans d'histoire*, 2 vols., Paris, 1911–20.

J. R. Levenson, *Confucian China and its Modern Fate*, 3 vols., 1958–65.

Bernard Lewis, *The Emergence of Modern Turkey*, 1961.

Mahmud al-Durra, *al-Harb al-iraqiyya-al-britaniyya* (The Anglo-Iraqi War), Beirut, 1969.

Mahmud Shukri al-Alusi, *Tarikh Najd* (History of Najd), Cairo, 1343 A.H.

Fu'ad Matar, *Russya al-nasiriyya wa Misr al-misriyya* (Nasserite Russia and Egyptian Egypt), Beirut, 1972.

Albert Memmi, *Portrait of a Jew*, 1963.

Mohamad Gamal-El-Din Ali Hussein El-Mesady, 'The Relations between Abbas Hilmi and Lord Cromer' unpublished Ph.D. dissertation, University of London, 1966.

Richard P. Mitchell, *The Society of the Muslim Brothers*, 1969.

Muhammad Anis, ed., *Safahat matwiyya min tarikh al-za'im Mustafa Kamil* (Secret Pages from the History of the Leader Mustafa Kamil), Cairo, 1962.

Muhammad Bahjat al-Athari, *A'lam al-Iraq* (Iraq Notables), Cairo, 1345 A.H.

Muhammad Ibrahim al-Jaziri, ed., *Athar al-za'im Sa'd Zaghlul* (Literary Remains of the Leader Sa'd Zaghlul), Cairo, 1927.

Muhammad Jalal Kishk, *Madha yurid al-sha'b al-misri* (What the Egyptian People Want), Beirut, 1970.

Muhammad Jalal Kishk, *Madha yurid al-talaba al-misriyyun* (What the Egyptian Students Want), Beirut, 1968.

Muhammad Khalil Subhi, *Tarikh al-hayat al-niyabiyya fi Misr* (Parliamentary History of Egypt), Vol. V, Cairo, 1939.

Muhammad al-Makhzumi, *Khatirat Jamal al-Din al-Afghani al-Husayni* (Memoirs of Jamal al-Din . . .) Beirut, 1931.

Muhammad Rashid Rida, ed., *Athar Rafiq al-Azm* (Literary Remains of Rafiq al-Azm), Cairo, 1925.

Muhammad 'Umara, ed., *al-A'mal al-kamila li-'Abd al-Rahman al-Kawakibi* (The Complete Works of 'Abd al-Rahman al-Kawakibi), Cairo, 1970.

Munif al-Razzaz, *al-Tajriba al-murra* (The Bitter Experience), Beirut, 1967.

Mustafa al-Hifnawi, *al-Sifr al-khalid* (The Everlasting Record), Cairo, n.d. (after 1936).

Nasir al-Din al-Nashashibi, *Safir mutajawwil* (Roving Ambassador), Beirut, 1970.

Jukka Nevakivi, 'Lord Kitchener and the Partition of the Ottoman Empire, 1915–16', in K. Bourne and D. C. Watt, eds., *Studies in International History*, 1967.

Niqula Yusef, *A'lam min al-Iskandariyya* (Notables from Alexandria), Alexandria, 1969.

Nizar Qabbani, *Fi'l-shi'r wa'l-jins wa'l-thawra* (On Poetry, Sex and Revolution), Beirut, 1966.

Jacob Obermayer, *Modernes Judentum im Morgen- und Abendland*, Vienna and Leipzig, 1907.

Stephen B. L. Penrose, Jr., *That They May Have Life*, New York, 1941.

Stephen B. L. Penrose, Jr., 'Building up the Voltage' in *The Arab World* (January 1954).

I. S. O. Playfair *et al.*, *History of the Second World War: The Mediterranean and Middle East*, vol. II, 1956.

E. E. Ramsaur, Jr., *The Young Turks*, Princeton, 1957.

Robert Rézette, *les Partis politiques marocains*, Paris, 1955.

Pierre Rondot, *Les Institutions politiques du Liban*, Paris, 1947.

Salim al-'Anhuri, *Sihr Harut* (Harut's Magic), Damascus, 1885.

Salim Khalil al-Naqqash, *Misr li'l-misriyyin* (Egypt for the Egyptians), Alexandria, 1884.

Sami al-Jundi *al-Ba'th*, Beirut, 1969.

Sayyid Qutb, *Ma'alim fi'l-tariq* (Signposts on the Road), Cairo, 1964.

Patrick Seale, *The Struggle for Syria*, 1965.

N. Slousch, 'Le nouveau régime turc et Tripoli' and 'Redjeb Pacha' in *Revue du monde musulman*, vol. VI (1908).

Wilfred Cantwell Smith, *Islam in Modern History*, Princeton, 1957.

M. W. Suleiman, 'The Lebanese Communist Party' in *Middle Eastern Studies*, vol. 3 no. 2 (January 1967).

Somerville Story, ed., *The Memoirs of Ismail Kemal Bey*, 1920.

Freya Stark, *Dust in the Lion's Paw*, 1966.

Freya Stark, *East is West*, 1945.

Leonard Stein, *The Balfour Declaration*, 1961.

V. R. Swenson, 'The Military Rising in Istanbul 1909', in *Journal of Contemporary History*, vol. 5, no. 4 (October 1970).

Tawfiq Ali Baru, *al-Arab wa'l-Turk fi'l-'ahd al-dusturi al-'uthmani* (Arabs and Turks during the Ottaman Constitutional Period), Cairo, 1960.

Abraham Twena, 'Diary', *The Scribe*, Vol. 2 no. 11 (May–June 1973).

Mayir Vereté, 'The Balfour Declaration and its Makers' in *Middle Eastern Studies*, vol. 6 no. 1 (January 1970).

A. J. B. Wavell, *A Modern Pilgrim to Mecca*, [1912], 1918 ed.

Yusuf al-Hakim, *Suriya wa'l 'ahd al-'uthmani* (Syria and the Ottoman Era), Beirut, 1966.

Zeine N. Zeine, *The Emergence of Arab Nationalism*, Beirut, 1966.

Index